RACE FIRST

The Ideological and Organizational Struggles of Marcus Garvey and the Universal Negro Improvement Association

TONY MARTIN

The New Marcus Garvey Library, No. 8

THE MAJORITY PRESS
P.O. Box 538
Dover, Mass. 02030, U.S.A.

Copyright© 1976 by Tony Martin

Library of Congress Cataloging-in-Publication Data

Martin, Tony, 1942-
  Race first.

  (The New Marcus Garvey library; no. 8)
  Reprint. Originally published: Westport, Conn.: Greenwood Press, 1976. Originally published in series: Contributions in Afro-American and African studies; no. 19.
  Bibliography: p.
  Includes index.
  1. Garvey, Marcus, 1887-1940. 2. Universal Negro Improvement Association--History. 3. Afro-Americans--Biography. 4. Intellectuals--United States--Biography. 5. Black nationalism--United States. I. Title.
II. Series: Martin, Tony, 1942-   . New Marcus Garvey library ; no. 8.
E185.97.G3M37 1986   305.8'96024 [B]   86-12853
ISBN 0-912469-22-6
ISBN 0-912469-23-4 (pbk.)

First published in 1976.

First Majority Press edition, 1986.

  9 8 7 6 5 4 3

The Majority Press
P.O. Box 538
Dover, Massachusetts 02030

Printed in the United States of America

To My Parents

OTHER BOOKS BY TONY MARTIN

Rare Afro-Americana: A Reconstruction of the Adger Library. (With Wendy Ball)

In Nobody's Backyard: The Grenada Revolution in its Own Words. Volume I: The Revolution at Home. (With the assistance of Dessima Williams)

In Nobody's Backyard: The Grenada Revolution in its Own Words. Volume II: Facing the World. (With the assistance of Dessima Williams)

Contents

Preface

This book is based on the simple premise that no one could have organized and built up the largest black mass movement in Afro-American history, in the face of continuous onslaughts from communists on the left, black reactionaries on all sides, and the most powerful governments in the world, and yet be a buffoon or a clown, or even an overwhelmingly impractical visionary.

Distortions are not new to Afro-American history, but one would be hard put to find a major black figure who has suffered more at the hands of historians and commentators. This study attempts to treat Marcus Garvey and the Universal Negro Improvement Association with the seriousness and respect which they deserve.

After a brief biographical introduction, the study examines the major features of Garvey's ideological outlook, as they manifested themselves both in theory and in practice. The last and longest portion of the book is taken up with an examination of the formidable battles which the UNIA was simultaneously involved in on a variety of fronts. Despite the personal animosities generated by these struggles, they were essentially ideological conflicts, for Garvey's revolutionary nationalism was perceived as a threat by a wide spectrum of opponents who had little affection for each other outside of their common desire to crush Garvey and extirpate his movement. Against all these disparate forces Garvey prevailed, and it was only with his deportation from the United States that his organizational grip n the black masses in North America and, to varying degrees elsewhere, slowly began to loosen. Even then, his ideological legacy continued to be a major force in black communities.

A large number of people helped me in a large number of ways, big and small, during the years that this book slowly took shape. I thank them all. In particular I would like to mention four professors who provided much encouragement during and after my sojourn as a graduate student at Michigan State University, when the foundations for this book were laid. They are Professors James R. Hooker, Joseph McMillan, Harold G. Marcus and Ruth Hamilton.

I would also like to include a special word of appreciation for the inspiration provided by the several persons with whom I spoke who had been active UNIA members in Garvey's day. They are the late Mrs. Amy Jacques Garvey of Kingston, Jamaica; Mr. J. Charles Zampty, once of Trinidad, but for over a half-century of Detroit, Michigan, a founder of the Detroit UNIA and one-time auditor to Garvey; Mr. J. R. Ralph Casimir of Roseau, Dominica, leader in the post-World War I years of the Dominica UNIA and one of the most active and influential of West Indian Garveyites; Queen Mother Moore, who saw Garvey in New Orleans in 1922; Colonel Von Dinzey of New York and the several members of the New York Vanguard Local and the Detroit UNIA with whom I chatted. Thanks also to Mr. Herbert Whiteman, friend of Kwame Nkrumah, the Schomburg Center for Research in Black Culture, the New York Public Library, Astor, Lenox and Tilden Foundations, for materials used in the appendix, and to the Association for the Study of Afro-American Life and History for materials contained in Chapter 9, which originally appeared in an article in the *Negro History Bulletin*.

To the fool or fools in Harlem who broke into my car, ripped off my first six months' notes and forced me to start over my research I say, "Why didn't you take the spare tire instead, man?"

June 1975   Tony Martin

RACE
FIRST

1

Introduction:
Marcus Mosiah Garvey,
1887–1940

What do I care about death in the cause of the redemption of Africa? . . . I could die anywhere in the cause of liberty: A real man dies but once; a coward dies a thousand times before his real death. So we want you to realize that life is not worth its salt except you can live it for some purpose. And the noblest purpose for which to live is the emancipation of a race and the emancipation of posterity.

           —Marcus Garvey[1]

History records that slaves—by virtue of their experiences and the knowledge gained in captivity in strange lands—have eventually become Masters of themselves, and in time enslaved others. Let us therefore use adversity as others have done. Take advantage of every opportunity; where there is none, make it for yourself, and let history record that as we toiled laboriously and courageously, we worked to live gloriously.

           —Marcus Garvey[2]

Marcus Mosiah Garvey was born in St. Ann's Bay, Jamaica, on August 17, 1887. His childhood was deeply rooted in the peasant environment

3

which largely surrounded him. He once described an uncle, for whom he
sometimes worked, as a sharecropper. His own parents also engaged in
small-scale peasant farming. Garvey's was not a typical peasant experience, however. His father, a descendant of the Maroons, Jamaica's
African ex-slaves who successfully defied the slave regime, was also a
skilled tradesman, a stonemason. Garvey's background further distinguished him from the typical peasant in that his father possessed a library
among whose volumes Garvey developed an early taste for reading.

His childhood was characterized by an adequate elementary education
supplemented by private tutors and Sunday school. His leadership ability
seems to have manifested itself from the very beginning, for his physical
prowess gave him a position of eminence among his peers.[3] At the age of
fourteen, by which time he had already become apprenticed to a local
printer, Garvey left school. Two years later he moved to Kingston,
Jamaica's capital city, where he obtained work. By the time he was eighteen he had achieved what he later described as "an excellent position
as manager of a large printing establishment." This was an outstanding
achievement, making Garvey the youngest foreman printer in Kingston,
and at a time when many foremen were still being imported from Great
Britain and Canada. Participation in a strike, during which he consented
to lead the workers despite assurances of favor from management, cost
him his job. He then obtained new employment with the government
printery.

In Kingston Garvey quickly immersed himself in the intellectual and
political life of the city. By 1909 his political involvement had brought
him into the National Club organized by a lawyer and legislative council
member, Sandy Cox. Garvey was elected one of the assistant secretaries
of this club, which sought to combat privilege and the evils of British
colonialism on the island.[4]

In 1910 Garvey embarked on the first of his many wanderings in
foreign lands. He went to Costa Rica, where he worked for a while as
a timekeeper on a United Fruit Company banana plantation and as a
laborer on the pier at Port Limón, edited a paper, *La Nación,* harassed
the British consul concerning his nonprotection of the many British
West Indian laborers working there, was arrested for urging workers to
fight for better conditions, and was eventually expelled from the country
(or left to escape the authorities).

He continued, for the next year or so, to wander through Latin America, going to such places as Panama and Ecuador where West Indian workers had migrated in large numbers in search of work. He observed the universal degradation of the black race, worked intermittently to finance his travels, started another small paper in Colón, Panama, and agitated among black workers. A black worker in Colón at the time remembers meeting Garvey around 1912 as he addressed the predominantly black Colón Federal Labor Union.[5] There is a possibility that Garvey may have stopped briefly, perhaps in transit at a seaport, somewhere in the United States during this period.[6]

From Central America Garvey returned briefly to Jamaica and by the autumn of 1912, undeterred by a lack of money, he was in England, where his only surviving sister, Indiana, was working as a governess. In England he indulged his love of public speaking at Hyde Park's Speakers' Corner, was a regular visitor to the House of Commons, and worked for the *Africa Times and Orient Review,* the foremost Pan-African journal of the day. He found the time to visit Scotland, Ireland, France, Italy, Spain, Austria, Hungary and Germany.[7] Garvey said later that he attended some lectures in law at Birkbeck College of the University of London.[8]

By July 1913 Garvey was, not surprisingly, almost destitute, and he applied for government assistance. Possibly because of his job at the *Africa Times and Orient Review,* however (his article for the magazine was published in the October issue), he was able to eke out an existence for almost another year. By May 1914, when he was probably again without employment, the Anti-slavery and Aborigines Protection Society intervened on his behalf, despatching him to the Colonial Office with an offer of a contribution from the society if the Colonial Office would put up some of the money to repatriate him to Jamaica. Early in June the society informed the Colonial Office that Garvey was "endeavouring to raise a fund to meet passage money" and offered to match equally any amount the Colonial Office proffered. Garvey managed to do without the largesse of these two agencies, however. He succeeded in raising his fare home and left England on June 17, 1914.[9]

Garvey's first sojourn in England was of great importance to his career. The workings of British democracy made a lasting impression on him and, like later generations of visitors from the colonized world to the metropolis, he noted the contrast to the autocracy which the very same colonizers maintained in their tropical dependencies. He was often to call, in the years to come, for an extension of "British justice" to the colonies. England gave him an opportunity, too, to enhance his already wide knowledge of the worldwide sufferings of black people. In the pages of the *Africa Times and Orient Review* there appeared regularly articles by and about such leading black figures as Booker T. Washington, Edward Wilmot Blyden, John Edward Bruce, W. E. B. Du Bois and William Ferris, to name but a few. Some of these would before long be his associates in the United States. Garvey also came into contact with black seamen and students, whose sufferings he observed, and with the many people of color who visited the offices of the journal. And the fact that the journal combined a Pan-African outlook with wide coverage of Middle and Far Eastern nationalist struggles, and indeed all anticolonial struggles, contributed further to Garvey's growth and influenced his future outlook.

Garvey arrived back in Jamaica on July 15, 1914, his head bristling with ideas on making a living and founding a racial movement. To secure the former he tried selling greeting and condolence cards and "monumental tombstones."[10] To secure the latter he formed, five days after his arrival, the Universal Negro Improvement and Conservation Association and African Communities (Imperial) League.[11] The title bore testimony to the enlarged vision brought about by his travels and the fear, which he never relinquished, that weak races were doomed to slavery and possibly extinction. In this regard he wrote:

> For the last ten years I have given my time to the study of the condition of the Negro, here, there, and everywhere, and I have come to realize that he is still the object of degradation and pity the world over, in the sense that he has no status socially, nationally, or commercially (with a modicum of exception in the United States of America). . . .[12]

Garvey became president and traveling commissioner of the new organization, among whose stated objects were the fostering of a "Universal Confraternity among the race," the establishment of a central nation for black people, the setting up of educational institutions, and a pledge "to work for better conditions among Negroes everywhere."

Amy Ashwood, whom he had met at the weekly meeting of the East

Queen St. Baptist Literary and Debating Society, became its secretary. The association was formed, she said, on their second meeting.[13] A few days later an inaugural meeting took place at the Collegiate Hall, Kingston, presided over by the mayor of Kingston. Recruiting was slow, even though Garvey worked tirelessly and succeeded in establishing himself in the minds of many as an agitator and a nuisance. Many "respectable Negroes" who had not yet learned to love their blackness opposed his movement. As Garvey wrote later, "I had to decide whether to please my friends and be one of the 'black-whites' of Jamaica, and be reasonably prosperous, or come out openly, and defend and help improve and protect the integrity of the black millions, and suffer."[14]

After about a year the organization could boast only about a hundred members.[15] Up to this time its activities were largely confined to Kingston. In November 1915, however, its first public meeting outside Kingston was held, in Garvey's hometown of St. Ann's Bay. The *Jamaica Times* reported, "Right merrily did the people of the town turn out to listen to their fellow townsman."[16] Garvey had planned to undertake a fund-raising lecture tour in the United States beginning this very month, having received an assurance of support from Booker T. Washington. But the latter's death caused him to postpone his trip until 1916.

Garvey arrived in New York on March 23, 1916, for a lecture tour which he thought would last five months and would be confined to black audiences mostly in the South. He arranged for his mail to be delivered to an address in Jamaica during his absence and let it be known wherever he went in America that he was raising funds for an industrial institute to be established in Jamaica.

Garvey's advent into the United States did not find him as much a stranger to conditions there as some are led to believe. For one thing his wide reading on racial matters had obviously included the race's condition in North America. More than this, though, Garvey's visit to the United States came in the midst of a large-scale migration of West Indians to that country. The to-ing and fro-ing of persons and ideas generated by this migration meant that adapting to the United States was probably not too much of a problem for new arrivals.

By March 1916 Garvey's sense of mission, his conviction that he had been called upon to emancipate his race, had developed to an uncanny degree. Shortly before leaving Jamaica he had written in a letter to

God - fantasy

Robert Russa Moton, Booker T. Washington's successor at Tuskegee,
"I am now talking with you as a man with a mission from the High God."
Even though he still thought that Jamaica would be the main field of
his exertions, he had nevertheless already mapped out the course he was
to follow over the next few years. He wrote in the same letter,

> I have many large schemes on my mind for the advancement of my
> people that I cannot expose at the present to the public as in such a
> case my hope of immediate success would be defeated, as my enemies
> are so many and they are ever anxious to misrepresent me. I have
> firstly to found a press of our own and to get some working [start?]
> so as to demonstrate my true intentions.[17]

Once in the United States, Garvey found lodgings with a Jamaican
family in Harlem, came down with pneumonia, obtained work as a printer, and saved enough to start out on his fund-raising tour through the
states. He gave his address at this time as 53 West 140 Street in Harlem.
By June he was lecturing in Boston and by November, demonstrating
again the amazing mobility which had characterized his Central American
and European visits, he had already visited, among other places, New
York, Boston, Philadelphia, Pittsburgh, Baltimore, Washington, D.C.,
and Chicago. He had also met a goodly number of prominent national
and local Afro-American leaders. Among them were John Edward Bruce,
whom he called "a true Negro," a man for whom he had "the strongest
regard," a Dr. R. R. Wright, Jr., Dr. Parks, vice-president of the Baptist
Union, Dr. Triley of the Methodist Episcopal Church of Philadelphia,
Reverend J. C. Anderson, whom he described only as being "of Quinn
Chapel," Mrs. Ida Wells-Barnett of antilynching fame, magazine editor
Fenton Johnson and William H. Ferris. Bruce had been an agent for and
a regular contributor to the *Africa Times and Orient Review*. Ferris had
once written an article for the same magazine in which he praised Garvey's
October 1913 article, which had appeared a few months before his.[18]
Ferris was later to edit Garvey's weekly *Negro World* from 1920 to 1923
and to hold a variety of high offices within the UNIA. Bruce, after an
initial period of skepticism, became a regular contributor to and member
of the editorial boards of both the *Negro World* and Garvey's *Daily Negro
Times*. Until his death in 1924 he remained the staunchest of Garvey's
supporters among the Afro-American intelligentsia.

Garvey's whirlwind tour took him through thirty-eight states and
lasted about a year. He returned at the end of it to New York City, where
he established a temporary base. Harlem, only recently converted into the
black section of New York, was already the virtual capital of the black
world. Its population, composed in the vast majority of southern and
West Indian-born immigrants, was possessed of a rare vitality, containing
as it did a high proportion of radicals of all types and a large number of
outstanding black creative artists. Race-uplift groups of all kinds abounded
and the main thoroughfare, Lenox Avenue, was a favorite haunt of soap-
box orators.

Harlem, however, was but a microcosm of the black world of the World
War I period. The subjugation of Africa by European imperialism was
still a fresh memory. In response to this an infinite number of nationalist
and Pan-Africanist organizations had come into being in Africa, Europe,
North America, the West Indies, Central and South America—everywhere
that black people lived and all looking toward the restoration of African
independence. Apart from the African question, black communities
everywhere had local problems of their own. The black man was almost
everywhere in a state of subjugation. Garvey, in his involvement in the
printers' strike, in his participation in Jamaica's National Club, in his
agitation among black workers in Central America, in his travels in Europe,
and in his formation of the UNIA ("Conservation" had dropped out of
the title along the way), had long embodied the spirit of black protest
which characterized the age. It was inevitable, therefore, that he should
be tempted by Harlem, the most highly politicized black community in
the world.

Garvey moved onto the center of the Harlem stage with all the ease
and self-confidence of the man with a mission. He took to the streets,
joining the soapbox and stepladder orators, and formed political alliances
with some of Harlem's prominent radicals. Someone who knew Garvey
at this time recalled that he "could throw his voice around three corners
without batting an eyelash."[19]

On June 12, 1917, Harlem intellectual Hubert Harrison invited Garvey
to address a mass meeting attended by two thousand held at the Bethel
AME Church for the purpose of organizing Harrison's Liberty League.
Garvey himself, before his tour through the states, had held a not too
successful meeting in the course of which he fell off the platform. The
Liberty League meeting was a windfall, however, for he was a tremendous

success.[20] Shortly before, or perhaps shortly after, Harrison's meeting, Garvey began to hold weekly meetings of his own every Sunday at 3 P.M. in Harlem's Lafayette Hall at 131 Street and Lenox Avenue. The meetings were slated to continue until October 1917 and Garvey was still being billed as head of the UNIA and ACL of Jamaica. At one of these Sunday meetings on July 8, less than a month after the Liberty League gathering, Garvey's address was devoted to a denunciation of the "Conspiracy of the East St. Louis Riots."[21] The first New York branch of the UNIA may already have been formed by this time, for the association's address was given as 235 West 131 Street. The subject of this lecture shows that Garvey had once again demonstrated the propensity, as in Costa Rica and Panama, of quickly becoming embroiled in the purely local issues of wherever he happened to be.

Garvey's first UNIA branch in New York, as well as a second attempted early in 1918, was envisaged as being auxiliary to the Jamaica headquarters. Garvey himself, as president of the Jamaica division, did not hold office in them. Both these efforts to establish UNIA branches were disrupted by attempts by socialists and Republicans to turn them into political clubs. On a third attempt based on the wishes of a nucleus of thirteen members, Garvey consented to become president of the New York branch, thus concretizing a decision that he had in all likelihood already contemplated—namely to cast down his bucket in the United States.[22] With this move New York City supplanted Kingston, Jamaica, as UNIA headquarters. A schism developed in this new attempt, too, but Garvey weathered the storm. The association's meetingplace had meanwhile moved from the Lafayette Hall to the Palace Casino where it remained for most of 1918.

Once Garvey had decided to remain in the United States, he moved on with renewed vigor. The UNIA was incorporated under the laws of New York on July 2, 1918. On July 31 the African Communities League was incorporated as a business corporation. A month or two later the *Negro World* appeared, destined to become the most widely circulated of race papers and the bane of European colonialists. Garvey initially edited it. The earliest issues were distributed free by being pushed under peoples' doors in the early hours.

During the year Garvey embarked on his first fund-raising tour outside of New York after moving the UNIA headquarters. His first stop was

Detroit, where he was hit in the head by a stone thrown by a heckler. On his return to New York his secretary, Amy Ashwood, who had accompanied him, was summoned to the district attorney's office a total, she wrote later, of seventeen times. The authorities, it seems, suspected Garvey of raising funds for a nonexistent "Back-to-Africa" enterprise.[23]

On November 11, 1918, the *New York Times* reported a meeting of five thousand persons presided over by Garvey at the Palace Casino. The meeting celebrated the end of World War I by calling on the Allied Powers to hand over the ex-German colonies in Africa to black rule. Several persons, among them socialist A. Philip Randolph and Ida Wells-Barnett, were nominated at the meeting to lobby on behalf of the UNIA at the upcoming Paris peace conference. The UNIA eventually despatched a Haitian as high commissioner to lobby during the conference since most Afro-Americans were being denied passports to France by the United States government.

Shortly after the November meeting Mrs. Wells-Barnett addressed a UNIA gathering in New York. On this occasion, however, she annoyed Garvey by advising against the idea of a return to Africa and the establishment of what was subsequently to become the Black Star Line Steamship Corporation. Like most people who saw Garvey in action, she later testified to the remarkable sway which he exercised over his audience.[24]

By 1919 Garvey was already firmly established as one of Harlem's most important radical figures. And it was during this year that his fame spread over the globe. Before the year had ended he would be regularly discussed in the press and in governmental circles in Europe, Africa, the West Indies, and elsewhere.

In March 1919 at another large meeting at the Palace Casino, Garvey claimed that W. E. B. Du Bois had humbugged the activities of his high commissioner in France.[25] The desire for an Afro-American lobby at the Paris peace conference was also responsible for bringing together a group of Harlem radicals and other prominent individuals at the home of wealthy but race-conscious Madame C. J. Walker. Garvey was among those present at this meeting, out of which grew the short-lived International League of Darker Peoples.[26]

In June 1919 Garvey incorporated his Black Star Line Steamship Corporation. By this time, Garvey claimed later, the UNIA had about thirty branches and over two million members.[27] This figure apparently

included sympathizers as well as members in any strict sense, but the
spread of his ideas by this time could not be gainsaid. As early as 1918
the *Negro World* had been reaching places as far as Panama and throughout 1919 Garveyites were blamed by colonial authorities for antiwhite
riots in Jamaica, Trinidad and British Honduras, among other places.[28]

In October 1919 Garvey, fast approaching the peak of his career, had
his closest escape from an untimely death. Several shots were fired at
him by one George Tyler, two of which found their mark. The wounds
were minor, however. Tyler died mysteriously, supposedly jumping to
his death from the cell where he was awaiting a court appearance. It was
widely suspected that he planned to implicate others in his assassination
attempt. A little over two months after this attempt on his life, on Christmas Day 1919, Garvey married Amy Ashwood during a lavish spectacle
at Liberty Hall, now the UNIA's own meetingplace. In 1916 she had
left Jamaica for Panama but had become reunited with Garvey in the
spring of 1918 when she moved to the United States. The marriage was
over by early 1920, the couple having parted company amid a welter of
accusations and counteraccusations concerning infidelity, financial mis-
dealings and political strategies.

The year 1920 witnessed the First International Convention of the
Negro Peoples of the World, organized by Garvey. At the opening session
at Madison Square Garden, New York, an overflow crowd of twenty-five
thousand filled the arena and spilled out into the streets. The other sessions took place in Liberty Hall in Harlem. Delegates, who came from
all over the black world, adopted the Declaration of Rights of the Negro
Peoples of the World. This declaration listed the main grievances of the
race and demanded their resolution. Notice was served on European
colonialists that the black man had an "inherent right . . . to possess
himself of Africa" regardless of the claims of any other race or nation.
Demands were made for the capitalization of the "N" in Negro, for the
teaching of black history in schools, and for an end to lynching and
sundry other discriminations. The red, black and green were adopted
as the colors of the race; August 31, the last day of the month-long convention, was proclaimed an international holiday for black people; and
the Universal Ethiopian Anthem was adopted. During the course of the
convention Garvey was elected president general of the UNIA and provisional president of Africa. The mayor of Monrovia, Liberia, Gabriel

Fantosy

Johnson, was elected supreme potentate, or ceremonial leader. Several others were elected leaders of various parts of the black world.

Also in 1920 was the birth of the UNIA's Negro Factories Corporation, which over the next two or three years managed a number of UNIA businesses, including laundries, restaurants, a doll factory, tailoring and millinery establishments and a printing press. Some of these ventures had been in operation since 1918, for Ida Wells-Barnett reported having been shown a UNIA restaurant and some unspecified smaller undertakings by Garvey in that year.

By 1921 Garvey was unquestionably the leader of the largest organization of its type in the history of the race. He had succeeded as no one else had in gathering up the worldwide feelings of dismay at the loss of independence and defiance against colonialism and oppression, which characterized the "New Negro" spirit of the age. As of August 1, 1921, the UNIA contained 418 chartered divisions (up from 95 a year earlier) plus 422 not yet chartered. There were in addition 19 chapters (none the previous year), making a total of 859 branches.[29]

Garvey's unparalleled success had the effect of arraying against him a most powerful conglomeration of hostile forces. The United States government was against him because they considered all black radicals subversive; European governments were against him because he was a threat to the stability of their colonies; the communists were against him because he successfully kept black workers out of their grasp; the National Association for the Advancement of Colored People and other integrationist organizations were against him because he argued that white segregationists were the true spokesmen for white America and because he in turn advocated black separatism. His organization also had to contend with unscrupulous opportunists who were not above sabotaging its workings for personal gain.

In 1921 opposition from all these forces escalated to a remarkable extent. First, the United States Department of State almost prevented Garvey from reentering the country after a short trip to the Caribbean area. He managed to make it back, however, barely in time for his Second International Convention. Then at his annual convention the communists, spearheaded by their black auxiliary, the African Blood Brotherhood, made an unsuccessful bid to capture his following. Meanwhile the NAACP, through its major black spokesman, W. E. B. Du Bois, was steadily in-

creasing its campaign of attacks in its organ the *Crisis* and elsewhere. The
black socialists, too, had begun to criticize Garvey, and the British authorities were busy pursuing the policy they had begun in 1919 of banning
the *Negro World,* prohibiting UNIA officials from entering their colonies,
and generally doing whatever they could to thwart the spread of Garvey's
influence. Finally on January 12, 1922, Garvey was arrested for alleged
mail fraud. This was a signal for redoubled efforts on the part of his
enemies who presumed his guilt and called for his arrest and deportation.
Despite all this, the UNIA managed to push ahead. *The Daily Negro
Times* appeared in 1922 and a *Black Man* magazine was projected but
did not in fact appear until much later. Garvey's second marriage took
place during this year, to his private secretary Amy Jacques.

In 1923 he was convicted on the mail fraud charges in connection
with the Black Star Line. Yet Garvey was now claiming a membership
of six million and nine hundred branches. Five hundred of the branches
and a little less than half the membership were said to be in the United
States.[30]

Garvey's last full year as a free man in the United States was 1924.
During this year the remarkable faith which his followers placed in him
was again demonstrated when they subscribed enough to launch a new
steamship line, the Black Cross Navigation and Trading Company. The
year 1924 also saw the blocking of Garvey's intention to set up a base
in Liberia. During this year too the UNIA launched its Negro Political
Union designed to bring its voting strength to bear on American and
other elections by endorsing candidates based on their record of dealings
with the race, irrespective of party affiliations.

In February 1925 Garvey's appeal was turned down and he entered
the federal penitentiary at Atlanta. What his enemies hoped to obtain
through his imprisonment did come to pass. Schisms appeared in the
American movement resulting, by 1926, in a splinter in the New York
branch, the largest of all (estimated at thirty-five thousand members at
one time). These strains occasioned by Garvey's departure were, however,
still relatively minor, for Garvey, even from jail, managed to maintain
some control, appointing and dismissing officers and conferring with his
aides. At an extraordinary conference in Detroit in 1926, the secretary
general, G. Emonei Carter, reported 814 "domestic" branches, 215 "foreign," and 91 "new" ones (whether foreign or domestic not specified),

for a grand total of 1,120. There were 25 pending applications for charters.[31]

The discovery in 1970 of UNIA records, including membership files, provides a unique opportunity to verify these figures. According to the data in these records (mostly compiled from about 1925 through 1928) there were 725 UNIA branches in the United States (possibly 723—see the appendix) and 271 outside of the United States (possibly 273), making a grand total of 996. The data (excluding eleven branches not cataloged according to location) is summarized in Tables 1 and 2.

Table 1.
Distribution of UNIA Branches in the United States, ca. 1926

State	Number of Branches	State	Number of Branches
1. Louisiana	74	20. Alabama	11
2. Virginia	48	21. Connecticut	10
3. North Carolina	47	22. Maryland	10
4. Pennsylvania	45	23. Tennessee	9
5. West Virginia	44	24. Texas	9
6. Mississippi	44	25. Kentucky	8
7. Ohio	39	26. Kansas	7
8. Arkansas	38	27. Massachusetts	7
9. Florida	32	28. Arizona	4
10. New Jersey	31	29. Colorado	3
11. Oklahoma	28	30. Delaware	3
12. Georgia	26	31. Washington	3
13. South Carolina	24	32. District of Columbia	2
14. Illinois	23	33. Iowa	2
15. Missouri	21	34. Rhode Island	2
16. California	16	35. Nebraska	1
17. New York	16	36. Oregon	1
18. Michigan	14	37. Utah	1
19. Indiana	13	38. Wisconsin	1

Source: Adapted from data in the UNIA Central Division (New York) files, Schomburg Collection, New York Public Library.

Note: "Miscellaneous" branches (see appendix) are omitted.

Several interesting and possibly surprising facts emerge from this new information. First of all, if the number of branches in a given area can be taken to indicate the extent of UNIA penetration, then the southern United States was the most thoroughly UNIA-organized area in the world. Louisiana was far and away the most thoroughly Garveyite state, with a total of seventy-four branches.[30] The top three states in the United States were in the South, and only three of the top thirteen were in the North.

Table 2.
Distribution of UNIA Branches Outside the United States, ca. 1926

Country	Number of Branches	Country	Number of Branches
1. Cuba	52	22. Canal Zone (Panama)	2
2. Panama	47	23. South West Africa	2
3. Trinidad	30	24. Wales	2
4. Costa Rica	23	25. Antigua	1
5. Canada	15	26. Australia	1
6. Jamaica	11	27. Bermuda	1
7. Spanish Honduras	8	28. Brazil	1
8. South Africa	8	29. Dominica	1
9. British Guiana	7	30. Dutch Guiana	1
10. Colombia	6	31. Equador	1
11. Dominican Republic	5	32. Grenada	1
12. Guatemala	5	33. Haiti	1
13. Nicaragua	5	34. Nevis	1
14. Barbados	4	35. Nigeria	1
15. British Honduras	4	36. Puerto Rico	1
16. Mexico	4	37. St. Kitts	1
17. Sierra Leone	3	38. St. Lucia	1
18. England	2	39. St. Thomas	1
19. Gold Coast	2	40. St. Vincent	1
20. Liberia	2	41. Venezuela	1
21. Bahamas	2		

Source: Adapted from data in the UNIA Central Division (New York) files, Schomburg Collection, New York Public Library.

Note: "Miscellaneous" branches (see appendix) are omitted.

These findings may be tempered somewhat, but only somewhat, by the fact that some of the largest single branches were probably in such northern cities as New York and Chicago. In all the UNIA was represented in thirty-eight of the United States. It was not only the organization of newly urbanized Afro-Americans. It was also the organization of the great mass of black peasants all over the South, Southwest and elsewhere.

Outside the United States Cuba led with fifty-two branches, more than any single United States state except Louisiana. The greater Caribbean area (including Central America and northern South America) was undoubtedly the biggest Garveyite stronghold outside of the United States. South Africa was the most thoroughly organized of the African countries. No area of significant black population in the world was without a UNIA branch. This included Canada, Europe and Australia.

The data suggests that the Detroit report of 1926 was accurate. The slight discrepancy in figures is probably due to no greater cause than the loss of some membership cards during the decades preceding their rediscovery. For there were branches in such places as Dahomey, the Belgian Congo and areas in Trinidad which do not appear among the records.

An important conclusion to be drawn from the figures in this chapter is that the UNIA continued to expand after Garvey's 1925 incarceration. Some branches were undoubtedly disbanding even as new ones were being added, but the evidence as to how many is inconclusive. Certainly by 1926 some branches were not sending up-to-date information to headquarters, but this had always been a problem and did not necessarily indicate lack of activity in those branches.

Meanwhile the clamor for Garvey's release mounted. At one demonstration in Harlem an estimated 150,000 people marched and jammed the sidewalks.[33] The government, bewildered by the depth of feeling shown for someone they liked to characterize as a crook and perhaps viewing with apprehension the upcoming election year, decided to commute his sentence but with deportation.

Five thousand loyal followers were on hand at New Orleans to listen to Garvey's farewell address from the deck of the vessel taking him to the Caribbean. They stood in the rain and sang the UNIA hymn, "God Bless Our President," as the ship pulled away, bearing their leader from the scene of his greatest triumphs, never to set foot in the United States again.

When the ship stopped in Panama Garvey was greeted by a delegation from the local UNIA and in Jamaica, where he arrived on December 10, 1927 he was given a hero's welcome as some of the largest crowds in the island's history turned out to greet him.

None dismayed by his deportation, Garvey set about making the most of his adversity. In 1928 he visited England, presented a renewed petition to the League of Nations and briefly visited Canada.

In August 1929 Garvey held the Sixth International Convention in Jamaica. It was as spectacular as the earlier ones in Harlem. A split occurring at the convention resulted in the formation of a separate UNIA Inc., headquartered in the United States. Garvey remained head of his faction, now calling itself the UNIA and ACL (August 1929) of the World. The American schismatics did not carry the whole American field with them. They failed, for example, to win control of the *Negro World,* which continued to carry Garvey's pronouncements. Units loyal to Garvey often changed their names to Garvey Clubs, Ethiopian Clubs and the like, and animosity between the two groups in the United States occasionally led to violence.

The year 1929 marked, too, Garvey's most direct incursion into Jamaican electoral politics. Between the convention and the end of the year he formed the Peoples' Political Party (PPP), began campaigning for a seat in the legislative council, was jailed for three months for contempt by British judges when he promised to reform the bench if elected, and was elected to the Kingston and St. Andrew Corporation (KSAC) council while in jail. Upon his release the corporation promptly declared his seat vacant, but he was returned unopposed early in 1930. Meanwhile, the British judges convicted him again, this time for supposedly libeling British colonialism in an editorial in his *Blackman* newspaper.

Garvey's bid for the legislative council was defeated in January 1930, largely because the majority of the black masses still had no vote under British colonialism. His PPP nevertheless successfully placed some candidates in both the KSAC and the legislative council. Garvey himself continued to serve on the KSAC council for the next few years, on one occasion (1931) being reelected while out of the country. During this period Garvey occasionally acted as a de facto trade union leader, taking up the causes of unorganized workers.

In 1931 Garvey made yet another trip to England and the League of Nations. Back in Jamaica he continued to hold political meetings, formed an amusement company and dabbled in real estate. A Seventh International Convention was held in Jamaica in 1934, followed some months later by a shift of his base of operations to England.[34]

In England Garvey contacted African students, harangued the crowds at Hyde Park's Speakers' Corner, and managed to keep together those divisions of the UNIA that had survived the depression, the schisms following his deportation from the United States, and the inroads into his erstwhile followers (especially in the United States) made by Father Divine, Muslims, the Peace Movement of Ethiopia, the communists and divers other groups.

His organization in the United States remained viable, and in 1936, 1937 and 1938 Garvey visited Canada to meet with his North American followers, who would on these occasions cross the border in large numbers and would, among other things, attend Garvey's School of African Philosophy, which provided crash courses for UNIA organizers. After his 1937 visit to Canada he toured the West Indies, speaking to enthusiastic audiences in St. Kitts, Nevis, Antigua, Montserrat, Dominica, St. Lucia, St. Vincent, Grenada, Barbados, Trinidad and British Guiana. During his 1938 visit to Canada he held his Eighth International Convention in Toronto from August 1 to 17.[35]

Despite his deportation and despite the increasing fragmentation of his membership, his ideas continued to hold sway among the black masses in America with remarkable tenacity. For one thing the fragmentation did not always mean a difference in ideology between the various splinter groups. Many of them, such as the Peace Movement of Ethiopia and the Moorish Americans, continued to regard Garvey as something of a patron saint even after they broke with the UNIA.

Garvey died in London in June 1940, active to the end in his efforts to emancipate a race.

NOTES

1. *Negro World,* April 28, 1923.
2. Amy Jacques Garvey, *Garvey and Garveyism* (Kingston: A. J. Garvey, 1963), p. 29.
3. Amy Ashwood Garvey, "Marcus Garvey—Prophet of Black Nationalism," n.d., Amy Ashwood Garvey Papers, London.
4. Garvey identified some of the leading figures in the club as

S. A. G. Cox, Alexander Dixon, H. A. L. Simpson, a Mr. DeLeon, and himself: *Blackman,* September 11, 1929; see also *Jamaica Times,* April 30, 1910, quoted in Rupert Lewis, "A Political Study of Garveyism in Jamaica and London: 1914-1940" (Masters thesis, University of the West Indies, 1971), p. 53. A contemporary remembered Garvey as one of the most frequent speakers at the club's weekly meetings. His speeches were usually antigovernment. See R. N. Murray, ed., *J. J. Mills-His Own Account of His Life and Times* (Kingston: Collins and Sangster, 1969).

5. Interview with Mr. J. Charles Zampty, Highland Park, Michigan, April 17, 1973.

6. The *Jamaica Times* of November 13, 1915, quotes Garvey as saying that he had traveled in "America, North and Central, Europe and parts of the West Indies." Another source claimed that Garvey first visited the United States in 1911. F. A. McKenzie, "Is There a Black Peril?" *Overseas* 6 (April 1921): 43. If the *Jamaica Times* article is correct and the *Overseas* one wrong, a further possibility may be an intransit stop on his way to or from England.

7. *Negro World,* September 10, 1921.

8. He claimed to have spent eighteen months here. *Negro World,* June 19, 1920.

9. Public Record Office, London, Colonial Office records, G/27424, Register of Correspondence for Jamaica, destroyed file, letter from M. Garvey, July 8, 1913; ibid., Misc/19729, May 28, 1914, "Repatriation of M. Garvey," destroyed file, June 9, 1914; ibid., destroyed file, June 19, 1914. In the case of all these destroyed files, the actual correspondence has been destroyed but a synopsis of their contents remains.

10. Amy Ashwood Garvey, "Prophet," p. 54.

11. *Negro World,* September 10, 1921.

12. Marcus Garvey, Jr., *A Talk With Afro-West Indians – The Negro Race and Its Problems* (Kingston [?]: African Communities League, 1915 [?]), p. 1.

13. Amy Ashwood Garvey, "Prophet," p. 41.

14. Amy Jacques Garvey, ed., *The Philosophy and Opinions of Marcus Garvey* (London: Frank Cass, 1967), II: 127.

15. Amy Ashwood Garvey, "Prophet," p. 60.

16. *Jamaica Times,* November 13, 1915.

17. Garvey to Moton, February 29, 1916, in Daniel T. Williams, *Eight Negro Bibliographies* (New York: Kraus Reprint Co., 1970).

18. *Africa Times and Orient Review* 1 (April 1914): 77-78.

19. *Negro World,* April 8, 1922.

20. *Emancipator,* March 27, 1920. The meeting was held at St. Mark's Hall, West 138 Street, New York.

21. Marcus Garvey, *Conspiracy of the East St. Louis Riots* (New York: UNIA, 1917).

22. Garvey, *Philosophy and Opinions,* II: 129, and *Garvey and Garveyism,* p. 25.

23. Amy Ashwood Garvey, "Prophet," pp. 111-113.

24. Ida B. Wells, *Crusade for Justice—The Autobiography of Ida B. Wells,* ed. Alfreda M. Duster (Chicago: University of Chicago Press, 1970), p. 381; Garvey, "Prophet," pp. 114-116.

25. *Crisis* 21 (December 1920): 60.

26. *Messenger* (August 1922): 470.

27. Garvey, *Philosophy and Opinions,* II: 129.

28. Tony Martin, "Revolutionary Upheaval in Trinidad, 1919," *Journal of Negro History* 58 (July 1973): 313-326.

29. *Negro World,* August 20, 1921.

30. *Evening World,* June 29, 1923.

31. *Negro World,* March 27, 1926.

32. Branches included divisions and chapters. A chapter designated a branch in an area that already contained a division. Chapters were kept to a minimum and could only be formed with the consent of the existing division.

33. *Negro World,* August 21, 1926. White New York papers (the *Herald, Tribune,* and *Journal*) estimated 100,000 in their August 16 edition.

34. For the Jamaica period, see Garvey, *Garvey and Garveyism,* chaps. 33-35.

35. The *Black Man* is the best source of information for this period.

2

Race First
and Self-Reliance

*In a world of wolves one should go armed, and one of the most
powerful defensive weapons within the reach of Negroes is the
practice of race first in all parts of the world.*

—Marcus Garvey[1]

What We Believe

*The Universal Negro Improvement Association advocates the
    unity and blending of all Negroes into one strong, healthy race.
(It is against miscegenation and race suicide.)
It believes that the Negro race is as good as any other, and there-
    fore should be as proud of itself as others are.
It believes in the purity of the Negro race and the purity of the
    white race.
It is against rich blacks marrying poor whites.
It is against rich or poor whites taking advantage of Negro women.
It believes in the spiritual Fatherhood of God and the Brother-
    hood of Man.*

—Marcus Garvey[2]

Marcus Garvey, unlike his major rivals in the United States, built a
mass organization that went beyond mere civil-rights agitation and protest and based itself upon a definite, well-thought-out program that he
believed would lead to the total emancipation of the race from white
dominion.

Central to the ideological basis underpinning Garvey's program was
the question of race. For Garvey, the black man was universally oppressed
on racial grounds, and any program of emancipation would have to be
built around the question of race first. The race became a "political
entity" which would have to be redeemed.[3] Against the rival suggestion
that humanity, and not the black race, should be the objects of his zeal,
he argued that it was not "humanity" that was lynched, burned, jim-
crowed and segregated, but black people.[4] The primacy of race characterized the UNIA from its beginnings in Jamaica[5] and by 1919 United
States government officials were drawing attention to what they considered this subversive doctrine.[6]

Garvey went about the task of converting the disabilities of race into
a positive tool of liberation with a thorough aggressiveness. "No man can
convince me contrary to my belief," he declared, "because my belief is
founded upon a hard and horrible experience, not a personal experience,
but a racial experience. The world has made being black a crime, and I
have felt it in common with men who suffer like me, and instead of making it a crime I hope to make it a virtue."[7] Accordingly, the consciousness of Garvey's followers was saturated with the new doctrine. Black
dolls were manufactured for black children; Garvey's newspaper proclaimed itself the *Negro World*; he encouraged his followers to support
their black businessmen and professionals; the race catechism used by
his followers disabused the minds of black folk concerning the claims of
the Hamitic myth by explaining that contrary to this myth, black people
were "certainly not" the recipients of any biblical curse; he frowned upon
advertisements of a racially demeaning nature,[8] the *Negro World* sponsored beauty contests and published photographs of beautiful black
women, a subject on which Garvey waxed poetic—"Black queen of
beauty, thou hast given color to the world."[9] Indeed, practically every
aspect of the organization was designed to bolster the black man's self-
esteem and to foster pride in self.

The primacy of race in Garvey's thought was coupled with a deep
pessimism concerning the future of the black man in America. He be-

lieved that the black man, with increasingly ample educational opportunities, would aspire to positions of influence, which would bring him
into direct competition with the white power structure. Within fifty to
a hundred years, he predicted, such confrontation would lead to a racial
clash which would end disastrously for the black race.

   This analysis led Garvey inevitably in the direction of racial separation.
His economic ventures in the United States amounted to an attempt
toward a nucleus of a self-sustaining (and therefore self-employing) black
race in America. But his gaze looked more longingly toward Africa as
the salvation of the African abroad. Even in Africa, though, he found
the European overlords attempting to increase the seeds of future racial
discord, as in 1938 when he protested British consideration of a proposal
to resettle European Jews in Tanganyika, Kenya or British Guiana.[10]

   Garvey's concern over the salvation of the race led him to harsh criticism of any weaknesses he perceived among black people, and there was
nothing that displeased him more than the black man who did not think
in racial terms. Such criticism brought out the finest of his invective—
"Yes, this an 'Uncle Tom Negro.' Yes, a 'yes boss Negro'—a 'howdi massa
Negro'—a 'yes Mass Charlie Negro.' A Negro who will be satisfied to black-
en a white man's shoes all the days of his life and lick the white man's
spittle if he orders him to do so."[11]

   Garvey's race-first doctrine found excellent expression in his acute
awareness of the role of culture as a tool for liberation. He himself was
a prolific poet of liberation.[12] Indeed, his poems are as good a source of
his ideology as any. They were replete with such themes as the beauty
of the black woman, the need for self-reliance, the glories of African
history, the necessity for an end to black participation in white wars,
and protests at the Italian invasion of Ethiopia. This experimentation
with the arts for purposes of politicizing the UNIA membership was also
indulged in by one of Garvey's closest associates, John Edward Bruce.
One Bruce play, *Preaching vs. Practice*, expressed Garvey's hostility toward
unscrupulous black preachers. Another, *Which One*, provided an excellent
example of the use of this medium for political education. The main characters were a Sennebundo Ajai, an African UNIA diplomat, and three
young ladies, one each from Martinique, the British West Indies, and
Afro-America, all of whom were in love with the hero, who was leaving
for Nigeria on UNIA organizational business. In between the romantic

escapades the audience was treated to monologues extolling the virtues of the UNIA. The set was liberally decorated with the red, black and green of the UNIA, and the hero and the lady of his choice eventually announced their intention to be married in a Liberty Hall in Africa.[13]

Garvey himself indulged in political play writing. His *The Coronation of the African King* was performed at his Edelweis Park headquarters in Jamaica in 1930. The three-act play included scenes in New York, Washington, Paris, London, the West Indies, Ashanti, Dahomey, Senegal and the Sudan. One scene showed the French premier and British Prime Minister David Lloyd George conferring over UNIA penetration into Africa. Another featured black voices delivering stirring oratory against a backdrop of African freedom fighters engaged in bloody struggle with French usurpers in the Sudan. The whole play was conceived as a dramatization of the results of UNIA propaganda since 1918.[14]

Such cultural activity was widely indulged in throughout the UNIA. The Dominica division had a literary club. The Black Cross Nurses in Norfolk, Virginia, in 1922 staged *An African Convention*, a play which "was full of race pride, and was staged to enthuse the public on the aims of the U.N.I.A. and A.C.L." In Newport News, Virginia, at about the same time, the Juvenile Black Cross Nurses and Boy Scouts put on a short play, *Coming Home to Africa*. In New York the UNIA Dramatic Club performed "the great race drama, 'Tallaboo,'" designed to "Interpret the Ideas of This Great Association."[15] The Philadelphia division sponsored *The New Negro*, described as "A Genuine Negro Melodrama." The *Negro World* commented on the play: "The old Uncle Tom type is shown as a servant of the Hon. Marcus Garvey, while the new Negro stands up man to man in the son of Marcus Garvey and demands an equal break with other races."[16]

Garvey's heyday in the 1920s coincided with the Afro-American literary efflorescence known as the Harlem Renaissance, for the race and Africa-consciousness of which Garvey himself was in no small way responsible. Indeed, some of the most important artists of the Renaissance were associated with the UNIA. Claude McKay was a Garvey supporter and a regular contributor to the *Negro World* in its early period; Eric Walrond was a *Negro World* editor; and Zora Neale Hurston was a columnist for the paper. *Negro World* readers were treated to excellent book reviews by editors William H. Ferris, Eric Walrond and Hubert H. Harrison.

Yet Garvey could not uncritically accept the exoticism and exaggerated Negritude which sometimes characterized writers of the period. He accordingly joined in the chorus of criticism against Claude McKay's *Home to Harlem.* Writing from France he disapproved strenuously of black writers who were "prostituting their intelligence, under the direction of the white man, to bring out and show up the worst traits of our people. . . ." He considered McKay's book "a damnable libel against the Negro" and postulated his conception of the type of artist the race needed: "We must encourage our own black authors who have character, who are loyal to their race, who feel proud to be black, and in every way let them feel that we appreciate their efforts to advance our race through healthy and decent literature."[17]

The *Negro World,* in similar vein, took Countee Cullen, another luminary of the Harlem Renaissance, to task. The paper deplored the fact that a Harvard graduate could overdo the Negritude idea to the extent of writing:

> Not yet has my heart or head
> In the least way realized
> It and I are civilized.[18]

During UNIA international conventions in New York and Jamaica, a literary censor was recommended who would safeguard black people from material unfavorable to the race.[19]

During the latter half of the 1930s Garvey increasingly focused his attention on Paul Robeson, the leading black motion picture actor of the period. Garvey paid due homage to Robeson's artistic ability but did not like the spectacle of the foremost black dramatic personality of the age being cast in a series of roles calculated to demean black folk. Robeson was reported in 1929 to be the projected star of a satire on Garvey's career written by two authors, Wallace Thurman and Willard Rapp, known for their sensationalism of Harlem's seamier side. Whether this had anything to do with Garvey's attitude is unclear. The play was to be titled *Jeremiah the Great.*[20] At any rate, 1935 found Garvey denouncing Robeson's appearances in such well-known stage and motion picture productions as *Emperor Jones, Sanders of the River,* and *Stevedore.* Readers of Garvey's *Black Man* magazine were informed that "Paul Robeson, the Negro actor, has left London for Hollywood. He is gone there to make another slanderous picture against the Negro." The point was made that in days gone by any black man who succeeded in white circles was automatically lionized. That day should be no more. The hope was expressed that Robeson was now making sufficient money "so that when he retires from the stage he may be able to square his conscience with his race by doing something good for it."[21] In 1937 Garvey protested to the British Broadcasting Corporation against antiblack programs and to the British Moving Picture Board against Robeson's films, while in 1939, one year before his death, he actually published a critical pamphlet aimed at Robeson's films.[22] Robeson withdrew from Hollywood the same year for the same reasons contained in Garvey's criticisms.[23]

Garvey's concern with the racial implications of culture embraced also vaudeville (the UNIA owned two follies companies in Jamaica), various UNIA choirs and bands (such as the Universal Jazz Hounds of the Jamaica UNIA), and sports, where Garvey expressed keen interest in the wider implications of the Joe Louis versus Max Schmeling bouts of the late 1930s. Outstanding black talent in any field was always welcome at Liberty Hall. Women's day at the 1922 convention featured Marian Anderson of Philadelphia, billed as "America's Greatest Contralto Soloist."

Garvey's doctrine of race first was severely tested by the presence within the race of large numbers of persons of mixed African and Caucasian origin. He took the position that "there is more bitterness among us Negroes because of the caste of color than there is between any other peoples, not excluding the people of India."[24] He even asserted that prejudice within the race probably exceeded that directed against the race by alien races.[25] This position brought Garvey into serious ideological conflict with middle-class leaders in the United States and the West Indies, many of whom were themselves of lighter hue. Such opposition was particularly hostile in the United States, where integrationist leaders such as W. E. B. Du Bois argued that this problem either did not exist or was relatively minor in the United States and that Garvey, because of his West Indian background, was erroneously importing this feature of island society into an Afro-American scene that he did not understand.

Garvey had indeed come out of a West Indian society stultified by an exaggerated three-tiered system of white-brown-black social stratification, and he himself regularly discussed the problem from at least as early as 1913.[26] His Jamaican daily, the *Blackman* editorialized in 1929:

Some people are afraid, some annoyed and others disgusted that we,
as they say,

RAISE THE COLOUR QUESTION

The question has long ago been raised and put into vindictive operation. The colour question is the one and only reason that we cannot
find a black girl or boy in store or office in this city when to our certain knowledge intelligent ones among them . . . have been refused at
places filled with half illiterate brown and mulatto girls and boys affecting the attitude of superiors in behavior. . . .

There is going to be fairplay in this country yet. "The Blackman" is
on the job and soon will blacken some of these stores and offices beyond recognition.[27]

As the editorial suggests, even in Jamaica, where the color-caste distinctions were acute, the tendency of the brown class was to deny its
existence, much as Du Bois and the Afro-American integrationists did.
But Garvey was relentless in his attempts to bring the issue to the surface.
"This hypocritical cry of 'Peace, Peace,' when there is no Peace is ruinous
to the peace and harmony of society," he declared.

We deny the existence of a condition that is woven into the warp and
woof of the fabric of our social and public life. We refuse to admit
the presence of a feature in our national life, the inescapable results
of whose insidious workings cause delay, irritation and annoyance.
We rave against, we forbid, we threaten those [who] dare to refer to
the evident, the patent facts and their glaring results. While the whole
land is leavened and permeated with the evils of colour distinction
and we cry out for harmony and peace. We are, to use a vulgar phrase,
a bunch of cheats. We are dishonest, immoral, liars, hypocrites.[28]

This type of assault on entrenched privilege brought Garvey a death threat
from a self-styled "Jamaican Secret Society of Colored Men," which considered him a "black swine."[29]
    In Afro-America, too, Garvey observed a preference among employers
for light-skinned people as clerks, waitresses, etc., and newspapers full

of advertisements for skin whiteners, often couched in the crudest possible language. Added to this, he discovered in New York, Boston, Washington and Detroit the Blue Vein Society and the Colonial Club. "The
West Indian 'lights' formed the 'Colonial Club' and the American 'lights'
the 'Blue Vein' Society."[30] These attitudes extended into the churches.
It would appear then, that Garvey, as one of his supporters pointed out,
did not "appeal" to intrarace color prejudice in the United States but
rather "revealed" it.[31]

Despite the similarities, of course, the situation in America, where the
majority did not need the support of the buffer mulatto element to the
same extent as the white minority in the islands, was not as serious as in
the West Indies. Garvey was fully aware of this. The situation in America
was serious enough to warrant exposure and attack, but in the West Indies
it more nearly approximated a rigid caste structure. Garvey himself pin-
pointed this difference better than any of his critics:

> In the term "Negro" we include all those persons whom the American
> white man includes in this appelation of his contempt and hate. . . .
> The contents of the term are much reduced in Jamaica and the West
> Indies, but it carries no less of reprobation against the persons. . . .

> The great curse of our Jamaica communal life is the failure of the
> hybrid population to realize their natural and correct identifica-
> tion. . . .[32]

So whereas the UNIA in the United States numbered among its ranks
people of all colors, excluding whites, and business and professional
people in addition to the great mass of workers and peasants, in Jamaica
it was largely confined to the "humbler sections" of humanity. This led
Garvey to surmise that "God seems to save from the bottom upwards."[33]
Garvey's experience with the light-skinned element, both in the West
Indies and America, led him to be hostile toward those who seemed to
portray the supercilious attitudes he abhorred. It led him, too, to consider
miscegenation to be an evil which should not be perpetuated—"We are
conscious of the fact that slavery brought upon us the curse of many
colors within our Race, but that is no reason why we of ourselves should
perpetuate the evil. . . ."[34]

The doctrine of race first had various implications for Garvey's attitude toward white people. It meant first of all the exclusion of white people from membership in the UNIA and affiliated organizations. Whites were also prevented from holding shares in Garvey's economic undertakings. His desire to build racial self-reliance led logically to the rejection of white financial philanthropy. In reply to a suggestion by a white reporter in 1921 that "certain negrophiles in Massachusetts" might be prevailed upon to contribute to the UNIA, Garvey replied, "We do not want their money; this is a black man's movement."[35]

Race first meant, however, not only race first for black people but for other races as well. As far as Garvey was concerned, white people of whatever political pursuasion put race before all other considerations. Accordingly he often preferred an honest expression of racism to the possibly transparent smiles of the philanthropist. He looked at the honest expression of racism as a blessing in disguise because it forced the black man into a heightened racial consciousness whereas the camouflaged variety could lull him into a sense of false security. Commenting in 1917 on the great strides Afro-Americans had made in independent racial endeavor, he wrote: "The honest prejudice of the South was sufficiently evident to give the Negro of America the real start—the start with a race consciousness, which I am convinced is responsible for the state of development already reached by the race."[36] Thus he could say, "We have to admire the white man who fixed the Bible to suit himself, and who even fixed tradition itself, telling us that everything worthwhile and beautiful was made by the white man; that God is a great white man, that Jesus was a white man, and that the angels, etc., whatever they are, are as beautiful as peaches in Georgia."[37]

By the same token, however, he saw white self-interest as largely detrimental to black self-interest. And within the confines of a country such as the United States, where whites formed a large ruling majority, white racial self-interest would tend inexorably toward the extermination of the black minority. These considerations strengthened Garvey's commitment to racial separation.

Despite the fact that Garvey would not accept white philanthropy or allow whites to join his organization, it did not follow that he could not work to a limited extent with white people. In fact, by maintaining an independent black power base, he had more freedom to work with or support widely differing types of white persons and organizations on specific projects or for limited objectives than some of his contemporaries who were straitjacketed in interracial organizations.

The first category of white people with whom Garvey could cooperate were certain types of radicals, usually those engaged in anticolonial, anti-imperialist or antiracist struggles. Often they were leaders of mass movements like his own and he could identify them as kindred spirits. Among persons in this category were Eamon De Valera, the Irish leader, who on one occasion was listed as a featured speaker at Garvey's Harlem Liberty Hall,[38] and the Russian revolutionaries Lenin and Trotsky. He often had a good word for historical figures such as John Brown, Elijah Lovejoy, and others of abolitionist inclination.[39] He also had great admiration for Captain A. A. Cipriani, white leader of the Trinidad Workingmen's Association (TWA), whose public career largely coincided with Garvey's in time and political outlook. Cipriani had become head of the TWA in 1919 at the invitation of the members, who were black. By this time the association had already become a Garveyite stronghold in Trinidad, and its struggles were being reported in the *Negro World*. Many of its meetings were held in Port-of-Spain's Liberty Hall and its second-in-command, W. Howard Bishop, as well as other members of its hierarchy were prominent Garveyites. Garvey corresponded with Cipriani, who made representations to the British government in 1937 to change their intention of barring Garvey from entry into the island.[40] Another well-known white radical for whom Garvey seems to have had some respect was Nancy Cunard, renegade member of a wealthy shipping family who became involved in a variety of black causes. In 1932 Cunard visited Jamaica to gather material for her *Negro Anthology* and was the guest at a reception arranged by Garvey.[41]

If Garvey could associate with some radical whites of the left in deference to their anti-imperialist stance or reputation as leaders of the masses, he could also associate, for different reasons, with segregationists on the far right. These latter shared one very crucial ideological tenet with Garvey: they, too, believed in race first and therefore in the separation of the races.

Despite Garvey's limited agreements with some white persons, however, the insistent black nationalist thrust of the UNIA ensured the hostility of the majority of whites. One white lady witnessing a UNIA parade on 125 Street in Manhattan in 1920 is said to have tearfully exclaimed, "And to think, the Negroes will get their liberty before the Irish."[42]

Garvey's race-first doctrine was essentially a stratagem to ensure self-reliance and equality for the downtrodden African race. Unlike the white preachers of this doctrine with whom he collaborated, he did not go a step further and preach racial superiority. He more than once stressed that "all beauty, virtue and goodness are the exclusive attributes of no one race. All humanity have their shortcomings; hence no statement of mine, at any time, must be interpreted as a wholesale praise of, or attack upon any race, people or creed."[43]

Self-reliance was a necessary corollary to race first. In his earliest extant pamphlet Garvey explained, in terms showing the probable influence of Booker T. Washington, that "the Negro is ignored to-day simply because he has kept himself backward; but if he were to try to raise himself to a higher state in the civilized cosmos, all the other races would be glad to meet him on the plane of equality and comradeship." He went on to express an idea which would later cause him much enmity from Afro-American integrationists: "It is indeed unfair to demand equality when one of himself has done nothing to establish the right to equality."[44] Garvey never abandoned this dual tendency to score the white race for its injustice while simultaneously utilizing the language of condemnation to spur the black race on to greater self-reliance.

Garvey's belief in the necessity for self-reliance led him occasionally to speak in the language of Social Darwinism. He attacked the pseudo-scientific racists who tried to justify genocide against black people in terms of the Darwinian "survival of the fittest" and turned their arguments to the cause of racial self-reliance. "White philosophers," he argued, "Darwin, Locke, Newton and the rest . . . forgot that the monkey would change to a man, his tail would drop off and he would demand his share."[45] And not only had these philosophers been mistaken, but black heroism in World War I had finally given the lie to such false assumptions. He reminded his black audiences that "that theory has been exploded in the world war. It was you, the superman, that brought back victory at the Marne."[46]

The urgency Garvey felt for racial independence and self-reliance led him to argue that in independent endeavor lay the only hope of eventual solution to the problem of race prejudice. The white race would cease its aggressiveness toward the black when it was met by independent black power of a magnitude equal to its own. White prejudice was manifested "not because there is a difference between us in religion or in colour, but because there is a difference between us in power."[47]

Furthermore, Garvey believed that the black man had little choice in the matter. If he did not continue going forward, spurred on by his own efforts, then he would slide backward into slavery and even extermination. "The days of slavery are not gone forever," he reminded his followers. "Slavery is threatened for every race and nation that remains weak and refuses to organize its strength for its own protection."[48]

The most important area for the exercise of independent effort was economic. Garvey believed, like Washington before him, that economics was primary. Successful political action could only be founded on an independent economic base. "After a people have established successfully a firm industrial foundation," he wrote, "they naturally turn to politics and society, but not first to society and politics, because the two latter cannot exist without the former."[49] Within months of his arrival in the United States in 1916, Garvey was already appraising, with approval, the efforts Afro-Americans had made in the economic field. At this early period, before he had made his decision to remain in the United States, he wrote, in a vein having prophetic implications for his own career, "The acme of American Negro enterprise is not yet reached. You have still a far way to go. You want more stores, more banks, and bigger enterprises. I hope that your powerful Negro press and the conscientious element among your leaders will continue to inspire you to achieve. . . ."[50]

This desire for economic self-reliance dominated Garvey's thought. The fact that the black man was a consumer and not an independent producer worried him. "Let Edison turn off his electric light and we are in darkness in Liberty Hall in two minutes," he once said, "The Negro is living on borrowed goods."[51]

Garvey made a valiant attempt to change this state of affairs. Between 1918 and the early 1920s Garvey's headquarters area in New York City sprouted a large assortment of UNIA businesses. The Black Star Line was incorporated in 1919. The Negro Factories Corporation followed not long afterward. Under its aegis there appeared Universal Launderies, a Universal Millinery Store, Universal Restaurants, Universal Grocery Stores, as well as a hotel, tailoring establishment, doll factory and print-

ing press. In addition, the UNIA in New York had by the first half of
1920 acquired three buildings, one lot and two trucks, and its weekly
organ, the *Negro World,* was already well established. By 1920, too, Garvey
was even contemplating a large bank.[52] By 1920, more than three hundred
persons were employed by the UNIA and its allied corporations in the
United States, and between 1920 and 1924 UNIA and allied employees
on occasion exceeded one thousand in the United States alone.[53]

The effort at self-reliance is well illustrated by the status of the Negro
Factories Corporation in mid-1922. There were three grocery stores.
Cooperative buying for all the stores and restaurants was done by one
manager, thus keeping prices competitive with the white-owned enterprises which proliferated in Harlem. At Universal Grocery Store No. 1
(47 West 135 Street) the manager reported a minority of white customers.
Grocery Store No. 2 (646 Lenox Avenue, between 142 and 143 Streets)
was reported to be doing all right, despite being surrounded by white
competition. Store No. 3, at 552 Lenox Avenue and 138 Street, was said
to be the most flourishing of the three. It included a meat, fish, and
poultry market, said to be the only one of its kind in Harlem. It also
boasted the first black butcher in Harlem. The groceries featured such
foods as West Indian yams, pigeon peas, eddoes, pumpkins and plantains,
and southern sweet potatoes and cane syrup.

Universal Restaurant No. 1 was situated in Liberty Hall at 138 Street.
Its seating capacity of fifty was being increased to a hundred. Mrs. Mary
Lawrence, a food chemist and former hospital dietician, presided over
the food preparation. Restaurant No. 2 at 75 West 135 Street was smaller
and still new and facing competition from eight other eating places in
the same block.

The corporation's Bee Hive Printing Plant at 2305 Seventh Avenue
was described as doing the bulk of Harlem's job and magazine printing.

At 62 West 142 Street was situated the corporation's Universal Mart
of Industry, which housed a variety of enterprises. These included the
Universal Steam and Electric Laundry, which employed two delivery
trucks; the Men's Manufacturing Department, which made UNIA uniforms, insignia, and the like; and a Women's Manufacturing Department
and Bazaar, which made Black Cross Nurses' uniforms, Panama hats and
other millinery, shirts and ties. Plans were afoot for a Universal catalog
and mail-order business, and indeed nurses' uniforms were already available on a mail-order basis.

Presiding over the Negro Factories Corporation, at that time employing about seventy-five people, was Ulysses S. Poston, UNIA minister of industries and a former editor of the black Detroit *Contender*.[54] Because of his position Poston found himself called upon to act as an unofficial adviser to Harlem businesses in general. During May 1922 alone, he reported, the UNIA Department of Labor and Industries had received at least forty visits from Harlem businessmen who wanted the UNIA to bail them out.[55]

In addition to the parent body in Harlem, local branches of the UNIA owned considerable amounts of property and sometimes launched into local business ventures. The encouragement of local businesses was in fact a prime motive for the enterprises established in Harlem by Garvey. These efforts were often successful. In 1927, for example, after several years of financial assault on the organization and two years after Garvey's incarceration, his attorneys stated that the organization still owned assets, usually real estate, valued at $20,000 in Philadelphia, $30,000 in Pittsburgh, $50,000 in Detroit, and $30,000 in Chicago, among other places.[56] Local units outside the United States participated in such economic activity also. The Colón, Panama, UNIA, for example, ran a cooperative bakery, while the Kingston, Jamaica, branch ran a laundry and an African Communities League Peoples Co-operative Bank, the shares of which were open only to UNIA members.[57]

The individual business enterprises established by UNIA branches all over the world were to be linked, according to Garvey's grand design, into a worldwide system of Pan-African economic cooperation. Such a trading community, when fully developed, would be so large that the economies of scale generated would enable it to thrive even in the face of hostility from the rest of the world. Garvey summed up this idea thus: "Negro producers, Negro distributors, Negro consumers! The world of Negroes can be self-contained. We desire earnestly to deal with the rest of the world, but if the rest of the world desire not, we seek not."[58] The Black Star Line (and later the Black Cross Navigation and Trading Company) was to be the carrier for this Pan-African trade.

Garvey's attempts to establish economic self-reliance went beyond cooperative business enterprises, for UNIA branches acted as mutual aid friendly societies for the payment of death and other minor benefits to members. In rural areas among poor communities, this aspect of the organization's operations assumed greater importance. Local divisions also were required to maintain a charitable fund "for the purpose of assisting distressed members or needy individuals of the race," a fund for "loans of honor" to active members, and an employment bureau to assist members seeking work.[59]

Economic self-reliance, especially on the American scene, acquired a special urgency for Garvey, for he foresaw a depression which he thought would finish the black man in America for good: "The readjustment of the world, as I have often said, is going to bring about an economic, industrial stagnation in America that is going to reduce the Negro to his last position in this nation."[60]

The UNIA quest for self-reliance led to sporadic attempts at educational facilities provided by the organization. Garvey's correspondence with Booker T. Washington and his visit to the United States were both motivated by a desire to establish in Jamaica an industrial and agricultural school along the lines of Washington's Tuskegee Institute in Alabama. This desire for an education geared toward independence continuously cropped up. The 1920 Declaration of Rights had demanded unlimited and unprejudiced education for black people, and UNIA locals in Port Limón (Costa Rica), Colón (Panama), British Guiana and elsewhere ran elementary and sometimes grammar schools.[61] One such school in Colón was described, two months after its inception in 1925, as being along cooperative lines (with free tuition for members' children), with an enrollment of more than three hundred and staffed by five British West Indian and one Panamanian teacher, the latter appointed to satisfy a government requirement for a Spanish-speaking teacher.[62]

In New York City the association owned a "Booker T. Washington University" in the early years, and in 1926 the association in the United States obtained the Smallwood-Corey Industrial Institute in Claremont, Virginia, afterward renamed Liberty University. The school was reported to be on property adjoining the James River and containing the wharf where the second lot of slaves landed in Virginia in 1622. It was transferred to the UNIA in consideration for assuming its outstanding indebtedness. At the time of its transfer the school's vice-president, J. G. St. Clair Drake, was the UNIA's international organizer, while its principal, Caleb B. Robinson, was a member of the Philadelphia division.[63] Liberty University was acquired amid high hopes that it would become a successful vehicle for imparting self-reliance and race pride and for rehabilitating black history.[64] The university, like many other Afro-American colleges

of the period, was in fact of high school standard, and it struggled on
for three years before being closed in 1929 due to financial difficulty.
Those students who did attend were often sponsored by local UNIA
units and were dedicated Garveyites.

In addition to its formally organized schools, the UNIA throughout
its history organized inservice training courses of various kinds. During
Garvey's American period, for example, the organization carried out
such programs for its civil servants, and ex-schoolmaster James O'Meally
wrote a special guidebook for prospective UNIA officers. During Garvey's
last years in London he organized a School of African Philosophy which,
by means of correspondence courses as well as intensive courses administered by Garvey himself in Canada, prepared UNIA workers for their
roles in the organization.

The insistent UNIA thrust for self-reliance can best be summarized in
Garvey's own words:

> The Universal Negro Improvement Association teaches to our race
> self-help and self-reliance, not only in one essential, but in all those
> things that contribute to human happiness and well being. The dis-
> position of the many to depend upon the other races for a kindly and
> sympathetic consideration of their needs, without making the effort
> to do for themselves, has been the race's standing disgrace by which
> we have been judged and through which we have created the strongest
> prejudice against ourselves. . . .

> The race needs workers at this time, not plagiarists, copyists and mere
> imitators; but men and women who are able to create, to originate
> and improve, and thus make an independent racial contribution to
> the world and civilization.[65]

NOTES

1. *Negro World*, July 26, 1919.
2. Ibid., January 5, 1924.
3. *Black Man* 2 (September-October 1936): 5.
4. *Negro World*, July 28, 1923.
5. A UNIA application form of 1915 required the applicant to state
his color. Enclosed in Marcus Garvey to Booker T. Washington, April 12,
1915, Box 939, Booker T. Washington Papers, Library of Congress.

6. U.S. Post Office, Translation Bureau, to Solicitor, Post Office Department, July 24, 1919, RG 28, Box 56, Unarranged #500, National Archives of the United States, Records of the Post Office Department.

7. Speech at the Ward Theatre, Kingston, Jamaica, *Negro World,* January 7, 1928.

8. After Garvey's imprisonment some such advertisements (e.g., for bleaching creams) did appear in the *Negro World,* no doubt a reflection of financial necessity; for a letter protesting this development, see *Negro World,* September 7, 1929.

9. Marcus Garvey, *Selections from the Poetic Meditations of Marcus Garvey* (New York: A. J. Garvey, 1927), p. 22.

10. Garvey to Viscount Halifax, Secretary of State, Foreign Office, November 22, 1938, FO 371/21637, Foreign Office Records, Public Record Office, London.

11. *Blackman,* September 3, 1929. *"Black Man"* refers here to Garvey's monthly magazine published for the most part in England. *"Blackman"* refers to his daily (subsequently weekly) paper published in Jamaica.

12. Garvey, *Selections;* Marcus Garvey, *The Tragedy of White Injustice* (New York: A. J. Garvey, 1927). The *Black Man* magazine also contains a large number of his poems.

13. *Preaching vs. Practice,* n.d., John E. Bruce Papers, F10, 8, Schomburg Collection, New York Public Library; *Which One,* Bruce Papers, BD 10, D. 1. Another Bruce creation, *The Odious Comparison,* was serialized in the *Negro World;* see the July 1, 1922, edition, for example.

14. *Blackman,* June 21, 1930.

15. *Negro World,* May 13, 1922; January 28, 1922; December 17, 1921; January 21, 1922.

16. *Negro World,* July 16, 1921.

17. Ibid., September 29, 1928.

18. Ibid., January 9, 1932.

19. Ralph Bunche, "The Programs, Ideologies, Tactics and Achievements of Negro Betterment and Interracial Organizations," unpublished manuscript prepared for the Cargegie-Myrdal study on *The Negro in America,* June 7, 1940 (Schomburg Collection), p. 419; *Negro World,* June 7, 1924, in FO 371/9633.

20. *Negro World,* November 9, 1929.

21. *Black Man* (late October 1935): 10-11.

22. *Panama Tribune,* February 14, 1937; Marcus Garvey, *Grand Speech of Hon. Marcus Garvey at Kingsway Hall, London, Denouncing the Moving Picture Propaganda to Discredit the Negro* (London: Black Man Pub. Co., 1939).

23. Paul Robeson, Jr., "Paul Robeson: Black Warrior," *Freedomways* 11 (1971): 26.

24. *Negro World,* December 8, 1923; Amy Jacques Garvey, ed., *The Philosophy and Opinions of Marcus Garvey* (London: Frank Cass, 1967), II: 128.

25. Marcus Garvey, *An Answer to His Many Critics* (UNIA press release "To the White Press of the World," January 1923).

26. Marcus Garvey, Jr., "The British West Indies in the Mirror of Civilization," *Africa Times and Orient Review* (October 1913): p. 159; Marcus Garvey, Jr., *A Talk With Afro-West Indians* (Kingston?, African Communities League, 1915), p. 6; Garvey to Moton, February 29, 1916, reprinted in *Eight Negro Bibliographies.*

27. *Blackman,* April 16, 1929.

28. Ibid., January 22, 1930.

29. Ibid., May 20, 1929.

30. Garvey, *Philosophy and Opinions,* II: 58.

31. *Negro World,* October 27, 1923.

32. *Blackman,* September 17, 1929.

33. Ibid.

34. Garvey, *An Answer to His Many Critics.*

35. Rollin Lynde Hartt, "The Negro Moses," *The Independent* 105 (February 26, 1921): 205.

36. Marcus Garvey, Jr., "The West Indies in the Mirror of Truth," *Champion Magazine* 1 (January 1917): 267.

37. *Negro World,* April 28, 1923.

38. Handbill in the John E. Bruce papers announcing a Liberty Hall meeting on Saturday, January 1 (year not given).

39. *Negro World,* March 7, 1925; Garvey, *Philosophy and Opinions,* II: 10.

40. *Negro World,* June 14, 1919, memorial of the T.W.A. to the British Government. *New Jamaican,* September 1, 1932, p. 2; minute of 21 July 1937, CO 323/1518; and see Tony Martin, "Marcus Garvey and Trinidad, 1912-1947," paper read at the International Seminar on Marcus Garvey, University of the West Indies, January 1973.

41. *New Jamaican,* July 12, July 18, July 29, July 30, 1932.

42. Truman Hughes Talley, "Garvey's 'Empire of Ethiopia,' " *World's Work,* 41 (January 1921): 265.

43. Garvey, *Philosophy and Opinions,* II: 134; *Blackman,* June 21, 1929.

44. Marcus Garvey, *A Talk with Afro-West Indians,* (Kingston [?] : African Communities League, 1915 [?]), p. 2.

45. St. Louis, Mo., *Star,* October 6, 1923.

46. British Guiana *Tribune,* May 15, 1921.

47. *Negro World,* February 24, 1923.

48. Ibid., May 22, 1926.

49. Ibid., May 17, 1924.

50. Marcus Garvey, "The West Indies in the Mirror of Truth," *Champion Magazine* 1, (January 1917): 267.

51. *Negro World,* January 26, 1924.

52. William H. Ferris, "Garvey and the Black Star Line," *Favorite Magazine* 4 (July 1920): 396; Amy Ashwood Garvey, "Prophet," pp. 153, 154; Michael Gold, "When Africa Awakes," *New York World,* August 22, 1920, p. 7; Wells, *Crusade for Justice,* p. 380; M.I. l.c., New York to Foreign Office, January 7, 1920, FO 371/4567; *New York Amsterdam News,* January 31, 1923; undated anonymous letter, "To the Editor," Bruce Papers, BL 11.

53. Ferris, "Garvey and the BSL"; *Negro World,* May 6, 1933.

54. *Negro World,* July 8, 1922, March 22, 1922.

55. Ibid., August 12, 1922.

56. RG 204, 42-793, Records of the Office of the Pardon Attorney, National Archives.

57. *Negro World,* June 30, 1923; *Blackman,* July 30, 1929; *Blackman,* August 23, 1930.

58. *Blackman,* April 10, 1929.

59. *Universal Black Men Catechism* (n.p., n.d.), p. 28.

60. *Negro World,* January 26, 1924.

61. *Negro World,* December 24, 1927; *Blackman,* August 5, 1929; ibid., June 21, 1930.

62. Odin G. Loren, American Vice Consul, Colon, to Secretary of State, Washington, D.C., April 22, 1925, Records of the Department of State, RG 59, 819.5032; *The Star and Herald* (Panama), April 19, 1925.

63. *Negro World,* July 24, 1926.

64. Ibid., August 7, 28, 1926.

65. Ibid., August 18, 1923.

3

Nationhood

When we, as members of the Universal Negro Improvement Association, talk about a government of our own in Africa, a flag of our own and a national anthem of our own, some Negroes laugh at us, but we have only pity for them, as they know not what they do. When Uncle Sam lynches her black boys with her uniform on their back, and John Bull calls her ex-soldiers aliens who helped her in the Ashanti and Zulu wars to take big slices of Africa, then it is high time for some dull, apathetic Negroes to think in terms of nationhood.

—Marcus Garvey[1]

. . . we are determined to solve our own problem, by redeeming our Motherland Africa from the hands of alien exploiters and found there a Government, a nation of our own, strong enough to lend protection to the members of our race scattered all over the world, and to compel the respect of the nations and races of the earth.

—Marcus Garvey[2]

Convinced that black people must seek salvation first as a race, Garvey set himself the task of doing this through the principle of nationhood.

He believed that black people should be brought into one active community encompassing the whole black universe. By belonging to this
Pan-African community of four hundred million (Garvey's critics often
took issue with his arithmetic) black people could rely on the force of
an overwhelming majority, even in areas, such as the United States, where
they were in a minority.

The idea of nationhood, like probably all of his major ideas, had already been formulated by Garvey before the UNIA was formed, as evidenced by his activity in the National Club in Jamaica. By the time that
the UNIA became operative in the United States, then, Garvey could
proclaim his disagreement with the limited strategies of his rivals—the
UNIA, he declared, did not speak "in the language of theology and religion; not in the language of social reform, but the Universal Negro Improvement Association speaks in the language of building a government: of
building political power and all that goes with it."[3]

And "all that goes with it" the UNIA did have. Indeed, during Garvey's
American period it became a microcosm of the African nation that Garvey
hoped to build. In the international conventions beginning in 1920 the
UNIA had, in Garvey's words, "the greatest Legislative Assembly ever
brought together by the Negro peoples of the world."[4] Issues were aired
and debated, usually for the full thirty-one days of August, and all officers,
including Garvey himself, were duly elected. Delegates, themselves usually
elected by UNIA branches and other race organizations, attended from
places as far apart as Australia, Africa and North America. Presiding over
the organization from 1920 on was a potentate, a kind of constitutional
monarch. The UNIA constitution stipulated that the potentate must be
an African from the Motherland. Garvey himself, the executive head, was
given the title of provisional president of Africa. The black world was sub-
divided into several broad geographical regions, each presided over by a
leader. The organization had its own "Universal Ethiopian Anthem,"
which in 1920 was adopted as "the anthem of the Negro race,"[5] as well
as its own Magna Charta in its Declaration of Rights of the Negro Peoples
of the World adopted at the 1920 convention. Garvey himself was bestowed with the title "honorable" at this convention. A UNIA civil service administered its own exams and prepared workers for service in the
organization. The UNIA demonstrated the trappings of nationhood, too,
by bestowing titles on deserving members of the race. White as well as

black critics ridiculed the practice, to which Garvey retorted, "I am accused of creating Dukes, Barons and Knights. Who gave the white man a monopoly on creating social orders?"[6] With similar logic Garvey insisted on wearing, on ceremonial occasions, uniforms and robes after the fashion of those worn by the leaders of sovereign states. Garvey lived long enough to see the Italian fascists install a Duke of Addis Ababa after their invasion of Ethiopia. He pointedly noted the lack of hostility to this occurrence from those who had ridiculed him in 1924 for appointing John E. Bruce a Duke of the Nile.[7] The external attributes of nationhood were evidenced also in the uniformed auxiliaries of the UNIA, such as the Universal African Legions, the Universal Motor Corps, the Universal African Black Cross Nurses, Juveniles, and so on.

The most extravagantly impressive item of Garvey's nationalist-inspired pageantry centered around the court receptions that marked his conventions. Such receptions were conceived of as "the biggest event in the social life of the Negro Peoples of the World." The 1929 reception was adorned with a statue of the Black Queen of Beauty holding aloft her torch of truth. Among the retinue at such court receptions were "Her Majesty Candace and Provisional Ladies of the Royal Court of Ethiopia of the UNIA."

The most enduring of the UNIA's external trappings of nationhood was its flag of red, black and green, adopted in the 1920 Declaration of Rights as the official colors of the African race. The question of a flag for the race was not as trivial as might have appeared on the surface, for in the United States especially, the lack of an African symbol of nationhood seems to have been the cause for crude derision on the part of whites and a source of sensitivity on the part of Afro-Americans. White derision over this deficiency was summed up in a popular American song, "Every Race Has a Flag But the 'Coon.'" A 1912 report appearing in the *Africa Times and Orient Review* (for which Garvey worked) documented the far-reaching consequences of this song.[8] A Bishop J. Lennox of the African Methodist Episcopal Church of Zion of Cleveland, Ohio, had emerged from a theater where the song had been sung to be met by a fistfight between an Irishman and an Afro-American who had objected to the white man's repeating the song. The bishop duly parted the contestants but was moved by the incident to design a flag for the race to remove this source of ridicule. His flag was subsequently endorsed by eighty-five thousand (according to the article) black people at a convention in Ontario, Canada. The general conclave of the bishop's church also endorsed the flag. The flag was a complicated affair of stars and bars and red, white, blue and purple, and was based largely on biblical symbolism (purple for Jesus' robe, white for the purity of the saints, blue for the loyalty of the Negro to the United States). The flag itself was apparently not a great success but the idea lived on with Garvey who was able to translate it into the more meaningful (and today universally adopted) red, black, and green.

Garvey was in all probability familiar with the bishop's article. In 1921 he declared,

> Show me the race or the nation without a flag, and I will show you a race of people without any pride. Aye! In song and mimicry they have said, "Every race has a flag but the coon." How true! Aye! But that was said of us four years ago. They can't say it now. . . .[9]

The race catechism Garveyites used explained the significance of the red, black and green as red for the "color of the blood which men must shed for their redemption and liberty," black for "the color of the noble and distinguished race to which we belong," and green for "the luxuriant vegetation of our Motherland."[10] On at least one occasion Garvey gave a different explanation for the colors. Here his purpose seems to have been to deliberately alarm his interviewer, Charles Mowbray White, a member of the conservative coalition of businessmen, moderate trade-unionists, and professional people known as the National Civic Federation. He told White that the red expressed the UNIA's sympathy with the "Reds of the World," the green expressed a similar sympathy for the Irish in their struggle against the British, and the black stood for people of the African race.[11]

The nationalist implications of Garvey's flag, like other aspects of Garvey's thought, were not confined to Afro-America but inspired nationalist struggles on the African continent too. Thus at the charter unveiling ceremony of the UNIA Woodstock division in Cape Town, South Africa, in 1924, the featured speaker, J. G. Gumbs, expressed particular gratitude for the red, black and green flag, a flag, as he expressed it, "of our own."[12]

In the next year the African National Congress, also of South Africa, adopted a gold, black and green flag—gold for the country's wealth, black for the people and green for the land. The flag was suggested by a Garvey admirer and influential ANC member, T. D. Mweli Skota.[13] In the 1950s the red, black and green could be seen in Kenya, this time with a shield, arrow and spear superimposed on it, as the flag of Jomo Kenyatta's nationalist Kenya African Union.[14]

One of the more important consequences of Garvey's doctrine of nationhood was the establishment of representatives of the race in strategic areas. To this end the Declaration of Rights of the Negro Peoples of the World had called "upon the various governments of the world to accept and acknowledge Negro representatives who shall be sent to the said governments to represent the general welfare of the Negro peoples of the world."[15] Just days after the adoption of this declaration the announcement was made that the UNIA's leader of the American Negroes would take up residence in a Black House in Washington since black people could not elect one of their own to the White House.[16]

But even before the declaration and the Black House proposal (which was not implemented) the UNIA had sent commissioners to France to the Paris peace conference of 1919. Their lobbying efforts did not succeed in obtaining any abatement in the zeal of the European imperialist powers to seize the ex-German African colonies. Perhaps for this reason the 1920 declaration wrote the League of Nations off as "null and void as far as the Negro is concerned, in that it seeks to deprive Negroes of their liberty."[17] Nevertheless, by 1922 the UNIA was ready to try the league again. A delegation consisting of Oxford-trained George O. Marke from Sierra Leone, Professor J. J. Adam from Haiti, who was educated at Tuskegee, William LeVan Sherrill from Afro-America, a graduate of Philander Smith College, Little Rock, Arkansas, and Professor James O'Meally from Jamaica, a former teacher at Calabar College, proceeded to Geneva to lay a petition before the league. The petition requested that the ex-German colonies be turned over to black leadership, since black soldiers had been responsible for their capture. The petition suggested that under black leadership they could make good within twenty years. Then four hundred million black people would not be serfs any longer.[18]

The delegation arrived in Geneva early in September 1922, secured

seats in the assembly hall, was admitted to all committee rooms, and met
with the director of the mandates section of the league, whom they urged
to appoint a black person to the permanent mandates commission. After
lobbying for three and a half weeks, they were able to interest the Persian
delegation in submitting the petition on behalf of the UNIA. The Persians
did so, but by this time the current session of the league was within three
days of ending, and the petition was therefore filed away for consideration at the 1923 session. The UNIA delegation succeeded in being seated
among the official delegates rather than in the gallery where nonofficial
delegates sat. According to a member of the delegation, of about three
hundred similar unofficial delegates attempting to present petitions, only
the UNIA representatives succeeded.[19]

For the 1923 league session the UNIA again despatched a representative, in the hope that the 1922 petition would be debated. This time the
sole delegate was Professor Jean Joseph Adam, a former president of the
San Francisco UNIA division and secretary and translator to the 1922
delegation. Now he was upgraded to the rank of first provisional ambassador of the Negro peoples of the world to France. He would reside in
Paris and would lobby at Geneva. He sailed from New York on August
23, and on August 24, the British consul general in New York City, who
kept a close watch on the UNIA, so informed the British ambassador in
Washington who so informed the Foreign Office in London.[20] By the
time that Adam got to Europe the league, probably at the instigation of
Britain and France, whose ex-German African territories were the objects
of the UNIA's race-conscious desires, had quietly thwarted Garvey's
plans. They had gotten around the UNIA's assumption of nationality by
resolving that all nationals with grievances should present them through
their respective governments. As far as Garvey was concerned, of course,
the African, wherever he lived, had no government to speak to his interests
and so he should be heard as a race. And the UNIA, with its aspirations
to nationhood, represented these racial interests.[21]

The petition could hardly have pleased European governments, calling
as it did for "racial political liberty" and recalling the heroic efforts of
black soldiers, supposedly in the cause of democracy. It showed that all
subject peoples had received something out of the war, except the majority of Africans:

We readily appreciate the fact that the League of Nations has taken into consideration the restoration of Palestine to the Jew. . . . Ireland has been given the consideration of a Free State Government, Egypt has been granted a form of independence, and there is still a great consideration for India, who was represented at the Peace Conference at Versailles through and by reason of the splendid service rendered by Indian soldiers.[22]

Garvey issued a renewed petition in 1928 and continued to try to attract the league's attention thereafter, but he never came any closer to success than in 1922.[23]

The UNIA drive for nationhood did not stop with commissioners to the League of Nations and a provisional ambassador to France. Traveling commissioners were constantly on the move, establishing personal contact with UNIA branches. There were also provisional ambassadors appointed and legations set up in other places besides France. One such place was Liberia, where a legation was set up in 1921. The resident secretary summed up his duties in a letter to Garvey, in the following terms:

The oral instructions of Your Excellency, being conceived from the point of view that the post was a diplomatic one, the Commissariat a Legation, and my position Secretary to the Legation, indicated that I should do all that a Legation Secretary would be expected to do— study the Liberian situation, the people and the government, ferret out all important news about whomsoever and whatsoever, and make confidential reports to Your Excellency direct, aside from other reports that I might send to the Council through Your Excellency.[24]

In the case of Liberia, Garvey had attempted to establish a legation without openly advertising it as such. In January 1924, however, he despatched an ambassador to Britain amid much fanfare. He had been distressed during his travels in Europe to discover that all peoples and races residing there had someone who could look after their interests—except the black man. The first UNIA ambassador to Britain was Sir Richard Hilton Tobitt. Tobitt, a former African Methodist Episcopal minister and schoolmaster in Bermuda had attended the 1920 UNIA convention and was one of the signers of the Declaration of Rights. He was elected leader of the eastern provinces of the West Indies and, as a result of his refusal to disavow the UNIA, he lost his position in the church and suffered a withdrawal of government support from his school.[25] On his appointment he was admitted by Garvey to the "exclusive order of Knight-Commander of the Sublime Order of the Nile," which entitled him to use the prefix "Sir."[26] He was charged with the task of representing the interests of the Negro peoples of the world at the court of St. James. He was to study the political situation in England as it affected the African race. Garvey considered the time propitious (Tobitt sailed in January 1924) because 1924 was a year of Labour party rule. A Labour government, Garvey surmised, would be less difficult to deal with than aristocratic Conservatives, since they should have some sympathy for the aspirations of the mass of people. For this reason, too, Tobitt was charged with creating favorable sentiment among the English working class, for, as Garvey explained, "If you can convince the English working man that he has no cause for complaint against the Negro it would be impossible for any government in Great Britain to do anything that would affect the interests of Negroes. . . ." If English workers refused to fight, then there was no way that Britain could go to war with the UNIA in Africa. Tobitt, like Adam in France, would be a provisional ambassador only and would give way when a truly independent Africa began sending ambassadors of its own.[27]

Garvey, with all the aplomb of the master propagandist, officially informed the British government of the appointment of the Honorable Richard Hilton Tobitt as "High Commissioner and Minister Plenipotentiary to His Britannic Majesty's Government" in a note that read: "Honourable Richard Hilton Tobitt is accredited by the Universal Negro Improvement Association to interest himself in all matters affecting the interest of the Negro race within Great Britain." It continued, "His credentials have been submitted to His Majesty's Prime Minister and Foreign Secretary and it is hoped that His Majesty's Government will accord to him such courtesies as are extended to other representatives of independent races and sovereign peoples."[28]

Upon arrival in England, Tobitt requested interviews with the prime minister and the secretary of state of the Colonial Office so that he might present the credentials of the UNIA and ACL. His request precipitated a debate over whether a response should properly come from the British Foreign Office or the Colonial Office. One Colonial Office official suggested that it was the business of his department "to keep Garvey and his associates out of West Africa—not out of No. 10." Keeping the UNIA out of No. 10 (the official residence of the British prime minister) should be the responsibility of the Foreign Office. Another Colonial Office official considered the adverse effects on British colonialism in the West Indies which would flow from any such official recognition of the UNIA: "The confidence of the West Indies in HMG [his majesty's government] would suffer a rude shock if any sort of official recognition were given to this Association, which has a record of fraud, sedition, and incitement to violence."[29]

Not surprisingly, Tobitt's request for an interview to present his credentials was finally turned down.[30] The high commissioner nevertheless did remain in England awhile, addressing meetings of UNIA branches in Manchester and London.[31] In 1925 as high commissioner of the eastern provinces of the West Indies he fared much better with the Dutch colony of Surinam, where he was received by the governor and given the freedom of the colony.[32]

One year before refusing to accept Garvey's high commissioner to the court of St. James, the British government had seriously considered extending quasidiplomatic recognition to the Cuban UNIA division. The situation in Cuba was unique. Here, thousands of black workers, especially Haitians and Jamaicans (the latter British subjects), had for years been recruited to work as laborers on Cuban sugar plantations. In Cuba these black workers were ruthlessly oppressed and were afforded practically no legal protection, either by the Cuban government or by British diplomatic personnel. In this situation the UNIA became firmly entrenched among the black workers in Cuba and in time became mutual aid society, race uplift organization, and quasigovernment for the black population. It was practically the only effective attempt to look after their interests.[33] Not surprisingly, by the mid-1920s Cuba had the largest number of UNIA divisions and chapters of any country except the United States (see appendix).

In this situation the British minister in Cuba bought the UNIA's idea of extending semiofficial recognition to it as the organization protecting the interests of British West Indian workers in Cuba. The Foreign Office in London, to whom the suggestion was forwarded, decided to sound out three governors of its West Indian colonies before coming to a decision. These governors, all of them well acquainted with the work of the UNIA in their own colonies, were mostly hostile to the idea. The governor of Barbados explained that there were but two UNIA branches in the island, one of which was composed of "more solid men" and lacked "any distinctly anti-white proclivities" while the other was allegedly very probably disloyal. Semiofficial recognition of the Cuban UNIA would give a fillip to the local branches, which might end in headaches for British colonialism. "If, however," he replied to the Foreign Office query,

> the Cuban branch were recognised as the centre of protection of the interests of the British West Indians in that Country I foresee that the Society would obtain a status in this Colony that might be very inconvenient. It would certainly result in a very large increase in membership and the hot heads in the Association would probably be awakened to renewed zeal to stir up trouble between the two races. The Barbadians are generally a quiet well behaved body of men, but they are very excitable and easily roused.[34]

He further indicated that UNIA members had recently sent threatening letters to planters and were encouraging the workers to strike, and with the approach of croptime in the sugar plantations, these hotheads might become restive. Furthermore, it would be inconsistent to recognize the UNIA in Cuba and repress it in Barbados (where it was subject to police surveillance and the *Negro World* was banned).

The British governor of Jamaica was somewhat less hostile to the idea, possibly because the Cuban UNIA was largely Jamaican in composition. He was inclined to be against recognition, but in the peculiar circumstances, "as a means of obtaining concerted action for the protection of British West Indians in that country," he could not "foresee how this Government would be embarrassed by semi-official recognition of the persons mentioned, provided that care is taken to prevent all idea that this Government is in any way party to the recognition."[35]

The governor of Trinidad, where the UNIA was usually most repressed among the British West Indian islands, replied briefly and with venom: "I am strongly averse to any action which might in any way lead to the

Universal Negro Improvement Association believing that His Majesty's
Government regarded the Association as one which could in any way
improve the position of His Majesty's negro population in the West Indies." He added that he had recently refused a petition from the Trinidad
UNIA to lift the ban on the *Negro World* "owing to the objectionable
character of the matter which this publication continues to contain."[36]
Based on these opinions, the British minister in Cuba was advised to
withhold recognition.[37] Thereafter the Cuban government, with the collusion of such American employers of black labor as the United Fruit
Company, increased its campaign against the UNIA which, among other
things, was responsible for strikes against these employers. UNIA officials
were sometimes jailed and branches were sometimes closed by the government.[38] In 1930 Garvey himself was refused permission to visit Cuba.
General Manuel Delgado, secretary of the interior, explained that there
was no race problem in Cuba, but the UNIA was nevertheless stirring up
same. He also issued a statement ordering the provincial governments to
close all UNIA branches.[39]

If Garvey's provisional government was well supplied with ambassadors
and traveling commissioners, he himself on his travels acted like a head
of state, requesting, and sometimes receiving, interviews with such digni-
taries as the governor of British Honduras and the president of Costa Rica.[40]

The UNIA's assumption of nationality was not without its humorous
incidents. In 1923 the organization despatched an official delegation to
the funeral of President Warren Harding. The delegation rode in a car
complete with a member of the Universal African Legions on each running
board. After the funeral the delegation amused themselves by driving
through the streets of Washington and watching the policemen salute and
hold up the traffic to let them pass. They had obviously been mistaken
for representatives of a sovereign state. William Sherrill, remembering the
incident a decade later, explained that "having never before enjoyed such
consideration at the behest of southern police, we took full advantage of
our mistaken identity."[41]

Underpinning Garvey's predilection toward nationhood were his own
speculations on political theory. He conceived the major problem of democratic practice to be the devising of a mechanism of government which
would ensure the permanent representation of the popular will, a popular
will that would be synonymous with the expression of the majority of

the population but which would somehow ensure "that all the citizens of that government will be satisfied and in sympathy with each other."[42] He found fault with American democracy on this score. He explained that often only a minority of the population actually votes for the president of the United States, so he does not necessarily represent the will of the majority. Furthermore, since the executive often controlled the judiciary, appealing from one to the other would sometimes be like appealing from Caesar to Caesar. Garvey once wrote a short essay, "Governing the Ideal State," on these problems of nonmajority government and insensitivity to the popular will. He proceeded on the premise that since all systems of government ultimately depend on human implementation, he would devise a system whereby representatives of the people would fulfill their trust or suffer immediate recall, disgrace, and execution:

> Government should be absolute, and the head should be thoroughly responsible for himself and the acts of his subordinates. . . . He should be the soul of honor, and when he is legally or properly found to the contrary, he should be publicly disgraced, and put to death as an outcast and an unworthy representative of the righteous will of the people.

The threat of instant recall and death should also hang over the heads of the ruler's subordinate officials.

To further ensure the incorruptibility of the ruler, Garvey suggested that he "be removed from all pecuniary obligations and desires of a material nature" through the device of a very large salary and allowances, both during and after his administration. In return, the ruler should devote himself entirely to the governance of the state, and, during the period of his administration, he should forestall the possibility of sectarian interest-group pressure by spurning the company of all friends outside of his immediate family. Rulers found to have abused their trust would be executed, and "images of them should be made and placed in a national hall of criminology and ill fame, and their crimes should be recited and a curse pronounced upon them and their generations."[43]

Furthermore, Garvey foreshadowed the unwillingness of a later generation of black activists to be restricted by established political ideologies (sometimes even to the point of random eclecticism) by insisting that he felt free to "pick out the best in every government, whether that government be monarchical, democratic or soviet."[44]

Garvey's thoughts on democracy led him inevitably to the consideration of capitalism and communism, since the concept of democracy is
meaningless without relation to the economic system underpinning it.
He considered capitalism to be a necessary stage in human advancement
while simultaneously expressing uneasiness at the results of its unrestrained
uses.[45]

Garvey's disapproval of unrestrained capitalism extended to the nas-
cent upper crust of his own race. Like Frantz Fanon three decades later,
he thought that this class among the black race was more destructive than
similarly circumstanced persons among the white and other races. For
while white millionaires endowed charitable foundations and otherwise
displayed some progressive characteristics, rich black persons tended to
be more parasitical and destructive to their own race. Garvey in 1924
expressed this idea thus: "We have not only to fight the white capitalist,
but we also have to fight the capitalistic Negro. He will sell his own people into Hell the same as anybody else." In 1929 he repeated similar sentiments: "The Negro or 'Coloured' race is developing a class of millionaires
or money hoarders, much more dangerous to the race's life and existence
than any similar group of men among any other race."[46]

For solutions to these problems Garvey leaned toward reforms of a
social democratic nature rather than toward the complete eradication of
the capitalist system. He favored ceilings of $1 million and $5 million for
investible funds controlled by individuals and corporations, respectively.
Sums accumulated above these figures should be appropriated by the
state. The state should also expropriate without compensation the assets
of capitalists and corporations who fomented wars and strife in the furtherance of their financial interests.[47]

In his own organizations Garvey attempted to implement these ideas
by organizing his business ventures along cooperative lines and by placing
a ceiling on the number of shares any one person could own. He seems
to have sometimes seen efforts such as these as attempts by poor people
to establish "a capitalistic system of their own" to "combat the heartless
capitalistic system of the masterly ruling class."[48] On one occasion, while
representing workers in Jamaica in a dispute with the United Fruit Company, he even described himself as a capitalist in an attempt to show that
he also was an employer of labor, but nevertheless found ways to avoid
the excesses concerning which the strikers he represented were complaining.[49]

Garvey's ideas on capitalism and communism can be illustrated also
by the company he kept, so to speak. For the Third World leaders he admired were generally those with a similar political outlook—people, like
himself, involved in nationalist struggles and attempting to walk a precarious tightrope between capitalism and communism. The most important
of these were Mahatma Gandhi in India, Clements Kadalie in South
Africa, and Captain A. A. Cipriani, leader of the Trinidad Workingmen's
Association. These leaders were usually lumped together with Garvey in
communist journals as "petit-bourgeois reformists" "misleaders" and
"fakers." Imperialist governments usually considered them dangerous
agitators.

Garvey's tendencies to social democracy can also be seen in his op-
timism concerning the election of Franklin D. Roosevelt in the United
States in the 1930s[50] and most of all in his long-standing fondness for
the welfare socialism represented by the British Labour party. As early
as 1923 Garvey was reported by the *New York Age* as being a member
of this party. His belief that the Labour party would show greater sensitivity to the aspirations of black people was a perennial dream of colonized peoples in the British empire but one that was usually betrayed. In
1923, for example, Garvey, rejoicing over the fact that the British Labour
party was now the official opposition in Parliament, editorialized on the
significance of this event for black British subjects:

Let us take new courage as well as firm confidence in our effort, and
let us be inspired through the achievement of the Labor Party in
England and the Labor forces all over the world.

The ascendancy of Labor in politics will bring about a new political
order which cannot be as senseless as the one to which they succeed.

. . . Labor may have enough sense to know that the best course it
could adopt toward its own prosperity is to be fair and friendly to
all human groups. We would not contemplate labor going out to fight
other peoples for the adventurous exploitation of that which is native
to such peoples. We could not think of Ramsay MacDonald as Premier of England declaring war against native Africans who seek to protect their native rights, but we would expect it of David Lloyd George
or an Arthur J. Balfour, who represent the Tory element and the cap-

italistic crowds of their country. . . . We are glad of the downfall, therefore, of the Tory Government of England. We also rejoice when other monopolist political organizations tumble down to be succeeded by the control of that element of the people who know what human love is, who know what justice is.[51]

In January 1924 Garvey celebrated the victory of MacDonald's short-lived government with a telegram informing the new prime minister that the UNIA looked to Labour as allies of the black race in the fight for national independence in Africa.[52] Almost simultaneously he despatched his UNIA ambassador to England. The propitiousness of the time and Garvey's generally favorable attitude toward the Labour party may have had something to do with the fact that at about this very time the London UNIA was expressing appreciation to the Labour party for assisting unemployed black persons in London to find work.[53]

This unusual endorsement of Labour in Britain was partly due to Garvey's lack of substantial distinction between the Labour party's welfare socialism on the one hand and Russian socialism as practiced under Lenin on the other. For, as will be seen later, despite his feuds with white communists in the United States, Garvey admired Lenin for his mass movement and his attempts to curtail capitalistic control, and he considered the British Labour party to be of the same stripe. In eulogizing Lenin at Liberty Hall in 1924 upon the Russian leader's death he said, "I believe, in time, that the whole world will take on the social democratic system of government now existing in Russia. It is only a question of time, I say. England is the first to have reached out for this perfect state of social democratic control among its peoples."[54] By 1932 he was willing to admit that the Labour party had not arrived at communism but that it was working diligently toward this goal and would soon be "Red Communists," a proposition that did not appear to alarm him.[55] In the meantime he had reiterated his support for the party during the 1929 elections.[56]

In 1927 the Labour party did receive an opportunity to reciprocate in a minor fashion. South African trade union leader Clements Kadalie, during a visit to Britain, succeeded in obtaining the party's assistance in the case of a Nyasalander, Isa Macdonald Lawrence, who had been sentenced by British authorities to three years at hard labor for importing into Central Africa six copies of Garvey's *Negro World* and two of the South African *Worker's Herald*. A Labour MP, Richard Wallhead, raised the question in the House of Commons, and Lawrence was released shortly after.[57]

Garvey's reflections on political theory, and especially on democracy, found expression in his conception of his own leadership. Though at times showing a tendency toward the autocratic, he was nevertheless imbued with a consuming notion of service, which led to a fatalistic acceptance of sacrifice as the inevitable consequence of leadership, despite occasional complaints concerning the difficulties of race leadership and the unworthiness of errant colleagues.

Garvey's concept of leadership as dedication, sacrifice, and even martyrdom was matched by a loyalty among large numbers of his followers which astounded observers. Kelly Miller of Howard University, one of the small number of non-Garveyite Afro-American intellectuals who attempted to analyze him with some semblance of objectivity, wrote that "it must be conceded that he has begotten for himself an intensity of discipleship which has no parallel among Negroes in this country."[58] Miller noted that on the death of Frederick Douglass, Howard University, of which Douglass had been a trustee, could raise only a few thousand dollars to endow a school in his honor. The Douglass home had similarly failed to become a mecca for the race. In the case of Booker T. Washington, too, his campfollowers, many of whom were indebted to him for their exalted positions, were indifferent to the attempt to raise an endowment of half a million dollars in his honor. This contrasted sharply with the devotion of Garvey's followers even, and indeed more so, after his incarceration. T. Thomas Fortune, veteran civil-rights fighter, dean of Afro-American journalists, former close associate of Booker T. Washington, and, for the last few years of his life editor of the *Negro World,* made a similar observation:

> The editor of the *Negro World* is in a position to judge of this matter because he has been actively engaged in race journalism for forty-five years and has known every leader of the race in America and in other lands during that time, personally or by reputation, from Frederick Douglass to Marcus Garvey. None of them had the magnetic personality of Mr. Garvey; none of them could draw men to him and hold them as he. None of them had a world-embracing slogan that appealed to the Negro people everywhere.[59]

A petition from the Jacksonville, Florida, UNIA division to President Coolidge for Garvey's release from prison expressed the same idea in more poignant fashion—"The world has never had a character, as a leader, such as Marcus Garvey, one of the most inspiring and courageous idealists in history. And this Marcus Garvey is all the Negro has ever had."[60] To the official mind of an attorney general of the United States, such loyalty was irrational and disturbing. He explained his perplexity in a memorandum to President Coolidge:

> The situation as presented in the Garvey case is most unusual. Notwithstanding the fact that the prosecution was designed for the protection of colored people, whom it was charged Garvey had been defrauding by means of exaggerated and incorrect statements circulated through the mail, none of these people apparently believe that they have been defrauded, manifestly retain their entire confidence in Garvey, and instead of the prosecution and imprisonment of the applicant being an example and warning against a violation of law, it really stands and is regarded by them as a class as an act of oppression of the race in their efforts in the direction of race progress and of discrimination against Garvey as a negro. This is by no means a healthy condition of affairs.[61]

Such loyalty manifested itself in thousands of letters, telegrams, petitions and the like which poured into departments of the United States and other governments whenever Garvey was unfairly dealt with.[62] It manifested itself too in such scenes as those enacted during Garvey's trial in 1923 for alleged mail fraud. Hundreds of his supporters knelt, prayed, lamented and allegedly threatened witnesses. The police wagon carrying Garvey to prison was obstructed by an estimated three hundred people, and, in the quaint language of the *New York Times*, "several negresses showed marked emotion."[63] This paper was as perplexed by these manifestations of devotedness as had been the attorney general of the United States, and, in an editorial entitled "A Hero More Sorry Unimaginable," it chided Garvey's supporters: "Surely there ought to be intelligence enough among the colored people to see that Garvey illustrated their worst and weakest qualities, not their best and strongest."[64] This loyalty was manifested, too, in the fact that only about eighteen persons out of the thirty-five thousand Black Star Line stockholders

written to by United States government officials who seized the company's books were willing to agree that they were dissatisfied with the
company's operations. All eighteen were, Garvey thought, in the employ
of the government.[65] Many of these same stockholders were among those
who subscribed $4,400 toward a defense fund the very same night of his
arrest.[66] Such fund-raising feats were quite commonplace. In 1921 Garvey
collected an estimated $25,000 in Costa Rica, most of it within forty-
eight hours.[67] The United Fruit Company at Puerto Barrios, Guatemala,
reported a sale of drafts destined to the UNIA and Black Star Line of
$2,941.08 between November 1921 and February 1922. This figure was
considered an understatement. The population of Puerto Barrios was given
as only 2,400.[68] Within a year of his release on bail in 1923, Garvey is
said to have collected 150,000 balboas from followers in Panama.[69]

Concerning such manifestations of loyalty, *Negro World* columnist
S. A. Haynes concluded that Garvey had demonstrated two things, namely that black people could be organized, and that they were indeed "eager
to repose confidence in and support sincere Negro leadership."[70] This is
graphically illustrated by a visitor to Garvey's Harlem offices in January
1920, who reported a line of people stretching over a hundred yards along
135 Street waiting to see Garvey, some for no other reason than to personally express their appreciation to him.[71]

Not surprisingly, such fierce unswerving loyalty was often branded
"fanaticism," and Garvey's critics and enemies did not hesitate to describe
the style of leadership existing within Garvey's provisional African nation
as fascist. These accusations were helped along by a strain of violence
that seemed to run among Garveyites. Apart from anticolonial struggles
in which they were implicated, such as the 1919 uprisings in Trinidad and
British Honduras, Garveyites, particularly in the United States, were often
implicated in violent confrontations with rival persons and groups. Possibly the most publicized of such cases involved the murder of former
UNIA leader of the American Negroes, J. W. H. Eason, in New Orleans
in 1923 after he had broken with Garvey. W. A. Domingo, Jamaican ex-
editor of the *Negro World* reported that "in New York City, as early as
the Fall of 1919, I raised my voice in protest against the execrable exaggerations, staggering stupidities, blundering bombast and abominable
assininities of our black Barnum, culminating in Thomas Potter and
myself being assaulted, kicked, and placed under arrest by Garveyites

in the Spring of 1920."[72] In August 1920 several hundred Garveyites invaded a revival meeting being held under a big tent at West 138 Street in Harlem by the Reverend Adam Clayton Powell, Sr. The cause of this disturbance was the Reverend Charles S. Morris, veteran missionary from Norfolk, Virginia, whose sermon contained a rejection of Garvey's African program because, in his opinion, the colonialist powers were too strong to be dislodged. Uniformed police and plainclothesmen had to escort the reverend gentleman home, and by a circuitous route, since the most direct route went past Liberty Hall.[73]

W. E. B. Du Bois appended his name to the list of real or potential victims of UNIA violence and threats. He "was not only threatened with death by men declaring themselves his [Garvey's] followers, but received letters of such unbelievable filth that they were absolutely unprintable." His friends were moved, he declared, to provide him with secret police protection when he landed in the United States from his trip to Africa.[74] Arguments over Garvey's trial sometimes turned peaceful gatherings such as house parties into brawls resulting in slashings and other injuries.[75] A case similar to the Eason murder occurred in Miami in 1928. Here a Laura Champion, alias Laura Koffey, a self-styled African princess whose unauthorized money-collection endeavors from UNIA branches had been denounced by the organization, was killed at an anti-Garvey meeting she was addressing. Her followers murdered a Garveyite in retaliation. The president and the colonel of legions of the Miami UNIA division were charged with and acquitted of first-degree murder.[76]

The violent streak was not the only point of similarity between Garveyism and the doctrines of fascism and nazism, which later flourished in Europe. In their fierce nationalism, in their doctrines of racial purity, in their uniformed indoctrinated youth groups, in their conversion of the crowd into disciplined uniformed units, with some qualifications in their anticommunism, in the impassioned oratory of their leaders, in the pageantry, the atmosphere of excitement surrounding their movements, European fascism and nazism bore certain resemblances to Garveyism. The similarities were not lost upon contemporaries. J. A. Rogers noticed these during a trip to Mussolini's Italy in 1927. Writing from Italy for the *Negro World,* he said, "The other thing that made me feel at home, as I said, was Fascism, or should I say Mussolini. I have been through the agitation that raged around Garvey in Harlem in 1922, and I have but to

shut my eyes and ears to color, the issues, and watch human conduct to
hear the same old tune sung to different words."[77]

Ten years later Garvey himself impressed upon Rogers the fact that
the UNIA had antedated Mussolini with the style of government associated with the latter. He said, "We were the first Fascists. We had disciplined men, women and children in training for the liberation of Africa.
The black masses saw that in this extreme nationalism lay their only hope
and readily supported it. Mussolini copied fascism from me but the Negro
reactionaries sabotaged it."[78] In a speech the same year (1937) delivered
in Canada, Garvey emphasized the same point—"The UNIA was before
Mussolini and Hitler were heard of. Mussolini and Hitler copied the program of the UNIA—aggressive nationalism for the black man in Africa."[79]
On other occasions he pointed out that he had preached race purity before Hitler, and in 1935 he told an interviewer in London, "They laughed
at me because I dressed my followers up in uniforms and paraded them
through the streets. But look what Mussolini and Hitler have done with
shirts and uniforms. If I had been left alone the Negro, too, would have
had a shirt."[80]

The question of fascism recurred often in Garvey's various publications.
In 1923, for example, the *New York Amsterdam News* quoted a *Negro
World* editorial which claimed that the UNIA had accomplished a blood-
less revolution more far-reaching than fascism.[81] In 1929 the *Blackman*
editorialized, while Garvey was in jail, to the effect that "Marcus Garvey
is the Mussolini of the Negro race and no other Negro can or has come
up to him as a fighter for the liberties and rights of a people."[82] Garvey
himself identified one trait he admired in Mussolini as his iron-fisted
rule, which Garvey considered necessary at some stages of history.[83]

Garvey's interest in Hitler coincided with his rise to influence in Ger-
many. Indeed, even before Hitler's journey to power Garvey, on a visit to
Germany in 1928, was impressed by German thoroughness and discipline.
He suggested that black people might profitably imbibe these qualities.[84]
In 1932 the editor of his *New Jamaican* praised Hitler's role as a patriot,
a view that Garvey shared.[85] Garvey hoped that the black race would
produce a Hitler and that black people would acquaint themselves with
Hitler's ideas. By 1934, though, mindful of his own experience in the
United States and Jamaica, he concluded that a black Hitler could be
permanently successful only in Africa, for Africa afforded a far greater

opportunity for an appeal along nationalistic lines than areas in the African dispersion.[86]

Garvey's admiration for Hitler and Mussolini was not, however, an unqualified one. His admiration was based on the objective consideration of their political style and philosophy. He was too astute not to realize, however, that their theories could spell only ruin for Africa, and he opposed them resolutely on this basis. As early as 1924 he despatched a telegram to Mussolini from the Fourth International Convention of Negro Peoples of the World, requesting a change in Mussolini's Africa policy and self-determination for Italian colonies in Africa.[87]

His dual attitude of limited endorsement and hostile opposition to Hitler and Mussolini can best be explained by a 1933 statement on Hitler:

Adolph Hitler, the German Chancellor, cannot be mistaken for anything else than a patriot. . . .

. . . We are interested in Hitler only from the point of view of Germany's relationship with our race. It is evident that if Hitler hates the Jew, he also hates the Negro. . . .

Whilst we admire him as a German Nationalist, or rather, Patriot, we must not do so to the loss of our nationalism or patriotism, therefore, it would be very unwise for us to encourage one as pronounced in his views as Hitler. Hitler stands for a greater Germany, which is his right, and the Negro should stand for a greater Africa which is also his right.[88]

His opposition to Mussolini was couched in similar terms.[89] And a *Negro World* editorial of 1928 argued that Mussolini was not only aware of Garvey but considered him a menace to his plans for Italian imperialism in Africa. The editorial quoted from a speech in which Mussolini had referred to a Harlem riot: "There is one great quarter in New York called Harlem where the population is exclusively Negro. A great riot broke out there last July which, after a whole night of sanguinary conflict, was finally controlled by the police, who found themselves opposed to compact masses of Negroes." The editorial commented that Mussolini's account was exaggerated and represented an indirect warning to the United States that Afro-American race consciousness was a menace to his schemes in Africa, especially since he knew that Garvey's program came out of Harlem. The editorial continued: "He may not call Marcus Garvey by name, but Negroes throughout the world know that he regards Garvey as the most potential hindering force to his scheming and planning to lay robber hands on Africa's wealth." It ended in prophetic vein: "We are somewhat puzzled, in common with other beholders, at the new attitude for Ras Taffari toward the ancient enemy of Ethiopia, but we will not take hasty judgement."[90]

When Mussolini invaded Ethiopia in 1935 Garvey's opposition became strident, and practically every issue of his *Black Man* was adorned with hostile articles and poems. The following, from "The Smell of Mussolini," is typical:

> Let all Italians live and die in shame,
> For what their Mad Dog did to our dear home:
> Their Mussolini's bloody, savage name
> Smells stink from Addis back to sinful Rome. . . .
>
> We'll march to crush the Italian dog,
> And at the points of gleaming, shining swords,
> We'll lay quite low the violent, Roman hog.[91]

Garvey's concept of nationhood was, therefore, extremely well developed. His was a provisional nation, biding the time of Africa's liberation. Within maybe fifty years, Garvey conjectured, while W. E. B. Du Bois and the NAACP "will be sending up petitions to Congress asking them to introduce another Dyer Anti-Lynching Bill, Marcus Garvey and the UNIA will be coming up the Hudson Bay with a flotilla of battleships, dreadnoughts and cruisers to land our first ambassador, and whilst they will be introducing bills in Congress, we will be entertained in the White House as being the first ambassadors from the great African republic. And let me tell you, they will hear us then."[92]

There can be no doubt that Garvey's assumption of nationality filled a great void in the lives of black people, especially during his most successful years. Almost nowhere on the globe did black people at this time have a government of their own race. And the UNIA, reaching as it did into every area where black people lived, sowed the seeds of nationalism and on occasion even acted as a provisional government.

NOTES

1. *Negro World,* January 30, 1926.
2. *Blackman,* December 30, 1929.
3. *Negro World,* February 24, 1923.
4. *Blackman,* September 7, 1929; *Negro World,* August 3, 1929.
5. Amy Jacques Garvey, ed., *The Philosophy and Opinions of Marcus Garvey* (London: Frank Cass, 1967), II: 140; *Negro World,* August 25, 1923. The anthem was composed by Arnold J. Ford, UNIA musical director, in 1919.
6. *Negro World,* February 4, 1928.
7. *Black Man* 2 (July-August 1936): 18.
8. "New Flag for Afro-Americans," *Africa Times and Orient Review* 1 (October 1912): 134.
9. *Negro World,* March 19, 1927 (reprint of a 1921 speech).
10. *Universal Black Men Catechism* (n.p., n.d.), p. 37.
11. National Civic Federation Papers, New York Public Library, Box 152.
12. *Negro World,* June 14, 1924.
13. Mary Benson, *South Africa: The Struggle for a Birthright* (Middlesex: Penguin, 1966), p. 46.
14. Donald Barnett and Karari Njama, *Mau Mau from Within,* (New York: Monthly Review Press, 1966), p. 75.
15. Garvey, *Philosophy and Opinions,* II: 141.
16. *New York World,* August 18, 1920; *New York Times,* August 18, 1920.
17. Garvey, *Philosophy and Opinions,* II: 141; *Catechism,* p. 39.
18. *Negro World,* June 11, 18, 1932.
19. Ibid., December 9, 1922, August 25, 1923.
20. H. G. Armstrong, H. M. Consul General, New York, to H. M. Chargé d'Affaires, Washington, D.C., August 24, 1923, FO 371/8513, Foreign Office Records, Public Record Office, London.
21. *Negro World,* October 27, 1928.
22. *Petition of the Universal Negro Improvement Association and African Communities' League to the League of Nations, Geneva, Switzerland,* n.p.—copy in RG 59, 800.4016/19, National Archives, Washington, D.C.
23. See, e.g., *Negro World,* October 27, 1928; August 3, 1929; November 14, 1931; J. V. Wilson, League of Nations to William Strang, Foreign Office, and related correspondence, May 1934, FO 371/18505.

24. Cyril Crichlow to Garvey, "Special Personal Report," June 24, 1921, RG 59, 882.00/705.

25. Governor of Bermuda to Secretary of State, Colonial Office, November 2, 1920, CO 318/356, Colonial Office Records, Public Record Office, London.

26. *Negro World*, January 26, 1924.

27. Ibid.

28. Marcus Garvey and P. L. Burrows, Secretary-General of the UNIA to Rt. Hon. J. H. Thomas, H. M. Colonial Secretary, January 25, 1924, CO 554/64.

29. Minutes, February 13, March 6, 1924, CO 554/64.

30. Ibid., private secretary of the Secretary of State, Colonial Office to Tobitt, March 8, 1924.

31. *Negro World*, April 5, April 19, May 10, 1924.

32. Ibid., May 19, 1925.

33. Ibid., February 2, 1924. A correspondent from Santiago de Cuba says that Jamaican UNIA members control the dispensing jobs in many hospitals and use their positions to provide medical care for Haitians and Jamaicans.

34. Charles Bain, Governor of Barbados, to Secretary of State, Colonial Office, January 16, 1923, FO 371/8450.

35. Governor L. Probyn to Duke of Devonshire, Secretary of State, April 25, 1923, FO 371/8450.

36. Governor Wilson of Trinidad to Secretary of State, 20 January 1923, FO 371/8450.

37. Under Secretary of State, Colonial Office to Under Secretary of State, Foreign Office, 29 May 1923, FO 371/8450.

38. *Negro World*, August 4, 1928; *Blackman*, June 28, 1930.

39. RG 59, 837.00–General Conditions/27; *New York Times*, January 30, 1930, January 31, 1930. Some branches were reopened six months later—*Blackman*, June 28, 1930.

40. F. Gordon, H.M. Consul, Port Limón, Costa Rica to A. P. Bennett, H.B.M. Minister, San José, Costa Rica, May 9, 1921, FO 371/5684; ibid., Governor Eyre Hutson of British Honduras to Secretary of State, Colonial Office, 14 July 1921.

41. *Negro World*, July 9, 1932.

42. Ibid., October 3, 1925.

43. Garvey, *Philosophy and Opinions*, II: 74-76.

44. *Negro World*, October 3, 1925.

45. Garvey, *Philosophy and Opinions*, II: 72.

46. *Daily Worker,* August 12, 1924; *Blackman,* September 5, 1929.

47. Garvey, *Philosophy and Opinions,* II: 72.

48. *Blackman,* January 8, 1930; see also *New Jamaican,* September 6, 1932.

49. *Blackman,* May 29, 1929.

50. *Black Man,* 1, (January 1934): 14.

51. *Negro World,* December 15, 1923.

52. Ibid., February 2, 1924.

53. Ibid., January 12, 1924.

54. Ibid., February 2, 1924.

55. *New Jamaican,* October 12, 1932.

56. *Blackman,* April 3, June 4, June 7, 1929.

57. Clements Kadalie, *My Life and the ICU* (New York: Humanities Press, 1970), p. 125; *Negro World,* August 20, 1927; George Shepperson, in Sylvia Thrupp, ed., *Millennial Dreams in Action* (The Hague; Mouton and Co., 1962), p. 153. Kadalie and the *Negro World* give the country of importation as Rhodesia; Shepperson says they were imported into Nyasaland.

58. *Negro World,* September 3, 1927.

59. Ibid., May 9, 1925.

60. Ibid., June 25, 1927.

61. John Sargent, Attorney General to the President, "In the Matter of the Application for Commutation of Sentence of Marcus Garvey," November 12, 1927, RG 204, 42-793, National Archives.

62. See, e.g., the many thousands of these still retained in RG 60, 198940; RG 204, 42-793; National Archives Sen. 69A-J25, Senate Judiciary Committee, 69th Congress—Petitions; also *Negro World,* December 19, 1925, and *Blackman,* October 10, 1929.

63. *New York Times,* June 22, 1923; *New York Herald,* June 23, 1923; *Negro World,* June 30, 1923; Lenford Sylvester Nembhard, *Trials and Triumphs of Marcus Garvey* (Kingston: The Gleaner Co., Ltd., 1940), p. 88.

64. *New York Times,* July 3, 1923.

65. Marcus Garvey, *Speech Delivered by Marcus Garvey at Royal Albert Hall* (London: Poets and Painters Press, 1968), p. 13.

66. Bruce to Editor, *The World,* January 17, 1922, Bruce Papers, BL 27, Schomburg Collection, New York Public Library.

67. F. Gordon, H. M. Consul, Port Limón, Costa Rica, to A. P. Bennett, H. B. M. Minister, San José, Costa Rica, May 9, 1921, FO 371/5684.

68. American Consul, Guatemala City, to Secretary of State, March 9, 1922, RG 59, 811.108 G 191/27, Records of the Department of State, National Archives.

69. "Panama and Canal Zone," annual report, 1924, FO 371/10632.

70. *Negro World,* May 6, 1933.

71. Hugh Mulzac, *A Star to Steer By* (New York: International Publishers, 1972), p. 81.

72. "The Policy of the *Messenger* on West Indians and American Negroes—W. A. Domingo vs. Chandler Owen," *Messenger* (March 1923): 639.

73. *New York Age,* August 28, 1920.

74. W. E. B. Du Bois, "A Lunatic or a Traitor," *Crisis* 28 (May 1924): 9.

75. *New York Amsterdam News,* June 27, 1923; February 18, 1925.

76. *New York Times,* March 21, 1928; *Negro World,* July 14, 1928; July 21, 1928; July 28, 1928.

77. *Negro World,* May 21, 1927.

78. J. A. Rogers, *World's Great Men of Color* (New York: J. A. Rogers, 1947), p. 602. Garvey said this during a conversation with Rogers in London in 1937.

79. *Black Man* 2 (December 1937): 12.

80. Ibid., (September-October 1936): 2; *New York Amsterdam News,* August 31, 1935.

81. *New York Amsterdam News,* September 19, 1923.

82. *Blackman,* December 14, 1929.

83. Ibid., April 4, 1929.

84. *Negro World,* August 25, 1928.

85. *New Jamaican,* July 28, 1932. *Black Man,* 1 (January 1934): 13.

86. *Black Man,* 1 (March-April, 1934): 3.

87. *Negro World,* August 9, 1924.

88. *Black Man* 1 (December 1933): 2.

89. *Blackman,* April 16, 1929; *Negro World,* May 7, 1932.

90. *Negro World,* October 6, 1928.

91. *Black Man* 2 (July-August 1936): 9.

92. *Negro World,* February 24, 1923.

4

Religion

God in the affairs of men is on the side of the strongest battalion.

—Marcus Garvey [1]

. . . in spite of all the evidence . . . Negroes still believe that
Garvey is not dead. What is wrong? Was he immortal? Was he
not human and subjected to sickness and death like the rest
of us?

—S. U. Smith, treasurer,
Harmony Division, Jamaica [2]

In March 1917, the Chicago-based *Champion Magazine* editorialized
on the need for a religion that would inspire the black man to do for
himself. It noted that "From a secular standpoint both Booker T. Washington and Dr. Du Bois with their different schools of thought supplied
it." Nevertheless, the article continued, "such faiths do not penetrate
so deeply into the nature of a man as those inspired by his spiritual self."
The editorial continued with an impassioned plea: "The Negro is crying
for a Mohamed, a Prophet to come forth and give him the Koran of
economic and intellectual welfare. Where is he?"[3] An article by Garvey

had appeared in this magazine two months earlier,[4] and within the next two years he would be on his way toward answering this plea.

Garvey seems to have had frequent contact with religion during his early years. At the age of seven he is supposed to have enjoyed affecting the role of preacher among his playmates. As a boy, too, he pumped the organ in the Wesleyan Methodist Church in St. Ann's Bay, Jamaica, the church to which his parents belonged.[5] Garvey later converted to Catholicism, which did not deter him from following an independent line in things religious.

Like many of the world's great revolutionaries and reformers, Garvey dreamed dreams, saw visions, and long before his dreams assumed worldwide importance, he was imbued with a self-conscious premonition of impending greatness. This phenomenon, coupled with his fascination for religion and religious ritual, gave his career a messianic quality which he himself was not reluctant to express. He was not loathe to compare his own career to that of Jesus Christ. In doing so, however, he was attempting to recapture what he considered to be the progressive and revolutionary essence of the early Christian church. As far as he was concerned, Christ was the leader of a mass movement for the uplift of oppressed people, and so was he. This explains why he could be proreligious and very often anticlerical at the same time. Christ's doctrine, he explained, "was simple but revolutionary. He laid the foundations of a pure democracy and established the fact, not a theory, of the Universal Brotherhood of man."[6] And just as he saw himself in the role of messiah, so he saw his doctrine of black nationalism as one that would survive and thrive even in the face of persecution. A favorite poetic quotation of UNIA orators was the line, "Truth crushed to earth shall rise again."[7]

This spiritual aspect of Garvey's movement distinguished it from the more important contemporary movements with similar goals. The universal feeling of oppression and resentment experienced by black people at their worldwide subjection to colonialism and oppression cannot be overemphasized. Garvey's uncanny ability to encompass all this worldwide racial sentiment and the spectacular success with which he channeled it into organizational form released emotions of hope and appreciation among black people which knew no bounds. Garvey's followers and admirers regularly hailed him as "the mightiest prophet who has appeared among us in fifty years," a great religious teacher, a John the Baptist.[8]

They regularly compared him to Christ. Like Christ he had been betrayed
for money and condemned by governments. And his gospel, too, would
be preached to every nation and would precipitate an end to barbarism.[9]
One preacher wrote a book wherein he essayed to show that Garvey had
brought the race the UNIA through the instrumentality of God.[10] Garveyites from Colón, Panama, seeking their leader's release from prison in the
United States, informed President Coolidge that "We the Negroes of the
World look upon Garvey as a superman; a demigod; and as the reincarnated
Angel of Peace come from Heaven to dispense Political Salvation" to an
oppressed people. "Yea," this message continued, "we love Garvey next
to our GOD."[11] One New York division went so far as to canonize Garvey
in his own lifetime after his expulsion from the United States.[12] This
tendency to apotheosize Garvey found expression in the words of the
UNIA creed: "We believe in God, the Creator of all things and people,
in Jesus Christ, His Son, the Spiritual Savior of all mankind. We believe
in Marcus Garvey, the leader of the Negro peoples of the world, and in
the program enunciated by him through the UNIA . . . the redemption
of Africa."[13] A similar creed found its way into a nationalist South
African church: "We believe in one God, Maker of all things, Father of
Ethiopia . . . who did Athlyi, Marcus Garvey and colleagues come to save?
The down-trodden children of Ethiopia that they might rise to be a great
power among the nations."[14] It was consistent with this veneration that
some of Garvey's followers at first refused to believe accounts of his
death (due in part to the fact that the first reports of his passing were
in fact false) and had to be reassured that Garvey had indeed passed on,
but remained in spirit to share the joys and sorrows of his people.

Garvey did not indulge in religion for its own sake, however, but
used it as he did art—for furthering his program of race pride and self-
reliance. His political use of religion began by the simple argument that
if, as established Christian churches preached, man was made in the image
and likeness of God, then black men should depict a God in their own
image and likeness, which would inevitably be black. Garvey pointed
out that the practice of Western Hemisphere Africans to worship a God
of another race had few parallels anywhere else. It was quite normal for
people to visualize and depict their gods in their own color. The foisting
of a white God onto black people was therefore a white distortion.
Garvey's close colleague Bishop George McGuire reinforced his argu-

ment by pointing out that Christ was historically reddish-brown rather than white. And furthermore, should Christ visit New York, he would not be allowed to live on Riverside Drive but would have to reside in Harlem because of his color.[15] Garvey reinforced this view by the argument that "Because He came as an embodiment of all humanity, and therefore was coloured," Christ was persecuted.[16]

This facet of Garvey's thought, like most others, was taken to its logical conclusion. At a religious ceremony marking the close of the 1924 International Convention of Negro Peoples of the World, Jesus Christ was canonized as a "Black Man of Sorrows" and the Virgin Mary as a "Black Madonna." The convention also agreed to "the Idealization of God as a Holy Spirit, without physical form, but a Creature of imaginary semblance of the black race, being of like image and likeness." Garvey explained that this did not mean that the UNIA was embarking upon a new religion. It was simply correcting the mistake of centuries.[17]

Garvey's black God elicited rebukes from a cross-section of the types of people who opposed his other programs. The pastor of the St. Philips Colored Episcopal Church in Harlem considered the idea absurd. Garvey was in his view holding the race up to ridicule. One British Foreign Office official considered that this religious program "beats the band." Another thought that "Bishop McGuire seems to have got some of his ideas from Chartres." Professor Kelly Miller of Howard University agreed that God was equally as black as he was white but thought that the remedy did not lie in "the vindictive alternative of Marcus Garvey." A correspondent to the *New York Times* pointed out that Indians and Africans in Brazil had long depicted Christ as black but minus what he considered Garvey's racial animosity.[18]

Since religion for Garvey was eminently political, the black God of the UNIA differed from many other Christian gods insofar as he was a God of self-reliance. The God of the UNIA concerned himself with spiritual matters. He endowed all races equally and left them to their own devices to solve the problem of survival. It appeared as though Garvey, in view of his own religious background and mindful of the entrenched position of religion in the lives of black people, opted to channel this religious fervor into the path of racial salvation rather than attempt to fight it. Therefore he incessantly repeated the message: "We blame God for many things that he doesn't even know about."[19] He was convinced

that in a thoroughly materialistic world mere religious precepts would
not sway the hearts of those in power. He even jokingly suggested that
if he thought religion alone could win justice for the black man, he would
be a bishop.[20]

This difference between Garvey's religion and mainstream Christianity
was not accidental. He considered white Christianity to be synonymous
with hypocrisy and assailed black people for giving up the world to the
white man for the dubious privilege of receiving Jesus: "The white man
has the world and gives up Jesus! Don't you know the white man has a
right to Jesus, too? Jesus belongs to everybody so you are foolish to give
up the world and take Jesus only."[21] Accordingly when, during the annual
International Convention of 1922 in New York, a white Bible society
pretentiously offered free Bibles to delegates, the offer was declined with
the suggestion that they be sent south to the racists who dwelt in those
parts, since all the delegates already possessed their own.[22] The bitterness
which Garvey felt toward white Christianity is eloquently summed up in
a *Negro World* editorial he wrote in 1923:

> The Negro is now accepting the religion of the real Christ, not the
> property-robbing, gold-stealing, diamond-exploiting Christ, but the
> Christ of Love, Justice and Mercy. The Negro wants no more of the
> white man's religion as it applies to his race, for it is a lie and a farce;
> it is propaganda pure and simple to make fools of a race and rob the
> precious world, the gift of God to man, and to make it the exclusive
> home of pleasure, prosperity and happiness for those who have enough
> intelligence to realize that God made them masters of their fate and
> architects of their own destinies.[23]

In 1937, in similar vein, Garvey described himself as a Christian driven
from the church by such actions as the pope's blessing of Italian fascists
en route to their invasion of Ethiopia.[24] And to black preachers who uncritically emulated their white counterparts, Garvey was equally hostile.
He considered them of little help to the UNIA since they confined their
activities mostly to preaching and collecting money.[25]

During his American period, Garvey's religious program was reinforced
and often implemented by the African Orthodox Church. While the UNIA
never adopted any specific religious denomination, Christian or otherwise,

to the exclusion of others, the African Orthodox Church (AOC) was the nearest approximation to such a state of affairs. The dominant figure in the AOC was George Alexander McGuire (also known as George Alexander), a naturalized American, once a Church of England minister in his native Antigua and elsewhere in the West Indies, and later an Episcopalian and chaplain general of the UNIA. McGuire was ordained first bishop of the AOC on September 29, 1921, by a functionary of the Russian Orthodox Church after duly being reordained and elevated to the episcopate in the American Catholic Church in order to ensure apostolic succession. The *Negro World* extended its congratulations to Bishop McGuire on this occasion and reminded its readers that this was in keeping with the decision of its recent convention to endorse all churches under race leadership while not allying itself with any. Bishop McGuire resigned as chaplain general of the UNIA upon his elevation to the episcopate.[26]

Despite a tiff with Garvey, which caused Bishop McGuire to become temporarily estranged from the UNIA, the AOC played an important role in disseminating Garveyism in North America, the West Indies, Africa, and elsewhere. It was Bishop McGuire who wrote the race catechism used by Garveyites, and which faithfully reproduced Garvey's (and McGuire's, for they seem to have been mostly the same) ideas on religion and religious history, as well as the fundamental principles of the UNIA. Garveyites, some high ranking, played important roles within the AOC. In 1924, for example, a former secretary general of the UNIA became vicar general of the African Orthodox Church.[27] During the "united synodal service" of the fourth general synod of the AOC held at Harlem's Liberty Hall in 1924, Bishop McGuire conferred the honorary degree of Doctor of Civil Laws on Garvey.[28] In 1923, with Garvey incarcerated in the Tombs prison in New York, McGuire was mentioned as a possible successor in the event that Garvey should be permanently denied bail.[29]

The AOC served often as a supplementary propaganda agency for the UNIA. The *Negro Churchman,* its official organ, regularly promoted such Garveyite ideas as race pride, colonization in Liberia, and the like. McGuire's editorials, "Ex Oriente Lux," usually began, "Churchmen of African Descent, Greeting in Christ," which bore obvious similarity to Garvey's "Fellowmen of the Negro Race, Greeting."

The AOC's activities in colonized territories proved no less embarrassing to colonial authorities than those of the UNIA itself, and indeed the two were sometimes represented by the same individual. An AOC clergyman who doubled as UNIA head in Santo Domingo was reportedly deported from that country for insulting the British flag, while another, a Ven Edward Seiler Salmon, was deported, according to the same source, from Trinidad to Jamaica for fomenting riots and strikes there and for stirring up workers in British Honduras against the United Fruit Company. The latter was assistant secretary of the Trinidad Workingmen's Association.[30] The source of this information was a renegade AOC clergyman who took it upon himself to inform the British authorities of his church's activities. Among the gratuitous information thus proffered was the fact that the AOC had ordained a bishop, ostensibly of Canada but who would in fact preside from Nova Scotia over the West Indian sections of the church. It was feared that the title "bishop of the West Indies" would cause the British colonialists to prevent him from entering the islands. McGuire told the AOC branches in the West Indies to change their name if molested by the authorities, if this would allow them to carry on their work.

The AOC was similarly engaged in various parts of Africa. In 1924 an application for membership was accepted from an "Archdeacon of Pretoria, South Africa" together with his congregation of five hundred. In accepting the application, Bishop McGuire is reported to have suggested that the archdeacon help effectuate Garvey's entry into South Africa, after which Bishop McGuire would consecrate him bishop of South Africa.[31] Shortly thereafter, from Griqualand West, South Africa, came word that an AOC clergyman intended to go to New York to attend the next international convention and to be elevated to the episcopate by Bishop McGuire.[32] In 1929 a branch of the AOC was begun in Uganda by Reuben Spartas Mukasa, a nationalist politician who had for some time been in correspondence with Bishop McGuire and who was also an admirer of Garvey.[33]

In 1925 McGuire summed up his religious belief in a nutshell: "I believe in God; I believe in the Negro race." And even though the UNIA was not a religion, he was sure that "the time has come when we shall all espouse it as a great, all-comprehensive, racial missionary movement, a holy cause to which every Negro should give undivided allegiance."[34]

Not unnaturally, UNIA meetings were characterized by religious overtones. They featured hymns, prayers, and sometimes processions, and every unit had a chaplain. Christian festivals such as Easter and Christmas were celebrated, but, in keeping with Garvey's reinterpretation of Christianity, they were turned around to the cause of Garvey's program. At a Christmas pageant at Liberty Hall in Harlem, for example, Christ was depicted as a black child. For the period before Easter, the UNIA produced its own moving picture to replace passion plays where white actors portrayed God. At Easter, Garvey made his annual speech on "The Resurrection of the Negro."[35] Even the Christian practice of baptism had its counterpart, for the association's catechism stipulated that infants should be brought by their parents to be dedicated by the chaplain of their division not later than three months after birth, "at which time they enter the general membership of the Organization."

Garvey the irrepressible, not content with being a poet and playwright of liberation, turned his hand also to political hymn writing. Among his religious verses there cropped up, inevitably, such titles as "Freedom's Noble Cause—1834-1934" and lines such as "Nevermore, as black footstool, Shall Afric's sons be sold."[36]

Garvey took his religious innovations seriously, and he and his colleagues were intolerant of religious cranks who were attracted to the organization. "The U.N.I.A. is flooded with a bunch of eccentric religionists," said *Negro World* columnist S. A. Haynes of a lady who complained that the organization was godless.[37] Garvey himself expressed disagreement with Father Divine, who proclaimed himself God, and his disapproval of the Jamaican folk religion "pocomania" was in one instance surprisingly strong.[38] He disapproved also of Jamaican "prophets and prophetesses who are going to fly Heavenward for the solution of the Negro problem,"[39] an apparent reference to the Jamaican prophet Bedward, with whom Garvey is on occasion somewhat controversially compared.[40] On another occasion Garvey declared, "They sent poor Bedward to the asylum, but they will have a hard time to send me there. . . ."[41]

As previously stated, the UNIA refused to exclusively adopt any single Christian denomination. This reluctance to split the race along denominational lines extended to the avoidance of distinction among religions. Though he adopted Christian forms for the UNIA, Garvey considered differences between religions such as Christianity and Islam inconsequential since they were but different ways of worshipping God.[42] An early copy of the preamble to the UNIA constitution enclosed in Garvey's correspondence to Booker T. Washington had referred to the promoting of "Christian" worship. This gave way in revised versions to "spiritual" worship.

This religious tolerance is interesting in the light of the rapid post-Garvey spread of Islam among Afro-Americans. For the UNIA presented the budding Islamic movement with a sympathetic forum. This tolerance toward Islam may have been indirectly due to Garvey's renowned predecessor in the cause of African redemption, Edward Wilmot Blyden. In his earliest extant pamphlet, Garvey carried a quotation from Blyden's *Christianity, Islam and the Negro Race,* which occupied about half of its few pages. The quotation itself dealt only peripherally with Islam, but the book from which it was taken is a clear expression of Blyden's admiration for Islam, despite Blyden's being a devout Christian.[43]

Blyden's favorable attitude toward Islam had also influenced John E. Bruce. Bruce had met Blyden (who died in 1912) and had been planning a biography of him. In an address to the Boston UNIA in 1923 Bruce compared Christian and Islamic attitudes to the African race to the detriment of the Christians. Another possible source for Garvey's tolerance toward Islam may have been Duse Mohamed Ali, who was a prominent member of London's Islamic community.

At the 1922 UNIA convention several delegates suggested that the association should adopt Islam as its official religion since three-quarters of the black world were Muslims and Muslims were better Christians than Christians. Garvey of course refused to legislate on this matter.[44] Some *Negro World* writers went so far as to occasionally compare Garvey with Mohammed. One such, in 1925, compared "the prophet of Allah, concentrating his inexhaustible incandescent energy on the spiritual-material liberation of his people and the 'Herald of the New Dawn,' Garvey, stressing with equal zeal the material-spiritual redemption of his race."[45] Another, in a paean of praise entitled "Sing of Garvey, Glorify Him, Ye Myriad Men of Sable Hue," referred to him as "a child of Allah."[46] Even the organization's Universal Ethiopian Hymnal, compiled by Rabbi Arnold J. Ford (a leader of Harlem's so-called Black Jews, no less), contained a hymn "Allah-Hu-Ak Bar" based on African lyrics.

Among the Muslims who established apparently close contact with the UNIA during Garvey's American period were adherents of the Ahmadiyya movement, a Muslim denomination founded in northern India a decade or so before the end of the nineteenth century. In 1920 Dr.

Mufti Muhammad Sadiq, a missionary from this group, arrived in the
United States. He purchased a property at 4448 South Wabash Avenue
in Chicago, part of which was converted into a mosque, and began proselytizing.[47] By 1923 we find Sadiq among the guests on the rostrum during a Liberty Hall meeting. He had recently converted forty Garveyites
in Detroit, an area of intense Ahmadiyya effort.[48] Sadiq returned to
India in 1923 and was succeeded by Mohammed Yusuf Khan, also of
India. Maulvi Muhammed Din, Sadiq's successor as editor of the
Ahmadiyya movement's *Moslem Sunrise*, reprinted pro-Moslem matter
from the *Negro World*, which in turn carried his discourse, "Has Christianity
Failed and Has Islam Succeeded?"[49] Din appeared in the *Negro World* again
in 1925, this time replying to a couple of editorials by T. Thomas Fortune in
which the latter disagreed with Blyden that Islam was preferable to Christianity. Fortune's argument rested on the alleged moral superiority of
monogamy over polygamy and the ease of divorce in Islam.[50] Din, described as belonging to the Moslem Ahmadiyya Mission, pointed out that
illegitimacy and divorce among Christian monogamists undermined
Fortune's argument. Fortune remained adamant, however. An associate
editor of the *Negro World* favored the Muslim position, and even Fortune
was by 1926 denouncing "the high-handed way in which the Christian
Americans and Europeans are and have been dealing with the African
and Asiatic Mohammedans."[51]

Possibly because of such favorable exposure in the *Negro World*, Islam
continued to be a subject of interest among UNIA members in the United
States after Garvey's deportation. In 1931 the Cleveland, Ohio, division
celebrated a "Mohammed Day" meeting, during the course of which they
were addressed by Dr. Abad M. D. Sty, listed as being from North East
Africa.[52]

The Ahmadiyya Muslims apparently did not succeed in building up a
mass movement, but those Muslims who did were also associated in some
respects with the UNIA. It has been suggested that Elijah Muhammad,
leader of the most successful of these Muslim organizations, the Nation
of Islam, was a corporal in the uniformed ranks of the Chicago UNIA
division.[53] Others remember him as an active member of the Detroit
UNIA.[54] Muhammad did some of his early proselytizing in Chicago in
1933 in a UNIA Liberty Hall.[55] He also apparently encouraged, or at
least did not object, to having his movement cast in the role of successor

to the Garvey movement.[56] It is also sometimes suggested that Timothy
Drew (later known as Noble Drew Ali), founder in 1913 of the Moorish-
American Science Temples, acknowledged Garvey's influence on his
movement. Drew's movement had for its major theological document a
Holy Koran compounded of the teachings of the Bible, Marcus Garvey
and the Quran. Garvey was apparently "eulogised at every meeting as the
John the Baptist of the movement."[57] Indeed, so successful were the
Moorish-Americans at attracting Garvey's followers after his deportation
that Philadelphian Garveyites actually wrote the United States authorities
in 1935 asking for Garvey's return to combat the usurpation of Garvey
by this group. The letter indicated that the Moorish-Americans were en-
ticing away UNIA members "under the pretense that they are doing
Garvey's work, as he no longer can return." The Moorish-American leaders
constantly reminded their converts of the injustices attendant upon Garvey's
deportation and went so far as to claim authority from Garvey, while denouncing orthodox Garveyites as crooks who had lost contact with Garvey.[58]

The essence of religion for Garvey was the imparting of race pride,
Black Nationalism and self-reliance. In this light, his willingness to tolerate Islam and the attraction he had for Muslims are not difficult to understand. Indeed, even Harlem's Black Jews could find a home in the UNIA
for the basic thrust of their doctrines boiled down in essentials to a similar message of race pride and self-reliance. And in religion, Garvey was
concerned primarily with essentials. Christian and non-Christian religions
approved by Garvey all simultaneously predicted and worked hard to
effectuate a return of the former glories of the African race. The UNIA
catechism expressed it thus:

Q.   What prediction made in the 68th Psalm and the 31st verse is
     now being fulfilled?

A.   "Princes shall come out of Egypt, Ethiopia shall soon stretch
     out her hands unto God."

Q.   What does this verse prove?

A.   That Black Men will set up their own government in Africa,
     with rulers of their own race.

NOTES

1. *Negro World*, January 30, 1932.
2. *National Negro Voice*, July 29, 1941.
3. *Champion Magazine* 1 (March 1917): 334.
4. Ibid., 1 (January 1917): 267, 268.
5. Amy Ashwood Garvey, "Marcus Garvey: Prophet of Black Nationalism," n.d., Amy Ashwood Garvey Papers, London, England; J. A. Rogers, *World's Great Men of Color* (New York: J. A. Rogers, 1947), II: 599; James L. Houghteling, Commissioner of Immigration, to Senator Theodore G. Bilbo, n.d. [ca. February 1938], RG 60, 198940, Records of the Department of Justice, National Archives.
6. *Blackman*, November 30, 1929.
7. Amy Jacques Garvey quotes it and the stanza from which it is taken in her *The Philosophy and Opinions of Marcus Garvey* (London: Frank Cass, 1967), II: iii.
8. *Arkansas Survey*, December 18, 1927; *Negro World*, December 24, February 19, 1927; March 10, 1923; May 15, 1926; *National Negro Voice*, July 26, 1941.
9. *Negro World*, April 4, 1925; speech by Mrs. Bruce, n.d., Bruce Papers, 69-6, Schomburg Collection, New York Public Library.
10. Rev. Zebedee Green, *Why I Am Dissatisfied—Part Two* (Pittsburgh, 1924), p. 6.
11. Colón UNIA to President Calvin Coolidge, June 20, 1927, RG 204, 42-793.
12. *Negro World*, January 10, 1931.
13. *Sixth Anniversary Drive, Cincinnati Division, No. 146* (1927), pp. 14, 15.
14. Quoted in Tony Martin, "Some Reflections on Evangelical Pan-Africanism, or, Black Missionaries, White Missionaries, and the Struggle for African Souls," *Ufahamu* 1 (Winter 1971): 84. The church was the Afro-Athlican Constructive Church.
15. *New York Times*, August 6, 1924.
16. *Blackman*, August 3, 1929.
17. *Negro World*, June 7, September 6, 1924.
18. *New York World*, August 23, 1920; *New York Age*, August 28, 1920; minutes, June 26, October 20, 1924, FO 371/9633, Foreign Office Records, Public Record Office, London; Pittsburgh *Courier*, August 8, 1924; *New York Times*, August 17, 1924.
19. *Negro World*, January 26, 1924.

20. Ibid., February 24, 1923.

21. The *Tribune* (British Guiana), May 22, 1921, reprinted from the *Gleaner* (Jamaica), March 26, 1921. Enclosure in Governor of British Guiana to Secretary of State, Colonial Office, June 7, 1921, CO 318/364, Colonial Office Records, Public Record Office, London.

22. Amy Jacques Garvey, *Garvey and Garveyism* (Kingston: A. J. Garvey, 1962), p. 99.

23. *Negro World,* November 3, 1923, May 21, 1932.

24. *Black Man* 2 (January 1937): 5.

25. *Negro World,* February 2, 1924; March 19, 1927; *Black Man,* 1 (1934): 10.

26. *Negro World,* October 8, 1921.

27. *Negro World,* March 29, 1924.

28. Invitation card to the ceremony in FO 371/9633.

29. *New York Amsterdam News,* June 27, 1923.

30. Rev. E. Urban Lewis to H. M. Consul, New York, September 24, 1924, FO 371/9633.

31. Lewis to H. M. Consul, November 1, 1924, FO 371/9633.

32. *Negro World,* February 7, 1925.

33. Robert I. Rotberg, *A Political History of Tropical Africa* (New York: Harcourt, Brace and World, 1965), pp. 340, 341.

34. *Negro World,* December 5, 1925.

35. Ibid., January 3, September 5, 1925; April 7, 1923; Garvey *Philosophy and Opinions,* I: 66; *Blackman,* April 6, 1929.

36. Marcus Garvey, Jr., *Universal Negro Improvement Association Convention Hymns* ([Kingston], 1934); some of the hymns in here were by Arnold J. Ford, who compiled the better-known *Universal Ethiopian Hymnal* (New York: Beth B'nai Abraham Pub. Co., 1920, 1921, 1923).

37. *Negro World,* March 19, 1927.

38. *Black Man,* 1 (late March 1936): 16.

39. Ibid., 2 (January 1937): 12.

40. E.g., Sylvia Wynter, "Garvey and Bedward," *Sunday Gleaner,* March 12, 1972, and related correspondence.

41. Lenford S. Nembhard, *Trials and Triumphs of Marcus Garvey* (Kingston: The Gleaner Co. Ltd., 1940), p. 117.

42. *Blackman,* August 31, 1929.

43. Marcus Garvey, *A Talk with Afro-West Indians – The Negro Race and Its Problems* (Kingston [?]: African Communities League, 1915 [?]); for Blyden's biography, see Hollis Lynch, *Edward Wilmot Blyden* (New York: Oxford University Press, 1967).

44. *Negro World,* September 2, 1922.

45. Ibid., August 15, 1925. The writer was Randolph P. Mercurius.

46. Ibid., June 4, 1927.

47. A. T. Hoffert, "Moslem Propaganda—The Hand of Islam Stretches Out to Aframerica," *The Messenger* (May 1927): 141, 160.

48. *Negro World,* September 1, 1923; *The Moslem Sunrise* 2 (January 1923): 167. I am indebted to Professor Khalil Mahmud of Ibadan University for copies of this journal.

49. *Negro World,* January 5, 1924; *The Moslem Sunrise* 2 (October 1923): 263.

50. *Negro World,* July 18, September 5, 1925.

51. Ibid., October 3, 17, 1925, July 3, 1926.

52. Ibid., August 8, 1931.

53. Leonard E. Barrett, *The Rastafarians* (Rio Piedras: Institute of Caribbean Studies, University of Puerto Rico, 1968), p. 62. The statement was told to Barrett by Mrs. Amy J. Garvey during an interview.

54. Interview with J. Charles Zampty.

55. *Muhammad Speaks,* Special Issue [n.d., ca. June 1972], p. 5.

56. See foreword by Daniel Burley, in Elijah Muhammad, *Message to the Blackman in America* (Chicago: Muhammad Mosque of Islam No. 2, 1965).

57. Arna Bontemps and Jack Conroy, *They Seek a City* (Garden City, N.Y.: Doubleday, 1945), p. 175.

58. Benjamin W. Jones, Secretary of Philadelphia UNIA to Joseph B. Keenan, Asst. Attorney General, May 21, 1935, RG 60, 39-51-821; for a similar complaint, see *Negro World,* April 15, 1933.

5

History

You assume a right to write history within the last 500 years, and simply because you have been able to dump so many tons of your history in the world and other people have not said anything by way of complaint, you think your history rests there. But a lot of things your Mr. Wells has said we Negroes treat as bunk. Mr. H. G. Wells may divert civilization for the benefit of his Anglo-Saxon group, but that does not make it the fact that the people who laid claims to the civilization he attributed to others are going to give up easily. The black man knows his past. It is a past of which he can be nobly proud. That is why I stand before you this afternoon a proud black man, who would be nothing else in God's creation but a black man.

—*Marcus Garvey*[1]

Out of cold old Europe these white men came,
From caves, dens and holes, without any fame,
Eating their dead's flesh and sucking their blood,

Relics of the Mediterranean flood;
Literature, science and art they stole,
After Africa had measured each pole,
Asia taught them what great learning was,
Now they frown upon what the Coolie does.

—Marcus Garvey [2]

Garvey's study of history seems to have assumed significant proportions during his teenage years, while serving his printer's apprenticeship. During this period he interested himself largely in black heroes of the Caribbean, of whom Toussaint L'Ouverture, leader of the Haitian revolution, was his favorite.[3] His early articles in the *Africa Times and Orient Review* and in *Champion Magazine* show this keen appreciation of West Indian history. Quite possibly before he first left Jamaica, he began to explore the history of Africa as well as that of Afro-America. His interest in African history was clearly stated in his early pamphlet, *A Talk With Afro-West Indians.* Here he commended his audience to a study of Edward Wilmot Blyden:

> You who do not know anything of your ancestry will do well to read the works of Blyden, one of our historians and chroniclers, who has done so much to retrieve the lost prestige of the race, and to undo the selfishness of alien historians and their history which has said so little and painted us so unfairly.[4]

Garvey's knowledge of and appreciation for the history of his race was reinforced by many of his early contacts. Duse Mohamed Ali was author of the well-known historical work on Egypt, *In the Land of the Pharoahs.* William H. Ferris, one of the earliest editors of the *Negro World,* had previously published *The African Abroad.* John Edward Bruce had in 1911 been among the founders of the Negro Society for Historical Research in Yonkers, New York, and was its president. This society disseminated historical knowledge and collected rare books and manuscripts on the history of black people. The society's Pan-African thrust was symbolized by the selection of King Lewanika of Barotseland as honorary president. Duse Mohamed Ali was among its corresponding members, as was Marie Du Chatellier of Bocas del Toro, Panama, later an important UNIA organizer. It antedated by four years the better-known Association for the

Study of Negro Life and History founded by Carter G. Woodson. The secretary-treasurer of the Negro Society for Historical Research was the famous historian and bibliophile Arthur A. Schomburg. Commenting on the appearance of Woodson's *Journal of Negro History* in 1916, Schomburg suggested that this journal was "stealing our thunder in which we are pioneer."[5] Woodson himself several years later became a *Negro World* columnist. And among Garvey's lifelong acquaintances, from his boyhood in Jamaica to his last years in England, was another of the leading black historians of the time, J. A. Rogers.

History, like everything else for Garvey, was a subject to be used for the furtherance of racial emancipation. He used history first to establish a grievance—to show that the black man had been wronged. Many of his writings were historical in this sense. In 1938, for example, he submitted a memorandum to the West India Royal Commission, a British government body which was investigating recent rioting and workers' revolts in the islands. Here he traced the history of the islands since emancipation— the denial of full equality to Afro-West Indians, their resultant migrations in search of work elsewhere, the usurpation of the island economies by alien races—in order to explain the recent upheaval.[6]

History, however, could also be used to instill self-confidence. He continually stressed the fact that the African had in former times enjoyed a creditable history and that this had been acknowledged by historians such as Herodotus who belonged to an era that felt less inclined to establish myths of African inferiority.[7] The African, therefore, had nothing to be ashamed of in the face of allegations of inferiority emanating from the white world. Indeed, black people should move from the defensive to aggressively rehabilitate their past. "The time has come," he declared, "for the Blackman to forget and cast behind him his hero worship and adoration of other races, and to start out immediately to create and emulate heroes of his own. We must canonize our own saints, create our own martyrs, and elevate to positions of fame and honor Black men and women who have made their distinct contributions to our racial history."[8]

Garvey's stress on the progressive nature of the black past was a reaction to the distortions he observed emanating from the pens of white historians in his era. He therefore carried on a constant campaign against white historical writing on the black past. In 1929 he declared that "History is written with prejudices, likes and dislikes; and there has never been a white historian who ever wrote with any true love or feeling for the

Negro."[9] He continued: "White historians and writers have tried to rob
the black man of his proud past in history, and when anything new is
discovered to support the race's claim and attest the truthfulness of our
greatness in other ages, then it is skillfully rearranged and credited to
some other unknown race or people."[10]

Garvey's rehabilitation of the black past, especially the ancient past,
and his acknowledgment of the greatness of black heroes past and present
in no way detracted from his ready admission that the black man had
fallen behind in the preceding few hundred years in the march toward
material progress. He incorporated this into a cyclical theory of history,
which was designed to give the black man hope. As in the case of all
major revolutionary theories, from Christianity to communism, Garveyism decreed that the attainment of its ultimate goals was inevitable, the
goals in this case being the resurgence of the black race: "In the cycle of
things he lost his position, but the same cycle will take him back to where
he was once."[11]

In the tradition of these major philosophies, however, the inevitable
success which awaited the black man would have to be activated by the
black man's own efforts. In other words, success was inevitable provided
the black man did not become complacent and did not cease to engage
in constant struggle, based on the lines of Garvey's program. As Garvey
himself expressed it, "We are bound to win. Black men and women are
bound to go forward; nothing can stop them but death and themselves."[12]
This same idea was succinctly expressed by Garvey during a debate with a
delegate at the Sixth International Convention of Negro Peoples of the
World held in Jamaica in 1929. The exchange went like this:

Mr. Garvey: You don't believe there is a literal interpretation to
               Ethiopia stretching forth her hands to God?

Mr. Bailey: I do.

Mr. Garvey: Then how can we do it except we attempt it?[13]

This idea was also the central theme of Garvey's long poetic saga, *The
Tragedy of White Injustice,* which recounted African glories at a time
when Europe was steeped in barbarism and cataloged a history of Euro-

pean genocide and rapine. It postulated the black man's inevitable resumption of glory and held out the hope of peace if the white man should mend his evil ways soon. Otherwise, Armageddon would ensue.

Garvey's interest in black history differed in one important respect from that of some cultural nationalists, to whose school of thought he is sometimes linked. For he avoided the pitfalls of living in the past. He used history to establish a grievance, instill black pride, and point a way for eventual race emancipation, and that was all. He refused to glory in the past to the extent of letting its exoticism become a hindrance to the struggle in his own time. By 1936 he was able to say, "It is an established fact that the Negro had a glorious past. We need not worry about it now, because outside of inspiring us with confidence and hope it will be of no material value to harp on it, for the present is what confronts us along with the future."[14] Thirteen years earlier he had expressed similar sentiments: "We may go back three thousand years ago and point to our civilization of that time. But WE CANNOT LIVE BY THE PAST."[15]

His interest in history was reinforced by a feeling of deep empathy with the historical suffering of the black race. The following expression was typical:

My firm purpose, my one purpose in life, is to work for the salvation of my race. Because of the cries from the grave—I hear the cry of 300 years. The cry of my great-grandparents in the cotton and cane fields; I see the hard taskmaster drawing his lash across their backs; I hear them cry out in mortal agony: "It pains; it pains; it pains." I see them fall under the lash; I see them fall to the ground; I see them buried, and I hear the wailing souls from heaven and from regions below. I hear the cry of my mother and father and millions of Negroes who have been brutalized: "Go on, Garvey! Go on! Go on!" And so, fellow men, because of that cry that comes from the grave I have given up all material desires; I have given up all temporal pleasures and have dedicated myself to the sacred principles of the UNIA, the emancipation of the Negro race and a free and redeemed Africa.[16]

This communion with the past was linked to a strong consciousness on Garvey's part of himself as an important historical figure. He often spoke in terms of future generations who would be inspired by his example, as well as of past generations whose sufferings would thereby be rendered not in vain.[17]

Not surprisingly history played an important role in the day-to-day affairs of the UNIA. The race catechism used by the organization was largely an encapsulation of historical knowledge concerning the race. The first of its four sections, Religious Knowledge, succinctly described Africa in antiquity, with particular emphasis on biblical references to Africa and Africans.

The second section, Historical Knowledge, provided a bird's eye view of Ethiopia, Meroe, Egypt, the slave trade, New World slavery and Africans in the Americas before Columbus. It also included brief biographical sketches of such famous historical figures as Edward Wilmot Blyden, James Africanus Horton, and Samuel Lewis of Sierra Leone, the Reverend Samuel D. Ferguson of Liberia, Conrad Reeves of Barbados, Toussaint L'Ouverture, Frederick Douglass, Prince Hall, Alexander Crummell and others.[18]

J. A. Rogers and Arthur A. Schomburg sometimes lectured to UNIA locals on Black history,[19] and Rogers' *From Superman to Man* was offered as a bonus with subscriptions to the *Negro World*.[20] Carter G. Woodson's Association for the Study of Negro Life and History was favorably reported by the paper's writers,[21] and Woodson himself had actually taken the initiative in writing Garvey requesting permission to publish in his paper.[22] Woodson had a similarly amicable relationship with Garvey's Harlem-based daily paper, the *Daily Negro Times*. John E. Bruce, who worked on this paper, was a friend of Woodson and sometimes plugged Woodson's historical efforts in his regular column appearing in the paper.[23] As early as 1920 the Declaration of Rights had demanded that Black history be taught in schools. And when the organization obtained Liberty University in Virginia, it was envisaged that this subject would be taught truthfully.[24] For juvenile readers of the *Negro World* the lives of famous black figures, such as entertainer Bert Williams and ex-heavyweight boxing champion Jack Johnson, were serialized in comic strip form. Black Star Line ships were named after black heroes, as were the Phyllis Wheatley Hotel and the Booker T. Washington University, both in Harlem. This interest in race history was not confined to Afro-American Garveyites.[25] Garvey himself was a collector of African art pieces, and on one occasion we find him spending an afternoon with Professor William Leo Hansberry at the latter's Howard University office reviewing pictures of ancient Ethiopian culture.[26]

An important feature of Garvey's makeup, which was illuminated by his use of history, was his deep feeling of humanity. He took the view that great civilizations in the past were destroyed by materialism and a submergence of human values, and he looked forward to an ideal society which would learn from these past mistakes. In this regard, he saw a chance for the black man to be humanity's saviour. For the black man had the double experience of his own ancient civilizations on the Nile as well as the white man's in which he currently lived. The former had been destroyed by materialism and feelings of racial superiority. The latter was in the process of disintegration for the same reason. In this situation the black man could not only emancipate himself but could perhaps save mankind in the process and "salvage the bankrupt civilization of white Europe." He could do this because "The heart of the Negro is deep and holy. Misdirected, it has been emotional and sentimental up to the present, but the recovery of the race in its sublimest thought will give it an urge, direct it toward an end that will bestow great blessings upon mankind."[27]

NOTES

1. Marcus Garvey, *Minutes of Proceedings of the Speech by the Hon. Marcus Garvey at the Century Theatre* (London: Vail and Co., 1928), p. 26.

2. Marcus Garvey, *The Tragedy of White Injustice* (New York: A. J. Garvey, 1927), p. 3.

3. Amy Ashwood Garvey, "Marcus Garvey—Prophet of Black Nationalism," n.d., Amy Ashwood Garvey Papers, London, England.

4. Marcus Garvey, *A Talk with Afro-West Indians—The Negro Race and Its Problems* (Kingston [?]: African Communities League, 1915 [?]), p. 3.

5. Schomburg to Bruce, June [?] 13, 1916[?], Bruce Papers, Ms. 23, Schomburg Collection, New York Public Library.

6. Marcus Garvey, Memorandum to the West India Royal Commission, September 24, 1938, CO 950/44, Colonial Office Records, Public Record Office, London.

7. E.g., Lenford S. Nembhard, *Trials and Triumphs of Marcus Garvey* (Kingston: The Gleaner Co., Ltd., 1940), p. 113; Garvey, *The Tragedy of White Injustice*, p. 6; Garvey, *A Talk With Afro-West Indians*, p. 3.

8. Marcus Garvey, "African Fundamentalism." This was an essay reprinted several times in the *Negro World* and elsewhere and sold as a poster for framing.

9. *Blackman*, June 20, 1929; Amy Jacques Garvey, ed., *The Philosophy and Opinions of Marcus Garvey* (London: Frank Cass, 1967), II: 82.

10. Garvey, *Philosophy and Opinions*, II: p. 82; see also H. W. Peet, "An Interview with Marcus Garvey," *The Southern Workman* 57 (October 1928): 424; *Negro World*, April 28, 1923, September 7, 1929; *Blackman*, November 28, 1929.

11. *Black Man* 2 (July-August 1936): 11.

12. *Negro World*, August 18, 1928.

13. Ibid., September 7, 1929; for similar sentiments, see Garvey, *A Talk With Afro-West Indians*, p. 6.

14. *Black Man* 2 (September-October 1936): 3.

15. *Negro World*, March 24, 1923.

16. Ibid., July 25, 1925.

17. E.g., *Blackman*, April 9, 1929; Garvey, *Philosophy and Opinions*, II: 183, 276.

18. The *Universal Black Men Catechism* used by the author is a reprint of the original catechism. It is mostly the same as the original, though Mrs. Amy J. Garvey informed the author that some changes were made. One major change is the substitution of "Black Men" for "Negro."

19. E.g., *Negro World*, January 23, 1932; UNIA Central Division, (New York), Files, Box 14, f. 4; handbill for a UNIA meeting of July 21, 1935; Schomburg Papers, Box 3, Rev. R. Felix, vice-president, New York division, UNIA to Schomburg, November 21, 1934 and November 26, 1934. Schomburg spoke on this occasion on "African Cultures in America."

20. *Negro World*, December 24, 1927.

21. E.g., ibid., June 18, 1927.

22. T. Thomas Fortune to Woodson, December 21, 1923, replying to Woodson to Garvey of December 15, 1923, Carter G. Woodson Papers, Library of Congress, Box 5, Folder 85.

23. Bruce to Woodson, January 17, 1923; Bruce to Woodson, January 20, 1923, Woodson Papers, Box 5, Folder 77.

24. *Negro World*, August 7, 1926.

25. E.g., *National Negro Voice* (Jamaica), August 9, 1941.

26. *Negro World*, February 2, 1924.

27. *Black Man* 2 (September-October 1936): 4; *Negro World*, July 17, 1926.

6

Propaganda

The great white man has succeeded in subduing the world by forcing everybody to think his way, from his God to his fireside. He has given to the world, from the Bible to his yellow newspaper sheet, a literature that establishes his right and sovereignty to the disadvantage of the rest of the human race.

The white man's propaganda has made him the master of the world, and all those who have come in contact with it and accepted it have become his slaves.

The Universal Negro Improvement Association is now calling upon the 400,000,000 members of our race to discard the psychology and propaganda of all other peoples and to advance our own. The white man taught that the best of the world was intended for him, and we now teach that all the beauties of creation are the black man's, and he is heir to all that God has given to man.

—Marcus Garvey[1]

Garvey sold the Negro to himself. . . .

—S. A. Haynes[2]

Among Garvey's greatest feats was the thoroughness and success of his propaganda effort. He set out with self-conscious candor to oppose the propaganda of race pride and nationhood to the contrary ideas of white supremacy, African inferiority, white man's burden and Caucasian manifest destiny. Garvey almost single-handedly took on the official propaganda machines of all the European and North American colonialist powers, as well as the myriad publications, agencies, universities and the like which helped in the dissemination of information inimical to the black man. "We are not afraid of the word *propaganda*," he declared, "for we use the term in the sense of disseminating our ideas among Negroes all the world over. We have nothing stealthy in this meaning."[3] As far as Garvey was concerned, everything—education, religion, history, the news media—was enlisted by the dominant race in the furtherance of propaganda designed to perpetuate its continuance in power. The time had come, therefore, for the black man not only to make his own propaganda available, but to refuse to be guided by those who did not suffer and could not empathize with him. He said, "It takes the slave to interpret the feelings of the slave; it takes the unfortunate man to interpret the spirit of his unfortunate brother; and so it takes the suffering Negro to interpret the spirit of his comrade."[4]

Garvey's propaganda effort was most earnest in the years of his greatest glory in the United States. He considered the war-induced turmoil with its political unrest, its Russian Revolution, and its rumors of self-determination for all peoples ideal for strident propaganda of his type. By 1924 he thought that the world scene had stabilized to the point where the UNIA effort would have to shift more toward silent organization with a deemphasis on loud propaganda. He informed his followers: "Remember, the policy of the Universal Negro Improvement Association for 1924 and 1925 as far as its objective goes is the same as it was in 1917 and 1918, only that we are using more careful judgment. The things that we could have said in 1914, up to 1920, we cannot say now, but we mean them just the same."[5] This attitude was doubtless influenced, too, by the escalating attacks on his organization, both from within and without. Yet there had been no essential change. The International Convention of 1924, for example, discussed, among other things, "the tabooing of all alien propaganda inspired to destroy the ideals of and the enslaving of the minds of the Negro."[6]

UNIA propaganda was disseminated in a variety of ways. In fact practically every aspect of the organization had propaganda value. Its artistic productions were largely geared toward political indoctrination. The same could be said for religion as practiced within the organization. Its businesses were designed to instill racial self-confidence and set an example. As Garvey said, you could not *tell* black people, you had to *show* them.[7] UNIA printed material, such as the black catechism, served a similar purpose. The UNIA was even in the business of moving pictures, some of its parades having been filmed for showing at Liberty Halls. Many of Garvey's speeches as well as selections rendered by the Black Star Line band were available on phonograph records.[8] At the 1929 International Convention delegates considered the feasibility of a broadcasting station to further disseminate the message.[9] Garvey's ambassadors, too, like all ambassadors, were charged with propaganda functions. His traveling commissioners toured much of the world spreading his message and disseminating his literature.

But the most effective of Garvey's propaganda devices were his newspapers. Having been trained as a printer and a journalist, Garvey was well qualified for his role as newspaper propagandist. He founded several papers and journals during his life in several different countries. Around 1910 and 1911 he started *Garvey's Watchman* in Jamaica, *La Nación* in Port Limón, Costa Rica, and *La Prensa* in Colon, Panama, and he was apparently a co-publisher of the *Bluefields Messenger* in Costa Rica. All of these were short lived.[10] The weekly *Negro World* was published in Harlem from 1918 to 1933. Between 1922 and 1924 the *Daily Negro Times* appeared in Harlem. Back in Jamaica after his expulsion from the United States, he published the *Blackman* from 1929 to 1931. This started, as it proclaimed in large type on its front page, as "A Daily Newspaper Devoted to the Uplift of the Negro Race and the good of Humanity." It was later converted into a weekly. Its demise was followed by the appearance in 1932 of the *New Jamaican,* "A Daily Evening Paper Devoted to the Development of Jamaica." This lasted until 1933, and was followed almost immediately by the *Black Man* magazine, first published in Jamaica in December 1933, and later in England up at least until 1939. To this list must be added his work on the *Africa Times and Orient Review* in London. The National Club which he helped found in his early days in Jamaica issued its own fortnightly *Our Own,* and his mentor of this period, Dr.

J. Robert Love, published the *Jamaica Advocate*. He also claimed to be
"connected with" the Kingston *Catholic Opinion*.[11]

The most important of Garvey's papers and possibly his single greatest
propaganda device was the *Negro World*. The paper considered itself "a
propaganda medium published in the interest of the awakened Negro,"[12]
and in its earliest period it bore the banner headline "NEGROES GET
READY," which appeared at the very top of the front page and even
dwarfed the paper's title. The title was followed by the explanation, "A
Newspaper Devoted to the Interests of the Negro Race Without the Hope
of Profit as a Business Investment." Throughout almost the whole life of
the paper, its front page was devoted to a Garvey polemic. A. Philip
Randolph in his campaign against Garvey derided this practice thus:
"What sort of a newspaper is the *Negro World* anyway, which devotes
its front page, the news page of every modern civilized, recognized newspaper in newspaperdom, to the vaporings, imbecile puerilities and arrant
nonsense of a consummate ignoramus?"[13] What Randolph did not know
was that Garvey's front-page ideological statements served as gospel for
black people throughout the world. The reading of Garvey's *Negro World*
message was a standard part of UNIA meetings wherever the organization
existed. A *Negro World* columnist in 1927, for example, explained that
"it is translated into scores of dialects twenty-four hours after arrival in
Africa and carried by fleet runners into the hinterland, up the great lakes
of Southeast Africa. . . "[14] In Trinidad the governor noted in 1920 that
at meetings of the Trinidad Workingmen's Association and elsewhere
verbatim quotations were utilized from the *Negro World* and other Garvey
writings.[15]

Apart from Garvey himself, the *Negro World* was helped in its efforts
by a succession of some of the finest editors in Afro-America. One of the
earliest was W. A. Domingo, who was for a while the paper's "editorial
writer."[16] He and Garvey parted company in 1919 over his socialistic
ideas (according to Garvey) and his disagreements over Garvey's business
schemes.[17] During 1920-1921 the paper had as a joint editor Hubert H.
Harrison, a lecturer activist and a highly respected member of Harlem's
intellectual community. From 1917 to 1919 he had published *The Voice*,
an organ of his Liberty League, founded in 1917.[18] William H. Ferris,
historian and graduate of Harvard and Yale, served three years as literary
editor and one as associate editor between 1919 and 1923. He claimed that

the paper's "bona fide" circulation grew from seventeen thousand to sixty thousand within his first year.[19] John E. Bruce was for some years a contributing editor up to his death in 1924, as was Eric D. Walrond, a successful literary figure in the Harlem Renaissance. But perhaps the most illustrious of the *Negro World* editors was T. Thomas Fortune, generally acknowledged dean of Afro-American journalists, who edited the paper from 1923 to his death in 1928. He dictated his last *Negro World* editorials from his sickbed during the last three weeks of his life.[20] Duse Mohamed Ali was also at one time associated with the paper. In the last years after *Fortune,* this high editorial standard was maintained under Hucheshwar G. Mudgal, an Indian who came to Harlem via Trinidad.

The *Negro World* penetrated every area where black folk lived and had regular readers as far away as Australia.[21] It was cited by colonial powers as a factor in uprisings and unrest in such diverse places as Dahomey, British Honduras, Kenya, Trinidad and Cuba. These powers therefore had no illusions concerning the appeal of its message of racial self-reliance and its anticolonialist tone to oppressed black people. During its entire existence, therefore, the paper was engaged in a running battle with the British, French, United States and other governments, all of which assiduously sought to engineer its demise, or, failing that, to restrict or prevent its circulation, especially in Africa, Central America and the West Indies. The attitude of the colonialist powers can be summed up in the words of a British official in Panama: "The whole paper bristles with racial antagonism."[22] Garvey and his followers for their part variously protested these attempts, joked about them, always tried to circumvent them, and, in Garvey's case, waxed poetic about them:

We will keep from them the "NEGRO WORLD"
That no news they'll have of a flag unfurled;
Should they smuggle copies in, and we fail,
We will send the sly agents all to jail.
This is the white man's plan across the sea
Isn't this wily and vicious as can be?[23]

In more prosaic fashion the 1920 Declaration of Rights protested the suppression of black papers all over the world, while a 1928 Garvey petition to the League of Nations specifically protested the banning of the

Negro World in some areas and the imposition of penalties, including life imprisonment and even death, for possessing it. Garveyite S. A. Haynes observed laconically and correctly, "It is read weekly by the British and French Foreign Offices."[24]

The British authorities were kept especially busy in their war against the paper. In 1923 the British acting governor of Nyasaland explained that "On the grounds that this paper was poisonous and mischievous to a degree which only those who have dealings with the crude African native can properly appreciate, it was placed in March last year on the list of prohibited papers in Nyasaland."[25] In 1923 copies were also being confiscated in Northern Rhodesia.[26] Around the same time, the acting governor of Sierra Leone was reporting that the paper "though not absolutely prohibited has been strictly controlled, and only a few copies have been allowed to circulate."[27] In the other British colonies in West Africa—the Gold Coast, Nigeria, and the Gambia—it was banned outright by this time.[28] It was still prohibited in these areas into the 1930s.[29] The British overlords were less successful in suppressing the local African press that supported Garvey's program. The *Gold Coast Leader* in an article in 1928 entitled, "Censorship of the *Negro World* a Sign of Weakness," praised the paper, supported its principles of Pan-African cooperation and actually quoted from the forbidden publication.[30] How its editor, J. E. Casely Hayford, was able to obtain the paper is illustrated by a letter of his to John E. Bruce. He wrote, "I do not get the *Negro World* regularly. When I see it it is much too late and I like to keep abreast of what is going on. Can you kindly make sure and send me a copy each week well wrapped up to my Seccondee address?"[31]

In South Africa, though the paper was not proscribed outright, a local agent in Kimberly reported that when he picked up his papers at the post office, he ran a gauntlet of "kicks, punches, sneers, insults and impertinent questions."[32]

In the West Indies, too, the heavy hand of British reaction fell upon the paper. Indeed, here the paper was attacked practically from its inception. As early as February 1919, when UNIA agents were discovered soliciting memberships and selling the paper in Trinidad, it was banned. In June 1919 the acting governor of Trinidad confided to his counterpart in British Guiana that in so doing "the action taken by this Government is not strictly covered by the law." It was not until 1920 that the legal

let written by Garvey specially to the people of Trinidad, hidden in between the cargo of a ship from New York.[51] C. L. R. James has said that despite the ban, he managed to buy a copy every Saturday morning in Port-of-Spain.[52] The police in Trinidad, and doubtless elsewhere, were kept busy looking for the paper, and houses were searched by detectives.[53]

The United States government, although it never actually banned the *Negro World,* nevertheless kept it under close surveillance from the beginning. In addition, Attorney General A. Mitchell Palmer in 1919 gave the *Negro World* pride of place in his Department of Justice report on "Radicalism and Sedition Among the Negroes as Reflected in their Publications." The *Negro World* was the first of the several Afro-American publications dealt with in the report.

By July 1919 officials of the Post Office Department were conferring among themselves and seeking the advice of their solicitor as to whether the paper was objectionable enough to be proceeded against. They were particularly alarmed at pro-Bolshevik and race-first articles, both of which were apparently considered equally dangerous.[54] Apart from the department's own observations, the occasional public-spirited American citizen sought to draw their attention to the radical effects of the paper. One such, an apparently white resident of Tower Hill, Virginia, sent the department copies of the *Negro World* and *Chicago Defender* to show what kind of matter was benefiting from the United States mails. He drew the attention of the officials to the fact that Negroes now would not work for white folks, presumably due to the influence of these papers.[55]

Many communications of this nature emanated from American consular agents abroad, who generally shared the feelings of their host governments that the United States mails should not be used for what they considered the subversion of friendly governments. In May 1919 the American consul in Georgetown, British Guiana, reported that the local inspector of police had called on him. This goodly British official explained that his government wanted to prevent the receipt and distribution of four publications—the *Negro World, Crusader, Monitor* (published in Omaha, Nebraska), and the *Christian Recorder* (official organ of the African Methodist Episcopal Church—apparently the combination of black and American was enough to cause fright among British colonial officialdom). The British official explained, in the words of the consul, that "owing to the fact that the black population is several times that of the white and includes some

prominent persons such as officials, lawyers, doctors and ministers, they
are uncertain as to the advisability of taking the necessary steps here to
prevent their circulation." They therefore preferred for the United States
to stop them at source, if not by banning them outright, then by denying
them the use of the mails. The consul reported that of the four, only the
Negro World and *Crusader* were dangerous.[56] Two years later the post
office solicitor got around to declaring that a publication could not be
subject to a blanket denial of mailing privileges. Each issue would have
to be separately ruled upon.[57] The British authorities in London itself,
in a 1919 document, "Unrest Among the Negroes," presumed to inform
Uncle Sam that there were radical black organizations in the United States.
The UNIA and the *Negro World* were mentioned and its British drafters
were careful to point out that "It is certain that the various negro organizations in the United States will not leave the British colonies alone."[58]

In the case of Trinidad, the American consul, Henry D. Baker, took
the initiative in suggesting that the paper be stopped at the source. He explained that "altho the local Postal Authorities burn every copy they
can find of this publication, which is obviously intended as propaganda
to cause race troubles, and general anarchy, nevertheless it is believed
that many copies escape destruction, and are circulated in a surreptitious
way throughout this Colony." He enclosed several wrappers in which
papers had been mailed by Garvey to persons in Trinidad to "show how
the United States mails are being used for the purpose of forwarding to
a friendly country, papers directly inciting the negro population to acts
of murder and anarchy."[59]

From Costa Rica, the Post Office Department found itself being prodded
into action by an anti-*Negro World* coalition of the United Fruit Company,
the British consul and the Costa Rican authorities. In September 1919 the
Washington counsel for the United Fruit Company wrote the secretary of
state and enclosed sample copies of the *Negro World*. Garvey's earlier sojourn in Costa Rica had evidently not been uneventful, for the company
remembered it clearly. The letter explained that Garvey "left Limón in
1912 and that he is a typical noisy Jamaican, and if allowed to go on as
he has been doing, there is a possibility of his attempting to repeat the
French experience in Haiti." He reported, too, that the governor of
Limón, with the agreement of the British consul, was planning to deport
all those present at the next UNIA meeting. The United Fruit Company

counsel suggested, finally, that the Department of Justice assign its secret service to the case, since the UNIA was inciting revolution and thereby violating the neutrality of countries at peace with the United States.[60] Similar correspondence was received from Costa Rican officials who, after banning the *Negro World,* requested the New York post office not to allow it to be mailed to Costa Rica.[61]

The *Negro World* propaganda spreading over the Caribbean area did not bypass United States colonies. Casper Holstein, a prominent figure in the United States-based Virgin Islands nationalist movement, was a regular contributor to the *Negro World,* which he found a cooperative medium. His brother-in-law, D. Hamilton Jackson, was president of the St. Croix Labor Union. After a short spell in the United States, Jackson was by 1923 back in St. Croix agitating, among other things, for universal suffrage. Officials became alarmed at the propaganda value of articles appearing in the *Negro World* praising Jackson's efforts. One judge ventured the opinion that "all the poisonous articles published in the *Negro World* by Holstein are inspired by Jackson."[62]

The course of events in the United States suggests that authorities apparently preferred to move against Garvey himself rather than possibly create an equally great furor by moving merely against the paper. Indeed, a move against the paper may have been very unpopular with the same establishment black leaders who were anxious to see the government move against Garvey himself, since many of them were involved in publications of their own and were sensitive to any precedents establishing press censorship. This had been the lesson of Attorney General Palmer's 1919 report against the Afro-American press. Some of those who later became Garvey's bitterest enemies (such as A. Philip Randolph and Chandler Owen of the *Messenger* and Cyril Briggs of the *Crusader*) were censured along with Garvey and the *Negro World* in that report, and the *Crisis,* edited by W. E. B. Du Bois, though disclaiming any brief for the *Negro World* and other publications, still came out in defense of their right to speak.[63] Similarly, in 1920, the Graham sedition bill was killed in Congress with the support of the conservative black *New York Age* and the NAACP. This bill had sought to muzzle and render nonmailable radical black publications.[64] A move against Garvey himself involved no such entanglements for the United States government, since the most important recognized leaders outside of the UNIA were almost totally arrayed against him.

The nearest that United States officialdom came to banning the *Negro World* was during and soon after Garvey's trial in 1923 for alleged mail fraud when they could have moved under the cloak of Afro-American establishment opposition to Garvey which had reached its zenith. Garvey reported that the prosecutor threatened to suppress both the *Negro World* and the *Daily Negro Times* during and after the trial. He also illegally seized the subscription lists of the *Negro World,* and subscribers soon began receiving enemy papers. The purpose of the threats was to scare the editors into not reporting the prosecutor's conduct during the trial.[65] The *Negro World* reporting of the trial was, indeed, unusually subdued.

If the *Negro World* was the greatest single propaganda device that the UNIA possessed, it had a close rival in Garvey himself. A handbill announcing a Garvey lecture in Atlanta, Georgia, in 1917 referred to him as "an orator of exceptional force." Before long, handbills would proclaim him "the World's Greatest Orator." A UNIA circular advertising a speech of his at the Albert Hall in London in 1928 proclaimed that the world's greatest orator was "to deliver one of the greatest speeches ever heard in any period of the world's history." Readers of the circular were assured that "Such a chance comes sometimes but once in a lifetime."[66] The most surprising thing about these statements is that few people would have quibbled with them. The excellence and power of Garvey's oratory was probably the single most uncontroversial of his attributes. Indeed it is difficult to think of any other fact concerning Garvey on which such diverse persons as communist leaders, J. Edgar Hoover of the Department of Justice, NAACP anti-Garveyites, British colonial police officers and Garvey's followers all agreed.

In their efforts to capture the tone of a Garvey oration, those who witnessed this singular experience often summoned up equally exquisite language to describe what they had seen. UNIA organizer Marie Duchatellier, in a letter to John E. Bruce said, on the subject of Garvey's oratory:

> I have noted what you say in your letter in re my writing to Mr. Garvey to bridle his language, but I think I have told you before that you ask of me an impossible thing. I told you I had just as well stop the flowing waters of Niagara Falls. You say you have written to Mr. Garvey on the subject, so that will have to suffice. All that you say is true and if Mr. Garvey was less Radical it might be better, but you had just as

well hope for the "Ethiopian to change his skin or the leopard his spots" as to ask Garvey to change his method or procedure. I am convinced that it is the outpouring of the pent up feelings of generations of his ancestors who have borne the oppression and injustice of the white man for centuries. The cry has come ringing down the ages and he is giving voice to the cumulative agonies our people have suffered during their slavery and since their emancipation. We are the "heirs of the ages."[67]

A reporter of the *Panama-American* expressed it this way:

He would probably pass unnoticed in a crowd—until he speaks. He has the most precious of all bounties, the gift of eloquence; and as he speaks his small, dark brown eyes seem to grow, his even white teeth flash through black lips. His speech is smooth and unctuous, without any touch of the American twang despite his long residence in the United States. His English is that of an Oxford scholar and when he speaks—his hearers listen.[68]

Even a British colonial police officer, detailed to observe a Garvey meeting in British Honduras, could not totally obscure his appreciation of Garvey's fine oratory behind his obvious contempt:

Marcus Garvey was introduced by the Chaplain and commenced his 1-¼ hours address. When he waxed hot I was reminded of Rider Haggard's "Winstopogoas" in his moments of animal feriousness [sic] but he nevertheless knew how to get his hearers and was cheered heartily time and again. Garvey in his serious moments did not lack humour which was appreciated. . . . There were moments of enthusiastic madness into which he worked himself while speaking when I thought the aid of a medical man would be absolutely necessary but, such was not to be.[69]

A newspaper report of a Garvey speech in Jamaica said, "Towards the end of his speech Mr. Garvey applied the well known prank of the platform speaker, 'I think I have kept you long enough for tonight,' he said, and the crowd roared for him to continue."[70] An apparently white United

States paper said of his equally apparently black audience on one occasion, "they cheered almost his every word. Men shouted and some even gave vent to an emotional 'amen.' " This article noted, "He pronounced such words as 'master' with the use of a long 'R' but ordinarily his flow of language was that of the educated southern negro."[71] Herbert J. Seligman, director of publicity of the NAACP, also commented on his "slightly English intonation that falls strangely upon the ears of Americans unaccustomed to natives of the British West Indies."[72] Robert Minor, covering Garvey's 1924 international convention for the Workers (Communist) party of the USA said, "I heard Garvey speak last night. He is one of the most powerful personalities that I have ever seen on the platform."[73] After a speech at Howard University in 1924, the head of the department of public speaking and dramatic art considered it one of the few good speeches he had ever heard. Dean Kelly Miller considered it one of the best ever delivered in the university chapel.[74] J. Edgar Hoover, soon to become head, for almost a half-century, of the Federal Bureau of Investigation, was less effusive. He wrote in 1919, "He is an exceptionally fine orator. . . ."[75]

The excellence of Garvey's early training as a printer and journalist was matched by his long and systematic study and practice of elocution. We are told that the young Garvey visited various churches to study and learn from the speaking styles of ministers.[76] During this period he also is said to have taken elocution lessons from his early mentor, Dr. J. Robert Love.[77] By 1910 Garvey was participating in elocution contests and himself training young orators and promoting such contests in West Kingston. A former president of the Jamaica Union of Teachers recalled having seen Garvey perform about this time during the finals of an all-Jamaica elocution contest in which he placed third.[78] During his first London years (1912-1914) he often spoke at Speaker's Corner in Hyde Park (as indeed he did during his other periods in London). Back in Jamaica in 1914 he frequented and participated in the weekly literary debates at the Baptist Church Hall in Kingston.[79] Indeed, as late as 1932, he was still organizing elocution contests in Jamaica.[80]

By the time he burst on the American scene, then, Garvey's preparation in the art of oratory had been long, varied and thorough. And his oratorical skill was put to the fullest advantage as a propaganda medium for the organization. More so than a writer, Garvey was first a speaker. A corps of very efficient shorthand writers copied his speeches verbatim and they filled many pages of the *Negro World* and his other papers. He was constantly on tour, so that in an age before television his followers, especially in the United States, but to some extent also in Canada, the West Indies, Central America and Europe, had fairly ample opportunities to see and hear him in person. Among Garvey's subordinates there were also several outstanding orators who also spent much time on tour, sometimes traveling with Garvey.

Garvey's propaganda caused, or was implicated in, nationalist and anticolonial manifestations all over the world. Many of the concessions to colonized people that followed were traced by Garvey ultimately to his propaganda.[81] He also credited his propaganda and the example of the *Negro World* with bringing about an improvement in the tone of Afro-American journalism. He said, "When I arrived in this country in 1916, I discovered that the Negro press had no constructive policy. The news published were all of the kind that reflected the worst of the race's character in murder, adultery, robbery, etc. . . . other features played up by the papers were dancing and parlor socials of questionable intent. . . ." After a few years of the *Negro World*, he thought that this trend was changing and that several papers were now "publishing international news and writing intelligent editorials on pertinent subjects."[82]

One result of Garvey's propaganda was to call forth an extensive counterpropaganda effort from colonial powers. They evidently felt that their efforts in banning the *Negro World* and imprisoning and deporting Garvey's agents were not enough, so they set out to deliberately counter Garvey's message. In New York in 1923 the British consul general actively promoted a pro-British magazine, the *British West Indian Review* to, in his own words, "offset, to some extent, the vicious propaganda being carried on by Garvey and the Universal Negro Improvement Association."[83] In Panama in 1925 the head of the British legation announced that he had mounted his own propaganda campaign among the West Indian population to counter Garvey's. He had enlisted the support of ministers with large West Indian congregations and was organizing the Boy Scouts as a medium for getting across pro-British and anti-Garvey sentiments.[84] A writer in the white South African *Cape Argus* in 1923 came to the same conclusion concerning the need to organize active anti-Garvey propaganda: "No doubt the government will watch very carefully the spread of this and other anti-White propaganda in the Union, but it will easily be realized that mere suppression of these movements as they arise will not be suffi-

cient. The native people are growing up, and some healthy counteracting
methods to enable them to express their growing ideals will be necessary."[85]

For Garvey to have had the great British propaganda machine on the
defensive must rank among his more noteworthy feats. While the black
W. E. B. Du Boises and A. Philip Randolphs of America called him a
clown and a buffoon and helped engineer his downfall, the arbiters of
the fate of black people in Washington and London were disposed to be
more realistic. As early as 1919 the British government had informed
Washington that the UNIA program was "being carried on by clever
propaganda directed principally by Marcus Garvey, a West Indian
negro. . . ."[86]

Garvey was aware of the existence of a counterpropaganda effort.
Around the same time as the British consul general in New York was
overseeing the first edition of the *British West Indian Review,* Garvey
was declaiming in Liberty Hall against "counter-propaganda to distort
and disrupt the minds and intentions of those who are behind the program."[87] In 1929 he issued a statement on the situation:

> Just at this time there is a well organized propaganda and conspiracy
> engineered by a combination of forces known and unknown, seen and
> unseen, in the United States of America, and different parts of the
> world, to undermine the powerful influence of the Universal Negro
> Improvement Association in uniting Negroes everywhere.
>
> This propaganda and conspiracy is being conducted on the one hand
> by some of our one-time slave masters, who have never been able to
> outlive the idea that the Negro should be anything else but a slave,
> and on the other hand by a cheap, brainless, conscienceless, treacher-
> ous, disloyal brand of Negro reprobates who, like traitors of all causes,
> national, secular and religious, are ever willing to sell themselves for
> the thirty dirty pieces of silver.
>
> It is difficult for me to explain thoroughly and as clearly as I would
> like to the complete make-up of the combinations that are now organ-
> ized to fight the Universal Negro Improvement Association. . . .[88]

Garvey's propaganda did not die with him. A surprisingly ample number
of black leaders in the 1960s, the era of independence and Black Power,
acknowledged his influence.[89]

NOTES

1. *Negro World*, November 3, 1923.
2. Ibid., May 6, 1933; A. J. Garvey, *Garvey and Garveyism* (Kingston: A. J. Garvey, 1963), p. 214.
3. *Blackman*, April 16, 1929.
4. Ibid., May 21, 1929.
5. *Negro World*, November 22, 1924; see also ibid., August 1, 1925; *Black Man* 3 (July 1938): 12.
6. *Negro World*, June 7, 1924.
7. Ibid., November 22, 1924.
8. For a list of these, see ibid., October 8, 1921.
9. *Blackman*, August 31, 1929.
10. A. J. Garvey, *Garvey and Garveyism*, pp. 7-8; *Crisis* 21 (December 1920): 58. Garvey said that *Garvey's Watchman* was weekly, had a circulation of about 3,000 and was published for between 12 and 15 months; *La Nación* was a daily; and *La Prensa* was tri-weekly—*Negro World*, June 19, 1920.
11. *Negro World*, June 19, 1920.
12. Ibid., August 10, 1929.
13. A. Philip Randolph, "Reply to Marcus Garvey," *Messenger* (August 1922): 468. What would Randolph have said of the London *Times'* use of its front page for advertisements?
14. *Negro World*, August 20, 1927.
15. Governor Chancellor to Viscount Milner, November 30, 1920, CO 318/356, Colonial Office Records, Public Record Office, London. The editors placed such a high premium on Garvey's messages that when he was away on tour and after he had left the country, they sometimes reprinted old speeches of his if his message did not arrive in time to go to press. Apparently there were even times when, in an emergency, they made up a message and placed Garvey's name to it, a practice that did not please Garvey. Lenford S. Nembhard, *Trials and Triumphs of Marcus Garvey* (Kingston: The Gleaner Co., Ltd., 1940), p. 77; Amy Jacques Garvey, ed., *The Philosophy and Opinions of Marcus Garvey* (London: Frank Cass, 1967), II: 200; *Black Man* 1 (December 1933): 19.
16. *Negro World*, July 19, 1919. Editors or editorial writers wrote regular editorials in addition to Garvey's front-page statements. Garvey was officially designated managing editor. Editions of June 7 and 14, 1919, bear only Garvey's name on the editorial staff. Domingo's name appears in issues for July 1919. The author came across only occasional copies of the paper for 1919.

17. *Messenger* (September 1919): 32. Domingo said that he was editor
from the paper's inception to "eleven months thereafter": *Emancipator,*
April 3, 1920.
  18. Hubert H. Harrison, *When Africa Awakes,* New York, The Porro
Press, 1920, pp. 8, 10.
  19. William Ferris, "The Spectacular Career of Garvey," *New York
Amsterdam News,* February 11, 1925. He says here the circulation grew
from 17,000 to 60,000. Elsewhere he gives the latter figure as 50,000.
See *Favorite Magazine* 4 (July 1920): 396.
  20. *Negro World,* June 9, 1928.
  21. A. Goldsmith (black Australian) to Woodson, September 6, 1920:
Woodson Papers, Box 5, G 86. The *Negro World* was not the only
Afro-American publication read by this race-conscious individual.
  22. Braithwaite Wallis, British legation, Panama, confidential memorandum to Austen Chamberlain, November 4, 1925, CO 554/66.
  23. Marcus Garvey, *The Tragedy of White Injustice* (New York: A. J.
Garvey, 1927), p. 12.
  24. *Negro World,* August 20, 1927.
  25. Acting Governor R. Rankine to His Excellency the Governor
General and High Commissioner, Cape Town, May 15, 1923, CO 525/104.
  26. Richard Goode, Acting Administrator, Livingstone, to Prince Arthur
of Connaught, High Commissioner for South Africa, Cape Town, May 2,
1923, CO 417/693.
  27. Acting Governor, Sierra Leone, to Duke of Devonshire, May 28,
1923, CO 267/600.
  28. Synopsis of a destroyed record, Register of Correspondence for the
Gold Coast, 1923, Public Record Office, London, Colonial Office
records, Gov/28913; *Negro World,* April 21, 1923; "The Universal
Negro Improvement Association and African Communities League,"
memo by Colonial Office, March 7, 1924, CO 554/64.
  29. C.O. 318/399/76634, "Memorandum—Marcus Garvey and the
Universal Negro Improvement Association and African Communities
League" [1930]; K.E.E. Baidoo, Abidjan, Ivory Coast to *Negro World,*
November 16, 1932, UNIA Central Division (New York) Files, Box 3, a 33.
  30. Reprinted in *Negro World,* December 1, 1928. The original
article was from the *Leader* of October 17.
  31. Hayford to Bruce, November 24, 1923, Bruce Papers H. 5, Schomburg Collection, New York Public Library. Hayford also received copies
from J. R. Ralph Casimir of Dominica, where it was not banned. Interview
with Mr. Casimir.

32. *Negro World,* September 13, 1924.

33. Governor J. R. Chancellor to Viscount Milner, November 30, 1920, CO 318/356. W. M. Gordon to Governor of British Guiana, June 10, 1919, Henry D. Baker, American Consul, Trinidad, to Secretary of State, March 5, 1920, RG 59, 844 g. 04417, National Archives. *Negro World,* October 4, 1924.

34. Governor Eyre Hutson of British Honduras to Secretary of State, Colonial Office, May 10, 1920, FO 371/4567, Foreign Office Records, Public Record Office, London.

35. Officer Administering the Government (OAG) C. Clementi, British Guiana, to Viscount Milner, P.C., G.C.B., G.C.M.G., etc., etc., September 2, 1919, confidential, CO 111/624.

36. Sir Wilfred Collet, Governor of British Guiana, to Milner, April 14, 1920, CO 111/630.

37. *Negro World,* June 26, 1920. Petition from British Guiana UNIA to Major E. F. L. Wood, n.d., CO 318/373.

38. Collet to Rt. Hon. Winston S. Churchill, July 6, 1922, CO 318/371.

39. Churchill to Governor Wilson of Trinidad, August 22, 1922, secret, CO 318/371; destroyed secret file of September 29, 1922—headnote refers to Trinidad's refusal to lift the ban, Gov/51931.

40. Collet to Churchill, July 6, 1922, CO 318/371.

41. OAG, Bermuda, to Milner, November 27, 1920, CO 318/356.

42. Governor G. Haddon-Smith of Grenada to Milner, October 8, 1920, CO 318/358.

43. American Consul, Port Limón, to Secretary of State, Washington, D.C., August 24, 1919, RG 59, 818.4016/ orig.

44. H. M. Consul, Colón, to Secretary of State, February 5, 1926, FO 372/2257.

45. Quoted in *Negro World,* June 26, 1920.

46. Ibid., February 2, 1929.

47. Garvey, *Philosophy and Opinions*; II: 385; *NegroWorld*, May 16, 1925, p. 4.

48. H. M. Consul-General, Dakar, Senegal to Secretary of State, August 17, 1922, FO 371/7286; *Negro World,* January 10, 1925; K.E.E. Baidoo, Abidjan, Ivory Coast to *Negro World,* November 16, 1932, UNIA Central Division (New York) Files, Box 3, a 33.

49. Interview with J. Charles Zampty.

50. Governor Hutson to Secretary of State, Colonial Office, May 10, 1920, FO 371/4567.

51. Governor Chancellor to Milner, November 30, 1920, CO 318/356.

7

Africa

*The white world may despise us; the white world may scoff and
spurn the idea of a free Africa because they say: "How dare you
talk about Africa when Africa is in the possession of England,
when Africa is in the possession of France, when Africa is in
the possession of Spain?" What logic have you, Mr. White Man?
Have you not before you the pages of history recording the
rise and fall of peoples, of races and of nations? White Man,
can you not learn by experience? Why talk about the permanency
of Great Britain in Africa? Why talk about the permanency of
France in Africa?*

—Marcus Garvey[1]

*How long do you suppose the colored people got to suffer in
this land? I pray that God will send a Moses to lead us out of
this land. . . .*

> *—Will Wright of*
> *Damascus, Georgia,*
> *to the American*
> *Colonization Society,*
> *April 5, 1920*[2]

Garvey was heir to a rich tradition of interest in international black unity which had flourished throughout the nineteenth century. In many ways Garvey belonged to this nineteenth-century Pan-African tradition and might even be called the last of the great nineteenth-century Pan-Africanists, despite the twentieth-century setting for his movement. His phraseology was unmistakably nineteenth century—his constant references to Ethiopia stretching forth her hands to God, his talk of an African nationality and the redemption of Africa, his slogan "Africa for the Africans," all of these were staples in the vocabularies of the Martin Delanys, the Bishop Turners, the Edward Blydens and other Afro-American and West Indian Pan-Africanists who preceded him. His preoccupation with Liberia, his interest in emigration and his desire to operate his own shipping company also placed him firmly in the nineteenth-century tradition.

Many of Garvey's speeches and writings reveal a familiarity with the careers of his predecessors. But more interesting is the fact that there were several direct or near-direct linkages between Garvey and some of the big names of the nineteenth and early twentieth centuries. Perhaps the most important link was provided by John Edward Bruce, who for many decades maintained contact, both through personal meetings and correspondence, with an amazing array of important figures from all over the black world. Among Bruce's many friends and major correspondents over the years were Edward Blyden, Alexander Crummell, Frederick Douglass, Dr. Mojola Agbebi of Nigeria and J. E. Casely Hayford of the Gold Coast, all major historical figures.[3] Garvey's mentor, Dr. J. Robert Love, provided another link. Not only had Love carried on a prolific correspondence with Bruce long before Garvey's rise to prominence, but during his many years in the United States he had been a close friend of Bishop Henry McNeal Turner, one of the most important Pan-Africanists of the nineteenth century and the one whose rhetoric perhaps comes closest to Garvey's. Love, as a clergyman, had also worked in Haiti under the well-known Afro-American emigrationist Bishop J. Theodore Holly.[4] The following 1901 quotation from Love could easily have been written by Garvey two decades later. He wrote, " 'Africa for the Africans' is the new shape of an old cry. . . . This cry will waken the so-called civilized world to a consciousness of the fact that others who are not accounted as civilized, think, with regard to natural rights, just as civilized people think. . . ."[5]

Love had also collaborated in 1901 with Henry Sylvester-Williams, organizer of the 1900 Pan-African Conference in London, when the latter visited Jamaica and established branches there of his Pan-African Association.[6] Garvey had another link with that 1900 conference in the person of the widow of the man who presided over the gathering, Bishop Alexander Walters. Mrs. Walters was an ardent Garveyite and a regular speaker at Liberty Hall meetings.[7]

Yet another link was Dr. J. Albert Thorne, a Barbadian who lived in the same parish as Garvey during the latter's boyhood. Thorne in the 1890s had attempted to organize the settlement of West Indians in Central Africa. He is said to have supported Garvey's early UNIA activity in Jamaica, and an assistant of his was one of the first to join the UNIA.[8]

Two of Garvey's most direct contacts were, of course, with Booker T. Washington, perhaps the most internationally famous black man of his time, and Duse Mohamed Ali of the *Africa Times and Orient Review.* Also, the name of Garvey's organization bore a suspicious similarity to the Universal Association for the Moral Improvement of Mankind, established in 1905 by the Haitian Pan-Africanist Benito Sylvain.[9]

Many of those who joined the UNIA, though not necessarily internationally famous, had belonged to or had led race uplift organizations, usually with a Pan-Africanist outlook. By way of example, James B. Yearwood, for some years a high-ranking UNIA official, had immediately prior to joining the UNIA led the Universal Loyal Negroes based in the Canal Zone, Panama.[10] Maurice Rouselle, leader of the Wilmington division, had many years before organized the Afro-American Improvement Company, in connection with which he visited Africa.[11] William Ferris from 1901 to 1903 had been a "lecturer and newspaper correspondent" for William Monroe Trotter's *Boston Guardian,* as well as being a foundation member of the American Negro Academy, the Niagara Movement, and John Edward Bruce's Negro Society for Historical Research.[12] Bruce himself in 1913 had formed the Loyal Sons of Africa to unite black folk all over the world and later popped up as a major figure in the Hamitic League of the World.[13]

One important precursor whom Garvey did not particularly appreciate being compared with was Chief Alfred Sam of the Gold Coast, who in 1914 had been thwarted in his attempt to establish a colony of Afro-Americans in his native land. Garvey's black enemies adopted the same

scurrilous attitude toward Sam that they adopted toward Garvey himself, and they often compared the two. Such a scurrilous comparison
was contained in a *Chicago Defender* article which formed the subject
of libel proceedings brought by Garvey.[14]

Garvey saw Africa essentially as the only place where black people
could launch a successful bid for equality with other races and nations.
Africa was the black man's ancestral home; he was still in a majority
there; the continent was rich in natural resources; and with some tech-
nical help from black people in other areas a determined drive for equality would have the best chances of success there. And if the black man
became powerful in Africa this would necessarily raise his status all over
the world. For, as Garvey was fond of saying, "A strong man is strong
everywhere."[15] As a means of consolidating its protection for the scattered members of the race, Garvey envisioned that such a strong African
government should extend citizenship to black people everywhere.[16]

The question of white exploitation of Africa naturally spurred Garvey
on to a sense of urgency. "If the oil of Africa is good for John D. Rocke-
feller's interest," he wrote; "if the rubber is beneficial to the Firestone
interests; if the iron ore is good enough for the Carnegie Trust, then,
surely, they are of interest to us."[17] On one occasion Garvey became
particularly incensed when English historian H. G. Wells suggested that
Africa was economically necessary to Europe. Garvey sent him an irate
telegram suggesting that Wells must have gotten his "old-time 'Uncle
Tom' information" from W. E. B. Du Bois.[18]

While people like Wells tried to justify the expropriation of Africa's
wealth, other segments of white opinion attacked Garvey's African program on pseudoethnological grounds. The *New York Times* took the
trouble to editorially admonish Garvey for not knowing that Africa never
entirely belonged to the "negro." If Garvey went to Africa, this curious
editorial reasoned, he would have to chase out the Hottentots, Zulus, and
Pygmies, among others, supposedly because they were not "negro."[19]

Garvey directed a lot of his propaganda effort to the African continent, and there is sufficient evidence to suggest that his influence was
widely felt, even in areas which never had UNIA branches. Some of this
African work was clandestine, of necessity, and the names of his agents
were sometimes withheld even from UNIA executive members. On occasion Garvey financed these agents from his own personal funds rather

than the organization's money in order to maintain secrecy.[20] Similarly, at the 1920 convention some African delegates registered under assumed names and were heard in private.[21]

Garvey's desire to keep some of his African undertakings secret can be appreciated in light of the constant colonial surveillance over his agents' activities. In January 1920, British military intelligence reported that a Gold Coast merchant, S. G. Kpakpa-Quartey, had spoken at a December 1919 UNIA meeting.[22] In August 1920 Nyasalanders in the United States preaching Garvey's slogan came to the attention of British authorities.[23] In 1921 one Wilson from the Gold Coast was deported from the Belgian Congo for UNIA activities.[24] Again, in 1922 colonial authorities were watching the movements of one John Kamara, a UNIA traveling commissioner who had held meetings in Dakar, Senegal, before departing for the Gambia and the rest of West Africa.[25] After Kamara's departure from Senegal the French authorities raided the dwellings of some of the local UNIA people with whom he had been in contact. Documents were seized which revealed the existence of UNIA branches in Dakar, Rufisque and Thies. Four Garveyites from Sierra Leone were deported.[26]

Such activity was only a small portion of the colonialist effort against Garvey. They denied visas to black persons they considered radical, as historian J. A. Rogers discovered when he applied for one to visit Sierra Leone.[27] Where possible they tried to counter Garvey's propaganda. Thus Sir Gordon Guggisberg, one-time British governor of the Gold Coast, let it be known on a visit to the United States that Africans were "suspicious of the American Negro." The *Gold Coast Leader,* which consistently refused to be awed by the British overlords, suggested instead that "far from the African at home being suspicious of the African abroad, it has been the constant wish of the latter to get into touch with the former in the development of their common nationality. Hitherto local governments have adopted every device to make contact difficult, if not impossible."[28]

Sir Harry Johnston, a longtime British administrator in Africa, in an article "Why A Nigger Republic Must Fail," preferred to see in Garvey's "somewhat fantastic" carryings on a warning to European governments to be on guard in Africa lest an Afro-American-African alliance engulf them.[29] But perhaps most damaging of all, a British judge in British

Honduras voided the bequest by Isaiah Morter of property to the value of about $100,000 to the UNIA for African redemption. The judge ruled that African redemption was "an illegal purpose and contrary to public policy...."[30]

It was in this same spirit that the British authorities reacted when in 1923 Garvey reduced them to a state of consternation by announcing his intention to undertake a world tour to defend his reputation. Governors of the West, East and Central African colonies all agreed to prohibit him entry should he attempt to land in their areas, and they prepared to draft special legislation to meet this contingency.[31] Such Garvey-induced legislation, the Undesirable Persons (Prevention of Immigration) Ordinance, 1924, actually came into being in Sierra Leone. It bore the ingenuous subtitle, "An Ordinance to Prevent Certain Descriptions of Persons from Entering Sierra Leone."[32] Shipping companies were also alerted to refuse passages to Garvey and his party should he attempt to sail to Africa.[33]

If anything the French colonial authorities reacted with even greater hysteria to the UNIA presence than did the British, and their information more frequently tended to be garbled.[34] The governor general of French West Africa was in 1921 convinced that the UNIA planned to massacre all the whites in the Gold Coast as a preliminary to a general uprising which would be financed from America.[35]

Perhaps French hysteria can be understood by reference to Garvey's taunts. In 1922, for example, he declared that the French ban on the *Negro World* had come too late, since he had already organized French Africa as well as the Senegalese troops on the Rhine.[36] And to supplement the work of his agents in Africa, Garvey maintained close contacts with Africans from the French colonies living in Europe. Perhaps his closest such contact was Kojo Tovalou Houénou, a Paris-based lawyer and nephew of King Behanzin of Dahomey who had once been exiled by the French to the West Indies. Kojo was a star attraction at Garvey's 1924 convention, where he suggested an alliance between the UNIA and his own Ligue Universelle pour la Défense de la Race Noire. This alliance would spearhead a worldwide federation of race organizations, in which the UNIA would provide the "heavy artillery."[37] Kojo is said to have led an abortive, UNIA-inspired revolt in Dahomey in 1925.[38] During his trip to France in 1928, Garvey claimed to have "cemented a working plan with the French Negro" and to have established a "sub-European head-

quarters" in France.[39] He also joined the Comité de Défense de la Race
Nègre, a Paris-based Pan-African organization associated with the French
Communist party and the Comintern.[40]

The Belgians also found in Garvey cause for alarm. One writer in 1922,
fearful of the effects of denunciations of the Belgian Congo at UNIA conventions, thought that the Kimbangu uprising might have been inspired
by Garvey's propaganda.[41] Up to the 1930s the Belgians routinely suspected Garveyites of being implicated in anticolonial riots, including
some ostensibly led by local converts of the International Bible Students
Association of Brooklyn, New York. Many Africans were thought to
belong both to this sect and to the UNIA.[42]

Other evidence of Garveyite influence in Africa is easy to come by.
Many pioneer nationalist politicians maintained Garveyite contacts. One
of the founders of the "first permanent African political body" in British
Central Africa was a Nyasa who had been in communication with Garvey.[43]
And in Kenya the important nationalist figure Harry Thuku wrote Garvey
in 1921 for "advice and help."[44] Thuku was jailed shortly after and read
Garvey's *Philosophy and Opinions* while incarcerated.[45] Thuku's arrest
by the British had been followed by a peaceful demonstration calling
for his release at which a large number of Africans were shot dead by the
colonialist forces. Garvey held a protest meeting, issued a press release
on the matter, and despatched a telegram to the British prime minister.
"You have shot down a defenseless people in their own native land for
exercising their rights as men," he wrote. "Such a policy will only tend
to aggravate the many historic injustices heaped upon a race that will
one day be placed in a position to truly defend itself. . . . Again we ask
you and your government to be just to our race, for surely, we shall not
forget you."[46]

In the Gold Coast Garvey had a powerful ally in J. E. Casely Hayford
and his *Gold Coast Leader*. Hayford, who was knighted by Garvey in
1922,[47] welcomed the emergence of the UNIA during his inaugural address on the founding of the National Congress of British West Africa
in March 1920.[48]

Yet another major West African political figure who had early contact
with the UNIA was Ernest S. Ikoli of Nigeria who in the 1930s was a
founder of the important Lagos Youth Movement (later the Nigerian
Youth Movement). Ikoli was secretary of the Lagos UNIA at its inception

in 1920 and was responsible for receiving the two hundred copies per week of the *Negro World* which this branch was ordering by November 1920. (There were also other agents of the paper in Lagos.) In 1920 this branch ordered five hundred UNIA badges and three hundred copies of the constitution, and in 1922 police sources estimated a membership of three hundred of whom only twenty-eight were financial.[49] These Nigerian Garveyites (there was also a branch in Kano)[50] were characterized by the governor as "mal-content Africans."[51]

Perhaps the best known cases of Garveyite contact with prominent African political figures concern Jomo Kenyatta of Kenya, who is said to have come into contact with Garvey's ideas as early as 1921 and who met Garvey in the late 1930s, and Kwame Nkrumah of Ghana who acknowledged his debt to Garvey's ideas on several occasions.[52]

In England, too, Garvey maintained contact with young activists, many of them future political leaders, in such London-based organizations as the West African Students Union and the International African Service Bureau led by Wallace Johnson of Sierra Leone, George Padmore of Trinidad and others.[53]

But the area on the continent where the UNIA seems to have flourished most was in South Africa. Perhaps this may have been an indication of the severity of South African racism, for UNIA branches always tended to proliferate in the most oppressive areas (e.g., the southern United States and Cuba). Perhaps, on the other hand, this may have been an indication of the advanced and more highly proletarianized nature of the black South African population, as compared with much of the rest of Africa. South Africa, too, had already established the habit of intimate contact with Afro-America through the African Methodist Episcopal Church (Bishop Turner had visited South Africa just before the turn of the century) and through several prominent figures who had received Afro-American educations. In South Africa also, as in so many other areas, the presence of a numerically insignificant but highly motivated and often mobile group of West Indians, veritable missionaries of Garveyism, may have influenced the situation.

One obvious indication of South African interest in the UNIA is provided by readers' letters to the *Negro World*. More letters appeared from South Africa (together with South West Africa) than from any other African country. A letter of 1929 amply demonstrates the spirit that

permeated these correspondents. It read, "It is mere stupidity and puer-
ility to say that South African natives are apathetic toward the UNIA.
Even the Draconian laws of Hertzog and Roos cannot, at this hour of the
day, discourage them in their determination to attain the noble ideals of
Garveyism."[54] The evidence provided by these letters is corroborated by
indications of great interest in Garvey, not only in major cities like Cape
Town and Johannesburg but in neighboring Bechuanaland, among boys
at a mission school in east Cape Colony and "even in remote corners of
the Ciskei and Transkei."[55]

   South African UNIA branches seem to have been as active as those
anywhere else. They sent delegates to Garvey's conventions in the United
States and were reported to be preparing to send delegates to his 1929
Jamaica convention.[56] The president of the Cape Town division edited
a publication called *The Black Man*,[57] and from the British enclave of
Basutoland came reports of large UNIA conventions in 1924.[58] Some
South African branches ran into problems which were familiar elsewhere.
Thus a member of the Evaton division explained in 1927 that meetings
were being held in the open because the division had not yet acquired
a hall. Furthermore, he wrote, "native ministers are against us, they
don't allow us to have or hold any meetings in churches or schools because they have this spirit of a white man, keep nigger down as much as
you can. . . ."[59] Some of these branches were very long-lived. As late as
1935 the first unsolicited contribution to a new Garvey fund came from
South Africa,[60] and at least one division remained active until 1958.[61]

   The UNIA was active in the struggle for human rights inside South
Africa. It was among the thirty organizations and two hundred delegates
represented at the 1927 Non-European Conference in Kimberly, described
by George Padmore as one of the first attempts at a nationwide united
front among South Africa's subject peoples.[62] Garvey's *Blackman* reported
that on June 15, 1930, twelve hundred Africans gathered under UNIA
auspices to protest the Riotous Assemblies Act.[63] The UNIA was also
to influence the struggle for human rights by infiltrating the very highest
echelons of the two major African organizations, the Industrial and Com-
merical Workers Union (ICU) and the African National Congress (ANC).

   UNIA representation in the ICU hierarchy seems to have been facilitated
by the presence of South Africa's West Indian community. Clements
Kadalie, leader of the ICU, reported that at its formation in 1919 there

were "a considerable number" of West Indians in Cape Town. Most were dockworkers—stevedores, shipwrights, foremen.[64] UNIA sources also provide occasional glimpses of West Indian Garveyites such as an unnamed man in Durban in the early 1920s who had been in Africa twenty years and spoke several African languages fluently. This person traveled about South Africa a lot and regularly received copies of the *Negro World* "in a way of his own."[65] Again, in 1925 the president of the Luderitz, South West Africa, division announced the death of one Arthur Cecil Grainger, aged forty-two, from St. Vincent. Grainger had come to South Africa during the Boer War and had stayed on.[66] And in 1939 we hear of the death of Jamaican-born Arthur McKinley, an agent for Garvey's *Black Man* in Capetown.[67] A white South African paper in 1923 also estimated that there were about two hundred Afro-Americans in Cape Town.[68] It is not improbable that some, possibly many, of these may have been West Indian born. West Indian Garveyites in Africa were often described, especially by the European authorities, as black Americans, and many had indeed lived in America for varying periods. Arthur McKinley was among those in Cape Town described on occasion as American.[69] In 1922 we hear of a Claremont, Cape Town, division being organized by T. L. Robertson of New York.[70]

Perhaps because of their strategic location on the docks, Cape Town's West Indians were heavily represented in the ICU hierarchy. Kadalie tells us that at its inception in 1919 the second chairman of the ICU, James King, and the third chairman, J. G. Gumbs, were both West Indians. The executive committee, he reported, often contained three or four West Indians. And J. G. Gumbs, a chemist and rigger at the Cape Town docks, was the ICU's president from 1924 to his death in 1929.[71] While the white *Cape Argus* thought that the language problem would restrict the effectiveness of Cape Town's Afro-American population,[72] Kadalie considered the foreignness of West Indians within the ICU to be an advantage. Gumbs, he said, "was well respected by all, since like myself he was free of tribal affiliations."[73] (Kadalie was a Nyasalander.) One resident of Cape Town ventured the opinion that "West Indians are tough, hard-backboned Negroes . . . of the he man type, aggressive and daring."[74]

The West Indians in the ICU were staunch Garveyites, indeed too much so for Kadalie, who had to prevent what he considered their attempt to turn the organization into a UNIA auxiliary. He did this, he said, because

he disliked serving two masters at the same time and because he disagreed
with the slogan "Africa for the Africans," preferring local to Pan-African
struggle.[75] Kadalie preferred, however, not to participate in the struggle
which developed within the ICU between the Garveyites, led by Gumbs,
and the communists, which ended with the expulsion of the latter.[76]
Despite his fears concerning a UNIA takeover of the ICU, dual membership in the two organizations continued. Gumbs in particular was for
several years a member of the advisory board of the Cape Town UNIA.[77]

Many Garvey admirers were also to be found in leadership positions
in the ANC. One was Professor James Thaele, president of the Cape
Western ANC. Thaele was a graduate of Wilberforce University and had
studied for fifteen years in the United States.[78] He began promulgating
the doctrines of Garveyism soon after his return,[79] and together with
J. G. Gumbs he seems to have been one of the most sought-after speakers
at important UNIA functions. (They spoke from the same platform on
occasion.)[80] We even find Thaele praising the African work of the UNIA
at a meeting of the ICU.[81]

In 1929 Thaele began editing *The African World,* which instantly became a major outlet for Garveyite propaganda. The very first issue editorialized, "I believe that it is essential to the early success of our cause that
the Africans here at home should seek co-operation with the Africans
abroad. The Universal Negro Improvement Association and African Communities League is the biggest thing today in Negro modern organizations.
Its program must be scrutinized, imbibed and assimilated by us." It went
on to suggest that the *"Negro World* must be a Bible to us. . . .[82] The celebration of Garvey day in Cape Town in 1925 was due at least in part to
the urging of *The African World.*[83] The work of *The African World* was
paralleled by another ANC publication, *Abantu Batho,* reprints of whose
pro-UNIA articles also found their way into the *Negro World.*[84] ANC
conventions between 1925 and 1927 passed resolutions demanding
Garvey's release from jail.[85]

There were yet other points of contact between Garveyism and South
Africans. Solomon T. Plaatje, who toured the United States in 1921
raising funds for his work among miners at Kimberly, was entertained
by Garveyites and spoke at Liberty Halls in many states.[86] On his return
home Plaatje seems to have alarmed British officials by his pro-Garvey
position.[87] The African Orthodox Church also found its way into South
Africa.[88]

The reaction of South African officialdom to Garveyite activity seems to have been somewhat less hysterical than that of their European counterparts. Prime Minister J. C. Smuts summed up his attitude in 1923. He knew that the UNIA had "attempted propaganda work in the Union, chiefly in Cape Town and Johannesburg, but . . . not with very conspicuous success." He continued, "No repressive action has been taken against the agents of this organization although its activities are being carefully watched." He considered the UNIA to be "without moral or financial stability." He concluded, in familiar enough vein, "That a certain amount of mischief is being done by misleading ignorant and credulous persons is beyond doubt and to this extent Ministers regard the organization with disfavour."[89] The UNIA does seem to have been subjected to sundry harassments, however, such as tamperings with its mail and, in some places, confiscation of the *Negro World*.[90] And it seems that it became almost impossible for Afro-Americans or West Indians to obtain entry into South Africa.[91]

One of the expressions most frequently used to describe the UNIA was the "Back to Africa Movement," a phrase that greatly displeased Garvey. Garvey more typically preferred to argue that the UNIA advocated the return of pioneers capable of making a contribution to African development.[92] Yet his utterances often went beyond this and seemed to suggest large-scale emigration, as his critics alleged. He sometimes suggested that this emigration would take place after the pioneers had completed their work.[93] And he certainly supported the Bilbo bill in 1939, which envisaged the gradual repatriation of the majority of Afro-Americans. Also we are told that the very second UNIA meeting in Jamaica had as its theme the "Return to Africa."[94]

In these ambiguous appeals to a return to Africa lay the source of a significant portion of the UNIA's mass appeal. The power of the emigrationist impulse in Afro-American history is yet to be fully appreciated. During Garvey's American years letters were still pouring into the offices of the American Colonization Society from black people who could not take American oppression anymore and yearned for an escape to Africa. "Now a few of us are begging you to send us back to Africa," wrote one such correspondent from Oklahoma in 1920. So anxious was he that he began selling his property before arrangements to send him were finalized.[95] This emigrationist impulse was still so great in 1927 and 1928 that an imposter, the so-called Laura Coffey, could fleece southern blacks by

claiming to be Garvey's representative sent to collect funds for emigrationist purposes. Some people actually disposed of their property to
await the ships which she said would be sent by African kings to Miami
and Jacksonville to transport them to Africa.[96]

The UNIA's activity at the League of Nations was mainly geared toward
obtaining a foothold in ex-German East Africa or South West Africa, but
it was on Liberia, the traditional home of returned New World Africans,
that the bulk of its emigrationist effort was concentrated. The UNIA was
from early fairly well connected in Liberia. John E. Bruce was an old
friend of Chief Justice J. J. Dossen. First Assistant President General
Dr. LeRoy Bundy was the brother of Richard Bundy, one-time secretary
to the United States legation in Monrovia.[97] Reverend Frances Wilcome
Ellegor, an early UNIA official, had been a professor at Liberia College.[98]
The UNIA's legal advisor in Liberia was ex-president Arthur Barclay.[99]

Attempts to woo the Liberian government were already in effect by
February 1919, when UNIA high commissioner in France, Eliezer Cadet,
left several copies of the *Negro World* with Liberian delegates to the Pan-
African Congress in Paris. He also interviewed C. D. B. King, who would
soon be president of Liberia. King is said to have suggested to Cadet that
if conditions in America were so bad then Afro-Americans should go to
Liberia.[100] In the United States later that year, King again called for Afro-
American emigration to Liberia.[101] Yet, if these statements seemed favorable to UNIA aspirations, there were other indications to the contrary.
British intelligence sources reported that the Liberian president claimed
not to feel any affinity with the struggles black people were waging in
America,[102] and King had apparently shown the same inclination in his
meeting with Cadet.[103] The tendency on the part of the Liberian authorities to express conflicting sentiments toward the activities of the UNIA
became more marked over the years. Before the end of 1919, however,
Garvey was announcing his intention to move his headquarters to Monrovia after the 1920 convention.[104]

In view of these conflicting reports of Liberian attitudes, Garvey took
the sensible step of despatching a commissioner, Elie Garcia, to Liberia
early in 1920 to apprise the government of the UNIA's intention and to
obtain official approval. Garcia informed the government of the UNIA's
size and program, of its desire to move its headquarters to Liberia, and
of its intention to help Liberia financially and otherwise, together with

its plan to encourage immigration into Liberia. Garcia explained that, "Owing to the rumors prevalent in the United States with respect to the unfriendly attitude of the people of Liberia to persons of other Negro communities, a statement which my organization had great reason to doubt, it was thought best to approach the Government of Liberia on the subject of lands before settling our future program."[105] Secretary of State Edwin Barclay, replying for President King, assured the UNIA "every facility legally possible in effectuating in Liberia its industrial, agricultural and business projects."[106] The government's attitude was corroborated by a Dr. Jordan of the National Baptist Convention, who informed a Liberty Hall crowd that while dining with President King, the latter had expressed approval of the UNIA's plan to relocate in Liberia.[107]

While in Liberia Garcia, an astute observer, made a confidential appraisal of conditions in the republic and incorporated his findings into a secret report to Garvey. He noted that though well endowed with natural resources, Liberia was extremely poor due to the lack of enterprise of the ruling Americo-Liberian minority. He cataloged a long list of social ills, including rigid class distinctions, slavery, de facto polygamy, graft and financial mismanagement. He warned that the UNIA should in the beginning play down any intention to interfere in the political life of the country, for "the Liberian politicians understand clearly that they are degenerated and weak morally and they know that if any number of honest Negroes with brains, energy and experience come to Liberia and are permitted to take part in the ruling of the nation they will be absorbed and ousted in a very short while." The UNIA should similarly conceal its intention of "enlightening the native tribes." Garcia also noted the precarious tightrope which Liberia had to walk between the United States, Britain and France.[108] This document contained within it all the major elements in the relationship which would develop over the next few years between the UNIA and Liberia, and its discovery by the Liberian government some time later would help ensure the failure of Garvey's Liberian program.

At the 1920 convention, meanwhile, Gabriel Johnson, father-in-law of President King and mayor of Monrovia, was elected potentate or ceremonial head of the UNIA, and King himself repeated his call for organized immigration, though making no reference to the UNIA.[109]

With no indication of any change of heart from Liberia, the UNIA pushed ahead with its plans, and in March 1921, while Garvey was in the West Indies and King was in the United States, a small advance party of UNIA officials and technicians arrived in Liberia. The technicians were to begin work on farms, buildings and a drug store, among other things, and it was hoped that the Black Star Line would soon bring over supplies and large numbers of immigrants. The workers would be under the dual control of Potentate Johnson and Cyril Crichlow, resident secretary of the newly organized UNIA legation.

Shortly after the arrival of this party a UNIA delegation, consisting of Johnson, Crichlow, and G. O. Marke, Sierra Leone-born supreme deputy potentate, met with the Liberian cabinet. The cabinet offered the association "certain settlements already laid out" and worried over whether British and French companies would refuse coal to Black Star Line ships. The question of a potential UNIA threat to Liberia's neighbors caused some concern, and the delegation felt the need to calm the fears of the cabinet on this score. Acting President Edwin Barclay then made the following statement:

> I must admit that the British and French have enquired from our representatives in America about it and have asked definite questions on the attitude of the Liberian Government towards the Universal Negro Improvement Association. I will say this among ourselves. There isn't a Negro in the world who, if given the opportunity and the power to do certain things, will not do them. But it is not always advisable nor politic to openly expose our secret intentions—our secret thoughts. That is the way we do—or rather don't do—in Liberia. We don't tell them what we think; we only tell them what we like them to hear—what, in fact, they like to hear.[110]

This Liberian Machiavellianism stunned an American official who feared that Barclay might adopt the same attitude toward Americans.[111] But it was the UNIA which seemed to be the real victim of this duplicity. By June Crichlow had concluded that the Liberians wanted no part of the UNIA but its money.[112] An American official came to the same conclusion,[113] as did Cyril Henry, a member of the UNIA group of technicians.[114] And on July 18, in response to a letter from the British consul general in Monrovia detailing Garvey's pro-Liberian activities in Costa Rica, Barclay wrote: "Mr. Marcus Garvey's movements and activities are however of no practical interest to this Government as they have not given and will not give endorsement to his fantastic schemes. Steps have already been taken by President King to put to an end Mr. Garvey's unauthorized and unwarranted exploitation of Liberia."[115] This amazing statement came one year after Barclay's letter of approval to Elie Garcia and four months after the cabinet interview with the UNIA commissioners. Perhaps he was merely telling the British what he thought they would like to hear, but more probably he was telling them the truth, possibly because of a growing impatience at the rashness of Garvey's statements, a fact which he had alluded to in his statement to the UNIA delegation.

While the UNIA advance party had been doing its work in Liberia, Garvey himself was stranded in the West Indies forcibly prevented by the Department of State from reentering the United States. Because of this, Crichlow was hampered in his efforts to maintain regular contact, and Garvey may well have been unaware for some time of the substance of the cabinet interview. In any case Garvey was reported as having said in British Honduras in July that black people would spread from their Liberian base until they dominated the whole continent.[116] In June, meanwhile, three months after he had warmly received a UNIA delegation in New York,[117] President King published an open letter in Du Bois' *Crisis* warning that "under no circumstances" would Liberia "allow her territory to be made a center of aggression or conspiracy against other sovereign states."[118] This was unequivocal enough, and after his return to the United States Garvey announced that "we are not trying to use Liberia as a wedge to conquer all Africa. But we believe Africa rightfully belongs to the Negro race."[119] This was followed up by messages to King and to the Liberian Plenary Commission denying political aims. The commission's secretary, replying to this "most opportune" statement, reiterated that Liberia could not "be used as a center of hostile attacks upon other sovereign states."[120]

While these events were transpiring, the UNIA within Liberia began to experience severe internal problems. On January 13, 1921, the association was incorporated by an act of the Liberian legislature.[121] Even this necessary and positive step was seen as a potential threat by Crichlow, since aliens could not own real property under Liberian law and in the event

of a dispute lands bought by the parent body could easily be taken by
the local branch.[122] Furthermore, relations deteriorated between Potentate Johnson and Crichlow. Johnson, interpreting the UNIA constitution
literally, took the position that he was the highest authority in the association and attempted to usurp some of Crichlow's powers, especially
over UNIA funds. Crichlow, for his part, could not deal with "the haughty,
aristocratic, dogmatic, domineering, conservative manner of the Potentate."[123] There was also some pique felt by the Liberian president and
high-ranking officials over the fact that as potentate, Johnson was supposedly head of all the black people in the world and drew a larger salary
than the president.[124] The question of insufficient funds for the work
of the resident secretary and the group of technicians further exacerbated
matters. Crichlow accordingly resigned in June 1921, but not before embarking upon the extraordinary step of taking his dispute with the potentate to the United States minister in Liberia, Joseph L. Johnson.

Minister Johnson requested all relevant correspondence and Crichlow
delivered a rich haul, including his confidential reports to Garvey, other
confidential correspondence, Garvey's instructions to him, and the transcript of the interview between the Liberian cabinet and the UNIA. All
this material was promptly forwarded to the United States Department
of State.[125] The United States minister meanwhile promised Crichlow
that "the whole force and power of the United States Government would
be brought in to prevent any injustice being done to an American citizen,"
and Crichlow actually deposited UNIA money in the United States government safe at the American legation where the potentate could not get
his hands on it.[126] Crichlow justified his recourse to the United States
minister by comparing it to Garvey's attempts to secure justice in United
States federal courts.[127]

In Harlem, meanwhile, outward appearances suggested that nothing
untoward was happening in Liberia. A $2 million UNIA Liberian con-
struction loan continued to be pushed.[128] And at the August convention
the auditor reported over $8,000 spent on a sawmill and other materials
for construction in Liberia.[129] Garvey also announced, based, he said,
on the potentate's assurance, that the pioneers were doing well and had
purchased a two-hundred-acre farm.[130]

The next major development came in March 1922 when the influential
London-based imperialist journal, *The African World,* published Elie
Garcia's secret report to Garvey and his letter to President King. The leak-

ing of the report, with its unfavorable comments on Liberian society and
its frank discussion of UNIA aims in Liberia, in all likelihood put an end
to Garvey's chances of success, even though he persisted in his efforts for
two years more. The *Liberian News* reported later that these documents
"gave a clear picture of the revolutionary purposes of the UNIA in Liberia,
and determined the Government's irrevocable attitude of opposition."[131]
The African World did not reveal how it had managed to obtain the documents but stated only that the correspondence had been "sent from New
York to Monrovia," suggesting that the Garcia report may already have
been in the hands of the Liberian government by the time this publication received it. Among those showing great interest in the documents
were American officials in Liberia.[132] Garvey seems to have publicly ignored this monumental setback.

After a period of relative inactivity occasioned partly by his trial and
imprisonment, Garvey in December 1923 despatched a new delegation
to Liberia consisting of Robert L. Poston, secretary-general and leader of
the delegation, Henrietta Vinton Davis, fourth assistant president general,
and Milton Van Lowe, a Detroit attorney. They traveled via Lisbon, where
they met with the Liga Africana, a group composed of Portuguese Africans,
and arrived in Liberia in February.[133]

In Liberia the delegation was accorded an enthusiastic welcome.[134]
Yet this 1924 mission was largely a repeat of the 1921 experience. The
Liberian government told them what they wanted to hear while apparently biding its time before destroying the UNIA Liberian effort. President
King assured the delegation members that they should ignore anti-UNIA
propaganda. He suggested that artisans and material should precede the
general body of UNIA colonists. (Garvey had already promised him
twenty thousand to thirty thousand families in two years starting about
September 1924.)[135] King also suggested the appointment of a local
liaison committee. This was immediately set up and met that same night.
It included Vice-President H. T. Wesley, Chief Justice James J. Dossen,
ex-Presidents Arthur Barclay and D. E. Howard, Controller of Customs
Dixon Brown, and two others.[136] Among other things the committee
engineered the lease of a building belonging to King's stepson as a UNIA
commissary.[137]

The delegation was given a warm and enthusiastic send-off and arrived
back in New York amid hopes that the first colonists would sail on a UNIA
ship immediately after the 1924 convention.[138] The elation was dampened,

however, by the death at sea of the delegation's leader, Robert Lincoln
Poston.[139] And simultaneously with the delegation's return in March
came ominous press reports that Liberia did not want immigrants and
that President King had refused to meet the delegation.[140] King had of
course met with the delegation but, according to the British consul in
Monrovia, had refused them a formal hearing, opting for a private audience instead.[141]

Garvey attempted to ignore these press reports while seeking some
clarification from King.[142] Beginning in June, the Reverend R. Van
Richards, chaplain to the Liberian senate and son-in-law of Chief Justice
Dossen, assumed the role of defender of the UNIA in a series of Liberty
Hall speeches.[143] But even as Richards was trying to discredit reports of
Liberian hostility, his government was moving to crush the UNIA effort
once and for all. On June 30, 1924, Secretary of State Edwin Barclay
informed shipping companies that no members of "the so-called Garvey
movement" would be allowed to land in Liberia.[144] By this time some
UNIA officials and technicians were already on their way over, as suggested by the King-inspired liaison committee. On July 25 three of them
arrived on a German ship. They were immediately arrested and deported
on the next German ship back to Hamburg. In response to an inquiry,
the British consul thought it unlikely that he would intervene on behalf
of one who happened to be a British subject, "in view of the known mal-
practices of the UNIA."[145] The American embassy reported that three
more, all British subjects, arrived on July 30 and were deported.[146] Two
more arrived on August 4 and were not allowed to land.[147] Meanwhile
on July 10 the Liberian consul general in the United States, Ernest Lyon,
had announced that Garveyites would not be permitted to land in Liberia
and that Liberian consuls in the United States would not visé the passports of such persons. Visa applicants were later required to furnish an
affidavit showing they were not connected with the UNIA.[148] In August
Lyons sought the assistance of the United States Department of State
to make the Liberian position better known. At the suggestion of Secretary of State Charles E. Hughes, representatives of the Associated and
United Press were called in. The result was widespread dissemination of
the Liberian position, which also received support from a statement prepared by the Department of State.[149]

In the midst of all this the anti-Garvey press received a further excuse to discredit the UNIA Liberia effort when it was widely reported that a UNIA representative in Liberia had been executed for murder. It turned out that the man, Milton J. Marshall, was an imposter who had collected money in the United States by falsely pretending to be a UNIA representative and had been imprisoned for a while in Nigeria before moving on to Liberia.[150]

Garvey's response to these setbacks was one of anger tinged with a little disbelief, since the Liberian government at no time paid him the courtesy of a direct communication repudiating the agreements. In a statement appearing on July 26, Garvey said that he was more determined than ever to go ahead with his Liberian plans.[151] On the previous day, July 25, the same day on which the first UNIA members were deported from Liberia, a shipment of UNIA materials left New York for Liberia on the S.S. *West Irmo,* owned by the United States Shipping Board and operated by A. H. Bull and Co. This, too, was in accordance with the suggestions of President King and the liaison committee. The shipment, consisting of two motor tractors, a sawmill and other equipment was valued at $6,169.82, although Garvey said that this and an earlier consignment of June 25 were together valued at more than $50,000.[152] The goods were shipped by the H. D. Taylor Company of Buffalo, New York, and were to be picked up in Liberia by the consignee, Chief Justice Dossen. On July 30 the UNIA delivered a check to H. D. Taylor Co. for the goods. There were not enough funds in the account to honor the check and so, on or about August 21 the company asked the United States Shipping Board to stop the goods *in transitu*. This was a mere one day before the cargo was scheduled to reach Liberia and so by the time the cable requesting stoppage arrived the goods had been unloaded. It was therefore decided to store them in the customs warehouse until the money was paid. The bill was in fact paid in December and the UNIA was now free to collect the cargo subject only to the payment of storage fees. To compound the association's misery, however, Chief Justice Dossen had died on August 17, a few days before the goods reached Liberia,[153] and they were never collected.[154] The customs authorities first threatened to sell the material to cover storage charges and apparently established contact with the Liberia UNIA on the matter.[155] As late as March 1925 the goods were still in storage and the government was said to be negotiating with the UNIA representatives (presumably of the Liberian branch) to purchase them.[156]

The goods were eventually sold by the Liberian government to pay over-due official salaries, according to some sources.[157] According to another source they were merely sold by the customs to cover storage charges.[158]

In Harlem, meanwhile, the annual convention began on August 1 and quickly despatched a telegram to President King expressing "alarm and surprise" at reports of Liberian hostility.[159] This was followed some weeks later by a resolution unanimously protesting the actions of the Liberian government.[160] Throughout the convention Reverend Van Richards sup-ported the UNIA position, even calling his government's ban on the asso-ciation "a stinking shame."[161]

One of the last acts of the convention was to despatch a petition to the Liberian Senate and House of Representatives. The petition restated the ideological basis for UNIA interest in Liberia. It read:

> For six years this association has carried on a continuous system of education among its people to the end that they be organized into one great movement looking forward to their return to Africa, from whence their forefathers were taken centuries ago, and to there re-habilitate themselves and once more possess themselves of the land, of which they were original owners. With this end in view, it was de-cided that the most convenient way of their being able to help their native land—Africa—was through assisting the Republic of Liberia to establish herself as a successful nation through her highest industrial, agricultural and commercial development, thereby proving completely the Negro's undisputed ability for self-government.

The petition also recounted the history of relations between the UNIA and Liberia and quoted from the Liberian constitution to the effect that "the great object" of starting the Liberian nation was "to provide a home for the dispersed and oppressed children of Africa and to regenerate and enlighten this benighted continent."[162]

The convention followed up all this with the appointment of a six-member delegation which presented President Coolidge with a "Petition of Four Million Negroes of the United States of America to His Excellen-cy the President of the United States Praying for A Friendly and Sympa-thetic Consideration of the Plan of Founding A Nation in Africa for the Negro People, And to Encourage Them in Assisting to Develop Already

Independent Negro Nations As a Means of Helping to Solve the Conflicting Problems of Race."[163]
    These efforts brought no appreciable benefit. The enemy press, on
the other hand, continued to have a field day. The *New York Times* expressed wonderment at Garvey's powers of persuasion. "A man who can
persuade several thousand American negroes that they would be better
off in Liberia, or anywhere else in Africa, than they are in this country,"
it editorially pontificated, "can tackle almost any problem with some
hope of success."[164] The *Liberian News,* which usually reflected official
attitudes toward the UNIA, published a long and partly untruthful account
of UNIA-Liberia relations, claiming, among other things, that Secretary
of State Edwin Barclay had in 1921 "frankly told [the UNIA delegation]
that the Government would give no countenance to their schemes."[165]
The *Chicago Defender* became the object of a UNIA libel suit for suggesting in July that the "soap-box orators and leather lunged wind-jammers
of the Garvey movement" were rebuffed in Liberia, and for claiming that
a UNIA agent in Liberia had murdered his fellow Garveyite colleague due
to poverty induced by the nonreceipt of their salaries. Libel suits for
similar cause were brought against the *Pittsburgh Courier* and the *Afro-
American* of Baltimore. They were all dismissed without prejudice by
the New York courts for lack of jurisdiction or for failure of the plain-
tiffs to produce sufficient evidence.[166]
    The strangest episode of all concerning the hostile press was the pub-
lication by the *New York Amsterdam News* of Elie Garcia's secret report
of 1920. According to this paper, secret UNIA correspondence relating
to Liberia was stolen from UNIA files and made its way to the paper's
offices and to Garvey's communist foe Cyril Briggs, who was about to
publish this material when it was stolen from him by Cyril Crichlow,
now turned anti-Garveyite. Crichlow sent it on to one Captain James
Jones. From there the correspondence made its way to "certain diplomatic quarters," from which it was in turn stolen by a detective agency
who returned it from Baltimore (where the Liberian consul-general lived)
to Garvey. The paper apparently had seen the documents long enough
to transcribe Garcia's report.[167] Garvey himself also published it.[168]
    And by way of making assurance doubly sure, the presidents of both
the United States and Liberia restated their hostility to Garvey's Liberian
plans. In a September 1924 press conference the former declared that he

would cooperate with Liberia in this matter and in December the latter expressed relief that the "Marcus Garvey spectre" was "now completely exorcised."[169]

The question remains as to why the Liberian government, after providing Garvey with initial encouragement, repudiated the agreements in so insulting a fashion. One major reason was the Liberian fear of her British and French neighbors. Acting President Edwin Barclay, it will be remembered, had in 1921 informed the UNIA delegation of British and French interest in Garveyite activity. And in his inaugural address of January 1924, President King included much fawning talk of cooperation with France and Britain for the uplift of Africa.[170] Shortly after the ban on the UNIA Edwin Barclay declared that the association had "a tendency adversely to affect the amicable relations" with adjacent countries.[171] In September, the Liberian consul general in the United States told Department of State officials quite frankly that the advocacy of a black empire in Africa by UNIA agents in Liberia always caused protests from the British and French in Sierra Leone and the Ivory Coast, respectively. The Liberians, he indicated, feared actual absorption by these powerful colonialists if such propaganda was permitted to continue.[172]

Garvey certainly contributed to this type of reaction. During the 1923 trial Captain Cockburn, formerly of the Black Star Line, testified that at their first meeting Garvey had enquired whether it was possible to "float a fleet of battleships in the harbor of Monrovia."[173] And despite his acknowledgment that the British and French neighbors of Liberia were among his most powerful enemies,[174] he still suggested in a 1924 pamphlet that they should hand over Sierra Leone and the Ivory Coast so that they might be joined to Liberia to form a great state.[175] Furthermore, the 1924 delegation to Liberia had asked for six settlements of five hundred families each, four on the French border, two on the British. The British consul reported that the five hundred acres actually granted at that time was on neither border, but the *Liberian News* reported that the Cavalla River site was where the French were strongest.[176]

The timing of these unsettling suggestions was rendered especially unfortunate since Liberia actually experienced a border problem with the French in 1924. President King reported later that his country feared a French invasion.[177] The British, for their part, were so sensitive about their borders with Liberia that in 1925 they opposed the establishment of railway, road or water communications between Liberia and French Guinea in the vicinity of Sierra Leone's southeast frontier.[178]

The extent of British and French paranoia over a UNIA presence so close can also be measured by their relief at Garvey's defeat. The governor of Sierra Leone sent King and his wife a warship to visit his country. At a banquet in King's honor the governor assured him that "by slamming the door on . . . men who sought to make Liberia a focus for racial animosity in this Continent," he had "deservedly earned the gratitude . . . of all who have the true welfare of the African at heart."[179] The French made King a chevalier of the Legion of Honour.[180]

Garvey was not impressed. He wrote, "Time was when the native African was induced to part with his valuables, his gold and diamonds and ivory, in exchange for red handkerchiefs and beads. And in the year 1925, when Africa is waking from her slumber, and it is becoming increasingly difficult to fool even the most simple-minded, an 'intellectual' black would lose his soul, if only he gain a title and a ride in a warship. Surely Charles Dunbar King will go down unhonored and unsung by black men."[181] In a speech to his convention Garvey was more explicit. "The damned audacity of it," he said. "That a bunch of Anglo-Saxon rapers, villains and scoundrels and felons to stay in Europe and say that we must not go to Africa."[182]

Another major consideration which influenced the Liberian attitude was the fear that Garvey might stage a political coup within Liberia. The evidence seems to suggest that Garvey may indeed have had designs on political power within the African republic. Here, too, however, Garvey may have overplayed his hand too early by the rashness of his statements.

As early as 1920, as has been seen, Elie Garcia had warned Garvey of Liberia's hostility to immigrants who might "show any tendency to take part in the political life of the Republic." Garcia counseled that UNIA agents would have "to deny firmly any intention on our part to enter into politics in Liberia." Garcia revealed probable UNIA intentions when he added, "This attitude will remove any possible idea of opposition and will not prevent us after having a strong foothold in the country to act as we see best for their own betterment and that of the Race at large."[183]

Garcia's advice was reinforced by the association's emissaries in 1921. Cyril Crichlow warned that the distribution of UNIA immigrants would be "in line with the purposes of the one-party political system to maintain

its existence and power unimpaired." In other words, Garveyites would
be spread thinly over already existing settlements rather than be allowed
to concentrate in a few areas. This would "allow the Liberians to be in
the ascendancy politically and dominate in the political elections."
Crichlow concluded that Garvey should be aware of this in order to
"understand to what extent it is proposed to waive aside the political
program of the Association."[184] One of the team of technicians expressed
a similar view.[185] And an American official monitoring the situation came
to the conclusion that "From the information at hand it may without
difficulty be implied that the U.N.I.A. have political aims in Liberia. This
is the point which should be carefully watched. A few hundred radical
American Negroes shipped to Liberia might overthrow the government
as now constituted and attempt to replace it by a regime dominated by
the sentiments of the Garvey movement if not under the actual control
of the organization itself."[186] The political impact which even a few
hundred UNIA settlers could make can be appreciated when it is realized
that the entire Liberian electorate in 1920 consisted of the adult males
among the approximately 5,000 Americo-Liberians, augmented by a
handful of indigenous Africans.[187] The problem was brought home to
Liberty Hall in December 1921 when the Reverend Dr. R. Harten, a
missionary in Liberia, informed Garveyites of the Liberian fear of a
UNIA government within a government.[188]

Yet in May 1922 (probably due to the recent exposure of Garcia's
secret report in London) Garvey openly attacked the "large number of
narrow-minded men" who were monopolizing power in Liberia for the
benefit of a few, and challenged them directly. "Liberia was founded
over one hundred years ago," he wrote, "for the purpose of helping the
refugee, slave and the exiled African to re-establish a foothold in his
native land; thererore, no Liberian, neither at home nor abroad, has any
moral or other right preventing Negroes to return to their home to do
the best they can for its development."[189]

There was another component to the Liberian fear of Garvey's political
ambitions, namely the effect that he might have on the oppressed indigenous Africans. Garcia had warned Garvey about this in 1920. In 1923 a
Reverend H. H. Jones, recently returned from fourteen years' work among
the native African population, testified to Garvey's popularity among them.
Africans in remote areas knew more about Garvey than he did, he said,
and their kings had talked with him for many hours about Garvey.[190]

The last UNIA delegation to be favorably received in Liberia (in 1924) felt the effects of these Liberian fears. The Liberian liaison committee in its written stipulations made sure that it would have final authority over the UNIA settlements. Garvey suggested amendments substituting UNIA parent body control.[191]

In their last-ditch petition to the Liberian government, the UNIA's 1924 convention claimed to have "absolutely no political designs."[192] But once the issue seemed irrevocably lost Garvey felt free again to criticize "the Negroes of the Barclay and King type" who kept the "natives poor, hungry, shelterless and naked." "Such Negroes," he declared, "are afraid of me, for they realize that they have no colleague in me to exploit the labor of the unfortunate blacks and build up class distinction.[193]

A final twist to this fear of political intentions was the feeling that Garvey might join with influential Liberians, such as ex-Presidents Arthur Barclay and D. Howard, or perhaps Chief Justice J. J. Dossen, all of whom were associated with the Liberian UNIA, in an effort to unseat the incumbent faction.[194]

Garvey had the last word. In 1928 he claimed to have "had enough influence to have unseated Charles King as President in the next Election."[195]

Yet another factor in Garvey's Liberian failure is the possible role of his rival, W. E. B. Du Bois. Upon learning in late 1923 that Du Bois was bound for Liberia, William H. Lewis, a black Boston attorney and former assistant attorney general, suggested to President Coolidge that it would be "a very graceful thing" and a help to United States-Liberian relations if Du Bois could be appointed a special representative to King's forthcoming second inauguration.[196] What Du Bois, who accepted, did not know was that the offer represented a political ruse by the Republican party to, as Lewis put it, "insure the support of the *Crisis,* the most widely read publication among the colored people, or stultify it, if it should come out against us" in the upcoming elections.[197]

Du Bois misguidedly exulted in this official "gesture of courtesy . . . one so unusual that it was epochal . . . the highest rank ever given by any country to a diplomatic agent in black Africa." He gloried in his Liberian military escort, in the fact that he was dean of the diplomatic service in Liberia, in the frock-coated Liberian president "with the star and ribbon of a Spanish order on his breast" and in the European consuls "in white, gilt with orders and swords."[198]

Du Bois claimed later that he did not mention Garvey to President
King during his stay in Liberia.[199] Yet, one year earlier he had taken the
trouble to write Secretary of State Charles Evans Hughes for two ships
to take over Garvey's Black Star Line. He wanted to know, he informed
Hughes, if there was "any feasible and legal way by which the United
States Government could aid or guide a plan of furnishing at least two
ships for the tentative beginning of direct commercial intercourse between
Liberia and America." Such intercourse would be directed by a private
company composed of blacks and whites. The company would "take up
and hold in trust, the Black Star Line certificates."[200]

So apprehensive were Garveyites of Du Bois' possible malignant influence in Liberia and nearby territories that John E. Bruce cabled J. E.
Casely Hayford as follows: "Du Bois—Crisis—on trip to Africa, bent on
mischief due to failure of his Pan-African congress scheme. Financed by
Joel Spingarn a Jew, and other interests (white) inimical to African independence. Watch him. Letter follows. Make no committals."[201]

Upon returning to the United States Du Bois, in his report of his mission to the secretary of state, suggested, among other things, that a small
team of United States agricultural and industrial experts be sent to Liberia.
Where possible they should be black. This was exactly what Garvey had
been suggesting and was in the process of doing. The only difference was
that Garvey's experts were all black. Du Bois also published further attacks on Garvey's Liberian plans.[202]

The ninety-nine-year lease by Liberia of a million acres to the Firestone
Rubber Tire Company of Akron, Ohio, added yet another possible explanation for the repudiation of Garvey's scheme. President King, with encouragement from Du Bois, was making up his mind to grant Firestone
the land about the same time as he was rudely thwarting Garvey's aspirations.[203] Du Bois' role in the rubber deal seems to have been fairly intimate. In January 1924 he had accompanied the United States minister,
Solomon Porter Hood, and a Firestone rubber expert on a trip to Liberia's
rubber lands to ascertain whether Firestone should invest in the area.
And in 1925 he sought to capitalize on all this by asking Harvey Firestone
to include blacks among his company's supervisory personnel in Liberia.
All he got was a meaningless reply from the company promising nothing.[204]
Meanwhile the 1924 UNIA convention warned that a Firestone concession
would ultimately mean "usurpation of the government, even as has been

done with the black Republic of Haiti after similar white companies entered there under the pretense of developing the country."[205] This warning may have contributed to Liberian hostility when Firestone offered a $5 million loan in exchange for the right to appoint twenty-two officials to run Liberia's financial, military, and native affairs.[206]

The seed that Garvey had planted was such that his followers never relinquished their interest in Liberia. In 1925, with Garvey in jail, a delegation sought the help of President Coolidge toward settling in Liberia.[207] And in 1926 an unsuccessful attempt was made to enlist the aid of the American Colonization Society.[208] In 1936 the New York UNIA offered to satisfy President Edwin Barclay's request for continued immigration, and indeed the interest never ceased.[209]

Despite these many failures, several Garveyites did in fact migrate to Liberia over the years. Some went before the Liberian ban.[210] Among these were UNIA technicians who stayed on.[211] One of these technicians, Reginald C. Hurley of Barbados, became the subject of a minor diplomatic opera bouffe in 1924 when the Liberian government determined to deport him but was reluctant to fork up the $1.70 needed to get him to the nearest British colony, Sierra Leone. Hurley could not pay, the British authorities refused to pay, and since Hurley had entered before the law requiring the shipping companies to pay, they could not be forced to pay either. To end the impasse, Hurley was given the option of remaining if he would only disavow the UNIA. This he refused to do since, he said, the principles of the UNIA were too firmly engraved on his heart.[212] Finally in 1925 the Liberian government decided to let him stay, thus avoiding the expense of deporting him. The comedy was not over yet, however, for the British consul general restricted Hurley's passport making it renewable annually and preventing travel outside Liberia without his permission. "In that way," reasoned this British functionary, "I can keep him in view and note what mischief if any he is engaged on in connection with the UNIA."[213]

Yet other Garveyites got into Liberia by going along with the requirement for a denunciation of their leader. In this they had Garvey's approval.[214] By the 1930s the ban seems to have been forgotten.[215]

The urge among Garveyites to reunite with Africa also found an outlet in Ethiopia. The *Negro World* in 1932 urged its readers to go, even individually, to places like Liberia and Ethiopia to "establish bases to spread further propaganda to create a united and liberated Africa."[216] A decade

earlier the 1922 convention had received a message from the Ethiopian
monarch inviting skilled Western blacks back home.[217] The unofficial
leader of the UNIA migrants to Ethiopia was Rabbi Arnold J. Ford, a
leader of Harlem's Black Jews and for many years musical director of
the UNIA, who arrived in Ethiopia in December 1930. Some of the migrants fared well, working as music teachers, governesses, school principals, and the like.[218]

Garvey's impact on Africa can thus be said to be wide and varied.
Those Africans who came into contact with his message were favorably
disposed and often wildly enthusiastic about it. Where there was opposition it came principally from the European overlords, or, in the case of
Liberia, from the local quasicolonialist black overlords. This is not to say
that there was no African opposition. In British West Africa, many of the
more conservative elements opposed his political program while whole-
heartedly embracing his economic initiatives.[219]

More active opposition came from Blaise Diagne, the Senegalese deputy
to the French assembly and sometime member of the French cabinet. Because of his position his opposition may perhaps more fruitfully be classed
as European than as African. In 1922 he addressed an open letter to
Garvey: "We French natives wish to remain French, since France has
given us every liberty and since she has unreservedly accepted us upon
the same basis as her own European children. None of us aspires to see
French Africa delivered exclusively to the Africans as is demanded, though
without any authority, by the American negroes, at the head of whom
you have placed yourself."[220]

Of a similar stripe were the attacks of J. E. Kwegyir Aggrey. Originally
from the Gold Coast, Aggrey spent many years being educated and working in the United States. His reasonableness gained him a position on
Phelps Stokes Educational Commissions to Africa. As the only black
member of these commissions he was supposed to demonstrate the heights
to which Africans could reach, given the proper conditions. His presence
seems also to have been for another reason, namely to combat Garvey's
popularity among the mass of Africans. At a meeting in South Africa
where he was roundly heckled he said to his African brothers: "They who
preach 'Africa for the Africans' are mad; if you stood alone you would
soon be in deep darkness again. That which we have, and what we are, we
owe to the Missionaries. I was born a pagan, and am not ashamed of it.

But if the Missionaries had not sought and found me I should today have, perhaps, a dozen wives."[221] After a 1921 Johannesburg speech in which he denounced the Black Star Line, the African *Abantu-Batho* wondered why an ostensibly private educational commission should spend so much time attacking Garvey. In fact Aggrey's main speeches so far had entirely neglected the subject of education. The paper thought that Aggrey's efforts were actually counterproductive. "Marcus Garvey has certainly come forward with something to unnerve Mr. Whiteman," the editorial opined. "The broad[cast?] advertisement by the white press, of Dr. Aggrey's speech on this particular subject is the outcome of no other reason than sheer nervousness. Wisely or unwisely, but for reasons best known to himself, Dr. Aggrey has been rather free in his utterances on this subject."[222] Although when prodded by an interviewer Garvey criticized Aggrey for following the line of least resistance,[223] he preferred not to waste any time attacking him, and UNIA publications were kind to the educator.[224]

The kind of vitriolic, unprincipled opposition to Garvey which developed in Afro-America has little if any parallel among Africans. A rare exception is provided by M. Mokete Manoedi from Basutoland, and even his opposition took place in the United States and under the auspices of Garvey's arch enemies in the African Blood Brotherhood, a black communist cadre.[225] In addition to holding street rallies and publishing a hostile book, Manoedi, on the advice of the British consul in New York[226] and probably with the approval of the ABB, complained to the British Colonial Office about Garvey. (This resort to white governments by Garvey's enemies was a not infrequently used tactic. Du Bois was among those who did it, as were several other major Afro-American figures.)

Manoedi addressed his letter to Winston Churchill, then secretary of state for the colonies. Garvey's propaganda, he wrote, "has taken some effect on the unthinking masses of Negroes in America, the West Indies, South and Central America, and, also, in Africa." He warned Churchill that "we can not afford" to let Garvey continue creating the impression "that the British African is dissatisfied with British rule." He requested financial help to continue the struggle.[227] Churchill had the British representative in Basutoland check out Manoedi's credentials and they were found to be impeccable. The government of South Africa was then approached for advice on the desirability of financing Manoedi from Basutoland funds. The Smuts government suggested to the British that

the money might be better spent within South Africa and declined to
make a contribution. This advice was accepted and Manoedi did not get
his money.[228] His information was not without effect, however. It was
sent on to the Nyasaland authorities and one Foreign Office official later
used it to justify British moves against Garvey in Liberia.[229] Manoedi's
own ideas on African development consisted of Afro-American and West
Indian assistance, reforms from the colonialists, and white capitalist
investment.[230]

NOTES

1. *Negro World,* August 20, 1921.
2. American Colonization Society Records, Series 6, Box 7, Library
of Congress.
3. See Bruce Papers, Schomburg Collection, New York Public Library.
For an overview of Pan-Africanist activity before Garvey, see Okon E.
Uya, ed., *Black Brotherhood* (Lexington, Mass.: D. C. Heath, 1971).
4. Love wrote, "Bishop Turner knows me well. We were very intimate in Georgia about twenty years ago." See J. Robert Love to Bruce,
June 6, 1893, Bruce Papers, Group A, LL; Rev. Dr. J. Robert Love, *Is
Bishop Holly Innocent? Charges, Specifications, Arguments, Canon Law,
etc., involved in an Ecclesiastical Trial Held in Holy Trinity Church,
Port-au-Prince (Hayti), the 4th September 1882: Showing What Episco-
pacy Claims the Right to Do and Does Do in Hayti, under the Canons
of the P.E. Church in the United States* (Hayti, 1883).
5. *Jamaica Advocate,* April 20, 1901, reference supplied to author
by Mrs. Amy Jacques Garvey.
6. Rupert Lewis, "A Political Study of Garveyism in Jamaica and
London: 1914-1940," Unpub. Masters Thesis, University of the West
Indies, 1971, pp. 28-34.
7. *Negro World,* May 8, 1920; May 7, 1921; June 17, 1922.
8. Hucheshwar G. Mudgal, *Marcus Garvey—Is He the True Redeemer
of the Negro?* (New York: H. G. Mudgal, 1932), p. 5; Rupert Lewis, "A
Political Study of Garveyism in Jamaica and London: 1914-1940," p. 17.
9. Letterhead on letter stuck to copy seen by author of Benito
Sylvain, *Du Sort des Indigènes dans les Colonies d'Exploitation,* Paris,
L. Boyer, 1901. The letterhead is in English, as is the letter, written in
New York.
10. *Crisis* (April 1918): 297; FO 371/3450; Theodore Vincent,*Black
Power and the Garvey Movement* (Berkeley: Ramparts, 1971 [?]), p. 110.
11. *Negro World,* September 1, 1923.

12. Ibid., September 3, 1921.

13. *Yonkers Daily News,* September 20, 1913, in Bruce Papers, Scrapbook 2; "Unrest Among the Negroes," October 7, 1919, RG 59, 811.4016/27.

14. *Negro World,* June 19, 1920; Marcus Garvey vs. Robert S. Abbott Pub. Co., Federal Court Records (New York), FRC 536137. For comparisons by Garvey's enemies see *Emancipator,* March 20, 1920, *Messenger* (November 1922): 522.

15. *Negro World,* December 17, 1921.

16. Ibid., August 15, 1925.

17. Ibid., April 30, 1932.

18. Ibid., December 17, 1921.

19. *New York Times,* August 4, 1920.

20. Told to the author by Amy Jacques Garvey, Kingston, 1972.

21. Amy Jacques Garvey, *Garvey and Garveyism* (Kingston: A. J. Garvey, 1963), p. 47.

22. M.I. l.c. to Foreign Office, January 7, 1920, FO 371/4567.

23. Colonial Office to Foreign Office, August 27, 1920, FO 371/4567.

24. Governor General of French West Africa to H. M. Consul-General, Dakar, 25 March 1921, CO 96/625; note on destroyed Colonial Office File, Gov./33358 (Secret), Register of Correspondence, Gold Coast, 1922.

25. H. M. Consul-General, Dakar to Secretary of State, Foreign Office, August 17, 1922, FO 371/7286.

26. Ibid.

27. *Negro World,* August 22, 1925.

28. *Gold Coast Leader,* December 17, 1927, reprinted in *Negro World,* February 4, 1928.

29. *Gold Coast Leader,* October 23, 1920, reprinting an article from the *Daily Sketch,* September 17, 1920.

30. *Negro World,* April 7, 1926; Amy J. Garvey, ed., *The Philosophy and Opinions of Marcus Garvey* (London: Frank Cass, 1967), II: 90.

31. Acting Governor, Nyasaland, R. Rankine to His Grace the Duke of Devonshire, Secretary of State, Colonial Office, May 15, 1923, CO 525/104; Register of Correspondence for West Africa, 1923, note on destroyed file, September 20, 1923, FO/46712; Register of Correspondence, Gambia, 1923, note on destroyed file, Gov./29153; Register of Correspondence, Kenya, 1923, note on destroyed file, May 29, 1923, OAG/32018; Register of Correspondence, Gold Coast, 1923, note on destroyed file, Gov./29813; note of March 7, 1924, CO 554/64; Acting Governor, Sierra Leone to Duke of Devonshire, secret, May 28, 1923, CO 267/600.

32. C. C. Roberts, U.S. Shipping Board, Freetown, Sierra Leone to State Department, September 15, 1924, RG 59, 648p. 00 2/1.

33. Manager, William H. Muller and Co., to Secretary of State, Colonial Office, July 12, 1924, CO 554/64.

34. E.g., Governor-General of French West Africa to H. M. Consul-General, Dakar, March 25, 1921, CO 96/625. Here it is suggested that Garvey is an American black who previously captained a boat in Nigeria.

35. Ibid.

36. *Negro World*, July 29, 1922.

37. Ibid., September 13, 1924. Articles from Kojo's *Les Continents* and his *L'Action Coloniale* appeared regularly in the *Negro World's* French section. Kojo reciprocated with UNIA material in his publications. See, e.g., *Negro World*, May 10, September 20, 1924.

38. Jabez Ayodele Langley, "Garveyism and African Nationalism," *Race* 11 (October 1969): 169.

39. *Negro World*, August 11, 18, 1928.

40. Vincent (*Black Power and the Garvey Movement*, p. 283) reports having seen Garvey's membership card in the CDRN in Amy J. Garvey's papers.

41. Ch. du Bus de Warnaffe, "Le Mouvement Pan-Nègre aux Etats Unis et Ailleurs," *Congo* (May 1922): 13.

42. Memo of June 20, 1932 relating opinions of M. Borel of the Belgian Embassy, FO 371/16355; ibid., Belgian Minister of the Colonies to Belgian Foreign Minister; Raymond Leslie Buell, *The Native Problem in Africa* (New York: Macmillan, 1928), II: 563. For what it is worth, while perusing Garvey's *Blackman* in Jamaica the author came upon a handbill announcing a meeting sponsored by the International Bible Students Association. The handbill was printed at 78 King St. The Kingston UNIA at the time was headquartered at 76 King St.

43. Robert I. Rotberg, *The Rise of Nationalism in Central Africa* (Cambridge, Mass.: Harvard University Press, 1967), p. 125.

44. Harry Thuku to Mr. Kamulegeya, September 9, 1921, CO 533/277.

45. Harry Thuku, *An Autobiography* (Nairobi: Oxford University Press, 1970), p. 38.

46. *Negro World*, March 25, 1922; Garvey to David Lloyd George, March 20, 1922, UNIA press release, March 20, 1922, FO 371/7286.

47. *Negro World*, August 19, 1922.

48. Magnus J. Sampson, ed., *West African Leadership: Public Speeches Delivered by J. E. Casely Hayford* (London: Cass, 1969), p. 65.

49. "Right Oh" to Bruce, November 1, 1920, Lagos, Bruce Papers, Ms. 188. G. H. Walker, Deputy Inspector General of Police, Southern

Provinces, Nigeria, to Inspector-General of Police, Lagos, March 28, 1922, CO 583/109.

50. *Negro World,* August 21, 1920. This Kano branch seems to have been started by West Indians living and working in the area. See also ibid., April 9, 1921, for interest in the UNIA from Minna, Northern Nigeria.

51. Gov. Clifford to Winston Churchill, Secretary of State, Colonial Office, April 12, 1922, CO/583/109.

52. C. L. R. James, *Black Jacobins* (New York: Vintage, 1963), appendix. See the epilogue to the Collier Books edition of A. J. Garvey, *Garvey and Garveyism* (New York: 1970).

53. D. G. White to L. S. Smith, Colonial Office, 13 July 1937, CO 323/1518. According to this report Garvey contributed 10 shillings and 6 pence and offered his advice to the bureau but declined to be further associated with it.

54. *Negro World,* February 9, 1929. Letter from Enock Mazilinko, Johannesburg.

55. Ibid., September 27, 1924; James Hardy Dillard, "Impressions from East Africa," *Southern Workman* 53 (August 1924): 360; Mary Benson, *The Struggle for a Birthright* (Middlesex: Penguin, 1966), p. 47.

56. *Negro World,* July 2, 1921 (re a delegate to the 1920 convention); *New York World,* August 3, 1921; *Daily Worker,* August 13, 1924; *Negro World,* January 26, 1929.

57. *Negro World,* March 5, 1921.

58. Ibid., January 10, 1925.

59. Ibid., April 30, 1927.

60. *Black Man,* 1 (Late December 1935): 6.

61. Gary Brown, "Interview With Thomas Harvey," *CORE* (Fall/ Winter 1973): 46.

62. George Padmore, *How Britain Rules Africa* (London: Wishart, 1936), p. 370.

63. *Blackman,* August 28, 1930.

64. Clements Kadalie, *My Life and the ICU* (New York: Humanities Press, 1970), p. 220.

65. *Negro World,* May 10, 1924.

66. Ibid., August 8, 1925.

67. *Black Man,* 4 (June 1939): 19.

68. *Cape Argus,* January 29, 1923, reprinted in *Negro World,* March 17, 1923.

69. A. P. Walshe, "Black American Thought and African Political Attitudes in South Africa," *Review of Politics,* 32 (January 1970): 65.

70. *Negro World,* March 18, 1922.

71. Kadalie, *My Life*, p. 220.

72. *Cape Argus,* January 29, 1923.

73. Kadalie, *My Life*, p. 161.

74. *Negro World,* July 16, 1932.

75. Kadalie, *My Life*, pp. 220, 221.

76. Ibid., pp. 99-101.

77. *Negro World,* March 18, 1922; June 14, 1924.

78. Walshe, "Black American Thought," pp. 63, 64; Benson, *Struggle,* p. 57.

79. Prof. James Thaele, B.A., "Garvey and Garveyism," in *Africa Voice,* Cape Town, September 22, 1923, reprinted in *Negro World,* November 17, 1923.

80. *Negro World,* November 8, 1924; October 24, 1925.

81. Ibid., September 4, 1926, reprinted from *The Johannesburg Star,* July 14, 1926.

82. Reprinted in *Negro World,* July 4, 1925.

83. Ibid., July 4, 1925; June 20, 1925.

84. Ibid., August 7, 1926; Walshe, "Black American Thought," p. 65.

85. *Negro World,* May 2, 1925, April 30, 1927; reprinted from *Abantu Batho*, Johannesburg, March 17, September 3, 1927.

86. *Negro World,* February 19, February 26, June 18, 1921.

87. E.C.F. Garraway, Resident Commissioner, Maseru, Basutoland to H. C., Pretoria, December 12, 1922, FO 371/8513.

88. *Negro World,* February 7, 1925.

89. J. C. Smuts, Prime Minister's Office, Cape Town, February 28, 1923, FO 371/8513.

90. *Negro World,* April 1, 1922, April 30, July 16, 1927.

91. Garvey, *Philosophy and Opinions*, II: 361.

92. "An Answer to His Many Critics," UNIA press release, Bruce Papers, Group E, 13-13; *Negro World,* April 28, 1923, February 20, 1932.

93. *Negro World,* March 10, 1923, August 14, 1920.

94. Amy Ashwood Garvey, "Marcus Garvey—Prophet of Black Nationalism," Unpub. manuscript, A. A. Garvey papers, London, p. 53.

95. H. G. Bonds to ACS, February 24, 1920, and other letters from Bonds, American Colonization Records, Series 6, Box 7.

96. *Negro World,* April 7, 1928.

97. *New York Age,* April 5, 1919.

98. *Negro World,* May 1, 1920.

99. Cyril Crichlow, "Special Personal Report," June 24, 1921, RG 59, 882.00/705.

100. C. G. Contee, "The Worley Report on the Pan-African Congress of 1919," *Journal of Negro History* 55 (April 1970): 141.

101. *New York Age,* September 20, 1919.

102. "Unrest Among the Negroes," October 7, 1919, RG 28, Box 53, Unarranged 398, National Archives.

103. Contee, "Worley Report," p. 141.

104. M.I. l.c. to Foreign Office, January 7, 1920, reporting a Garvey meeting of December 14, 1919, FO 371/4567.

105. Garvey, *Philosophy and Opinions,* II: 363.

106. Ibid., p. 365.

107. *Negro World,* May 8, 1920.

108. Garvey, *Philosophy and Opinions,* II: 399-405.

109. Minutes of meeting of board of directors, March 10, 1921, American Colonization Society Records, Series 5, Box 13. King was present.

110. Interview With the Acting President of Liberia . . . By the Commissioners of the Universal Negro Improvement Association, Tuesday, March 22, 1921, RG 59, 882.00/705.

111. "Memorandum on Garvey Movement" [1921?], RG 59, 882.00/705.

112. Crichlow, "Special Personal Report," June 24, 1921, Crichlow to Dr. Joseph L. Johnson, July 5, 1921, RG 59, 882.00/705.

113. Ibid., "Memorandum"

114. Ibid., Henry to O. M. Thompson, July 1, 1921.

115. Edwin Barclay to H. B. M. Consul General, Monrovia, July 18, 1921, FO 371/5684.

116. Superintendent of Police, British Honduras, to H. J. Cavenaugh, July 4, 1921, FO 371/5684.

117. *Negro World,* March 12, 1921.

118. *Crisis* (June 1921): 53.

119. *New York World,* August 4, 1921.

120. *Negro World,* August 20, 1921.

121. H.B.M. Consul General, Monrovia to Secretary of State, Foreign Office, April 17, 1921, FO 371/5579. Crichlow to Garvey, July 4, 1921, RG 59, 882.00/705.

122. Crichlow to Garvey, July 4, 1921, RG 59, 882.00/705.

123. "Special Personal Report," June 24, 1921, RG 59, 882.00/705.

124. Ibid., Cyril Henry to O. M. Thompson, July 1, 1921; Garvey, *Philosophy and Opinions,* II: 366.

125. Minister Resident Joseph L. Johnson to Secretary of State, July 16, 1921, RG 59, 882.00/705.

126. "Special Personal Report."

127. Crichlow to Garvey, "Supplementary Report," July 4, 1921, RG 59, 882.00/705.

128. E.g., *Negro World,* April 16, June 18, 1921.

129. Ibid., August 13, 1921.

130. Ibid., August 20, 1921.

131. *Liberian News* (August 1924): 10.

132. H. F. Worley, General Receiver of Customs and Financial Advisor to Liberia, to Hon. Solomon Porter Hood, American Minister Resident, Monrovia, May 2, 1922, U.S. National Archives, RG 84, American Legation, Monrovia—Diplomatic Correspondence, 1922, File No. 840. The documents are in *The African World,* supplement, March 31, 1922. Garcia's report here contains several paragraphs omitted from Garvey's version in the *Philosophy and Opinions.*

133. *Negro World,* December 22, 1923, September 6, 1924.

134. Ibid., April 19, 1924, p. 2, reprinted from the *Liberian News* of February 1924; *Negro World,* September 6, 1924.

135. Garvey, *Philosophy and Opinions,* II: 368.

136. Ibid., p. 372; *Negro World,* September 6, 1924.

137. *Negro World,* September 6, 1924.

138. Ibid., March 29, 1924, April 19, 1924, reprinted from the *Liberian News,* February 1924.

139. *Negro World,* March 29, 1924. He was given a state funeral at Liberty Hall.

140. Garvey, *Philosophy, and Opinions,* II: 374.

141. Francis O'Meara, British Legation, Monrovia, to H. M. Principal Secretary of State for the Foreign Office, February 22, 1924, FO 371/9553.

142. Garvey, *Philosophy and Opinions,* II: p. 374.

143. *Negro World,* June 21, 1924 (he is described here as Dossen's brother-in-law); July 5, 1924.

144. Barclay to Agent, Messrs. Elder Dempster and Co., Ltd., Monrovia, June 30, 1924, FO 371/9553; Barclay to shipping companies, June 30, 1924, RG 59, 811.108 G 191/38.

145. Francis O'Meara to Secretary of State, August 8, 1924, FO 371/9553.

146. Telegram, American embassy to Secretary of State, July 31, 1924 RG 59, 811.108 G 191/37.

147. C. A. Wali, Clerk of Legation in charge of archives, to Secretary o State, August 8, 1924, RG 59, 811.108 G 191/38. *Negro World* October 11, 1924.

148. *Crisis* (August 1924): 154, 155; Garvey, *Philosophy and Opinions,* II: 394.

149. Memorandum, September 6, 1924, enclosed in Charles E. Hughes to President, September 6, 1924, RG 59, 882.5511/10; memorandum of August 25, 1924, RG 59, 811.108 G 191/34.

150. *Negro World,* May 10, 24, 1924; *Liberian News,* August 1924; O'Meara to Secretary of State, Foreign Office, July 7, 1924, FO 371/9553.

151. *Negro World,* July 26, 1924.

152. O'Meara to Secretary of State, Foreign Office, August 23, 1924, CO 554/62 and FO 371/9553. H. M. Gray, Asst. Admiralty Counsel, to A. M. Boal, Admiralty Counsel, U.S. Shipping Board, Emergency Fleet Corporation, September 21, 1926; National Archives of the United States, records of the United States Shipping Board, RG 32, 1091-4805. *Negro World,* September 6, 1924.

153. O'Meara to Foreign Office, August 23, 1924, CO 554/62 and FO 371/9553. Garvey thought that the shock of Liberian treachery killed him—*Negro World,* September 20, 1924.

154. Most of the material in the paragraph is from Gray to Boal, September 21, 1926, RG 32, 1091-4805; G.R. Snider, Admiralty Counsel, to Lincoln Tyler, December 10, 1924, RG 32, 1091-4805.

155. Gray to Sydney De La Rue, Receiver General of Customs, Monrovia, July 29, 1926, RG 32, 1091-4805.

156. E. L. M. Archey, Assistant Counsel, to Parker, May 3, 1929, RG 32, 1091-4805.

157. Garvey, *Philosophy and Opinions,* II: 379; George Padmore, *Pan-Africanism or Communism?* (New York: Roy Pubs., [1956?]), p. 100.

158. Gray to Boal, July 8, 1926, RG 32, 1091-4805.

159. *Negro World,* August 9, 1924.

160. Ibid., September 6, 1924.

161. Ibid., August 23, 1924.

162. Ibid., September 20, 1924; Garvey, *Philosophy and Opinions,* II: 386-394.

163. RG 59, 882.5511/10; *Negro World,* September 13, 1924.

164. *New York Times,* August 28, 1924.

165. *Liberian News,* August 1924.

166. UNIA v. Chicago Defender (L. 34, p. 86), July 25, 1924; Federal Court Records, New York, FRC 536323; UNIA v. The Afro-American (L. 34, p. 23), June 25, 1924, FRC 536321; UNIA v. Pittsburgh Courier (L. 34, p. 39), September 25, 1924.

167. *New York Amsterdam News,* September 10, 1924.

168. Garvey, *Philosophy and Opinions,* II: 399-405.

169. Memorandum, September 6, 1924, enclosed in Charles E. Hughes, Secretary of State, to President, September 6, 1924, RG 59, 882.5511/ 10; *Crisis* (April 1925): 261.

170. Inaugural Address of Charles Dunbar Burgess King, January 7, 1924, RG 59, 882.00/738.

171. News release, Department of State, August 25, 1924, RG 59, 811.108 G 191/34.

172. Memorandum in Charles E. Hughes to President.

173. *Negro World,* June 2, 1923.

174. *Evening World,* June 29, 1923.

175. Garvey, *Philosophy and Opinions,* II: 40.

176. Francis O'Meara to Secretary of State, Foreign Office, February 22, 1924; FO 371/9553; *Liberian News,* August 1924.

177. *Crisis,* April 1925, p. 260.

178. War Office to Secretary of State, Foreign Office, May 23, 1925, Foreign Office to O'Meara, June 3, 1925, FO 371/10621.

179. Raymond Leslie Buell, *The Native Problem in Africa* (New York: Macmillan, 1928), II: 733. King was traveling through Sierra Leone to the Liberian hinterland.

180. Garvey, *Philosophy and Opinions,* II: 385.

181. *Negro World,* March 28, 1925.

182. Ibid., September 6, 1924.

183. Garvey, *Philosophy and Opinions,* II: 399.

184. "Special Personal Report," June 24, 1921, RG 59, 882.00/705.

185. Ibid., Cyril Henry to O. M. Thompson, July 1, 1921.

186. Ibid., "Memorandum on Garvey Movement," unsigned [1921]

187. M. B. Akpan, "Liberia and the Universal Negro Improvement Association: The Background to the Abortion of Garvey's Scheme for African Colonization," *Journal of African History,* 14 (1973): 108.

188. *Negro World,* December 31, 1921.

189. Ibid., May 20, 1922.

190. Ibid., October 27, 1923.

191. Garvey, *Philosophy and Opinions,* II: 375, 376.

192. *Negro World,* September 20, 1924.

193. Garvey, *Philosophy and Opinions,* II: 397, 398.

194. Ibid., p. 379; *New York Times,* August 5, 1924.

195. Marcus Garvey, *Speech at Royal Albert Hall* (London: Poets and Painters Press [1968?]).

196. Herbert Aptheker, ed., *The Correspondence of W. E. B. Du Bois* (Amherst: University of Massachusetts Press, 1973), I: 278-279.

197. Quoted in Frank Chalk, "Du Bois and Garvey Confront Liberia," *Canadian Journal of African Studies* 1 (November 1967): 137.

198. W. E. B. Du Bois, *Dusk of Dawn* (New York: Schocken, 1968), pp. 123, 124.

199. Aptheker, *Correspondence,* p. 465.

200. Du Bois to Hughes, January 5, 1923, in Aptheker, *Correspondence,* p. 261.

201. Bruce to Florence (his wife), January 2, 1924, Bruce Papers, Ms L 33.

202. *Crisis* (July 1924): 106, (August 1924): 154, 155.

203. King to Du Bois, June 30, 1924; Du Bois to King, July 29, 1924, in Aptheker, *Correspondence,* pp. 280-283.

204. Du Bois to Harvey S. Firestone, October 26, 1925, W. D. Hines to Du Bois, November 10, 1925, in Aptheker, *Correspondence,* pp. 320-323.

205. Garvey, *Philosophy and Opinions,* II, p. 392.

206. Buell, *The Native Problem in Africa,* II: 822, 823.

207. UNIA delegation to President Calvin Coolidge, April 28, 1925, RG 59, 882.5511/16; William L. Sherrill, chairman, Liberian delegation to President Coolidge, May 5, 1925, RG 59, 882.5511/15.

208. P. L. Burrows to A.C.S., April 20, 1926; "Memorial from UNIA to American Colonization Society," April 26, 1926; statement from Fred A. Toote, et al.; W. A. Wallace, Secretary-General, UNIA., to A.C.S., September 28, 1926; Secretary, A.C.S., to UNIA., September 29, 1926; W. A. Wallace to Paul Sleman, Secretary, A.C.S., November 1, 1926; Secretary, A.C.S., to UNIA, November 16, 1926. American Colonization Society (A.C.S.) Records, Series 3, Box 3. Minutes of Special Meeting of the Board of Directors of the A.C.S., November 4, 1926, Ibid., Series 5, Box 14.

209. A. L. King to Edwin Barclay, October 22, 1936, UNIA Central Division (New York) Files, Box 9, d. 36. Senator Bilbo's proposed Greater Liberia Act of 1939 obtained UNIA support. Today (1975) the remaining UNIA units are still involved in work in Liberia.

210. E.g., *Negro World,* April 23, 1921—farewell meeting for two emigrants from the Sydney [probably Nova Scotia] division.

211. Alien declaration for Israel Saunders Mc Cleod, who came to Liberia as a UNIA engineer and became a Liberian citizen, RG 84, Consular Correspondence, Monrovia, 1922, Vol. II, File No. 811.1.

212. Francis O'Meara to Secretary of State, Foreign Office, August 23, 1924, FO 371/9553.
213. O'Meara to Secretary of State, Foreign Office, March 5, 1925, CO 554/66.
214. Garvey, *Garvey and Garveyism*, p. 258.
215. E.g., *Negro World*, September 26, 1931.
216. *Negro World*, April 9, 1932.
217. Amy Jacques Garvey, *Garvey and Garveyism*, p. 99.
218. William R. Scott, "A Study of Afro-American and Ethiopian Relations: 1896-1941," Unpub. Ph.D. dissertation, Princeton University, 1971.
219. E.g., G. H. Walker, Deputy Inspector General of Police, Southern Provinces, Nigeria, to Inspector General of Police, Lagos, March 28, 1922, CO 583/109. (Here Ernest Ikoli resigned as secretary of the Lagos UNIA because he favored the industrial but not the political aims of the association); Langley, "Garveyism," pp. 159-161; Akinbami [Agbebi] to Bruce, May 18, 1920, Bruce Papers, Ms 267.
220. *Revue Indigène* (1922): 275, quoted in Buell, *Native Problem*, p. 81.
221. William J. W. Roome, *Aggrey – The African Teacher* (London: Marshall, Morgan and Scott, n.d.), p. 67.
222. Editorial from *Abantu-Batho*, April 21, 1921.
223. H. W. Peet, "An Interview With Marcus Garvey," *Southern Workman*, 57 (October 1928): 425.
224. E.g., *Negro World*, August 20, 1927; *Blackman*, February 8, 1930.
225. Vincent, *Black Power and the Garvey Movement*, p. 192.
226. Manoedi to Winston Churchill, September 30, 1922, CO 417/691.
227. Manoedi to Churchill, September 30, 1922, FO 371/8513.
228. E.C.F. Garraway, Resident Commissioner, Maseru, Basutoland to High Commissioner, Pretoria, November 30, 1922, CO 417/683; H. J. Stanley, Imperial Secretary, H.C. Office, Pretoria to Secretary to the Governor General, Pretoria, December 8, 1922, FO 371/8513; Arthur Frederick, High Commissioner, Cape Town to the Duke of Devonshire, Colonial Office, March 23, 1923, CO 417/696.
229. Minute of November 1, 1922, CO 417/691; minute by Charles Dodd, FO 371/9553.
230. M. Mokete Manoedi, *Garvey and Africa* (New York: New York Age Press, n.d.) pp. 3, 19, 20.

8

The Black Star Line

Remember, the Black Star Line Steamship Corporation is not a private company. The ships that are owned by this corporation are the property of the Negro race.

—*Marcus Garvey* [1]

The white man controls cable and wireless,
Connections by ships with force and duress:
He keeps black races of the world apart,
So to his schemes they may not be smart:
"There shall be no Black Star Line Ships," he says,
"For that will interfere with our crooked ways:
"I'll disrupt their business and all their plans,
"So they might not connect with foreign lands."

—*Marcus Garvey* [2]

The story of the Black Star Line Steamship Corporation and allied shipping ventures illustrates the strongest and weakest features of the Garvey movement. On the one hand, the mere launching of four ships by

151

a black man in itself constitutes a remarkable feat with little if any parallel in New World black history. In the Black Star Line story we also see, more clearly than probably in any other aspect of the movement's history, the amazing sacrifices that black people were willing to make for a racial movement they perceived as being seriously about the business of effecting their emancipation. And the prospect of a black-owned shipping undertaking stimulated in many young black people an interest in a field which was hitherto mostly closed to them.[3] On the other hand the corporation's history reveals the extremes of thievery and corruption that black people could resort to, even within a movement for racial uplift. It illustrates too the relentless pressure of Garvey's external enemies, black and white, and the carelessness with which the organization's financial affairs were managed.

In the Black Star Line Garvey was attempting to fulfill a long-felt need. Black passengers were routinely subjected to racist practices on existing shipping lines. First-class tickets often did not prevent black people from having to eat after white passengers had finished.[4] Black seamen, the last hired and the first fired, also had reason to welcome a black company.[5] And for the few black seamen with advanced nautical qualifications, life was especially hard.[6]

For these kinds of reasons the Black Star Line was greeted with boundless enthusiasm by black people. African and West Indian merchants saw in it the hope of independence from racist white companies,[7] missionaries saw in it an end of the long trip via Europe to get to Africa,[8] Liberians saw in it the hope of a coastwise service between Liberia and Sierra Leone,[9] and most saw in it a triumph for black self-esteem. Garvey thought that the line would fear little from white competition since it would ideally operate within a self-contained black world.[10] Not surprisingly, the Black Star Line proved to be Garvey's greatest single device for UNIA recruitment.[11]

Garvey began work on the line in May 1919 and was promptly summoned before Assistant District Attorney Edwin P. Kilroe in New York. Kilroe, egged on by some of Garvey's ex-associates, informed him that he was illegally soliciting funds for a nonincorporated commercial venture.[12] He also accused Garvey of wrongly using Black Star Line funds for a UNIA restaurant and the *Negro World*.[13] The line was accordingly incorporated on June 27, 1919, in Delaware with a capital stock of $500,000.[14] The shares had a par value of $5.00 each, and individuals could buy a maximum of two hundred.[15] Garvey described himself as the biggest share-holder.[16]

Within less than three months of incorporation, the line had amassed enough money (mainly from stock sales) to enter into a contract for its first ship. This was on September 17, 1919 and the ship, the *Yarmouth,* was to cost $165,000.[17] The *Negro World* announced that the *Yarmouth* had previously operated from Boston and was the very ship on which the black civil-rights activist William Monroe Trotter had sailed as a waiter and cook, in order to overcome the government's refusal of a passport for his trip to the Paris peace conference.[18] It was in poor condition however. According to one of its black officers, it had been used during the war as a coal boat and was not worth a penny above $25,000.[19] The prosecution for Garvey's mail fraud case claimed that it had been used as a cattle boat, was in a filthy condition, and was not equipped for passenger service when bought.[20] To captain the ship Garvey was able to find one of the few qualified black men in this field, Joshua Cockburn, who had sailed extensively to African ports.[21]

A crowd of several thousand witnessed the *Yarmouth*'s launching on October 31, 1919, from the 135 Street dock, not far from Garvey's offices. This trip, by prior arrangement with the owners, lasted as far as 23 Street, since Garvey had not yet settled outstanding financial problems, including difficulties in obtaining insurance.[22] Most of the money for this first BSL venture, Garvey said, had come from his followers in New York, Philadelphia, Newport News (Virginia), Colón, Panama City and Bocas-del-Toro (Panama), and Cuba.[23]

The *Yarmouth* (unofficially renamed the *Frederick Douglass* by the BSL) eventually sailed on November 24 with some passengers (many stock salesmen among them) and a cargo of cement for Sagua La Grande, Cuba.[24] From Cuba Cockburn informed Garvey that the white engineers had tried to run the ship aground.[25] A few days later, on December 5, Cockburn again complained that the white engineers were causing trouble. He reported also that the people in Sagua La Grande were wild with enthusiasm for the ship. The persons on board were not allowed to land, for some unspecified reason, but the stevedores quickly bought up $250 worth of shares.[26] The ship remained in the West Indies for a while, traveling to Jamaica and Panama, with no new cargo beyond Cuba.[27] On its return trip, it carried a full complement both of passengers and cargo (logwood).[28]

Two days after its return in mid-January 1920 the *Yarmouth* received
orders to transport a cargo of whiskey to Cuba before the imminent arrival of prohibition. Garvey claimed that the contract (which he had already
turned down) had been entered into by his subordinates while he was on
honeymoon in Canada.[29] For carrying this cargo, variously valued at up
to $5 million,[30] the BSL was to receive the paltry sum of $7,000 ($11,000
according to some sources),[31] not enough to even cover the ship's expenses
for the trip. Furthermore, there were repairs to be done. As Garvey put
it, "I was therefore called upon to spend $11,000 for repairs in order to
have the ship sail with the cargo valued at $5,000,000 on which the com-
pany was collecting only $7,000 as freight, all because of the disobedience
of two officers of the company."[32]

Shortly after putting to sea the ship was sabotaged by an engineer and
Cockburn ordered five hundred cases of whiskey and champagne thrown
overboard, where they were picked up by small boats which suspiciously
happened to be on hand.[33] The ship had to return for repairs. It was also
held up for a while by United States revenue officers.[34] Garvey was able
nevertheless to salvage much publicity from these vicissitudes. "I want to
tell you that we have really made history," he declared, "for that whiskey
is from the South and it belongs to Southern crackers, too."[35]

The voyage was finally resumed on February 27, 1920, and the *Yarmouth,* with its whiskey as well as passengers, arrived in Havana on
March 3 to a fantastic welcome. It was unable to get a berth right away
but people came out in boats showering the ship with flowers and fruit.
When the ship did dock after five days it was "overrun with visitors from
dawn until sunset." The Cuban welcome included a banquet at the presidential palace given by President Menocal in honor of this signal event
in the history of black people, and promises of commercial support from
government officials, including the president, and businessmen.[36]

The enthusiastic Cuban welcome was offset, however, by heavy and
unnecessary expenses incurred as a result of the financial incompetence
(and possible deliberate dishonesty) of the line's officials who had entered
into the whiskey contract. In their haste to get the whiskey out before
prohibition the owners had failed to obtain a Cuban consignee, which
caused delays in discharging the cargo. Other delays were caused by the
five days at anchorage and a two-week longshoremen's strike. Normally
the shipper should have been protected, to the tune of several thousand

dollars a day, from such delays by a demurrage clause in the contract.
There was no such clause in this contract, however, so the cost, including
the upkeep of the thirty-five passengers bound for Jamaica and other
ports, had to be borne by the Black Star Line. The whiskey was finally
discharged in bond, and the *Yarmouth* departed after thirty-two days
in Havana.[37]
   The next stop was Jamaica, where hundreds of enthusiastic supporters
again greeted the ship. The boilers were repaired and supplies taken on
during the short stay here.[38] From Jamaica the *Yarmouth* headed for
Colón, Panama, where the welcome eclipsed even that in Havana. Hugh
Mulzac, a black officer on the ship, later described the scene: "Literally
thousands of Panamanians swarmed the docks with baskets of fruit,
vegetables and gifts. I was amazed that the *Yarmouth* had become such
a symbol for colored people of every land."[39] At Colón the ship took
on five hundred passengers, all West Indian immigrants who were tired
of American racism in the Canal Zone and wished to try Cuba's sugar
plantations. Makeshift arrangements were necessary to accommodate
them all.[40]
   Further scenes of heartrending enthusiasm awaited the ship at Bocas
del Toro and Almirante in Panama and Port Limón, Costa Rica, as oppressed
black people greeted this sign that maybe the race would yet be the equal
of other races. Mulzac described the scene at Bocas del Toro, where

> thousands of peasants came down from the hills on horses, donkeys,
> and in makeshift carts, and by a special train provided by the United
> Fruit Company, which, since it was going to lose its employees for
> the day anyway, declared a legal holiday. The crowd on the dock was
> so thick that when we threw our heavy lines ashore the peasants seized
> the hangers as they came out of the water and literally breasted us
> alongside the dock. In the tumult that followed dancing broke out
> on the deck, great piles of fruit and flowers mounted on the hatch
> covers, and U.N.I.A. agents signed up hundreds of new members.[41]

   From Central America the *Yarmouth* headed for Santiago de Cuba
where the five hundred passengers were discharged, and then back to
Jamaica for a cargo of seven hundred tons of coconuts and further repairs. Wartime restrictions limiting the export of food from Jamaica

made it impossible to secure enough for the homeward voyage, so Captain Cockburn stopped at Nassau and Norfolk, Virginia, for stores and fuel. At Norfolk Garvey ordered the ship to Philadelphia and Boston for UNIA celebrations. After some delays[42] the ship made it to these ports. By the time it was allowed to take its cargo and passengers to New York, however, the coconuts had rotted. The resultant financial loss was augmented by the fact that "the contract did not contain any limit upon company responsibility. Further," as Mulzac explained, "no one in the office knew how to check damage claims submitted by the owners of cargo, placing the company completely at the mercy of the shipper and forced to depend on *his* estimate of the value of the cargo instead of its own."[43]

The *Yarmouth*'s third and final trip began in May 1920 after Cockburn had been fired for dishonesty; his replacement was a white Canadian, Captain Dixon. A cargo of fertilizer was taken to Cuba after which the ship visited Port-au-Prince, Haiti, to be met by more enthusiastic crowds. Jamaica was the next stop. Here the financial ineptitude of the line's management again showed itself. The line's Jamaican agent, Mr. Wilson, contracted to assist in refloating a Japanese vessel which had run aground five hundred miles south of Jamaica on the Serrana Banks. Dixon and Mulzac suggested charging the cargo's owner, Lloyds of London, $45,000, which, according to Mulzac, was reasonable given the value of the cargo and other considerations. Wilson, who as Mulzac put it "was a building contractor who understood even less of the shipping business than Mr. Garvey," settled for $12,000, which barely covered the cost of the undertaking. The *Yarmouth*, with its thirty-two passengers on board, had little difficulty in refloating the stricken vessel. It then returned to New York.[44]

Later that summer the ship was taken out of service as a result of having been libeled by several creditors. It was sold by the United States Marshal in November 1921 for $1,625.[45] Yet litigation concerning the *Yarmouth* dragged on for another decade. This grew out of a collision on September 21, 1920 involving the ship. The line claimed that the United States marshal was in charge at the time. The government claimed that the master and crew of the vessel were at fault. A BSL appeal against an unfavorable decision in this case was dismissed with costs for nonprosecution in 1931, and a bonding company had to pay, because the line by then obviously could not.[46]

The line's second boat, the *Shadyside,* was purchased in April 1920 for $35,000 and carried passengers on excursions along the Hudson River two or three times a week.[47] Like the line's other ships, it was deemed seaworthy by the maritime authorities when purchased.[48] At the end of the summer excursion season it was put up at Fort Lee on the river but sprang a seam during a severe ice storm and sank.[49]

The line's third vessel, the *Kanawha* (unofficially renamed the *Antonio Maceo*) was being negotiated for at about the same time that the *Shady-side* was bought. By May 9, 1920, it was on display at 129 Street and North River Pier in Harlem,[50] Garvey having contracted to pay $65,000 for it.[51] At this stage, with two ships operating and a third about to go into service, the Black Star Line was probably at its peak. The *Kanawha,* however, was soon to become the most ill fated of the line's vessels. In June, on a maiden voyage up the Hudson it blew a boiler, resulting in the death of one person.[52] From July 1920 it made several attempts to sail to Cuba, all of which were frustrated by mechanical trouble.[53]

It was not until March 25, 1921, that the *Kanawha* finally left New York in a successful effort to reach the West Indies. The problems be-setting the ship for the next two and a half months were described in detail by Garvey (who was a passenger for part of the time) in a complaint against the crew and officers lodged with the American consul in Kingston, Jamaica, on June 7, 1921. Despite its certificate of seaworthiness, a valve in the engine blew out the same night the ship left New York. It was the chief engineer's watch, but he was nowhere to be found. The ship returned for repairs and sailed again on March 28. Between Norfolk and Jackson-ville (May 31 to April 3) the fan engine broke down despite warning signals which were ignored, requiring a stop at Jacksonville on April 3 for repairs. The ship departed once more on April 5 at 2 P.M., only to have the fan engine break again at 4 A.M. Twenty-four hours out of Jackson-ville the chief engineer damaged the boilers by taking in salt water, des-pite the presence of an evaporator capable of providing an indefinite supply of fresh water. The ship arrived in Havana on April 9. More repairs were necessary but no sooner had the ship departed than the fan engine broke again. The first-assistant engineer had apparently tampered with it even before leaving Havana. About five hours out of Havana piston rods and other parts of machinery were damaged due to the previous intake of salt water. On April 28 a dynamo expired.

On April 29 the ship put in at Sagua La Grande for further repairs and sailed the next day for Santiago de Cuba. Three and a half hours out there was more engine trouble, but no engineer was in the engine room. On May 1 the boilers were found to be without water and hot enough to catch the ship afire. Again no engineer could be found, so the boilers were soon out of commission. On May 2 the engineer put into Gibaro for water. The ship departed on May 4 and reached Santiago on May 6, by which time more salt water had been introduced into the boilers, necessitating further repairs. From Santiago the next stop was Kingston, where it was ascertained that the engine had multiple damages, and where extensive repairs were carried out.

The *Kanawha* departed Kingston on May 28 for Colón. After thirty hours the engineer demanded that they return to Kingston for lack of water, though he previously claimed to have had enough. More salt water was put in the boilers, and the chief engineer closed one engine because of a banging noise, which he failed to investigate. On May 29 the first-assistant engineer let the fan run at excessive speed, raising the boiler room steam pressure to such an extent that it blew a boiler tube. Then the starboard engine stopped working, so the banging port engine was revived. For the rest of the journey back the engineers on occasion absented themselves from the engine room. The chief engineer was sometimes drunk, continually used obscene language even in the presence of "ladies of refinement and culture," and on one occasion slapped the second mate.

Against the black captain, Adrian Richardson, Garvey had equally serious complaints. He carried a crew of forty, including stowaways, instead of the twenty-five stipulated by American regulations. They were being paid very high wages without the company's consent. He had kept the ship at a standstill in midocean all day on March 26. He had put into Norfolk on false pretenses and then absented himself to see his wife. He had taken on a friend at Norfolk and given him a ride to a destination out of the ship's route. In delivering the friend he collided with a pier, damaging both the pier and the ship's stern. At Jacksonville he ordered the wrong kind of coal and slowed the boat down.

Furthermore, Garvey charged, Richardson maintained the crew in a state of ill discipline. He himself gambled on deck with them, and they congregated on deck using obscene language when they should have been at work. On one occasion Richardson had permitted a fifteen-minute fight within view of the passengers. There was a charge of nepotism, too, in that the captain had taken on his brother as chief steward, lack of qualifications notwithstanding. All in all, the ship had consumed three months, Garvey charged, on a thirty-day journey which was still only half complete. He formally charged the officers with gross neglect and sabotage.[54]

Richardson denied those charges pertaining to him or explained them away. There had been discipline, he alleged, until Garvey came aboard. "Mr. Garvey," he explained, "wanted to be Purser, Engineer, Steward and Master, President and Owner."[55] The chief engineer, Charles Harris, similarly denied Garvey's charges.[56] Inspectors of the United States Steamboat Inspection Service later heard the case and found against Garvey.[57]

Despite these setbacks, the ship had received the customary warm welcome in Cuba, including friendly overtures from Governor Alfredo Lora of Oriente province.[58] It was at Santiago (in Oriente) that Garvey had joined the ship, hurrying over from Jamaica to head off an ugly confrontation between local stockholders and the captain and crew.[59]

Detailed as they were, Garvey's charges did not tell the whole story. An engineer in Kingston concluded that the ship's problems could only have been due to "sheer neglect."[60] And it was later revealed that Richardson had engaged in two fistfights with Garvey and had even pulled a gun on him.[61] The chief engineer supposedly had a nervous breakdown, which did not prevent him from attempting to sink the ship by opening the sea cock.[62]

After more than a month's delay in Jamaica the *Kanawha* finally headed back to New York but made it only as far as Antilla, Cuba, where it broke down and was abandoned. There it remained for years, a wreck and a menace to shipping. A watchman was placed on board but his pay was not forthcoming, and in 1924 a lien was obtained against the ship to satisfy the amount. The American consul at Antilla therefore arranged for a local dealer to store alcohol on board in return for employing the watchman. Over the years local persons offered sums ranging from $350 to $4,000 for the ship, but thieves stripped it of everything of value, even its nuts and bolts. In 1925 a storm swept the ship from its moorings and it began to sink. At this juncture the consul declared it a total loss and suggested it be written off the register. As of February 1927 it was still half-submerged in shallow water one and a half miles from the Antilla beach and the consul was considering an offer to salvage it in return for 15 percent *ad valorem* on anything of value recovered.[63]

The Black Star Line's fourth ship never came into the possession of the company but its history was nevertheless depressingly similar to that of the previous three. It involved the loss of a large sum of money, entangled the company in litigation for over a decade, and was finally sold as scrap. The *Phyllis Wheatley,* as this ship was to be named, was intended for the New York-Liberia route and its purchase had been promised several times, from as early as November 1919.[64]

Attempts to procure the ship began in earnest after Garvey's departure for the West Indies in 1921. After negotiations for a British ship broke down the company hired a white agent, A. Rudolph Silverston, who received $20,000 for a down payment on the S.S. *Hong Kheng,* which never materialized.[65] Silverston then turned to the United States Shipping Board. On April 28 he offered $190,000 for the *Orion,* a captured ex-German vessel, a bid which he increased to $225,000 about a month later. On May 26, believing that the *Orion* was already chartered to someone else, he bid $175,000 for the *Porto Rico,* another ex-German ship. This was refused as too low, and he upped his bid to an acceptable $225,000. The shipping board was at the time in fact negotiating with other parties for the charter of both ships, in the case of the *Orion* for $56,655 for six months plus a promise to purchase during this period for $200,000.[66]

After requesting a detailed report on the financial ability of the Black Star Line, the shipping board on August 2, 1921, decided to sell the *Orion* to Silverton's New York Ship Exchange on behalf of the line. Ten percent was payable in cash on delivery of the vessel and 10 percent each month thereafter until the price was paid, with an interest of 5 percent per annum on deferred payments. The purchasers were "to furnish a performance bond satisfactory to the shipping board to guarantee fulfillment of the contract."[67]

In the meantime Garvey had announced that Hugh Mulzac would be captain of the *Phyllis Wheatley,* "for propaganda reasons," Mulzac thought,[68] and advertisements had appeared announcing its sailing for Havana, Santo Domingo, St. Kitts, Dominica, Barbados, Trinidad, Demerara and Monrovia, first "on or about" March 27 and later "on or about"

April 25.[69] $8,900 was actually collected from persons who booked passages. The money was not kept separate from general Black Star Line funds and was never refunded.[70]

Instead of the $22,500 required under the contract, Silverston deposited $12,500 with the shipping board,[71] although he already had at least $20,000 of the line's money from the aborted *Hong Kheng* affair. Elie Garcia, the line's secretary, in 1928 swore an affidavit in which he recalled that Silverston was given $22,500 of the line's money in all. Silverston and Orlando M. Thompson, the line's vice-president, misappropriated $10,000. To cover up the fraud Thompson secured a $10,000 loan from the International Finance Corporation, proffering as authority a false resolution of the line's board of directors, which no other director saw. When these facts came to light a warrant was issued for Thompson's arrest, but with Garvey's arrest early in 1922 all the papers and records of the line were seized by the federal government, making it impossible to pursue the matter.[72]

In any event the line revoked Silverston's power of attorney around August 28, 1921.[73] With the weeks passing and no sign of the outstanding $10,000 or the performance bond, the shipping board began to weigh the pros and cons of cancelling the sale and forfeiting all or part of the $12,500 in its possession. It was decided to give the line another chance but the shipping board now delayed in sending on the necessary papers indicating the form of contract and bond because, they said, they were in the process of introducing a new form of contract.[74]

A further possible explanation for the delay is the fact that the United States government had by now intruded into the negotiations. On August 31 William J. Burns, director of the Justice Department's Bureau of Investigation, warned the shipping board that Garvey was a radical communist agitator who "advocates and teaches the over-throw of the United States Government by force and violence." Somebody at the shipping board initialed a brief handwritten note at the end of Burns' letter—"Recommended sale to this party be cancelled."[75]

The British government was not far behind. The British consul general in New York on January 17, 1922, informed the shipping board that the Black Star Line still owed money to the Canadian Department of Marine and Fisheries on the *Yarmouth*.[76] The vice-president of the shipping board was thereby strengthened in his resolve that the line would not acquire a ship.[77]

A check signed by Joseph P. Nolan, the line's attorney, and dated August 30, 1921, was deposited by the shipping board in December of that year.[78] Nolan complained that the check had indeed been delivered in August and linked this delay to that involving the form of contract and bond. And when, after some further delay these latter were finally delivered, the line now found itself asked to furnish a bond for $450,000, twice what had been agreed upon.[79] The manager of the board's ship sales division explained later that though the check had been proffered to him many times, he had refused for some time to accept it since his conditions concerning insurance and the bond had not been met. He eventually accepted it "as a matter of courtesy."[80] Garvey's arrest in January 1922 and the suspension of activities by the line more or less extinguished any remaining hope that the line would be able to fulfill the contract. Fortunately, the War Department expressed interest in the *Orion* for interisland service in the Philippines, and the shipping board began to think in terms of a complete or near-complete refund of the line's down payment.[81] The major problem was who to pay the money to.

On April 5 Orlando Thompson advised the shipping board to pay the money to attorney Nolan. On April 12 Garvey revoked Nolan's power of attorney in favor of attorney William C. Matthews. (Elie Garcia in his affidavit stated that neither Thompson nor Nolan had any interest in the money.) The board was willing to talk with Matthews though not satisfied enough with his credentials to pay him the money. On April 20 Silverston reappeared on the scene, claiming $12,500. The board now decided that it would not give over any money without full releases from each claimant. Yet the claims continued. Attorneys Matthews and Nolan surprisingly made a joint bid to recover it. When this failed Nolan continued on his own, now claiming that the $10,000 was his own money which he had lent the Black Star Line. Then some of the line's creditors attempted to attach the money to realize unsatisfied judgments. On August 17, 1923, Garvey asked the board to hold the money, since the stockholders wished to apply it to the purchase of a ship, and he did not want those "broker sharks" to deprive "poor Negroes" of what they had sacrificed for. As late as 1926 Casper Holstein, a prominent Harlem figure and for long a UNIA supporter, attempted to recover $1,000 which he said he had lent the line toward purchase of a ship.[82]

In 1926 and 1927 some thirty creditors, mostly ex-officers and seamen of the Black Star Line who had obtained judgments against the company, attempted to enforce a writ of attachment and garnishment against the shipping board to recover their arrears of pay. The attempt failed after going to the Court of Appeals for Washington, D.C.[83] The creditors then turned to Congress and procured the passage of a private act, approved by the Senate on March 1, 1929, which conferred jurisdiction on the court of claims to adjudicate "as a matter of equity and justice" claims of judgment creditors to the line's money.[84] Several persons recovered sums from this court.[85] As of July 1936, $17,722.79 of the line's $21,624.66 (a few hundred dollars having been deducted for expenses) had been paid out.[86] Enquiries from creditors were still being made in 1939.[87] Meanwhile, in 1930, the *Orion* was sold as scrap for $27,665.[88]

The *Negro World* of April 1, 1922, announced the suspension of the Black Star Line. By August the UNIA convention agreed in principle to launch a new shipping company and to establish a Black Star Line Redemption Corporation to pay back stockholders.[89] The new Black Cross Navigation and Trading Company was officially announced at Liberty Hall on March 20, 1924, and it was reported that this new venture brought the largest and most enthusiastic crowds to Liberty Hall since the old Black Star Line days.[90] In June Garvey offered to buy the *Susquehanna* by installments from the United States Shipping Board, despite the *Orion* mess. Inquiries by the board's credit department revealed that the UNIA treasury contained around $20,000, enough to ensure the initial payment but not enough to obviate the possibility of problems in raising the rest of the $140,000 purchase price. The board therefore decided to sell only for cash. They seem to have ignored Garvey's earlier request to apply the *Orion* deposit to a new ship, nor did Garvey repeat this request.[91]

Garvey purchased instead the *General Goethals* (referred to in UNIA circles as the *Booker T. Washington*) for $100,000 from the Panama Railroad Company and spent $25,000 reconditioning it. The ship was christened in January 1925, and so many people turned up to tour the boat that a thousand had to be turned away.[92] This remarkable display of devotion on the part of his followers was underscored by Garvey's statement that 90 percent of the money came from former BSL stockholders.[93]

The crew was all black. All but two of the officers were white. Garvey explained that qualified black officers were hard to find.[94] In an attempt to prevent a repetition of former problems, he made both the captain and the company's treasurer on board agree not to contract debts without the company's approval.[95] Garvey lost his mail fraud appeal and was jailed shortly after the ship left New York in late January for the usual Cuba-Jamaica-Panama run. The usual attempt was made to finance the trip largely from stock sales along the way. The result was yet another failure. The passengers and crew had conflicts with the white officers; these latter tried to have themselves discharged in Jamaica; there were long delays in Jamaica and Colón due to lack of money; the crew almost mutinied in Colón for lack of pay; in Charleston on the way home there was no money to pay for supplies and the chief engineer jumped ship causing a problem in obtaining clearance to resume the journey; and there were reports of the crew setting the forecastle afire to keep warm.[96] The ship returned to New York around the beginning of June.[97] It was later sold for debts.[98] In 1926 the UNIA auditor declared that the gross amount received for the company was $287,432.95, excluding monies received by an operating agent.[99] The launching of a steamship line assumed the proportions of an obsession among UNIA members, akin to the desire to relocate in Liberia. The steamship committee of the 1929 convention in Jamaica suggested the formation of an African Steamship Navigation Co. Ltd.[100]

The Black Star Line collected nearly $750,000 in its first ten months, prompting Garvey to increase its capital stock from $500,000 to $10 million in December 1919.[101] By August 1922 Garvey said that about $900,000 had been paid up for stock.[102] If to this is added the monies collected for the Black Cross Navigation and Trading Company, we have a loss to black people of almost $1.25 million. The question arises as to why this enormous loss was sustained. The reasons are of two kinds: those for which Garvey may have been directly responsible and those over which he had little control.

Among the former may be his lack of sound judgment in appointing subordinates. A possible case in point concerns the Black Star Line's Nigerian representative, Akinbami Agbebi, whose selection was criticized by his own cousin in the following terms: "A likely and suitable agent for the Black Star Line should be one who has a stake in the country, a shipper who can divert produce to your ships and take over the ballast cargo in his import trade. There are several such persons in Lagos but Akinbami is not one of them."[103]

Garvey's overexuberance also played into the hands of his enemies. The prosecution at his mail fraud trial made much of the fact that he was promising huge dividends while the BSL was in financial difficulty, promising to take up to a million emigrants to Africa in his ships, and so on. He was also too precipitate in buying new ships before the existing ones were paying concerns.

Garvey was also partly to blame for the losses resulting from lack of knowledge of maritime finance and the general unbusinesslike running of his shipping companies. The rotting of the cargo of coconuts is a particularly blatant example of this. Much of this kind of incompetence was of course due to Garvey's subordinates, and he tried to disassociate himself from their actions by explaining that he hired two of the best firms of accountants in New York to help start and audit the BSL books. Furthermore, the line's directors, though engaged in humble work prior to joining the line, were well qualified persons forced to do such jobs because of racial discrimination. Their incompetence, Garvey thought, was deliberate.[104]

Such general incompetence and sloppiness included the loss of stock certificates.[105] It can be illustrated too by the case of the Nigerian BSL representative, who could not commence business under the local laws until he had a registered office. Repeated entreaties to New York for the necessary papers for obtaining registration met with unreasonable delays, even though hundreds of pounds were coming in daily for stock. The money had to be returned.[106] A later Nigerian agent withdrew because of difficulty in communicating with the company.[107] A possible reason for some of this incompetence is the fact that the growth of the BSL was phenomenal, probably catching even its directors offguard. By May 1920 there were offices in New York, Cuba, British Guiana, Haiti, Jamaica, Bocas del Toro, Port Limón, Lagos, Monrovia, Sierra Leone, and fifteen states in the United States.[108] And money was coming in from other areas too.

Closely allied to general business incompetence was the hand-to-mouth financing often resorted to. "I vividly recall my own experiences upon the voyages of the 'Yarmouth' and sojourn in Panama," one BSL representative recalled. "But for my ready sales of stock to liquidate debts, we would have met disaster on more than one occasion."[109] By the summer of 1920 the line was already in enough financial trouble to cause

the establishment of a new corporation known as the Black Star Steamship Company in New Jersey in an effort to sidestep the Black Star Line's
problems.[110]
    Even more serious were those factors beyond Garvey's direct control.
Among these were the persistent and malicious attacks of his enemies.
The black mass-circulation *Chicago Defender* kept up a tirade against the
line. Garvey won a suit against the paper but the jury awarded him six
cents nominal damages.[111] Communist Cyril Briggs, in between denouncing Garvey as a tool of the British and other assorted imperialists, felt
no qualms at importuning these same imperialists with enquiries designed
to increase their opposition to the Black Star Line. He published the
replies of these imperialists in his anti-imperialist *Crusader.*[112] His socialist friend W. A. Domingo did likewise in his anti-imperialist *Emancipator.*[113]
Both these publications were dominated by anti-Black Star Line and anti-
Garvey material.
    White governments were a major source of opposition. The British
administration in Dominica passed a law aimed specifically at BSL stockholders, against the remittance overseas of more than ten dollars in a fort-
night.[114] Letters to the line from the Belgian Congo were intercepted and
destroyed.[115] And the role of the British and American authorities in the
Orion case has been noted.
    The greatest blow of all to Garvey's shipping ventures came from the
graft, thievery and sabotage of many of his employees. There can be little
doubt that the white engineers of the *Yarmouth* and *Kanawha* practically
destroyed those ships. The inflated bills brought the officers kickbacks
of up to 30 percent. Similar kickbacks were procured on other supplies.[116]
A BSL case against a New Jersey-based company for charging $11,791.74
for a negligently executed $2,500 repair job was dismissed for lack of
jurisdiction.[117] Captain Cockburn admitted to being one of five who
shared an $8,000 kickback out of the $16,500 down payment on the
Yarmouth. He and Edward Smith-Green, an official of the line, shared
a $2,000 bribe to expedite departure for Cuba with the whiskey cargo.[118]
"That man Cockburn!" Garvey said later. "May God damn him in eternal
oblivion. That man had in his hands the commercial destiny on the seas
of the black man. He sold it, every bit of it, for a mess of pottage."[119]
Neither Cockburn, nor Silverston, nor Orlando Thompson, nor any of
the other major figures involved here were ever convicted. Fraudulent

salesmen passing themselves off as BSL employees also hurt the company. The *Negro World* carried large advertisements against these, and some were successfully prosecuted.[120]

There was nothing inevitable about the failure of the Black Star Line and allied ventures. The few trips of the *Yarmouth* proved that the possibilities for substantial cargoes and a profitable passenger business were there. Without the problems enumerated above there is no reason why the UNIA shipping ventures could not have been at least modestly profitable.

NOTES

1. *Negro World*, May 1, 1920.
2. Marcus Garvey, *The Tragedy of White Injustice* (New York: A. J. Garvey, 1927) p. 15.
3. Hugh Mulzac, *A Star to Steer By* (New York: International Publishers, 1963), p. 92 (reference to Mulzac's Nautical Academy); *Negro World*, July 2, 1921, refers to the Universal Institute of Technology, Captain H. Mulzac, principal.
4. E.g., *Negro World*, July 19, 1924.
5. Ibid., June 26, 1920, letter from Brother H. Steed in England.
6. Mulzac, *A Star to Steer By*, passim.
7. Ibid., pp. 84, 85; *Negro World*, June 28, 1919.
8. *Negro World*, May 8, 1920.
9. Amy Jacques Garvey, ed., *The Philosophy and Opinions of Marcus Garvey* (London: Frank Cass, 1967), II: 403.
10. *Negro World*, March 5, 1921.
11. Marcus Garvey, "Why the Black Star Line Failed," in John Henrik Clarke, ed., *Marcus Garvey and the Vision of Africa*.(New York: Random House, 1974), p. 139.
12. *Negro World*, June 14, 21, 28, 1919.
13. United States Circuit Court of Appeals for the Second Circuit, Marcus Garvey vs. United States of America, brief for the United States, RG 204, Pardon Case File 42-793, National Archives. The May 1919 date for the beginning of the BSL is at p. 2.
14. Brief for the U.S., p. 3, RG 204, 42-793.
15. *Negro World*, June 26, 1920.
16. Garvey's application for executive clemency, June 5, 1925, RG 204, 42-793.

17. Brief for the U.S., p. 5, RG 204, 42-793.

18. *Negro World*, May 8, 1920.

19. Mulzac, *A Star to Steer By*, p. 82.

20. Brief for the U.S., p. 5.

21. *Emancipator*, April 10, 1920, p. 2.

22. Brief for the U.S.

23. *Negro World*, January 14, 1922.

24. Ibid.

25. Cockburn to Garvey, December 2, 1919, FRC 539440, Federal Court Records, New York, New York.

26. Ibid., Cockburn to Garvey, December 5, 1919.

27. *Negro World*, June 19, 1920.

28. Edmund David Cronon, *Black Moses* (Madison: University of Wisconsin Press, 1955), p. 82.

29. John Henrik Clarke, ed., *Marcus Garvey and the Vision of Africa* (New York: Random House, 1974), pp. 144, 145.

30. Mulzac, *A Star to Steer By*, p. 82 says "in excess of" $1,000,000. Garvey says $5,000,000 (Clarke, *Marcus Garvey*, p. 144, *Negro World*, June 19, 1920).

31. $7,000 according to Garvey (Clarke, *Marcus Garvey*, p. 144); $11,000 according to Mulzac, *A Star to Steer By*, p. 82.

32. Clarke, *Marcus Garvey*, p. 145.

33. Amy Jacques Garvey, ed., *The Philosophy and Opinions of Marcus Garvey* (London: Frank Cass, 1967), II: 196.

34. *Emancipator*, April 10, 1920; *Negro World* [1920—date missing from fragment seen by author].

35. *Negro World* [1920].

36. Mulzac, *A Star to Steer By*, pp. 83-85; *Negro World*, May 1, 1920.

37. Mulzac, *A Star to Steer By*, pp. 84, 85.

38. Ibid., p. 85.

39. Ibid.

40. Ibid., p. 86. The *Negro World*, May 8, 1920, says the ship arrived in Bocas del Toro, the next stop, with 40 crew and 280 passengers.

41. Mulzac, *A Star to Steer By*, p. 86.

42. *Negro World*, May 8, 1920.

43. Mulzac, *A Star to Steer By*, p. 87.

44. Ibid., p. 88.

45. Brief for the U.S., p. 11.

46. W. Davis Conrad, Assistant Admiralty Counsel to Erskine Wood, Admiralty Counsel, October 20, 1920, Conrad to J. A. Gibson, May 26,

1921; Interlocutory Decree, U.S.A., Libellant vs. Steamship Yarmouth, case heard June 26, 1926; George Z. Medalie, U.S. Attorney to Massachusetts Bonding and Insurance Co., August 10, 1931; William E. Collins to Chauncey G. Parker, General Counsel, U.S. Shipping Board, September 9, 1931, Record Group 32, File No. 553-1410, Records of the U.S. Shipping Board, U.S. National Archives.

47. Brief for the U.S., p. 9; *Negro World*, June 19, 1920.

48. Report of seaworthiness for S.S. Shadyside for inland waters for one year, Federal Court Records, Manhattan, FRC 539440, April 7, 1920.

49. Brief for the U.S., p. 9; Cronon, *Black Moses*, p. 85.

50. *Negro World*, May 1, 1920.

51. Brief for the U.S., p. 11.

52. Ibid., p. 12.

53. Ibid.; Cronon, *Black Moses*, pp. 86, 87.

54. Garvey to American Consul, Kingston, June 7, 1921, Garvey to American Consul [June 1, 1921], RG 41, 122539, Records of the Bureau of Navigation and the Steamboat Inspection Service (Department of Commerce), National Archives.

55. Richardson to American Consul, June 9, 1921, RG 41, 122539.

56. Charles Harris to Charles L. Latham, American Consul, June 8, 1921, RG 41, 122539.

57. Garvey to Commissioner, Steamboat Inspectors, Department of Commerce, September 7, 1921, U.S. Local Inspectors, Steamboat Inspection Service to Garvey, November 2, 1921, FRC 539440; U.S. Local Inspectors, New York to U.S. Supervising Inspector, Second District, New York, N.Y., October 31, 1921, RG 41, 82156.

58. *Negro World*, April 30, July 30, 1921.

59. Ibid., July 30, 1921.

60. A. M. Mc Innes, Ship and Engineer Surveyor, to Garvey, June 7, 1921, FRC 539440.

61. *New York Times*, May 25, June 7, 1923.

62. American Consul, Kingston to Secretary of State, June 17, 1921, RG 41, 122539. Governor L. Probyn of Jamaica to Winston Churchill, Secretary of State, Colonial Office, 11 July 1921, CO 137/749.

63. Garvey to Director of the Consular Service, Department of State, January 2, 1922, RG 59, 195.91/2163; D. B. Carson, Commissioner, to Collector of Customs, New York, April 28, 1924, RG 41, 139262; Horace J. Dickinson, American Consul, Antilla, to Secretary of State, March 31, 1924, RG 32, 1091-3520; Frederick W. Hinke, American Vice Consul, Antilla, to Secretary of State, May 10, 24, 1924, S. B. Davis,

Acting Secretary of Commerce to Secretary of State, June 28, 1924,
RG 41, 139262; Dickinson to Secretary of State, April 4, 8, 10, 1925,
February 8, March 24, 1926, RG 32, 1091-3520; Dickinson to Secretary
of State, February 25, 1927, RG 41, 139262.
    64. Brief for the U.S., p. 13.
    65. Cronon, *Black Moses*, pp. 94, 95.
    66. Silverston to Alfred D. Lasker, Chairman, U.S. Shipping Board, June
30, 1921, RG 32, 1091-1250; ibid., J. Harry Philbin, Manager, Ship Sales,
Memorandum, May 25, 1921; Lasker to Silverston, July 25, 1921, RG 32,
605-1-653.
    67. Clifford W. Smith, Secretary, U.S. Shipping Board, Memorandum,
July 10, 1921; Smith, "Memorandum for the Manager of Ship Sales,"
August 2, 1921, RG 32, 605-1-653.
    68. Mulzac, *A Star to Steer By*, p. 88.
    69. *Negro World*, February 19, April 23, 1921.
    70. Brief for the U.S., p. 15.
    71. J. Harry Philbin, Manager, Ship Sales Division to the Treasurer,
August 3, 1921, RG 32, 605-1-653.
    72. Ibid., Elie Garcia, affidavit of February 16,1928, in *Petition*
filed April 5, 1929, in the Court of Claims, John O. Garrett, claimant,
v. the United States. No. k132, pp. 18-20.
    73. Ibid., Joseph P. Nolan [B.S.L. counsel] to Philbin, August 28,
1921.
    74. Philbin to the Board, September 6, 1921, Elmer Schlesinger,
General Counsel, to Clifford W. Smith, Secretary, October 5, 1921,
Schlesinger to Philbin, October 5, 1921, Edward P. Farley, Vice-President,
U.S. Shipping Board Emergency Fleet Corporation, to General Counsel,
December 2, 1921, Schlesinger to Nolan, December 8, 1921, Nolan to
Schlesinger, December 9, 1921, RG 32, 605-1-653.
    75. William J. Burns to Frank Burke, Director, Bureau of Investiga-
tion, U.S. Shipping Board, August 31, 1921, Burke to A. J. Frey, Vice-
President in Charge of Operation, September 1, 1921, RG 32, 605-1-653.
    76. G. Armstrong, British Consul General, New York, to Secretary,
U.S. Shipping Board Emergency Fleet Corp., January 17, 1922, RG 32,
605-1-653.
    77. Ibid., J. B. Smull, Vice-President, U.S. Shipping Board to Clifford
W. Smith, January 21, 1922.
    78. Ibid., Philbin to Treasurer, January 5, 1922, Joseph P. Nolan to
Arthur W. Graef, Assistant Counsel,USSB, August 25, 1922.
    79. Nolan to Clinchfield Navigation Co., February 3, 1922, quoted
in E. Powis Jones, Assistant Counsel, USSB, to Stanford H. E. Freund,

Chief Counsel, March 8, 1922, Nolan to Arthur W. Graef, August 25, 1922, RG 32, 605-1-653.

    80. Philbin to General Counsel, April 12, 1927, RG 32, 605-1-653.

    81. Jones to Freund, March 7, 1922, Freund to Nolan, March 10, 1922, Philbin to N. A. Smyth, February 23, 1922, Quartermaster General to Manager, Operating Department, January 20, 1922, quoted in Jones to Freund, March 6, 1922, RG 32, 605-1-653.

    82. Thompson to Philbin, April 5, 1922, Philbin to Freund, April 13, 1922, quoting Garvey's telegram of April 12; Elie Garcia, affidavit of February 16,1928, Jones to Freund, April 19, 1922, Silverston to Philbin, April 20, 1922, Jones to Freund, April 29, 1922, Matthews to Freund, June 27, 1922, Nolan to Freund, December 19, 1922, Anton Gromich, attorney, to USSB, August 23, 1922, Edgar G. Wandless, Assistant Counsel to H. S. Brosh, District Comptroller, Building, June 25, 1923, Wandless to Purrington and Mc Connell, June 25, 1923, Secretary to General Counsel, August 29, 1923, quoting Garvey's letter of August 17, 1923, Casper Holstein to USSB, March 27, 1926, RG 32, 605-1-653.

    83. Ibid., Reeves T. Strickland, attorney, to Chauncey G. Parker, Counsel General, USSB, June 22, 1926, Speiser and Speiser to Fleet Corporation, July 1, 1926, Parker to Strickland, July 2, 1926; Parker to Speiser and Speiser, July 6, 1926, Samuel Goodacre, Secretary, to General Counsel, July 27, 1926; I. Lloyd Letts, Assistant Attorney-General to Parker, August 16, 1926; Acting Chairman to Jacobsen and Jacobsen, March 14, 1927.

    84. Ibid., T. V. O'Connor, Chairman to Mrs. Sophia Cox, April 24, 1928, "An Act for the relief of certain seamen and any and all persons entitled to receive a part or all of money now held by the Government of the United States on a purchase contract of steamship Orion who are judgment creditors of the Black Star Line for wages earned . . . ." Private—No. 459—70th Congress, S. 2291.

    85. Ibid., Parker to General Comptroller, May 13, 1929, In re John O. Garrett v. U.S.: In the Court of Claims No. 4-138; A. A. Ballantine, Assistant Secretary to the Treasury to Chairman, USSB, April 23, 1931. Among those suing was ex-B.S.L. attorney Joseph Nolan—Parker to Attorney-General, October 30, 1929.

    86. Ibid., J. M. Johnson, Assistant Secretary of Commerce to Hon. Royal S. Copeland, U.S. Senate, July 30, 1936.

    87. Arnold S. Cunning, Jamaica to Department of Justice, June 28,1939, RG 60, 198940.

    88. Manager, Ship Sales Division to Bureau of Navigation, January 16, 1930, Parker to Ship Sales, January 27, 1930, RG 32, 1091-1250.

89. *Negro World,* September 9, 1922.

90. Ibid., March 29, 1924.

91. Philbin to President, Emergency Fleet Corporation, June 16, 1924, Philbin to General Counsel, June 11, 1924, Garvey to Chairman, USSB, June 3, 1924, RG 32, 605-1-653.

92. New York *Daily News,* January 19, 1925. The figure for reconditioning is given as $60,000 in Garvey, *Philosophy and Opinions,* II: 264 (photo).

93. *New York Amsterdam News,* January 21, 1925.

94. Ibid.

95. Agreement between Captain Hiorth and Garvey, January 28, 1925, Garvey's instructions to George Williams, RG 41, 144621.

96. Ibid., G. Emonei Carter, Secretary, B.C.N.T. Co. to José de Olivares, March 9, 1925; Odin G. Loren, American Vice Consul, Colon to Secretary of State, April 22, 1925, RG 59, 819.5032; RG 41, 145456; C. V. Vaughan, Master, S.S. General Goethals to Secretary of Commerce, May 14, 1925, RG 41, 145301; *New York Amsterdam News,* June 3, 1925.

97. *New York Amsterdam News,* June 3, 1925.

98. Amy Jacques Garvey, *Garvey and Garveyism,* p. 164.

99. *Negro World,* March 27, 1926.

100. *Blackman,* August 28, 1929.

101. Clarke, *Marcus Garvey,* p. 142; Brief for the U.S., p. 8.

102. *Crisis,* 25 (November 1922): 35.

103. E. M. E. Agbebi to Bruce, February 12, 1920, Bruce Papers, Ty 238, Schomburg Collection, New York Public Library.

104. Clarke, *Marcus Garvey,* p. 143.

105. *Negro World,* February 19, 1921.

106. A. Agbebi to the President, The Black Star Line Inc., Bruce Papers, Ty 238C; Akinbami Agbebi to Bruce, July 4, 1920, ibid., Ms 372, Adeotan Agbebi to Bruce, June 25, 1920, ibid., A-7.

107. Messrs. A. and D.O.S. Dappa were the B.S.L., agents—Public Record Office, London, Colonial Office Files, W. 26068. Register of Correspondence, Nigeria, 1922, file destroyed but synopsis remains.

108. *Negro World,* May 8, 1920.

109. Cyril Henry to O. M. Thompson, July 1, 1921, RG 59, 882.00/705.

110. Brief for the U.S., p. 16.

111. *Negro World,* June 19, 1920.

112. *Crusader,* 5 (November 1921): 25.

113. *Emancipator,* March 27, April 10, April 17, 1920.

114. Interview with Mr. J. R. Ralph Casimir, Roseau, Dominica, August 31, 1974.

115. G. Ashio-Nikoi to Editor, *Times of Nigeria*, February 21, 1922, CO 583/109; Governor-General of French West Africa to H. M. Consul-General, Dakar, March 25, 1921, CO 96/625.

116. Clarke, *Marcus Garvey*, p. 145.

117. B.S.L. v. Irvine Engineering Co., Inc. February 18, 1920, FRC 536150.

118. Amy Jacques Garvey, *Garvey and Garveyism* (Kingston: A. J. Garvey, 1963), p. 81; Garvey, *Philosophy and Opinions*, II: 195, 196.

119. *Negro World*, January 7, 1928.

120. Ibid., November 6, 1920, February 19, 1921.

9

U.S.A. versus UNIA

*Garvey is a West-Indian negro and in addition to his activities
in endeavoring to establish the Black Star Line Steamship Corporation he has also been particularly active among the radical
elements in New York City in agitating the negro movement.
Unfortunately, however, he has not as yet violated any federal
law whereby he could be proceeded against on the grounds of
being an undesirable alien, from the point of view of deportation. It occurs to me, however, from the attached clipping that
there might be some proceeding against him for fraud in connection with his Black Star Line propaganda. . . .*

—J. Edgar Hoover[1]

*Only crooks and thieves and cowards fear to go to prison. Men
with principles don't care about jails.*

—Marcus Garvey[2]

The United States provided Garvey with the large black population
base, the financial and technological resources, and the strategic location

174

at the center of world and Pan-African affairs that were the objective
conditions against which he could rise to world prominence. His appearance in the United States, however, coincided with savage official repres-
sion against radical organizations. And it was not long before Garvey himself was the object of official scrutiny. In his 1917 pamphlet denouncing
the East St. Louis riots there appeared, without comment, the information
that the speech had been delivered "before a large and enthusiastic gathering of Negro Americans and West Indians, at which the Police Captain of
the Borough Precinct attended by more than ten detectives, police lieu-
tenants, and secret-service men were present."[3]

Such immediate official interest in Garvey is not difficult to explain.
For Garvey was, after all, provoking officialdom at a time when the
official mind usually saw, in the desire of black people to be free and
equal, a problem of law and order, and precious little else. To this kind
of mentality, even the National Urban League, the NAACP, and black
Republicans trying to enfranchise members of the race could on occasion
be viewed as threats to the peace.[4]

These attitudes were expressed by Attorney General A. Mitchell
Palmer in his 1919 report, "Radicalism and Sedition Among the Negroes
as Reflected in their Publications," which found fault with a Garvey speech
"which preached a doctrine of the negro for the Negro."[5] Similar attitudes
were also expressed in the 1920 report of the Lusk committee of the New
York State legislature into "Revolutionary Radicalism." Their acknowledgment of the oppression of Afro-Americans was most explicit: "The
most interesting as well as one of the most important features of radical
and revolutionary propaganda," they stated, "is the appeal made to those
elements of our population that have a just cause of complaint with the
treatment they have received in this country." This admission notwithstanding, the eradication of racism was predictably passed over in favor
of a law-and-order solution: "The very fact that the negro has many just
causes of complaint adds to the seriousness of the propaganda, and should
encourage all loyal and thoughtful negroes in this State to organize to
oppose the activities of such radicals, which cannot but lead to serious
trouble if they are permitted to continue the propaganda which they
now disseminate in such large volume."[6] The same ideas cropped up in
the opinions of the American consul at Kingston, Jamaica, who saw Garvey
as a "clever scoundrel" whose civil-rights activity made him a menace. In

the words of this official: "While he is clever enough to temper his propaganda with statements that he is for the negro rather than against the white man or any Government, his speeches are not lacking in many references to fighting for negro rights and I believe that a tendency of his propaganda is to alienate the loyalty of American and British negroes to his Association."[7] Thus did fighting for the black man's rights become a crime.

Garvey, for his part, did precious little to calm the fears of United States officialdom. It could not be otherwise. For in order to reach and stir the black masses, he had to say the things that needed to be said. In his 1917 denunciation of the East St. Louis riots, for example, his language gave no indication of the fact that he was an alien in the country for little more than a year, addressing an assemblage that contained a goodly share of police officers, in the era of deportation for foreign-born radicals. He condemned the collusion of civil authorities in the massacre as a crime against humanity. "For three hundred years," he said, "the Negroes of America have given their life blood to make the Republic the first among the Negroes of the world, and all along this time there has never been even one year of justice but on the contrary a continuous round of oppression."[8]

Many of his early speeches, too, urged black men not to participate further in white men's wars after their vain sacrifices in the world war. In a speech delivered not long after the termination of hostilities, he declared, "The first dying that is to be done by the black man in the future will be done to make himself free. And then when we are finished, if we have any charity to bestow, we may die for the white man. But as for me, I think I have stopped dying for him." This speech scandalized the Lusk committee. Their comment was not unexpected: "These extravagant and bombastic utterances may look trivial in cold print, but the continuous utterance of such sentiments has a very disquieting and pernicious effect upon the untutored element of the negro population."[9]

Not least of Garvey's provocations to United States officialdom were his ambiguous flirtations with communism. Like many other black leaders he resolutely prevented the communists from coopting his organization while at the same time hesitating to condemn them, and, at times, openly endorsing the system of government in Russia.[10]

In many other ways Garvey seems to have gone out of his way to

harass United States officialdom. The Washington Conference of the
Limitation of Armament, for example, was greeted by a Garvey telegram
to the effect that 400 million black people were unrepresented, and com-
mending to them President Harding's promise of democracy for black
folk.[11] Again, in 1922, Garvey wrote Secretary of State Charles E. Hughes
asking for a Department of State representative to attend the session on
colonialism at his international convention. The offer was declined.[12]

There was little about Garvey's program that could not be construed
as a threat, direct or indirect, to the United States. His doctrines of militant racial struggle could sometimes be transferred into strikes against
such powerful United States corporations as the United Fruit Company
in several Latin American countries. His African program too, with its
anti-imperialist and nationalistic implications would, if successful, augur
ill for American financial interests. Garvey took the position that American
capital would seek to expand its influence in Africa. In 1929, he wrote,
"Europe today is bankrupt and cannot advance much capital for the development of African industries, and therefore they are trying to interest
American capitalists in the exploitation of the wealth of the great Continent."[13]

Having determined, practically from the inception of his sojourn in
the United States, that Garvey was a dangerous character, various governmental, police, quasi-official and corporate agencies subjected Garvey and
the UNIA to a constant surveillance of international proportions. Where
possible their surveillance was supplemented by infiltration into the UNIA.
Garvey's charge that "agents of governments, organizations, corporations
and individuals, interested in the exploitation of Negroes operated among
the membership and officers of the Association in several cities" was hardly an exaggeration.[14] One UNIA counsel general, Garvey noted, upon
whom he depended for legal advice, was appointed an assistant attorney
general after his conviction.[15] White reporters who interviewed Garvey
were also suspected of being intelligence men.[16] At a speech in Jamaica
shortly after his deportation from the United States in 1927, Garvey
declared: "The Great United States Government got men to investigate
me; all manner of Secret Service people were set after me, and 20 percent
of my employees were United States Secret Service. I believe that I must
have cost the United States Government about five million dollars in ten
years."[17]

Evidence of official surveillance of Garvey sometimes cropped up in unexpected places. At hearings before a congressional subcommittee on appropriations in 1921, for example, the question came up of overload pay for a black Treasury Department employee who had been hired to transcribe proceedings at "some radical Negro meetings." A first-class stenographer was required, and a white one would not do since he would be liable to be thrown out of the meeting or killed. A qualified black stenographer had been sought outside of the government service, but in vain. The Department of Justice, which commissioned his work, therefore had to use a government employee. These meetings took place in Washington, D.C., in July and September 1920. The stenographer's task was described by a chief clerk of the Treasury Department as "very important and confidential stenographic work" consisting of "discreetly taking verbatim reports of the proceedings of negro radicals."[18] It transpired that this person had previously been employed as early as 1918 to cover a UNIA meeting in Baltimore, Maryland.[19]

The role of the Department of Justice in this case was not an isolated event. For much of the official surveillance of Garvey emanated from this department. In 1919, for example, officials of the Panama Canal contacted the department's Bureau of Investigation on the question of the Garvey threat to both areas.[20] The correspondence soon found its way to the bureau's J. Edgar Hoover, who demonstrated a more than passing acquaintance with Garvey. He expressed genuine regret over the fact that Garvey had not yet violated any federal law making him liable to deportation. He suggested, however, that proceedings might be sustained against him for fraud in connection with the Black Star Line. Hoover did not fail to acknowledge his adversary's mettle, describing him as "one of the most prominent negro agitators in New York" and "an exceptionally fine orator, creating much excitement among the negroes through his steamship proposition." Hoover concluded his observations in predictable fashion: "In his paper the 'Negro World' the Soviet Russian Rule is upheld and there is open advocation of Bolshevism."[21] By 1920 British officials, who regularly shared information on Garvey with their American counterparts, were cognizant of the fact that the Justice Department's agents were watching Garvey closely.[22] The department's surveillance extended to Garvey's economic undertakings.[23] The director of its Bureau of Investigation even attempted to influence the manner in which the prosecutor conducted the case against Garvey after he was arrested in 1922.[24]

Garvey was made painfully aware of the department's surveillance through the zeal of a black agent of the Bureau of Investigation's New York office, special agent James E. Amos, an ex-bodyguard of former President Theodore Roosevelt. Garvey's complaints against Amos included collusion with anti-Garvey individuals, membership in the NAACP, authorization of prejudicial news releases during the 1923 trial, encouragement of civil litigation against Garvey, an unjustified raid on the Harlem Liberty Hall, and much more.[25] Amos' harassments continued to 1926 when J. Edgar Hoover, now director of the department's Bureau of Investigation, sent on a secret report from Amos who now alleged, wrongly, that Garvey was instructing his wife from jail to collect monies in circumstances amounting to a use of the mails to defraud.[26]

Hoover maintained his interest in Garvey even after the latter's deportation. In 1928 he received a report of Garvey's doings in England from "a confidential source."[27] In 1929, presumably because of his continuing interest in Garvey, Hoover's aid was enlisted in the case of *John O. Garrett* v. *United States,* where an attempt was being made to recover portions of the $22,500 of Black Star Line money still impounded by the United States Shipping Board.[28] As late as 1930, Hoover was still dealing with the UNIA, this time proffering information to the Department of State, which was investigating the activities of a Trinidadian in Chicago suspected of being connected with Garvey's movement.[29]

United States surveillance of Garvey's activities abroad was as diligently pursued as surveillance at home. American consular agents and "confidential sources" from Sweden to Liberia, from Canada to Trinidad, kept a close watch on Garvey, his organization, and its ramifications in their respective areas.

In 1919, the American embassy in Stockholm, Sweden, informed Washington by telegram that a Swedish paper had published a "sensational despatch" from London on the Black Star Line and Garvey's boast of imminent race war.[30] Reports came from elsewhere in Europe, too, such as a 1930 report from the ambassador to France on the radical black movement in France and an instance of its connection with Garvey.[31] And when in 1919 the London embassy passed on to Washington the British secret intelligence report, "Unrest Among the Negroes"[32] (includ-

ing data on Garvey and his associates), the Department of State was highly
appreciative of British attention to "the problem of negro unrest throughout the world" and expressed a desire to obtain all possible information
from London.[33] This is interesting since much of the British information
was obtained through surveillance of their own carried on inside the
United States. In 1920 the presence in London of Garvey's ex-spouse,
Amy Ashwood Garvey, who was on her way to Liberia, occasioned a
telegram from the United States embassy to ascertain from the Department
of State whether she was involved in "Garvey's anti-white activities." The
department thought she was not.[34] In 1921 United States officials in
London, acting on Department of State advice, refused temporarily to
allow Garvey's former employer, Duse Mohamed Ali, to obtain a visa to
enter the United States, despite Mohamed's willingness to say uncomplimentary things about Garvey when interviewed by the United States
consul general.[35] White Englishman Dr. Charles Garnett came under
investigation by virtue of having chaired Garvey's Royal Albert Hall
meeting.[36]

The Department of State's interest in Garveyism in Liberia could not
have been more explicit. In May 1921 the United States minister resident
and consul general was instructed "to watch closely and report fully all
activities" of the UNIA. His instructions continued, "The Department
desires to know the names of persons in Liberia connected with this apparently subversive movement and wishes to be informed especially with
regard to Gabriel Johnson, Mayor of Monrovia, who is reported to have
taken an active part in furthering the aims of this movement." This United
States representative was in the happy position of being able to report
to Washington that he had embarked on the Garvey trail even before being
ordered to do so.[37] Reports on Garveyism also reached the Department
of State from United States officials in Sierra Leone.[38]

After Garvey's deportation from the United States he visited Canada
on several occasions. Not unnaturally, he did not escape the ubiquitous
gaze of Uncle Sam's representatives on these occasions. In late October
1928, less than a year after his expulsion from the United States, he arrived in Canada and spoke in favor of Al Smith, Democratic presidential
candidate in the imminent United States elections. He was promptly
arrested, brought before a board of enquiry of the local immigration
authorities in Montreal, and ordered deported under regulations prohibiting political agitators. Upon explaining that he was in transit, he was

placed on a $100 bond, given until November 7 to leave, and ordered
not to indulge in any more public statements.[39] The *Negro World* presumed that all this must be the handiwork of the Republican party,[40]
and it was right. The American consul general in Montreal unknown,
of course, to the public, claimed credit for the action of the Canadian
authorities. Writing to Washington on the day after the deadline for
Garvey's departure, he informed his superiors that Garvey had arrived
in Canada two weeks previously and had delivered his speeches in support
of the Democratic party. Garvey then, for some unexplained reason,
called at the consul general's office but left before he could be interviewed. At this stage the office contacted the Canadian immigration
authorities and informed them that Garvey was an ex-convict and inad-
missable into Canada. Whereupon the Canadian authorities, in this official's words, acted "quietly and promptly."[41]

From the anglophone West Indies came periodic observations on Garvey
and Garveyites, from such places as Jamaica[42] and the United States Virgin
Islands, where no less a person than the president of the United States in 1923
requested a report on a local political figure suspected of being a Garveyite.[43]

Surveillance in this area was particularly keen in Trinidad, especially
in the two years or so immediately after World War I. This was due largely
to the serious character of the upheaval and riots which occurred there
in 1919. The American consul in Port-of-Spain conferred regularly and
swapped information on Garveyite influence with the British governor
and police authorities. Not much escaped his attention. Characteristic of
his zeal was his request from the local police authorities in 1920 for confidential character sketches of two young Trinidadians mentioned in a
local black newspaper as seeking employment in the Black Star Line.[44]
The consul in Trinidad was among the strongest critics of what he considered Washington's tolerance in allowing Garvey's propaganda to leave
New York for the islands. In 1920 he admonished the Department of
State: "I have several times lately in despatches to the Department, mentioned the pernicious effects here already of this propaganda from New
York, which was probably largely responsible for the recent riots in
Trinidad and Tobago. I cannot too strongly express my own opinion to
the effect that this propaganda from New York should not be tolerated
by our government."[45]

This worldwide surveillance extended inevitably into Latin America,
where some of the strongest UNIA branches existed. Reports flowed

regularly into the Department of State from such places as Costa Rica,[46] Panama,[47] and Cuba, where in 1921 the American chargé d'affaires requested an informal investigation of the UNIA and the nationality of its officers.[48] In Santo Domingo, then an occupied country, United States marines at the beginning of the 1920s suppressed the UNIA and arrested its leaders.[49]

In Latin America, Department of State surveillance was supplemented by that of the United Fruit Company. In January 1920, for example, Marie Duchatellier, writing from Panama City where she was engaged on a promotional tour for the UNIA and Black Star Line, explained that the United Fruit Company had used its influence with the governments of Panama and the Canal Zone to try to prevent the UNIA delegation from landing. She reported that the local blacks, together with the West Indians and led by a radical Spanish Panamanian, Morales, forced the hand of the authorities by threatening to strike on the canal and burn down the city of Colón.[50] The company also kept a check, on occasion, of monies remitted by its workmen to Garvey's organizations. Such information was turned over to the local United States consul.[51]

The United Fruit Company was not the only nongovernmental or quasigovernmental body supplementing official surveillance. Another was the National Civic Federation. In August 1920, in the midst of Garvey's First International Convention of Negro Peoples of the World, the federation embarked on a novel means of ascertaining Garvey's position. A representative simply visited and interviewed several of the most important Afro-American political figures over the period of a few days.[52] The first person visited by the interviewer, Charles Mowbray White, was none other than Garvey himself. Garvey presented him with a copy of the Declaration of Rights of the Negro Peoples of the World and regaled him with stories of UNIA sympathy with communists and Irish liberationists. Garvey also explained that he did not advocate the return of all black people to Africa and relegated W. E. B. Du Bois to the status of "ante-bellum Negro." To Garvey's intimation of an intention to visit Africa soon, White responded by appending to his report a warning that the British government should be advised to keep him out of that continent.

Two days later White was at the offices of the *Messenger,* where he met with A. Philip Randolph and Chandler Owen. Owen did most of the talking but White reported that Randolph concurred in his partner's sentiments. Here White learned that Garvey could not possibly be Bolshevik because "he has made no effort to study the socialist movement headed by us." Garvey, they said, was an uneducated ignoramus who knew nothing about the Afro-American, being leader of a "purely West Indian" movement. Owen and Randolph even advanced the hypothesis that Garvey might be working with the Department of Justice to destroy black solidarity by siphoning away money from rival organizations. They also expressed the conviction that Garvey's slogan of "Africa for the Africans" was unscientific, whereas they were scientific internationalists. They predicted that Garvey's schemes would collapse within three months.

Two days later White visited W. E. B. Du Bois, who, like Randolph and Owen, considered the UNIA a West Indian rather than an Afro-American movement. According to White's transcript, Du Bois attributed a large following to Garvey not only in the Caribbean but also in the East Indies. Du Bois thought that Garvey was allied with Bolsheviks and Sinn Feiners and predicted a not-too-distant demise for the UNIA.

White's mission took him next to Frederick Moore of the well-established black weekly, the *New York Age*. He, too, considered the UNIA a West Indian affair. He boasted about how nice and conservative his paper was and expressed puzzlement at the authorities' reluctance to pounce on the "mountebank" Garvey, whom he accused of utopian and socialistic preachings.

The line between surveillance and harassment of Garvey and the UNIA was a thin one. Official surveillance obviously was not an end in itself. It was merely the backdrop against which a protracted war of attrition was enacted as a result of which, over an eleven-year period, Garvey and his organizations were relentlessly harassed, culminating in the arrest, trial, imprisonment and deportation of Garvey himself.

This process started not long after Garvey's arrival in the United States. The *Negro World* of June 14, 1919, carried a Garvey account of his recent appearance before an official described as a state attorney of New York at the latter's behest. Garvey claimed that some "political grafters and conscienceless crooks" had informed the New York police authorities that the *Negro World* was responsible for mailing bombs through the post to certain persons. These charges were not proved and the informers were expelled from the UNIA.

During this same month Garvey's tribulations involving Assistant District Attorney Edwin P. Kilroe began. Out of the conflict between the two came a libel action brought against Garvey by Kilroe. A retraction followed in the *Negro World*. Kilroe later admitted that the only person he could find to testify against Garvey during his investigation of the Black Star Line was Tyler, Garvey's attempted assassin.[53] According to Garvey, Tyler announced that he was sent by Kilroe to get him before firing the shots.[54]

One of the more interesting offensives in the continuing campaign against Garvey was the attempt by the Department of State to prevent him from reentering the United States after a visit to the West Indies and Central America in 1921. For all its seriousness, the case was heavily overlaid with melodrama as Garvey and the department and its consular representatives played hide and seek all over the Caribbean for five months.

Garvey left New York in February 1921 and journeyed by train to Florida, from where he proceeded by sea to Havana, Cuba. He made a triumphant tour of Cuba and was received by the island's president.[55] From Cuba he went to Jamaica. Then the plot thickened. On March 1 the American consul in Kingston, Charles L. Latham, had informed the secretary of state in Washington that the *Daily Gleaner* announced Garvey's impending arrival. He requested instructions concerning the visaing of Garvey's passport, should he intend returning to the United States, this in view of what he considered Garvey's subversive record.[56] On March 25, the State Department despatched its reply: "In view of the activities of Garvey in political and race agitation, you are instructed to refuse him a visa and to inform at the same time the Consul at Port Antonio [Jamaica] of your action."[57] On April 11 Garvey duly presented himself at Latham's office and requested a visa to travel to the United States Canal Zone and then back to the United States. He was accompanied by Cleveland Augustus Jacques and Amy Euphemia Jacques (later his second wife), who was then secretary of the Negro Factories Corporation. All three had booked passages for the same afternoon. Latham informed Garvey that he could not grant him a visa without time for due consideration and advised him to return the following day. He issued visas to Garvey's two companions, however. All three therefore canceled their bookings for the Canal Zone and sailed the next day for Port Limón, Costa Rica, instead. Latham informed Washington of all this and of the fact that all American consular officials in Caribbean ports had been notified by mail that Garvey was not to be granted a visa.[58] More details of this notification were despatched to the State Department on April 13 from Jamaica. Washington was advised that the consul general at Panama had been telegraphed because Garvey might yet attempt to land there. In such a case the view was expressed that "he would arouse considerable racial antagonism among the negroes" in the Canal Zone and the Republic of Panama, should he succeed.[59]

Once in Costa Rica Garvey attempted, as the United States officials had predicted, to obtain a visa for Panama. Secretary of State Charles E. Hughes on April 26 informed his legation in San José, Costa Rica, by telegram that Garvey must not be granted a visa.[60] On May 2, the legation at San José replied, advising Hughes that Garvey had already left for Bocas del Toro, Panama, by the time that Hughes' communication had arrived. He had entered Panama with a visa from the Panamanian consul in Boston.[61] In Panama he was again refused entry into the United States Canal Zone. He therefore boarded a launch and set out from Panamanian territory for Colón, where he arrived in full view of the American authorities.[62]

From Panama Garvey returned to Jamaica and by May 7 American consul Latham was informing Washington that Garvey might attempt to enter the United States as a crew member of the Black Star Line's *Kanawa,* then in Cuba.[63] On May 10 a secret urgent note was despatched from Secretary of State Hughes in Washington: "Refuse visa crew list SS *Kanawha,* if Garvey's name appears thereon, unless his name is removed therefrom."[64]

Latham's perturbation increased shortly thereafter when he was informed that Garvey had shipped from Santiago de Cuba as purser without the knowledge of the American consul there. He suspected that Garvey might try to sail for Port Limón on this vessel on or about May 20 and telegraphed instructions as to preventing Garvey from shipping as a member of the crew or a passenger.[65] The secretary of state on May 20 admitted that the Department of State could not prevent Garvey from traveling to Costa Rica, but he reminded the American consul at Port Limón to refuse Garvey a visa for the United States if he should show up there.[66]

In the United States, meanwhile, a UNIA attorney had obtained a hearing at the Department of State, requesting Garvey's return on the ground that he was needed to transact Black Star Line business.[67] A week and a half after this interview, however, a memorandum from the office of the solicitor of the department was still referring to Garvey as a troublemaker and suggesting "that he should be kept out of the United States if possible," though expressing doubt about the legality of refusing a bill of health to the *Antonio Maceo (Kanawha)* as suggested by Latham, if Garvey should attempt to ship to the United States as a crew member. In such a case though, it would be sufficient to refuse to visa the crew list to ensure that all aliens would be kept on board if it arrived without a visaed crew list.[68]

Nevertheless, by this time this elaborate farce was about to play itself out. On June 22 Garvey, still in Jamaica, despatched a telegram to Secretary of State Hughes requesting that he instruct his consul to visa his passport.[69] By this time, fortunately for Garvey, a new person had assumed Latham's position in Kingston. Garvey presented this new consul on June 23 with a request from the directors of the Black Star Line in New York that his passport be visaed.[70] By some coincidence the Department of State found itself temporarily with an acting secretary of state replacing Hughes at the same time as a new face appeared at the Kingston consulate. This new combination of actors first authorized the granting of Garvey's visa on June 25 and then finally issued it to him in Kingston on June 28.[71]

Still, Garvey's problems were not yet over. On arrival in New Orleans on a banana boat by way of Guatemala, he was detained by the immigration authorities who were surprised at his valid passport and were evidently playing for time while they could devise some new scheme to hinder him further. He was finally allowed to enter the country after despatching telegrams to the president and the secretary of state on July 13, 1921.[72]

The reason for the sudden granting of Garvey's visa is not clear. Perhaps the fortuitous and simultaneous change of personnel handling his case both in Kingston and in Washington may have been the stroke of good fortune that saved him from an indefinite enforced stay outside of the United States. After his imprisonment in 1925 an immigration officer in Atlanta provided another explanation, namely that Garvey was allowed back in order that he might be proceeded against.[73]

Garvey himself, obviously not fully aware of the nature of the correspondence emanating from Washington during his exclusion concluded, and not necessarily wrongly, that his black enemies had goaded Washington into this action but that the real culprit was the consul in Kingston, Charles Latham. Being thus cast into the role of villain displeased Latham, and he complained to Washington that New York papers were carrying Garvey's opinions that it was his recourse to the Department of State that led to a reversal of Latham's intentions to prevent his reentry. Latham reminded the department of its role in the affair,[74] and his pique was understandable. Amy Jacques Garvey, discussing her husband's imprisonment in 1927, thought that the British government was implicated in the episode.[75]

Official harassment also included annual efforts to disrupt Garvey's annual conventions. He was tried for criminal libel during the first (1920) convention.[76] The Department of State effort to keep him out of the United States in 1921 almost succeeded in causing him to miss the convention for that year. He managed to obtain reentry into the country just over two weeks before the convention was due to begin. The refusal of a visa to Duse Mohamed Ali in April may possibly have been influenced by a fear that he might attend the convention. Certainly this was a motive in attempts by immigration authorities some weeks before the convention began to deny entry to UNIA potentate Gabriel M. Johnson.[77] The 1923 convention had to be canceled altogether because Garvey had been refused bail after his conviction for alleged mail fraud. On August 4, 1924, with that year's convention barely begun, a grand jury indicted Garvey for an allegedly fraudulent income tax return for 1921.[78] Garvey was arrested while presiding over the assembly but this time managed to obtain release on bail and was able to continue the convention. Special agent Amos of the Department of Justice bragged that the arrest had been a deliberate attempt to embarrass the convention.[79]

It was not uncommon for Liberty Halls to be raided by the authorities. Possibly the most serious of these episodes was one which came to be known in UNIA circles as the Chattanooga Outrage. The incident took place on August 4, 1927, when, in the words of the *Negro World,* "a mob of white devils raided a peaceful meeting of the Chattanooga, Tenn., division and killed, wounded and imprisoned several Garveyites."[80] Apparently the police had previously prohibited UNIA meetings (street meetings only, according to the *Negro World*). On the night in question the police invaded an indoor meeting. Members of the Universal African

Legions stationed at the door requested the police to produce warrants
authorizing their entry, whereupon the police refused and opened fire.
The legionnaires returned the fire. The result was a number of casualties
on both sides.[81] The Baltimore *Afro-American,* normally hostile to Garvey,
expressed its indignation at the action of these southern police. It editorialized: "The Chattanooga riot represents the typical Southern white reaction to colored organizations provided with military uniforms and weapons. In Tennessee a Negro cannot join the State Militia, but he can join
the African Guards of Garvey, and the women are recruited as Black
Cross Nurses."[82] Four UNIA members were subsequently tried and convicted on charges arising out of this incident. They were assisted by a
UNIA defense fund set up to meet the emergency.[83]

In Fort Smith, Arkansas, the charter of the local UNIA division was
seized, and seven of its officers fined and imprisoned in 1924.[84] A year
earlier, in the wake of the shooting death of ex-Garveyite J. W. H. Eason,
a Department of Justice raid took place on a mass meeting of the New
Orleans division. The New York *Amsterdam News* reported that twenty-
one persons were arrested.[85] The records of the division were seized and
a nationwide anarchistic plot among black people was supposedly un-
covered. The Department of Justice announced that it would examine all
of the two thousand to eight thousand persons they suspected were members of the New Orleans division.[86] Garvey immediately despatched a
telegram and a letter to the United States attorney general protesting
the raid and informing him that the UNIA was not only not anarchistic
but actually loyal.[87] A top national official of the UNIA, Thomas W.
Anderson, assistant secretary general, expressed the satisfaction of martyrdom felt by Garveyite victims of such raids:

> We have been to prison for the Universal Negro Improvement Asso-
> ciation, thank God! If our going to prison or even suffering death
> would advance the cause of Negro freedom, as advocated by the
> Universal, we would as willingly enter the prison cells or the vale of
> death as we would take a drink of water when thirsty.[88]

A meeting of the Charleston, South Carolina, division was invaded by
police in 1922 because members refused to furl the red, black and green
flag. The president was arrested and placed in ball and chains.[89] On Decem-

ber 8, 1921, a white police inspector addressed the Detroit, Michigan, division and apologized for a previous police assault on Liberty Hall in which some Garveyites were arrested and one, a Mr. Carry, badly beaten.[90] Garvey himself was subject to similar harassments. On tour in 1922 he had to obtain an injunction to prevent the police chief in Oakland, California, from banning his meeting, and he ran into similar trouble in Los Angeles. When he arrived in New Orleans the police prevented his first meeting from taking place, and Garvey once more had to resort to an injunction. The meeting took place the following night with 2,500 people inside the Longshoremen's Hall and 4,000 outside. The police chief and several dozen officers lined themselves up in front of the platform facing Garvey. Undaunted, Garvey launched into an attack on the chief, who promptly threatened to lock him up. Garvey thereupon ordered the chief to sit down. "For the first time," Garvey commented a few weeks later, "we made a Southern police chief eat his own words and sit down in the heart of the South."[91]

The official campaign against Garvey reached into his private life. Garvey charged that the prosecution for his mail fraud trial had brought his divorced first wife, "one Amy Ashwood, who sometimes uses the name of Amy Ashwood Garvey," as he put it, back into the country, even waiving some immigration procedures, to enlist her aid in an anti-Garvey campaign.[92]

In the period while Garvey was courting prior to each of his two marriages, enterprising persons came up with the idea that he could be charged under some immorality statute such as the Mann Act (which prohibited the interstate transportation of women for immoral purposes). In 1919, a few months prior to his marriage to Amy Ashwood, an anonymous writer to the Department of Justice had suggested he be charged with violating the Mann Act since Ashwood had accompanied him on tour across state lines.[93] The United States consul in Kingston, Charles Latham, made a similar suggestion to the Department of State concerning his then secretary Amy Jacques, a mere month after Garvey had slipped away from him and reentered the United States in 1921.[94] In July of that same year a telegram to the Department of State originating in New York had again mentioned the Mann Act as a possible means of proceeding against Garvey because of his courtship of Amy Jacques.[95] Garvey himself was aware of such schemes.[96]

The post office, a long-standing tool in the fight against radicals, some-times figured in the official struggle against Garvey. In 1919 a copy of the British espionage report, "Unrest Among the Negroes," was forwarded by the Department of State to the postmaster-general for any action the latter might deem advisable.[97] In that year Assistant Attorney General R. P. Stewart and J. Edgar Hoover also suggested the use of post office laws against Garvey.[98]

But Garvey's tribulations at the hands of the post office continued and in some respects even escalated after his deportation in 1927. Toward the end of 1928 it was reported that the postal authorities were investigat-ing what was described as a census of the Afro-American population. Garvey was said to be directing this census from Jamaica and 40,000 letters were said to have already been sent out.[99] Shortly thereafter a group of persons signing themselves "Sufferers" wrote to the attorney general requesting that a stop be put to monies destined for Garvey since he was still, in their opinion, fraudulently fleecing black people in the United States.[100]

It was not until 1932, though, that the postal authorities finally clamped down on Garvey's mail. On May 28 a postmaster in Yonges Is-land, South Carolina, wrote the Post Office Department at Charleston, South Carolina, stating that for the previous four to six weeks a large amount of first-class mail had been coming in. It was all addressed to "negroes" and in care of a gentleman who did "not do any manual labor" but made a living as an organizer "among the more ignorant negroes in their various societies."[101] A remarkably rapid correspondence ensued between Yonges Island, Charleston and Washington, D.C., and a mere five days later the postmaster-general in Washington issued a fraud order by virtue of which all of Garvey's mail was to be stamped "fraudulent" and returned to Jamaica undelivered. Also, no money orders intended for Garvey or any of his concerns was to be issued, certified or paid.[102] Garvey had on this occasion indeed unknowingly infringed the rules since some of the offending letters contained raffle tickets, which could not be mailed without official permission. As always, Garvey and his supporters in the United States embarked on the accustomed path of protest letters to the authorities, since the ban involved all mail to and from Garvey. The order was finally revoked two years later, in April 1934.[103]

The means by which the United States was finally able to remove Garvey from the American scene once and for all was through the mechanism of the courts, and more specifically through the celebrated mail fraud trial in New York in 1923. The conviction handed down at this trial was affirmed by the United States Circuit Court of Appeals in 1925. This case was the most important but by no means the only one involving Garvey in the United States. From fairly early in his American period, he and his concerns were practically continuously involved in litigation of some sort or another. There were libel suits, some against him, some initiated by him. There were divorce suits and countersuits involving Amy Ashwood Garvey. There were suits brought by the Black Star Line against those who had defrauded the corporation. There were numerous suits brought by Black Star Line and other employees for arrears of pay. There was the income tax case which was not officially declared nolle prosequi until 1932. There were cases against former employees for embezzlement or other dishonesty. Garvey had no friend in the courts, as almost all these cases were determined in a manner unfavorable to him.[104]

The 1923 case marked the denouement in the long struggle between the United States and Garvey. The trial began one year after Garvey had been arrested on the charge of using the mails to defraud in connection with promotion of the Black Star Line.[105] Garvey had initially been indicted alone, after which the books and records of the Black Star Line and the UNIA had been seized by the authorities. The prosecution had used the lists of stockholders thusly obtained to send out circulars soliciting complaints against the corporation. Garvey complained that *Negro World* subscribers also mysteriously began receiving rival black newspapers at this time. Upon realizing that the Black Star Line was a corporation rather than a private firm, the government withdrew the original indictment against Garvey alone and substituted two new ones, naming Garvey as president, Orlando Thompson as vice-president, Elie Garcia as secretary, and George Tobias as treasurer respectively. This was apparently nothing more than a procedural move to safeguard the prosecution's case from dismissal on a technicality. Garvey was quite obviously the target, and his three co-defendants were eventually acquitted.

The case attracted much sensational publicity. Garvey himself attracted much of this when, very early in the trial he accused his lawyer of counsel-

ing a deal inimical to his client's best interests. Garvey fired his lawyer
at this point and thereafter defended himself, often in flamboyant fashion.
    The case itself was marked by many irregularities, all working against
Garvey. Right at the beginning Garvey made application to the trial judge,
Julian Mack, to disqualify himself on the grounds that he was a member
of or contributor to the NAACP. This organization, of course, was hostile
to Garvey, and its organ, the *Crisis,* had devoted much space to attacks
on Garvey. Many of its high-ranking members had for many months been
holding public meetings as part of a "Marcus Garvey Must Go" campaign
and had actually written the attorney general of the United States asking
him to get rid of Garvey.[106] Judge Mack admitted his connection with
the NAACP but did not consider himself biased thereby and denied the
motion. Again, under cross-examination by Garvey, a government witness,
Schuyler Cargill, who claimed to have worked for the Black Star Line
from 1919 to 1921, could not name a single fellow employee or the
timekeeper during this period. He even admitted in answer to questions
by Garvey and the judge, that he had been told by the prosecutor to
testify to these dates of employment. When this witness could not give
the location of the College Station post office where he claimed to have
regularly mailed Black Star Line letters, he admitted having been told
to give his testimony by Post Office Inspector Shea. Prosecution witnesses
in general were characterized as "for the most part dishonest, dismissed
and disgruntled ex-employees" of Garvey.[107] Garvey's case was further
prejudiced by the appearance in New York newspapers during the duration
of the trial of unsubstantiated stories of threatening letters being sent to
the judge, prosecutor and jury. The prosecutor, for his part, concluded
his remarks to the jury with the plea, "Gentlemen, will you let the tiger
loose?" The tiger, of course, was Garvey. The co-defendants were ignored.
    The two indictments contained thirteen counts and alleged a scheme
to defraud by means of sending certain letters through the mail. Some
counts also alleged a conspiracy on the part of the defendants to implement the same scheme. Garvey was convicted on only one count, namely
that for the purpose of furthering his scheme, he caused to be sent, on or
about December 13, 1920, "a certain letter or circular enclosed in a post-
paid envelope addressed to 'Benny Dancy, 34 W. 131 St.' " in New York
City. The prosecution produced an empty envelope bearing the Black Star

Line stamp and claimed that a particular letter promoting the Black Star
Line had been posted in it. Dancy, a Pennsylvania Station cleaner, testified that government agents had come to his house and he had handed
over the envelope to them there. He could not remember what had been
in that particular envelope though he often received mail from the Black
Star Line, the UNIA, and the Negro Factories Corporation. Some of
this mail he did not read, but some of what he read, he was sure "said
invest more money in the Black Star Line for the case [sic] of purchas-
ing bigger ships and so forth."

Garvey's lawyers, in setting forth their grounds for appeal, summarized
their objections to the Dancy evidence and to the case and verdict in
general as follows:

> And when we seek to understand how it was that the jury, by some
> inexplicable, absurd process found that Garvey was guilty of mailing
> a circular or letter to Dancy, when there was not in the evidence any
> such circular or letter, and when there was not in the evidence any
> means by which the circular or letter could be identified, and when
> the sole exhibit consisted of an envelope, that did not even appear to
> have been addressed by Garvey, or through his procurement, then we
> feel fully justified in stating that the verdict was unjust, that it was
> the result of speculation, if not of passion or prejudice.[108]

With the conclusion of the trial Garvey was on June 21 given the
maximum sentence of five years plus a thousand dollar fine. He was also
ordered to pay the entire cost of the trial. The trial had been a long one,
and this fact had apparently added to the judge's irritation, since he had
other business to attend to. At the close of the second week Judge Mack
had requested the attorneys for both sides to speed up proceedings so
that he could charge the jury at the end of the third week since he wanted
to attend an international Jewish convention in Chicago. Garvey's response was to jump up and shout, "What? And jeopardize the liberty
and freedom of Marcus Garvey!"[109]

Garvey's problems did not end with his conviction. Despite his notice
of appeal, he was lodged in the Tombs prison and was denied bail. Prosecutor Mattuck further argued that if even bail were set it should be in a

high amount, since UNIA monies were being used to purchase guns and
ammunition for the Universal African Legions, who would go to any
means necessary to secure Garvey's release.[110]

Garvey's followers spared no pains in their efforts to secure his release
on bail. A Marcus Garvey Committee on Justice was immediately set
up. Some of its members journeyed to the Department of Justice to request bail for Garvey. During their discussions with department officials,
Attorney General W. G. Crim became irritated and expressed the desire
to see a quick appeal so that Garvey could be sent to the federal jail in
Atlanta.[111] When bail was finally allowed after three months, it was set
in the high figure of $15,000. The extra three-months incarceration pend-
ing bail was not afterward deducted from Garvey's five-year sentence.[112]
Even after bail was granted Garvey's supporters were still faced with unusual frustrations, for no bonding companies would handle Garvey's bail
and the money had to be raised in cash.[113] In a further effort to harass
the UNIA, the bail was forfeited by prosecutor Mattuck in February
1925 when he issued a bench warrant for Garvey and had him arrested
at the 125 Street station in Manhattan.[114] Garvey was on his way from
Detroit to surrender to the authorities after being informed by telegram
that his appeal had been lost. He had been caught unawares because the
appeal had suddenly been brought forward from the previously intimated
date. The arrest and forfeiture of bail took place despite an agreement
between Garvey's lawyer and the district attorney that Garvey was on his
way to surrender and would be produced on the following morning.[115]
The forfeited bail money was returned only after several more months
of legal battles.[116]

Garvey's conviction received its ultimate seal of finality when the
supreme court in March 1925 refused to review his case.[117] Of this whole
legal episode, Garvey's counsel (whom he had retained to advise him
after he assumed his own defense during the 1923 trial) remarked, "In
my twenty-three years of practice at the New York Bar, I have never
handled a case in which the defendant has been treated with such manifest unfairness and with such a palpable attempt at persecution as this
one."[118]

With this resolution of his appeal Garvey was despatched to the federal
penitentiary in Atlanta, never to return to New York. But even the ques-

tion of which prison he should go to involved behind-the-scenes official deliberation. After passing sentence Judge Mack had agreed to a change of prison from Atlanta to Leavenworth in Kansas if possible, since the southern prison might be unbearable for somebody of Garvey's reputation. Garvey himself expressed a preference for Leavenworth. The court was advised that special authority would have to be sought from the attorney general, and such authority was requested. Washington denied the request on the grounds that it stated as its only reason the fact of Garvey's color.[119]

With Garvey in Atlanta, a defense committee was quickly formed, and from the time of his incarceration until his eventual deportation in 1927 an intense pressure was brought to bear on United States officialdom for his release. UNIA branches from all over the world despatched thousands of petitions, letters, resolutions, telegrams and the like to various government departments and to the president of the United States requesting Garvey's release without deportation. Mass rallies were held in Harlem and elsewhere. Many black churches regularly celebrated "Marcus Garvey Sunday" when prayers were offered for his release. Many black, and some white newspapers lent their editorial columns to protests against the irregular aspects of the trial and the need for justice to be seen to be done. The UNIA sent delegations to various officials, including one to Pardon Attorney James A. Finch.[120] At headquarters Liberty Hall, Garvey's chair was left empty at meetings with his robes of office draped over it. Some middle-of-the-road black intellectuals denounced Garvey's imprisonment as politically motivated. Dean Kelly Miller of Howard University wrote, "It is a dangerous principle to impose legal punishment upon men for their belief rather than for their behavior. This trick is as old as political cunning and chicanery. . . . Did they not treat Socrates, Jesus and John Brown so?"[121] Professor W. H. H. Hart of the Howard University law school showed that Garvey was wrongly incarcerated.[122] Even some of Garvey's bitterest enemies, such as William Pickens of the NAACP, had second thoughts in the light of the injustice which had been perpetrated. To cap it all, in January 1927 nine of the twelve jurors who had returned the verdict of guilty against Garvey signed a declaration stating that Garvey had been sufficiently punished. (Two of the jurors could not be located and one declined.) One juror, Martin J. Cregan,

admitted that he had held out for a long time in the jury room against
convicting Garvey. He had preferred convicting co-defendant Orlando
Thompson instead but was eventually dissuaded by his fellow jurors.[123]

Garvey, of course, agreed concerning the political nature of his conviction. While still lodged in the Tombs prison in 1923 he declared, "I
am here because I dared to tell the Negro that the time has come for
him to lift up his head and be a man."[124] He never ceased referring to
his trial as a frame-up by the United States government because of his
influence.[125] In February 1925 he solicited the aid of Senator James E.
Watson for a review of the inequities in his case, adding, "It will make
interesting American history." The senator took the matter up with the
Department of Justice but was informed that there was no basis for
Garvey's complaint.[126] Garvey also despatched applications for executive
clemency in 1925, 1926 and 1927.[127]

In jail, meanwhile, the authorities tried to shield Garvey from the
curious, such as a stranger who wanted to interview him for a book he
was writing; from his enemies, such as the Baltimore *Afro-American,*
which requested information on what work was assigned to Garvey,
what kind of food he was eating, etc., no doubt for yet another sensational article; and from his more solicitous friends, who requested a
medical certificate showing Garvey's current health condition.[128]

The most important consequence of Garvey's trial and conviction, in
terms of the protracted struggle waged against him by the United States
government, was that it finally cleared the way for his deportation. In
1921 the government had almost succeeded in keeping Garvey out of
the country, and official circles had been considering ways and means
of getting rid of him through deportation even before that. As early as
August 1919 Assistant Attorney General R. P. Stewart transmitted an
anonymous letter he had received informing on Garvey's allegedly unlawful
activities to the secretary of labor inquiring whether any action could be
taken under the immigration laws. The Department of Labor promised
to look into the matter.[129]

Garvey's narrow escape from unofficial deportation in 1921 had
brought home to him in a most pertinent manner the vulnerability of
his position as a British subject. Immediately upon re-entry into the
United States he had, therefore, obtained his first citizenship papers in
New York City and looked forward to obtaining his full citizenship two

years later.[130] But before his citizenship could become final he was arrested, indicted, tried and convicted. The result of all this was that with a crime involving "moral turpitude" now against his name, he was not only hindered in his bid to obtain full citizenship, but became immediately exposed to the danger of deportation. Thus Garvey argued in an application for pardon in June 1925 that not only had he been framed on the mail fraud charge, but that the 1924 income tax charge had been introduced as a standby in case the mail fraud case should fail. And if they both failed, Garvey thought that he would still be charged with immorality under the Mann Act or anything else that could render him deportable.[131]

The official attempt to move against Garvey before he could become a United States citizen was facilitated by the simultaneous clamor for his deportation raised by his black detractors from the "Marcus Garvey Must Go" campaign. Chandler Owen, for example, in 1922 sought to distinguish between his magazine's objections to the deportation of foreign-born European radicals on the one hand, and its advocacy of deportation for Garvey, by arguing that radicals should only be against the deportation of class war prisoners, which Garvey, in his opinion, was not. He then examined several clauses of the immigration laws to show their applicability to Garvey. The laws rendered deportable "Persons who are directly or indirectly members of or affiliated with any organization entertaining and teaching disbelief in or opposition to organized government." He argued that Garvey's dialogue with the Ku Klux Klan qualified him here. Garvey also qualified, in his opinion, under a clause relating to people likely to become a public charge, in view of his Black Star Line dealings. Again, the law referred to "all idiots, imbeciles, feeble-minded persons" and the like. Here, too, he thought that Garvey would qualify.[132]

Accordingly, no sooner was Garvey's conviction upheld on appeal in 1925 than the government made known its intention to deport him after the expiry of his jail term.[133] Shortly after his arrival in Atlanta he was brought before the immigration authorities there for a hearing as a result of which a warrant of deportation was issued against him, ready to be executed whenever he should be released from jail.[134]

The question of the legality of Garvey's deportation is shrouded in considerable uncertainty. According to immigration authorities Garvey was deported (on December 2, 1927) on the following grounds:

That he was a person likely to become a public charge at the time of his entry; and

That, subsequent to May 1, 1917, he has been sentenced to imprisonment for a term of one year or more because of conviction in this country of a crime involving moral turpitude commited within five years after entry, to wit: using the mails to defraud.[135]

This was nothing but a recitation of the provisions of the relevant statute. Garvey's date of entry into the country was given here as 1921, which did not make too much sense since the crime he was accused of having committed was allegedly committed in December 1920, even though he was not arrested until 1922. Thus, according to this statement the crime was committed not within five years of entry but before entry. The 1921 date, of course, was the date of last entry, Garvey having initially entered in 1916.

Perhaps because he considered his deportation inevitable, Garvey seems not to have offered any objections during the deportation hearings in March 1925, even though he testified on that occasion.[136] This is borne out by his willingness, expressed in the following month, to waive his right to remain in the country although under protest since he was sure he was not in a legally deportable category. He wrote on this occasion (as part of an application for clemency):

> That I am cognizant of the fact that I do not fall under the deportable statute, yet for the purpose of satisfying my enemies who are politically powerful enough to frame, indict and convict me without ordinary hope of redress and for showing my willingness to obey the laws as interpreted by those in authority, I have waived my rights to contest, beyond the allotting of a reasonable time for me to straighten out all my many business affairs in the interest of my race in America, by signifying my willingness to leave the country, the land of the Pilgrims and of Liberty. . . .[137]

He wrote in similar vein to the pardon attorney in December 1925, giving ill health (asthma) as the reason for his renewed application. He noted that his earlier application for clemency had been refused and had not been submitted to the president. Since, he said, he heard that he was to

be deported he would leave on his own accord if given two weeks to
gather his belongings and remove his family. "This I respectfully request,"
he stated, "so as to save the further humiliation of arrest by the Department of Labor and deportation as a criminal to my home where I have
never committed crime and where my character is unimpeached."[138]
Yet by late 1926 we find him complaining that since he has been in jail
his enemies visited the Department of Labor to press for his deportation.[139]

Garvey's uncertainty over what position to adopt concerning his deportation was matched by a similar uncertainty in at least some official quarters.
In January 1926 Attorney General John Sargent briefed the president on
Garvey's application for commutation of sentence. He pointed out that
Garvey, as an alien, was ineligible for parole and was in any case under a
deportation order. Assistant United States Attorney Mattuck, the prosecutor in the mail fraud case, was still, Sargent wrote, opposed to deportation. Judge Mack, however, was not opposed to commutation with deportation, but not before Garvey should have served two years of actual imprisonment. The attorney general then went on to state his own very unique objections to deportation:

> Garvey undoubtedly holds today an important and controlling influ-
> ence over many thousands of the Negro Race in the United States,
> and while it may be that his further imprisonment will result in dis-
> satisfaction to a greater or less extent, his release and deportation
> would by no means eliminate him as a menace. While a prisoner, his
> activities are subject to control, but with unrestricted freedom in
> another country to continue his propaganda, he might become even
> a greater menace to his own race and to society generally.[140]

He counseled denial of Garvey's application. His argument is rendered
doubly interesting by the fact that the British acting governor of Jamaica,
Garvey's own country, shortly afterward inquired of the Foreign Office
in London whether it would be feasible to ask the American authorities
not to deport Garvey back to Jamaica, presumably because he feared
the effect that Garvey would have on that island. The Foreign Office
thought that any such representations would serve no useful purpose.[141]

However, with the chorus of voices clamoring for Garvey's release
building up to a crescendo, the attorney general was ready to change his

mind by 1927. In a memorandum to President Coolidge dated November 12, 1927, he counseled immediate commutation together with deportation. This time his advice was based on the "most unusual" and "by no means . . . healthy condition of affairs" induced by the Garvey case. He pointed out to the president that far from the imprisonment of Garvey serving as a deterrent to wrongdoing, the black population saw his continued incarceration as "an act of oppression of the race in their efforts in the direction of race progress." He pointed out that his advice would have been different were Garvey to remain in the United States.[142] So whereas in 1926 he had been fearful of the influence which Garvey might continue to have from abroad, by 1927 the attorney general considered the situation caused in the United States by Garvey's continued incarceration so critical that it was imperative to get him out of the country immediately. President Coolidge accordingly commuted Garvey's sentence on November 18, 1927. The official wording of the relevant parts of the document was as follows:

> Whereas it has been made to appear to me that the ends of justice have been sufficiently met in this case by the imprisonment already served: I, Calvin Coolidge, do hereby commute the sentence of the said Marcus Garvey to expire at once.[143]

Under normal circumstances Garvey's sentence would have expired on October 14, 1928, with good conduct.[144]

Despite the fact that the President commuted the sentence on November 18 "to expire at once," it was not until November 21 that the pardon attorney got around to writing the warden of the prison to this effect. He enclosed the original warrant of commutation but told the warden not to deliver it until the immigration authorities called to take charge of Garvey for deportation.[145] The warrant of commutation, of course, made no mention of deportation. Garvey meanwhile remained in jail totally ignorant of the fact that his sentence had several days previously expired "at once," and indeed several months after his release he seems to have believed that it was commuted on November 24, even though he claimed not to have been notified until even after that date.[146]

While Garvey was being held in jail despite the commutation, his wife and lawyers were making feverish attempts to obtain at least a temporary

respite for him to settle his affairs in New York. Armin Kohn, Garvey's
lawyer, recalled his efforts in a long letter to Mrs. Amy Jacques Garvey.[147]
On February 24, 1927, Kohn and Mrs. Garvey journeyed to Washington,
D.C., where on February 25 Kohn, in the presence of Mrs. Garvey, presented arguments before Attorney General Sargent for the commutation
of Garvey's sentence. This was followed by a long conference with Mr.
Finch, the pardon attorney. A supplemental brief was submitted to
Finch on behalf of Garvey. The following day Kohn submitted yet another brief to Finch. Yet Kohn's first intimation of the president's November 18 commutation came on November 23 when evening papers carried the story.

   Kohn thereupon despatched a telegram to Atlanta penitentiary asking
for further information. He was referred to the Immigration Department,
to which he despatched a telegram which remained unanswered. He nevertheless presented himself a few days later at a hearing of the Board of
Review of the Department of Labor, Immigration Division. There he was
able to peruse the files on the Garvey case. Among the material in the
files was a telegram from the Commissioner of Immigration at New York
advising that Garvey's port of departure be changed from New York to
New Orleans. The files showed also that on November 25 (a day or two
previously) the Immigration Department had reconsidered a previous
decision to release Garvey on a thousand dollars bail. Instead they would
detain him for immediate deportation.

   Later that same day Kohn presented his arguments to the board of
review. The chairman of the board replied that he could not release Garvey
on bail because the president's commutation was dependent on immediate
deportation. (Kohn did not yet know that the warrant of commutation
did not in fact bear any such proviso.) Kohn's letter continued, "After a
lengthy pro and con, in which it appeared that the Chairman of the Board
was the attorney arguing in opposition to the application, a decision upon
the application was reserved." This appeared to be a delaying tactic and
Kohn objected, apparently in vain. He therefore hurried to New Orleans
hoping to lodge a writ of habeas corpus and argue against the government's
right to deport Garvey. His argument would be based on the fact that
Garvey's residence in the United States should date from 1917 [sic] rather
than 1921 as the government alleged. He would argue that Garvey in
1921 had been issued a green tax clearance receipt stating that he would

be returning soon. This, Kohn would argue, was tantamount to acceptance as a resident alien, and thus Garvey's return did not constitute reentry within the meaning of §4298 1/3 of the United States Revised Statutes which provided, inter alia, that an alien resident of five years or less was deportable upon commission of a crime. He would argue that since Garvey had arrived in the United States in 1917 and was convicted six years later in 1923, he was not within the provisions of this law. Kohn does not seem to have addressed himself to the fact that Garvey's alleged crime was in fact committed in 1920, well within the five-year period based on 1917, even though the conviction came in 1923; or, for that matter, the contrary consideration which may have reduced the government's case to an absurdity, namely that if, as they alleged, Garvey's entry into the country could only date from 1921, and if the five-year period began with that date, then the crime would have been commited before entry.

Presumably on his way to Louisiana, Kohn stopped in Atlanta and visited Garvey where he was held at a United States Immigration station. For some strange reason Garvey decided against the habeas corpus attempt because he did not want to obstruct the Immigration Department. This action may possibly be explained by the fact that both Garvey and Kohn still thought that the warrant of commutation was explicitly contingent upon deportation. In fact immediately prior to his deportation he did despatch telegrams of protest to the president and the secretary of labor.[148] He may possibly already have boarded the ship at New Orleans when he despatched these telegrams, for he explained a few months later that it was only then that he learned the true conditions of his commutation.[149]

With Garvey against the habeas corpus procedure, Kohn decided that his last chance lay in persuading the "authorities at Washington to voluntarily and without court order give Garvey a reasonable respite" to visit New York and settle his affairs. So he left Atlanta immediately for Washington, where he argued his case before Judge Smeltzer at the Department of Labor. The judge refused a short release on bail, citing the alleged presidential deportation stipulation. Kohn next headed for the Department of Justice where he met with no success. What happened next is best related in his own words:

However, at this office, the writer saw the copy of the commutation
of the President and not a single word is set out in that commutation
for deportation. In other words, the commutation of sentence is a
clear-cut unconditional commutation and is not, as was stated repeatedly by various officials in the Immigration Department, subject to immediate deportation.

The authorities, of course, were fully aware of their deception. A
"Memorandum In Re Marcus Garvey" lodged in the files of the office of
the pardon attorney and dated December 14, 1927, explains that the commutation was indeed unconditional but points out that Garvey, in an application for clemency, had expressed his desire to leave voluntarily after some
time to arrange his affairs in New York. The memorandum concluded,
however, that the deportation was effected "by operation of law" rather
than through the president or the Department of Justice.[150] Presumably
this was a reference to deportation for crime committed within the five-
year period.

The question remains as to why the Immigration Department lied to
Kohn if the "operation of law" would have secured Garvey's deportation
in any event. The answer may be that they were not unaware of possible
flaws in the "operation of law" argument, based as it was on the possibly
unsound premise that Garvey had entered the United States in 1921
rather than in 1916. Had Kohn seen the warrant of commutation in time
there might well have ensued a lengthy legal battle, during all of which
time Garvey would have been free. Such freedom may have been in time
to arrest the splits which were beginning to develop within the UNIA.
Certainly, in view of the mantle of martyrdom (which Garvey knew to
exploit so well) and in view of the broadly based support for his release,
he might have pushed the UNIA in America on to deeds rivaling its early
years.

One point worth making, however, from the point of view of officialdom, is that the presidential commutation, though devoid of any reference to deportation, was not necessarily any indication of presidential
opposition to deportation, since the president had been advised by the
attorney general that commutation plus immediate deportation was the
best course. Still, it would appear that by taking no chances and lying

about the warrant of commutation, the authorities bought barely enough
time to get Garvey out without what would have been a much more formidable fight. So that in 1927 the United States succeeded as narrowly in
deporting Garvey as he himself had possibly narrowly succeeded in reentering the country in 1921.

Attempts to enable Garvey to reenter the country were made throughout the rest of his life, up to shortly before his death.[151] A report of 1929
stated that a black Chicago congressman, Oscar de Priest, and Robert L.
Ephriam, president of the Chicago UNIA, had met together with others
to discuss the possibility of bringing Garvey back to the United States.
Garvey at about the same time said that he would not want to return to
the United States except as a private citizen, since rotten United States
politics had been a source of great trouble to him.[152] In 1931 the *Negro
World* started a campaign to gather 100,000 signatures to support a petition for Garvey's return. The move was opposed by veteran black anti-
Garveyist George S. Schuyler and the conservative *New York Age,* which
thought that Garvey's return would be a calamity.[153] In January 1935
Garvey himself wrote the secretary of state and the attorney general informing them that he wished to spend thirty-five days in transit in New
York on his way to England. He wished to obtain medical treatment for
diabetes and to see friends while there.[154] For several months in 1934
and 1935 the secretary of the Philadelphia UNIA sent a steady stream of
letters to President Roosevelt, the Department of Justice and the Department of Labor's Immigration and Naturalization Service asking for Garvey's
return in spite of his conviction, or, failing that, that his conviction be set
aside to facilitate his return. He was met by stony official assurances that
Garvey's conviction for a crime involving "moral turpitude" made him
mandatorily excludable. He therefore found it necessary to remind the
assistant attorney general who was answering his correspondence that
"regardless of whether Mr. Garvey be allowed to return, the programme
will still go on, for Africa shall still be redeemed even if the Divine Creator
has to raise up supermen in our stead; or use the elements in our behalf
as in the days of Pharoah. . . ." However, neither his assurances that Garvey
had been framed nor the reminder that black people had voted Democrat
nor anything else could make any impression on official stoniness.[155]

Other elements within the UNIA kept up the effort, however, and in
1937 consideration was even given to having a special bill introduced if

all else failed.[156] Out of these attempts in 1937 and 1938 arose the Second Regional Conference Committee on Mr. Marcus Garvey's Visit to America, chaired by Thomas W. Harvey. This committee sought a temporary permit which would allow Garvey to remain in the United States from June 1 to August 31 in order to hold an international convention from August 1 to 17. These efforts also failed, despite the assistance of Senator Bilbo and some of his fellow segregationists, and despite the blessing of Garvey himself.[157] Representations were still being made to government officials in the latter part of 1939, but by this time Garvey was less than a year away from his grave. Only death could extinguish the hopes of his faithful followers in the United States that he might yet one day return to rescue them from their misery.

NOTES

1. J. E. Hoover, "Memorandum for Mr. Ridgely," October 11, 1919, RG 60, 198940, National Archives.
2. *Daily Worker,* August 18, 1924.
3. Marcus Garvey, *Conspiracy of the East St. Louis Riots* (New York: UNIA, 1917), p. 2.
4. E.g., Memorandum on black radicals, August 1920, National Civic Federation Papers, Box 152, New York Public Library.
5. A. Mitchell Palmer, "Radicalism and Sedition Among the Negroes," in *Investigation Activities of the Department of Justice* (Washington, D.C.: Government Printing Office, 1919), p. 163.
6. *Revolutionary Radicalism, Report of the Joint Legislative Committee Investigating Seditious Activities, Filed April 24, 1920, In the Senate of the State of New York* (Albany, N.Y.: J. B. Lyon, 1920), p. 1476.
7. Consul Latham to Secretary of State, August 24, 1921, RG 59, 811.108 G 191/24.
8. Garvey, *Conspiracy,* pp. 2-3.
9. *Revolutionary Radicalism,* p. 1514.
10. E.g., *Negro World,* February 2, 1924.
11. Amy Jacques Garvey, ed., *The Philosophy and Opinions of Marcus Garvey* (London: Frank Cass, 1967), II: 110-117.
12. Garvey to Hughes, May 3, 1922, William H. Beck, private secretary to Hughes, to Garvey, May 13, 1922, RG 59, 811.108 G 191/28.

13. *Blackman,* September 4, 1929.

14. Garvey, *Philosophy and Opinions,* II: 406.

15. Marcus Garvey, *Speech at Royal Albert Hall* (London: Poets and Painters Press [1968?]), pp. 13-14.

16. Told to the author by Amy Jacques Garvey (Kingston, Jamaica, 1972). This tactic was by no means unusual and has been documented in the case of the Lusk committee. See J. M. Pawa, "Black Radicals and White Spies: Harlem, 1919," *Negro History Bulletin* 35 (October 1972): 130.

17. *Negro World,* January 7, 1928.

18. "For Payment to Woolsey W. Hall for Reporting Proceedings," extract from "Hearings before Subcommittee on Appropriations . . . First Deficiency Appropriation Bill for 1921," p. 630, January 10, 1921, Sims Ely, Chief Clerk and Administrative Assistant to Secretary of Treasury, February 21, 1923, RG 60, 198940.

19. W. H. Cowles, Chief MI 4, War Department, Office of the Chief of Staff, Washington, to the Secretary of the Treasury (Division of Appointments), August 29, 1922, RG 60, 198940.

20. A. L. Flint, Chief of Office, The Panama Canal, Washington Office, to the Chief, Bureau of Investigation, Department of Justice, October 9, 1919, RG 60, 198940.

21. J. E. Hoover, "Memorandum for Mr. Ridgely," RG 60, 198940.

22. Minute on report on Garvey, September 15, 1920, FO 371/4567, Foreign Office Records; Foreign Office to Colonial Office, October 1, 1920, CO 318/358, Colonial Office Records, Public Record Office, London.

23. William J. Burns, Director, Bureau of Investigation, Department of Justice, to Frank Burke, Director, Bureau of Investigation, United States Shipping Board, August 31, 1921, Burke to A. J. Frey, Vice-President in Charge of Operation, interoffice memorandum, September 1, 1921, RG 32, 605-1-653.

24. Resume of memorandum from Director, Bureau of Investigation, to Assistant Attorney General Crim [the memo is "restricted" and is not in the file], and Assistant Attorney General, United States, to Attorney for State of New York, March 27, 1922, RG 60, 198940.

25. Garvey, *Philosophy and Opinions,* II: 242-259.

26. Director, Bureau of Investigation, to Assistant Attorney General Luhring, November 6, 1926, enclosing report of special agent at New York City of October 26, 1926 [only a brief resume is in the file, since it is "restricted"], H. C. Heckman, Administrative Assistant to John W.

Snook, Warden, U.S. Penitentiary, Atlanta, Snook to Heckman, Assistant Superintendant of Prisons [sic], Department of Justice, Washington, D.C., November 16, 1926, Garvey to Snook, ca. November 16, 1926 [date hidden by file binding], RG 60, 198940.

27. Robert F. Kelley, Division of Eastern European Affairs, Department of State, to J. Edgar Hoover, Director, Bureau of Investigation, July 19, 1928, confidential, enclosing memorandum, "To Mr. Hoover, Justice," from U.S. Embassy, London, July 6, 1928, RG 59, 811.108 G 191/47.

28. Statement re delivery of documents served on the U.S. Shipping Board in re John O. Garrett vs. the U.S., May 3, 1929 (in the Court of Claims), RG 32, 605-1-653.

29. Hoover to Kelley, December 17, 1930, RG 59, 800.00B—International Negro Improvement Association of the World/4.

30. Telegram, American Embassy, Stockholm to Secretary of State, November 3, 1919, RG 59, 811.4016/28.

31. Excerpt from Despatch No. 585, "Alleged Negro Revolutionary Organization in Paris" from Ambassador Walter E. Edge, Paris, May 29, 1930, RG 60, 198940.

32. Secret document, "Unrest Among the Negroes," Special Report No. 10, Directorate of Intelligence (Home Office), Circulated by the Home Secretary, October 7, 1919, RG 59, 811.4016/27.

33. William Phillips, for the Secretary of State, to John W. Davis, American Ambassador, London, November 14, 1919, RG 59, 811.4016/27.

34. Telegram, "Davis," London, to Secretary of State, July 24, 1920, "Colby," Department of State, to American Embassy, London, July 27, 1920, RG 59, 811.108 G 191/-.

35. Telegram, U.S. Embassy, London, to Secretary of State, April 6, 1921, Secretary of State Hughes to U.S. Embassy, London, April 8, 1921, RG 59, 811.108 G 191/3, Embassy to Secretary of State, April 9, 1921, RG 59, 811.108 G 191/4. Ali was allowed in later that year. See *Crusader* 5 (November 1921): 16.

36. Secret memorandum to State Department from U.S. Embassy, London, June 16, 1928, RG 59, 811.108 G 191/51.

37. Robert Woods Bliss for Secretary of State to Joseph L. Johnson, Minister Resident and Consul General, Liberia, May 25, 1921 RG 59, 882.00/703A; also RG 84, American Legation, Monrovia—Diplomatic Correspondence, 1921, Vol. II, file no. 840; Johnson to Secretary of State, July 16, 1921, RG 59, 882.00/705.

38. C. C. Roberts, Port Superintendent Engineer, U.S. Shipping Board, Freetown, Sierra Leone, to State Department, September 15, 1924, RG 59, 648p. 00 2/1.

39. Memorandum [1930], CO 318/399/76634; *New York Times,* November 1, 8, 1928; *Negro Champion* (November 3, 1928): 8; *Negro World,* November 10, 1928.

40. *Negro World,* November 17, 1928.

41. Wesley Frost, American Consul General, Montreal, to Secretary of State, November 8, 1928, RG 59, 811.108 G 191/50.

42. E.g., Charles L. Latham, American Consul, Kingston to Secretary of State, September 12, 1920, RG 59, 811.108 G 191/1; José de Olivares, American Consul, Jamaica, to Secretary of State, September 27, 1929, RG 60, 198940; ibid., Paul C. Squire, American Consul, Jamaica, confidential, "Subject: Garvey, Marcus: Whereabouts and Activities" to Secretary of State, [1932?].

43. Henry H. Hough, Governor, U.S. Virgin Islands, to Secretary of State, February 23, 1923, Hough to President of U.S., February 24, 1923, RG 59, 811 G.00/37.

44. American Consul Henry D. Baker to Inspector Costello, Constabulary headquarters, February 16, 1920, enclosing clipping from *Argos* of February 13, RG 84, American Consulate, Port-of-Spain, 1920 Correspondence, 840.1/2052; see also, Costello to Baker, February 18, 840.1/2053, and Sgt. Sylvester to Detective Inspector, February 18, RG 84,840.1/2054.

45. Baker to Secretary of State, February 7, 1920, RG 59, 811.108/929.

46. E.g., American Consul, Port Limón to Secretary of State, August 24, 1919, RG 59, 818.4016/orig.

47. E.g., American Minister, Panama to Secretary of State, May 18, 1921, RG 59, 811.108 G 191/24.

48. Philander C. Cable, American Chargé d'Affaires ad interim, Havana to Secretary of State, September 30, 1921, RG 59, 837.504/218.

49. Cyril V. Briggs, "Lessons in Tactics," *Crusader,* 5 (November 1921): 16.

50. Etta [Marie Duchatellier] to Bruce, Panama City, January 12, 1920, Bruce Papers, Ms 189, Schomburg Collection, New York Public Library.

51. American Consul, Guatemala City, to Secretary of State, March 9, 1922, RG 59, 811.108 G 191/27.

52. National Civic Federation Papers, Box 152.

53. *Negro World,* June 19, 1920. Kilroe was giving evidence in a Garvey libel case against the *Chicago Defender.*
54. Ibid., December 8, 1923; Garvey, *Philosophy and Opinions,* II: 130, 197.
55. A. J. Garvey, *Garvey and Garveyism,* p. 58.
56. Charles L. Latham, American Consul, Kingston, to Secretary of State, March 1, 1921, RG 59, 811.108 G 191/2.
57. Wilbur J. Carr for Secretary of State to Latham, March 25, 1921, RG 59, 811.108 G 191/2.
58. Latham to Secretary of State, April 12, 1921, RG 59, 811.108 G 191/8.
59. "Gray," Kingston to Secretary of State, April 13, 1921, RG 59, 811.108 G 191/5.
60. Hughes to American Legation, San José, April 26, 1921, RG 59, 811.108 G 191/9.
61. American Legation, San José to Secretary of State, May 2, 1921, RG 59, 811.108 G 191/11.
62. A. J. Garvey, *Garvey and Garveyism,* p. 59.
63. Latham to Secretary of State, May 7, 1921, RG 59, 811.108 G 191/10.
64. Hughes to Latham, Urgent, Secret, May 10, 1921, RG 59, 811.108 G 191/10.
65. Telegram, Latham to Secretary of State, May 18, 1921, RG 59, 811.108 G 191/12.
66. Telegram, Hughes to American Consul, Kingston, May 20, 1921, Hughes to American Consul, Port Limón, telegram, May 20, 1921, RG 59, 811.108 G 191/12.
67. William C. Matthews to State Department, June 11, 1921, attention Mr. McBride, RG 59, 811.108 G 191/29. See also Affidavits, "In the Matter of Marcus Garvey Returning to the U.S., " submitted by William C. Matthews, Assistant Counsel-General, UNIA, May 9, 1921, RG 59, 811.108 G 191/33.
68. Memorandum, Department of State, Office of the Solicitor, June 21, 1921, RG 59, 811.108 G 191/31.
69. Telegram, Garvey to Hughes, June 22, 1921, RG 59, 811.108 G 191/30.
70. Heard [no first name given] to Secretary of State, June 23, 1921, RG 59, 811.108 G 191/19.
71. Ibid., Acting Secretary of State Fletcher to American Consul, Kingston; Heard to Secretary of State, June 28, 1921; Latham to Secretary of State, August 14, 1921, RG 59, 811.108 G 191/24.

72. A. J. Garvey, *Garvey and Garveyism*, p. 60; *Negro World*, August 23, 1924; Garvey, c/o Immigration Authorities, New Orleans to Hughes, July 13, 1921, telegram, RG 59, 811.108 G 191/32.

73. H.B.M. Consul, Atlanta, to H.M. Ambassador, Washington, D.C., April 3, 1925, FO 115/3027. I am indebted to Professor Ernie Mkalimoto of the University of Massachusetts for this reference.

74. Latham to Secretary of State, August 24, 1921, RG 59, 811.108 G 191/24. For Garvey's accusation against his black enemies see *Negro World*, August 23, 1924.

75. *Negro World*, August 27, 1927.

76. Ibid., August 14, 1920. Delegates raised $700 for his legal expenses.

77. Bruce to the editor of an unnamed paper, July 18, 1921, Bruce Papers, BL 9.

78. Grand Jury Indictment 38/771, U.S. vs Marcus Garvey, filed August 4, 1924, Southern District of New York, Federal Court Records, New York, FRC 539461; complaint, U.S. vs Marcus Garvey, filed March 30, 1925; *nolle prosequi*, C 38-771, May 1932.

79. Garvey, *Philosophy and Opinions*, II: 256.

80. *Negro World*, January 14, 1928.

81. Ibid., August 20, 1927; *Indianapolis Recorder*, August 29, 1927, reprinted in *Negro World*, September 3, 1927.

82. *Afro-American*, August 13, 1927, quoted in *Negro World*, August 20, 1927.

83. *Negro World*, December 24, 1927, March 3, 1928.

84. J. W. Ross to Charles E. Hughes, Secretary of State, January 8, 1925, RG 60, 198940.

85. *New York Amsterdam News*, January 24, 1923.

86. *New York Times*, January 20, 1923.

87. Telegram, Garvey to Hon. Harry M. Daugherty, U.S. Attorney General, January 22, 1923, Garvey to Daugherty, January 24, 1923, RG 60, 198940; *New York Times*, January 21, 1923.

88. *Negro World*, March 10, 1923.

89. Ibid., September 16, 1922.

90. Ibid., January 7, 1922.

91. Ibid., July 15, 1922. Three of the persons interviewed for this study were at that New Orleans meeting—Amy Jacques Garvey, J. Charles Zampty, and Queen Mother Moore. Queen Mother Moore thinks that Garveyites in the hall brandished their guns when the chief interrupted Garvey. The others do not remember this, though Zampty, who was traveling with Garvey, says that the persons guarding Garvey in his lodgings opposite Longshoremen's Hall were armed.

92. Garvey, *Philosophy and Opinions*, II: 253.

93. Anonymous to Department of Justice [August 1919?], RG 60, 198940.

94. Latham to Secretary of State, August 24, 1921, RG 59, 811.108 G 191/24.

95. William Smith, New York to Secretary of State, July 1, 1921, RG 59, 811.108 G 191/21.

96. Garvey, *Philosophy and Opinions*, II: 255.

97. "Unrest Among the Negroes," enclosure in Assistant Secretary, Department of State, to Postmaster-General, November 17, 1919, RG 28, File No. 398, Box 53, Unarranged.

98. Stewart to Secretary of Labor, October 15, 1919, RG 60, 198940.

99. *New York Times*, December 29, 1928.

100. "Sufferers" to U.S. Attorney General, ca. January 17, 1929, RG 60, 198940.

101. John W. Geraty, Postmaster, Yonges Island, S.C., to F. A. Ricky, Inspector, Post Office Department, Charleston, S.C., May 28, 1932, Ricky to Geraty, May 28, 1932, Geraty to Chief Post Office Inspector, Washington, D.C., May 1932, RG 28, Fraud Order Jacket 5929.

102. Fraud order of Postmaster-General, Walter F. Brown, June 2, 1932, fraud order to solicitor, Horace J. Donnelly, June 3, 1932, RG 28, Fraud Order Jacket 5929.

103. Ibid., Garvey to Karl A. Crowley, Solicitor, Post Office Department, Washington, D.C., March 28, 1934, and enclosed memorandum, Harlee Branch, Acting Postmaster-General, April 23, 1934; Nugent Dodds, Assistant Attorney General to Postmaster-General, January 16, 1933, RG 60, 198940; Benjamin W. Jones, Secretary of UNIA, Philadelphia to President F. D. Roosevelt, September 17, 1934, RG 60, 39-51-821.

104. For more on these cases, see, e.g., Federal Court Records, New York, FRC 536150, FRC 536137; *New York Amsterdam News*, January 24, March 14, 21, July 11, October 17, 1923, February 4, 1925.

105. Most of the following information on the trial and appeal, except where otherwise stated, is taken from "United States of America vs. Marcus Garvey: Was Justice Defeated?" Garvey, *Philosophy and Opinions*, II: 144-179.

106. Ibid., II: 293-309.

107. Ibid., p. 147.

108. Ibid., p. 169.

109. *Negro World*, September 3, 1927.

110. *Negro World*, June 30, 1923.

111. D. E. Tobias of the Marcus Garvey Committee on Justice to Augustus T. Seymour, Assistant Attorney General, July 27, 1923, RG 60, 198940.

112. *Negro World,* August 27, 1927.

113. Garvey, *Garvey and Garveyism,* p. 118.

114. *New York Times,* February 6, 1925.

115. Garvey, *Garvey and Garveyism,* p. 154.

116. Ibid., p. 155.

117. *New York Times,* March 24, 1925.

118. Garvey, *Philosophy and Opinions,* II: 150.

119. William Hayward, U.S. Attorney, New York to Attorney General, Washington, D.C., June 22, 1923, Mabel Walker Willebrandt, Assistant Attorney General to Hayward, June 28, 1923, Hayward to Attorney General, July 10, 1923, RG 60, 198940.

120. *Negro World,* May 1, 1926.

121. Ibid., September 3, 1927.

122. *New York Amsterdam News,* March 18, 1925; *Negro World,* March 28, 1925.

123. Affidavit, George Featherstone, January 14, 1927, and attached statement, RG 204, 42-793.

124. *Evening World,* June 29, 1923.

125. E.g., *Negro World,* October 27, 1928.

126. Garvey to Senator James E. Watson, February 28, 1925, H. C. Heckman, Acting Superintendent of Prisons, "Memorandum for Colonel Donovan," March 13, 1925, William J. Donovan, Assistant Attorney General to Watson, March 14, 1925, RG 60, 198940.

127. Application for executive clemency, June 5, 1925, Garvey to President Coolidge, January 17, 1927, Garvey to Attorney General John G. Sargent, January 17, 1927, RG 204, 42-793; *Negro World*, February 6, 1926.

128. A. H. Shannon to Superintendent of Prisons, October 20, 1926, W. T. Hammack, First Assistant Superintendent to Shannon, October 21, 1926, Shannon to Hammack, October 25, 1926, Perry W. Howard, Department of Justice to Attorney General, February 16, 1925; H. C. Heckman, Acting Superintendent of Prisons, "Memorandum for Mr. Martin," February 20, 1925, Eugene J. Sartorious, attorney to Attorney General, June 23, 1927, A. H. Connor, Superintendent of Prisons to Sartorius, July 1, 1927, RG 60, 198940.

129. Assistant Attorney General R. P. Stewart to Secretary of Labor, August 15, 1919, and reply from Louis Post, Assistant Secretary, Department of Labor, to Attorney General, RG 60, 198940.

130. "Petition for Pardon of Marcus Garvey," enclosed in Amy Jacques Garvey to Schomburg, Schomburg Papers, Box 3.
131. Garvey, *Philosophy and Opinions*, II: 255.
132. Chandler Owen, "Should Marcus Garvey Be Deported?" *Messenger* (September 1922): 479.
133. *New York Times*, February 3, 1925.
134. Ibid., August 3, 1925.
135. Edward J. Shaughnessy, Deputy Commissioner, Department of Labor, Immigration and Naturalization Service to Attorney General, October 17, 1934, RG 60, 39-51-821.
136. Garvey to James A. Finch, Pardon Attorney, December 24, 1925, RG 204, 42-793.
137. Garvey's application for executive clemency, June 5, 1925, RG 204, 42-793.
138. Garvey to Finch, December 24, 1925, RG 204, 42-793.
139. Garvey to J. W. Snook, Warden of Atlanta jail, ca. November 16, [date hidden by file binding] 1926, RG 60, 198940.
140. John Sargent, Attorney General, to the President, "In the Matter of the Application for Commutation of Sentence of Marcus Garvey," January 27, 1926, RG 204, 42-793.
141. Summary of destroyed correspondence of March 31, 1926, OAG/8674, summary of destroyed correspondence of May 6, 1926, Colonial Office records, Public Record Office, London, FO/8674.
142. Sargent to the President, "In the Matter of the Application for Commutation of Sentence of Marcus Garvey," November 12, 1927, RG 204, 42-793.
143. Copy of warrant of commutation in Amy Jacques Garvey Papers, Kingston, Jamaica.
144. James A. Finch, "Memo for the Attorney General," November 22, 1927, RG 204, 42-793.
145. Finch to John W. Snook, Warden, U.S. Penitentiary, Atlanta, November 21, 1927, RG 204, 42-793.
146. Garvey, *Speech at Royal Albert Hall*, p. 20.
147. Armin Kohn to Amy Jacques Garvey, December 2, 1927, copy in Amy J. Garvey papers. Also reprinted in *Negro World*, December 10, 1927 and Jamaica *Gleaner*, December 15, 1927.
148. James L. Houghteling, Commissioner of Immigration to Senator Theodore G. Bilbo, n.d. [ca. Feb. 1938], RG 60, 198940.
149. Garvey, *Speech at Royal Albert Hall*, p. 20.
150. "Memorandum In Re Marcus Garvey," December 14, 1927, RG 204, 42-793.

151. Ibid., Daniel M. Lyons, Pardon Attorney to Hon. George Gordon Battle, July 12, 1939.
152. *Blackman,* June 22, August 16, 1929.
153. *Negro World,* August 1, 1931.
154. Garvey to Secretary of State, January 7, 1935, RG 60, 198940.
155. Benjamin W. Jones, Secretary, UNIA, Philadelphia, to President F. D. Roosevelt, September 17, 1934, Edward J. Shaughnessy, Deputy Commissioner, Department of Labor, Immigration and Naturalization Service, to Attorney General, October 17, 1934, Keenan to Jones, October 22, 1934, Jones to Keenan, October 27, 1934, Jones to Roosevelt, October 27, 1934, January 4, 1935, Keenan to Jones, January 28, 1935, Jones to Keenan, June 3, 1935, and other letters in this correspondence, RG 60, 39-51-821.
156. A. L. King to Thomas Harvey, November 9, 1937, UNIA Central Division (New York) Files, Box 16, h. 10.
157. Ibid., Garvey to Harvey, January 5, 1938; Earnest Sevier Cox to Garvey, February 17, 1938, Cox to King, February 18, 1938, Bilbo to King, February 23, 1938, Harvey to King, March 31, 1938, Harvey to King, May 11, 1938, Ethel Waddell to King, December 1, 1938; Harvey to Senator George McGill, April 8, 1938, RG 60, 198940.

From Amy Ashwood Garvey Papers

THE UNIVERSAL AFRICAN LEGIONS ON PARADE

Courtesy of the African Studies Association of the West Indies

MARCUS GARVEY

BETWEEN THE FRYING PAN AND THE FIRE

NEGRO WORLD **CARTOON**

BLACK STAR LINE ADVERTISEMENT

NEGRO WORLD **CARTOON**

THE RAGAMUFFIN

NEGRO WORLD **CARTOON**

10

Garvey and the Communists

We have sympathy for the Workers Party. But we belong to the Negro party, first, last and all the time. We will support every party that supports us, and we appreciate the attention the Workers Party has given us in sending this friendly communication. But the Communists have a long time ahead of them before they can do anything for themselves in this country. When they get there we will be for them. But meantime we are for ourselves.

—Marcus Garvey[1]

We are working with the Universal Negro Improvement Association not because its President, Marcus Garvey, has improved enuf or even changed at all in the last two years to suit our view of what the American Negroes must do to win their freedom. As a matter of fact, the reason for our working with the Universal Negro Improvement Association is because we desire to win over the masses, organizationally and ideologically, following this association for the Communist program.

—Daily Worker[2]

The Russian revolution took place in 1917, one and a half years after Garvey's arrival in the United States. The Communist (or Third) Inter-

national was formed in March 1919 and was followed six months later
by the birth of the communist movement in the United States. The year
1919 was Garvey's first year as a full-fledged international headache for
white governments. After two years of persecution and factionalism, a
large portion of the American communist movement surfaced as the
Workers party in 1921. By this time Garvey was an established leader of
an unprecedented mass movement among African peoples all over the
world.

The bulk of Garvey's followers in the United States, as elsewhere, were
workers and peasants. These were the types of people upon whom the
communists would necessarily hope to build a mass movement. The
necessity of winning over the black workers and peasants would assume
even greater importance for the communists when they belatedly awoke
to the realization that the black masses, as the most exploited section of
American society, would have to occupy a critical position in their thinking if they were ever to seriously entertain any hope of overthrowing
American capitalism. But between the communists and the American
black masses stood Garvey. They tried to infiltrate the UNIA by "boring
from within," they attempted to woo and win over Garvey himself, they
tried launching frontal assaults against him in their press, they discussed
him at their meetings from Moscow to Chicago, they even tried to plagia-
rize facets of his nationalistic philosophy, but they could not prevail.
Garvey, displaying great tact and political cunning, would not be com-
promised. He usually refrained from open denunciation of the communists, but he would not be coopted.

There seems to be no evidence of black participation in the founding
of the American communist movement in 1919.[3] The program adopted
by the Communist party of America, one of the two founding factions,
nevertheless included the following paragraph: "The Negro problem is a
political and economic problem. The racial oppression of the Negro is
simply the expression of his economic bondage and oppression, each
intensifying the other. This complicates the Negro problem, but does
not alter its proletarian character."[4] This statement, with its attempt to
subordinate race to class, but with its uneasy realization that the racial
factor complicated the Negro Question, contained the basic elements in
the central dilemma which puzzled communists in their approach to black
noncommunist organizations in general and to Garvey and the UNIA in

particular. The question was not an easy one, and the difficulty faced by the communists in resolving it was understandable, especially since the analysis of these early American communists was restricted by a narrow interpretation of the orthodox Marxist doctrine of the primacy of class struggle. This rigidity in American communist analysis made difficult an objective analysis of the nationalist and racial components in a successful ideology such as Garveyism. The solution to the race problem was seen as an automatic by-product of a socialist revolution, and that was all. In 1920 the United Communist party (representing a merger between one of the 1919 factions, the Communist Labor party, and a split-off from the other faction, the Communist party of America) showed this tendency in its program. It recognized that the Afro-American population was a super-exploited one and declared,

> The United Communist Party will actively support the negroes in their desperate struggle against these hellish conditions. It points to the only possible solution of the negro problem, namely: the abolition of wage slavery through the overthrow of the capitalist State and the erection of a Communist society.

> The task of the United Communist Party is to break down the barrier of race prejudice that separates and keeps apart the white and the negro workers, and to bind them into a union of revolutionary forces for the overthrow of their common enemy.[5]

The Workers party, the "legal" manifestation of American communism which surfaced late in 1921, resolved in similar vein at its formation to show black people that "the interests of the Negro workers are identical with those of the whites."[6]

Nevertheless, by this time the first feeble recognition in communist circles that the race question affecting black people possessed a character other than a purely class one was manifested—not in America, but in Russia. At the second congress of the Communist International (Comintern) held in 1920 a white American delegate, journalist John Reed, volunteered some remarks on the national character of the Afro-American struggle. His remarks were prompted by a discussion of Lenin's ideas on "The Negroes in America," which formed part of his draft "Theses on the National and Colonial Question."[7] Reed's consideration of the national question, however, was merely to repudiate it. He said, "The Negroes have no demands for national independence. All movements aiming at a separate national existence for Negroes fail, as did the 'Back to Africa Movement' of a few years ago. They consider themselves first of all Americans at home in the United States. This makes it very much simpler for the Communists."[8]

What is interesting about Reed's opinion is that Lenin ignored it and incorporated into his final theses a statement far in advance of the position then being held by American communists. Because of the controversy which has surrounded this very brief reference it will be quoted together with the whole paragraph from which it came, as well as the paragraph which came afterwards:

> Offences against the *equality of nations* and violations of the *guaranteed rights of national minorities,* repeatedly committed by all capitalist States despite their "democratic" constitution, must be inflexibly exposed in all the propaganda and agitation carried on by the communist parties, both inside and outside parliament. But that is not enough. It is also necessary: first, to make clear all the time that only the Soviet system is able to ensure real equality for the nations because it unites first the proletarians, and then all the masses of the working people, in the struggle against the bourgeoisie; *secondly, communist parties must give direct support to the revolutionary movements among the dependent nations and those without equal rights (e.g., in Ireland, and among the American Negroes, etc.), and in the colonies.*

> Without this last particularly important condition the struggle against the oppression of the dependent nations and colonies, and the recognition of *their right to secede as separate States,* remains a deceitful pretence, as it is in the parties of the Second International.[9] [Emphasis mine.]

It seems quite clear that Lenin was referring to the Afro-American population here, if not as a nation, then at least as a national minority denied equal rights and possibly having a right to secede. That he should have taken such a position concerning Afro-Americans is not surprising since he had for some time leaned in this direction in regard to national minorities in the Soviet Union. This may well explain why Garvey could maintain an admiration for Lenin while simultaneously fighting the American communists. Lenin followed up these themes with advice to his American comrades on the urgency of the need for propaganda and organizational work among Afro-Americans.[10]

The fleeting nature of Lenin's reference to the national character of the Afro-American situation and its unavailability in translation for some time ensured that there would be no immediate follow-up of this idea. During the final session of the third congress in 1921, however, the South African delegation proposed that the executive committee should study "the Negro question or the proletarian movement among the Negroes as an important aspect of the Eastern problem."[11]

The Negro Question was accordingly considered by the fourth congress in 1922. The theses were introduced by Otto Huiswoud, a black member of the party in the United States, who operated under the pseudonym "Billings." They were adopted unanimously and revealed no change from the normal American approach. The Negro Question was seen as primarily economic, though the racial question still played an important role. Huiswoud considered the "Negro problem" to be "a vital question of the world revolution" and the cooperation of black peoples to be essential for proletarian success. He suggested a world organization of the black race which sounded suspiciously like a Garveyless UNIA.[12]

Huiswoud considered the Afro-American population to be a likely source of manpower for the counterrevolution, in the event of an uprising, not an uncommon opinion in early American communist circles, where the phrase "reserve of capitalist reaction" was once used to describe the Afro-American population.[13] An article appearing in the Soviet paper *Izvestia* two weeks before Huiswoud presented his theses expressed a similar view. The black race was here seen as "an obedient weapon" in the hands of international capitalism and hence a threat to the white proletariat.[14]

Comintern congress discussions of the Negro Question continued at the fifth congress in 1924. This time the national characteristics of the Afro-American struggle intruded into the discussions. An American delegate argued that the problem confronting Afro-Americans was psychological as well as economic and transcended class lines. It was therefore futile, he argued, to direct the same literature toward black and

white workers.[15] The program commission of the congress grappled
with this problem, too, and concluded that it was impossible to define
the concept of nation in such a way as to adequately cover every national
situation. None of this prevented American delegate John Pepper from
denouncing the Garvey movement in typically unrealistic fashion as "a
Negro-Zionist movement in America which wishes to go to Africa" despite the desire of Afro-Americans for social equality.[16]

The most concerted attempt to clarify the communist position on
the race question came at the sixth congress of the Comintern held in
Moscow in 1928. By this time Garvey had recently been deported from
the United States, and the communists, with little to show for their
previous efforts, were anxious to join the general rush for Garvey's
followers. Much of the earlier confusion manifested itself but this time
the debates culminated in the laying down of a definite policy. Stalin,
as a longstanding Soviet expert on the question of national minorities,
was largely responsible for the importance attached to the question. His
interest had apparently manifested itself as early as 1925 when he explained to a group of black students from the United States that the
American attitude to the question was all wrong. Afro-Americans, he said,
were a national minority with some of the characteristics of a nation.[17]

Preparatory work for the 1928 examination of the race question had
begun well in advance, and references to it appeared regularly from the
earliest sessions. John Pepper admitted at the very beginning that American communists had made some mistakes,[18] while another American
retracted the idea that southern black people were a reserve of capitalist
reaction.[19] Nevertheless, the views expressed in the debates varied widely.
Weinstone, a United States delegate, thought that the question could be
solved by advancing slogans of full social and political rights for Afro-
Americans.[20] *Pravda* of August 24, 1928 quoted Jones, a black United
States delegate, as saying that two tendencies had been expressed in the
Negro commission of the congress. One argued that Afro-Americans in
the United States were a racial minority, while another denied the national unity of the Afro-American and pointed to increasing class stratification within the race, especially since the World War. This delegate also
addressed himself to the suggestion for an independent Soviet-Socialist
Republic for Afro-Americans. He did not object to this idea but considered

a slogan for equal rights to be more fundamental at that particular time.[21] Afro-American James W. Ford referred to United States blacks as "an economically backward national minority, having no territory of their own." This did not prevent him from arguing that the interests of black and white workers coincided, as did those of the black and white bourgeoisie. He therefore opposed "at present any national movement among the Negroes" since it would "only be a trump in the hands of the bourgeoisie" and would "trammel the revolutionary class war of the Negro masses, and still more deepen the gulf between the whites and the oppressed groups."[22]

Out of such debate came the new Comintern line of self-determination for the black population in the "Black Belt" of the southern United States. The new line was stated at length in a resolution of the Comintern's executive committee shortly after the end of the congress. It pointed out that 86 percent of the Afro-American population lived in the South and that approximately half of these lived in the Black Belt where they comprised more than 50 percent of the entire population. From this it argued that "The various forms of oppression of the Negro masses, who are concentrated mainly in the so-called 'Black Belt,' provide the necessary conditions for a national revolutionary movement among the Negroes. . . . The great majority of Negroes in the rural districts of the South are not 'reserves of capitalist reaction,' but potential allies of the revolutionary proletariat." This belated recognition of the national character of the Afro-American struggle was thus limited to a question of territorial autonomy in this one area. Furthermore, the slogan of "full social and political equality" would remain the "central slogan." The implications of black nationalism for those outside the Black Belt, as demonstrated by Garvey, were ignored. The resolution noted, as Garvey had long done, that due to worldwide imperialist oppression, "a common tie of interest is established for the revolutionary struggle of race and national liberation from imperialist domination of the Negroes in various parts of the world."[23]

The adoption of this 1928 national line by the Communist International is usually presented as having proceeded from Stalin's famous definition of a nation—"A nation is an historically evolved, stable community of language, territory, economic life, and psychological make-up

manifested in a community of culture."[24] It is noteworthy that during
the congress debates most American communists, black and white, seem
not to have advocated a national approach to the race question. George
Padmore, at that time an active member of the American party, later
argued that the 1928 change had been motivated by the long-standing
attempt to get at Garvey's followers. He wrote, "It was therefore decided
that, since Marcus Garvey had rallied popular support by promising to
establish a 'National Home' for blacks in Africa, the American communists should go one better and offer the American Negroes a state
of their own in the Black Belt. . . . It was hoped by this manoeuvre to
satisfy the nationalist aspirations of those Negroes who still hankered
after 'Black Zionism' and turn them away from Garveyism to Communism." He continued, "With Stalin's blessing, this amazing piece of nonsense was imposed upon the American party."[25]

The American party certainly was not tardy in accepting the new line.
Indeed, the Workers party issued a statement on self-determination simultaneously with the last stages of the congress, prompted no doubt by the
fact that 1928 was an election year in the United States and the Workers
party had several black candidates in the field. The statement read in part,

> The Workers (Communist) Party of American puts forward correctly
> as its central slogan: Abolition of the whole system of race discrimina-
> tion. Full racial, social and political equality of the Negro people.
> But it is necessary to supplement the struggle for the full racial, social
> and political equality of the Negro with a struggle for their right of
> national self-determination. Self-determination means the right to
> establish their own state, to erect their own government, if they choose
> to do so. In the economic and social conditions and class relations of
> the Negro people there are increasing forces which serve as a basis for
> the development of a Negro nation (a compact mass of farmers on a
> contiguous territory, semi-feudal conditions, complete segregation,
> common traditions of slavery, the development of distinct classes and
> economic ties etc. etc.).

This Workers party statement, much more explicitly than the Comintern
statement, acknowledged (though in a grudging fashion) the part that
Garvey had played in inducing this new line. It continued:

There are many national movements of the Negro city petit-bourgeoisie and intelligentsia. The fact that the most important mass movement, was a sort of Negro Zionism and had such reactionary, extremely harmful slogans as leaving the United States and back to Africa, should not blind us to the revolutionary possibilities of the Negro national liberation movements of the future.

The resolution endowed Garvey with a measure of unintended legitimacy when it sought authority for the new national line in a Lenin quotation to the effect that all national liberation movements are bourgeois democratic. As the movement developed, though, they presumed that it would be taken over by proletarian elements.[26]

By 1930 in an effort to clear up once and for all the *"lack of clarity"* on the Negro question" which they still recognized within the American party, the political secretariat of the executive committee of the Communist International drafted a further resolution "On the Negro Question in the United States." This resolution recognized more clearly than before the peculiar features of the Afro-American nation. It stated:

In the interest of the utmost clarity of ideas on this question the Negro question in the United States must be viewed from the standpoint of its peculiarity, namely as the question of an *oppressed nation,* which is in a peculiar and extraordinarily distressing situation of national oppression not only in view of the prominent *racial distinctions* (material differences in the colour of skin, etc.), but above all because of considerable social antagonism (remnants of slavery). This introduces into the American Negro question an important, *peculiar* trait which is absent from the national question of other oppressed peoples.

The resolution nevertheless continued to distinguish between Afro-Americans in the South and those in the North. It saw tendencies and prospects for separateness as most likely in the South. Rather than self-determination, it saw the demand for equal rights as the more important slogan in the North, where it was "under no circumstances the task of the communists to give support to bourgeois nationalism in its fight with the progressive assimilation tendencies of the Negro working masses."

Yet it contradictorily admonished the party to "resist all tendencies
within its own ranks to ignore the Negro question as a national question
in the United States, not only in the South, but also in the North."
This resolution, then, was not itself a model of clarity. The distinction
between South and North meant, of course, that some way had to be
found around the uncomfortable reality of Garveyism, which had flourished both North and South and which, in 1930, three years after Garvey's
deportation, still presented a formidable obstacle to communist work in
the black North. Garvey was accordingly smothered in a torrent of rhetoric
which was made to substitute for analysis. Despite the advocacy of self-
determination in the Black Belt, even to the point of separation, communists were warned that they could not "associate themselves at present, or
generally speaking, during capitalism, indiscriminately and without criticism with all the separatist currents of the various bourgeois or petty-
bourgeois Negro groups," for there was "not only a national-revolutionary,
but also a reactionary Negro separatism, for instance, that represented by
Garvey." This led up to a statement of the main objection to Garvey's
nationalism, namely its racial exclusiveness. Having already stated the
progressive nature of assimilation in the North, it now drove home its
attack on Garvey's "utopia of an isolated Negro State (regardless if in
Africa or America, if it is supposed to consist of Negroes only)." Such a
state would serve only the "political aim of diverting the Negro masses
from the real liberation struggle against American imperialism."

So this, then, was the crux of their quarrel with Garvey. A separate
black-controlled state with a white minority would be supported in the
Black Belt, even to the point of complete secession from the United
States, and even if that state opted not to follow the communist program.
But an all-black Garvey state anywhere, even in America, would be
utopian and reactionary. The point was reinforced by another parting
blast at Garvey: "All national reformist currents as, for instance, Garveyism, which are an obstacle to the revolutionization of the Negro masses,
must be fought systematically and with the utmost energy."[27]

American Trotskyists also grappled with the national question. Trotsky
himself had in 1922 impressed Harlem renaissance poet Claude McKay
as viewing the race question in a more intelligent fashion than any of the
other Russian leaders. He had granted McKay an interview in Moscow
and among other things had proposed training some black men as Red

army officers.[28] Discussing the national question in Mexico with Ameri-
ćan comrades in 1939, Trotsky adopted a position somewhat more amen-
able to self-determination than most communists were wont to. He argued
that the success of the Garvey movement was explicable in its propensities
for self-determination. And rather than attack the petit-bourgeois leadership of race organizations, he preferred to see this phenomenon as a
necessary stage in the emancipation of the race, necessitated by the
racism manifested by white workers. He even envisaged the possibility—
very unusual for a communist at this time—that black people, through
the route of self-determination, might even leap-frog over the white
proletariat and assume a vanguard role. He expressed this view as follows:

> It is very possible the Negroes also through the self-determination
> will proceed to the proletarian dictatorship in a couple of gigantic
> strides, ahead of the great bloc of white workers. They will then
> furnish the vanguard. I am absolutely sure that they will in any case
> fight better than the white workers. That, however, can happen only
> provided the Communist party carries on an uncompromising merci-
> less struggle not against the supposed national prepossessions of the
> Negroes but against the colossal prejudices of the white workers and
> gives it no concession whatever.[29]

Communists usually tended to see Garvey in simplistic terms as a
petit-bourgeois figure preaching reactionary nationalism and diverting
the black masses into utopian channels. There was obviously, as has already been seen, much more to Garvey than this inaccurate picture suggested. Much of Garvey's hold on the masses was due to ideas not very
different from some espoused by communists. Despite his firm espousal
of the race-first principle, for example, there was a persistent class component to Garvey's thinking. As against the white race, he saw the need
for intraracial solidarity but within the race he demonstrated quite
clearly that he identified with the oppressed masses against those with
pretentions to more exalted status. Against a charge by W. E. B. Du Bois
that he was born in humble circumstances he declared, "Admitting that
Marcus Garvey was born poor, he never encouraged a hatred for the
people of his kind or class, but to the contrary devoted his life to the
improvement and higher development of that *class within the race* which

has been struggling under the disadvantage that DuBois himself portrays in his article."[30] [Emphasis mine.] UNIA members in New Orleans on one occasion eloquently expressed this same attitude. "We are not members of the Negro 400 of New Orleans," they wrote, "composed of the class that are spending their time imitating the rich whites. . . ."[31] On one occasion Garvey could even consider workers' revolts in white countries as an example for the black race to follow. In a 1926 editorial he commented, "The royal and privileged classes of idlers who used to tyrannize and oppress the humble hordes of mankind are now experiencing difficulty in holding their control over the sentiment of the people." He thought that the black man should also strike against royalty and privilege.[32] He once went so far as to versify:

> The downtrodden poor whites and blacks should join
> And prevent rich whites our rights to purloin.[33]

The class appeal of Garvey's propaganda was recognized by a State Department official who considered it more dangerous than communism. This official wrote in 1921, "Though he is certainly not an intellectual his particular propaganda and agitation is considered dangerous in that it will find a more fertile field of class divergence than Bolshevism would be likely to find in the United States."[34]

Nor was the race-first aspect of Garvey's philosophy difficult to explain in class terms, for it was based on a recognition that the overwhelming majority of the black race corresponded with the workers and the peasants everywhere. Garvey analyzed this situation in relation to his native Jamaica.

> Jamaica is a British Colony with a population of nearly one million people of this number, more than 850,000 are black people. There are 15,000 white and the rest are offsprings of white and black—coloured people. In this population there is a social arrangement whereby all positions of influence are held by a minority class. The bulk of the black people are kept in conditions bordering on serfdom, they are made up generally of the labouring class who receive but a pittance of a wage, ranging from six-pence for women a day to 9 [pence], and for men from 1 [shilling] a day to 2 [shillings]. Because of this low scale of wages among the people crime is rife, our poor houses are filled. . . .

In the midst of this distress of the black majority we have a prosperous minority of white, coloured and a few black persons who have been taken under the patronage of the privileged minority.[35]

Complementing his sentiment for the masses was an intolerance of privilege not too different from that of the communists. And Garvey's attack on privilege extended to appropriate persons within the race, his race-first doctrine notwithstanding. In 1924, for example, speaking against the candidacy of black Harlem Republican Charles H. Roberts, he accused him of being backed by black capitalists and grafters. He went so far as to assert that "as the white folks in the labor unions, the Socialist group and the Progressive group are keeping their eyes on that selfish group of white people who are attempting to rob and exploit, so have you to keep your eyes on those selfish Negroes who have been crushing you for the last 20 years." He clinched his argument by explaining to his audience that "you, the workingman, have nothing in common with Dr. Charles Roberts at this time."[36] On this occasion Garvey's Negro Political Union actually backed a white candidate against Roberts.

Such hostility toward privilege extended quite naturally toward landowners. His election platform during his 1929 campaign for the Jamaica legislative council included suggestions for land reform. Recalling the experiences of his own uncle who had been a sharecropper and subject to the caprice of a dishonest landlord, he proposed methods to compel large landowners to make surplus land available to small holders.[37]

In the light of all this it is not surprising that he objected to the titles bestowed by the UNIA being viewed as a hankering after aristocracy. UNIA titles, he observed, were not based on wealth but on service to the race. They were distinctions conferred on worthy individuals by an appreciative race.[38]

These class sentiments on Garvey's part were reinforced by a long history of struggle in and on behalf of workers' organizations. Communists and others who knew him only in the American context believed that his hostility toward white American labor unions was indicative of a general hostility toward workers' organizations. Yet in his hostility to the racist practices of the American Federation of Labor, Garvey was acting no differently from practically all Afro-American leaders and indeed the communists themselves. Where he differed from them and expressed what they considered heresy was in his advice to the black work-

ingman in America that he should have no compunction in playing on
the capitalist's greed by underselling the white worker and thereby obtaining employment. "It seems strange and a paradox," he wrote, "but
the only convenient friend the Negro worker or laborer has, in America,
at the present time, is the white capitalist."[39] This position, however,
was strictly in relation to the peculiar situation induced in America by
racist white labor unions. In other situations Garvey had a record of
struggle in labor organizations that was undoubtedly more outstanding
than that of many communist critics. His early involvement in workers'
struggles in Jamaica, Costa Rica, and Panama has already been noted.
During the early Jamaican years of the UNIA (1914-1916) he attempted
unsuccessfully to implement a scheme setting up unemployed workers
as peasant farmers on crown lands. He also attempted in this period to
enlist the aid of the Jamaica Federation of Labour.[40] He maintained his
interest in the Jamaican labor scene after moving to the United States.
In 1920, during a police strike in Kingston, he upset authorities by despatching a telegram expressing sympathy with his friend A. Bain Alves,
chairman of the Jamaica Federation of Labour, who had been very
active in workers' struggles that year.[41] Back in the Caribbean in 1921,
Garvey advocated the unionization of Jamaica labor and labor sponsor-
ship of representatives to the legislative council.[42]

Garvey's most sustained activity in the labor movement came during
his Jamaican period of 1927-1935. His *Blackman* newspaper became an
organ for the exposure of labor grievances. In May 1929, a little over a
month after its appearance, it took up the case of a young banana carrier
who had been kicked and cuffed on the wharf by an assistant wharfinger.
Garvey remonstrated with the other laborers on the wharf for not having
thrown the culprit into the sea. When the men attempted to strike a few
days later he supported them. They therefore marched to his Edelweis
Park headquarters and asked him to represent them in the dispute with
their employers, the United Fruit Company. Their wage was one shilling
and nine pence per hundred bunches of bananas loaded. Nor did they
receive overtime for night work, Sundays or holidays. Garvey spoke to
them on the necessity of unionization and condemned the social structure in Jamaica, as a result of which, he declared, "a large number of
your people, my people, our race form the unemployed." In view of the
lack of an organization strong enough to sustain a strike and the easy

availability of strikebreakers, Garvey suggested that the laborers resume
work while he negotiated on their behalf.

During his negotiations with J. G. Keifer, head of the United Fruit
Company in Jamaica, Garvey extended his grievances to include the
ragged and half-nude condition of female laborers on the wharf, whom
he said formed a favorite subject for tourist photographers. Keifer
threatened labor-saving machines and boasted of his ability to break
a strike. The *Daily Gleaner,* described by Garvey as "the mouthpiece of
special privilege and cold blooded capital in the Island of Jamaica," encouraged the adoption of the suggested devices, causing Garvey to warn
its editor to "keep his monstrous 'paws' off the situation," lest the
Blackman "tell him where he ought to get off at," as it was "always
ready to tell him without any hesitation."[43]

The demand for a minimum wage was featured on the 1929 manifesto
of Garvey's Peoples Political Party, and during his stay on the Kingston
and St. Andrew Corporation Council he regularly campaigned for an
eight-hour day.[44] Out of this and allied activity, including a delegation
to the governor and a petition to a visiting imperial sugar commission,[45]
emerged his Jamaica Workers and Labourers Association, conceptualized
as a body which would pave the way for unions, rather than itself being
a union.[46] Garvey's interest in Jamaica labor continued after his departure
from Jamaica, and in 1938 he approved of the entry into politics of labor
leader Alexander Bustamante, who was for the next three decades to play
a central role in Jamaica's political life.[47]

Garvey's ubiquitous presence, as has been seen, was felt in workers'
organizations in other parts of the world, such as Trinidad and South
Africa. This involvement extended to yet other areas. In British Guiana
the UNIA maintained close contact with pioneer labor leader Hubert
Crichlow and his British Guiana Labour Union.[48] Similar links between
the UNIA and workers' struggles were reported from Barbados[49] and the
United States Virgin Islands.[50] Indeed it has been said by one active in
the movement that most of the important working-class leaders who
emerged onto the political scene in the 1930s in the West Indies had been
influenced by involvement to a lesser or greater degree in the Garvey
movement.[51]

In Garvey, therefore, the communists were faced with an adversary
whose knowledge of the black working class, both from the standpoint

of the UNIA and the standpoint of labor unions, was very extensive. And
Garvey's field of operations was truly as universal as the communists'
was international. The bodies of thought represented by Garvey and
the communists were deceptively similar. Both were to a greater or lesser
degree anticapitalist and anti-imperialist. Both were anticlerical (Garvey,
of course, being at one and the same time somewhat anticlerical but very
much proreligious). They both sought to organize around the great mass
of workers and peasants, and they both (all claims of the communists to
the contrary notwithstanding) had their fair share of petit-bourgeois
leadership. Indeed Garvey held better claims to a humble background
than many of the communist intellectuals who glibly wrote him off as
petit-bourgeois. Both had, at least by 1928, come to recognize, though
in varying degrees, the national character of the so-called Negro Question.
Between them, however, stood the vast chasm of race. Just as the communists, in their formulation of the national question, felt the need to
hedge their attitude around with assimilationist requirements and thus
withdraw from an acknowledgment of the primacy of the race factor,
so Garvey, while recognizing the class character of society, always viewed
it within the constraints of the race factor, which in his opinion overrode
and transcended class differences. Thus, however near the two bodies of
thought might sometimes appear to be, the race/class question presented
a fundamental point of disagreement. These similarities and differences
manifested themselves in practice in an intricate relationship of hostility
interspersed with tolerance between the UNIA and the communists, as
all the while the communists tried to win over Garvey's following and
the UNIA deftly avoided falling into communist hands.

Some of the earliest contact between communism and the UNIA came
in the persons of early UNIA members. The first editorial writer (apart
from Garvey himself) of the *Negro World* was W. A. Domingo, a socialist.
Domingo was responsible for some at least of the Bolshevik propaganda
appearing in the paper which alarmed authorities in 1919. He was, in the
words of Garvey six years later, "dismissed from my employ as editor of
one of my newspapers because of his dangerous communistic principles."[52]
Another UNIA hanger-on was Cyril Briggs, who, through his African Blood
Brotherhood (ABB) provided the American communists with some of
their first black cadres. Still another was Otto Hall. A veteran of World
War I, he sympathized with the militant Industrial Workers of the World,

joined the UNIA in Chicago not long after the end of the war and became
a member of the Universal African Legions. From there he went into the
ABB and later followed Briggs into the Communist party.[53]

Communist attempts at capturing the UNIA began practically from
the inception of the communist movement in the United States. The
program of the United Communist party in 1920 urged black communists
to enter black unions, lodges, clubs, and churches "to expose the reactionary leaders, who, for the purpose of betraying their race, infest these
institutions." Communists were urged, on the other hand, to support all
radical black organizations.[54] The UNIA was not specifically mentioned
but could not fail to have been considered under one of those two cate-
gories. In subsequent years similar pronouncements encouraged infiltration into black organizations. The fourth congress of the Communist
International in Moscow in 1922 urged support for "every form of Negro
Movement which tends to undermine capitalism and Imperialism or to
impede their further progress."[55] In similar vein the executive committee
of the Communist International in 1928 laid down the line of "united
front tactics for specific demands" in dealing with "existing Negro petty
bourgeois organizations." The purpose of such tactics, it was clearly
stated, should be to mobilize the black masses under communist leadership and expose and undermine their "treacherous petty bourgeois leadership."[56]

Nor were the communists reluctant to consider utilizing bits and
pieces of Garvey's program and tactics. In 1921 a communist journal explained that "The Negro has a great love of display, show, pomp, ostenta-
tion, brass bands, mysticism, decorations, buttons, social frivolities and
military display. (In this regard it is only fair to say that he is not alone.)
These contraptions catch his imagination and act as an inducement for
organization as nothing else can at the present time."[57] This article suggested that such Afro-American aspirations as a free Africa, race equality,
and the like should not be opposed but directed into "effective channels."
At the fifth Comintern congress in 1924, Israel Amter, an American delegate, even suggested linking Africa and Afro-America by sending pamphlets
for distribution by Africa-bound sailors.[58]

One of the earliest attempts at infiltrating the UNIA came through
the use of Cyril Briggs' African Blood Brotherhood. Though this attempt
failed, Briggs and the Brotherhood were to continue to be a source of

harassment for the UNIA up to Garvey's death. Briggs organized the ABB in New York in 1919 and became its "paramount chief." An immigrant from Nevis in the West Indies, he had previously been an editor of the *New York Amsterdam News* before being fired for the militant nationalism expressed in his editorials. During his sojourn at the *Amsterdam News* he had toyed with various nationalistic solutions to the race problem, such as a separate state for Afro-Americans in the West, or in Africa, South America or the West Indies. His *Crusader* magazine, established in 1918 after his expulsion from the *Amsterdam News,* originally proclaimed itself the publicity organ of the Hamitic League of the World. The ABB was organized around this magazine, and though never a large organization (three thousand members at its height), it established branches in such places as Trinidad, British Guiana and Santo Domingo, in addition to several locations in the United States. In 1921, Briggs also claimed the affiliation of 153 organizations, such as churches, in the United States, the West Indies, Africa, and elsewhere. The organization saw itself in the beginning as radical, though not communist.[59]

Perhaps in early 1921, if not before, Briggs was approached by American communists who thereby succeeded in obtaining a handful of recruits from the ABB. These recruits were some of the earliest black communists in the United States and continued for long to be among the most prominent. They included, apart from Briggs himself, Richard B. Moore, Otto Hall, Lovett Fort-Whiteman, and Harry Haywood. Another outstanding Harlem socialist within the ABB was ex-*Negro World* editor W. A. Domingo. Domingo did not enter the Communist party. Otto Huiswoud joined the ABB from the party.[60]

The ABB cadre proved a boon to the American communists at a time when the powers that be in Moscow were wondering at the absence of black representation in the American movement. By 1922 the Harlem West Side Branch of the Workers party was run by ABB members: Huiswoud, organizer; Briggs, recording and financial secretary; and persons described as comrades Moore, Campbell and McKay, members of the propaganda and educational committee.[61] By November 28, 1922, Huiswoud, masquerading as Comrade Billings, was praising the ABB at a session of the commission on the Negro Question at the fourth Comintern congress. He distinguished the ABB from Garveyism, to the detriment of the latter.[62] Back in the United States, the Communist *Worker* saw in the ABB a great help in building a united front of black and white workers.[63]

The first important task for the ABB in building this desired united front was to infiltrate the UNIA. This they attempted to do during Garvey's 1921 International Convention. Before the convention, possibly for tactical reasons, Briggs had taken a position moderately favorable toward Garvey.[64] With the convention in progress Briggs on August 15 despatched a letter to Garvey. Assuming for the occasion an attitude of due deference, he addressed Garvey as "His Excellency, the Provisional President of Africa." He offered Garvey a proposition—that Garvey (with his international mass movement, perhaps millions strong) should enter into a program of joint action with the ABB (an obscure organization of a thousand or two) for African liberation. "But think of what we might be able to do for the race," he cajoled, "through conscious cooperation were we to adopt a program which would jointly represent us, without any serious compromise on either side of important tactical points or principles."[65] Briggs then took the opportunity provided by Garvey's assembled multitude to do a little recruiting for himself and passed around copies of the ABB program.

The next ploy in Briggs' attempt to impose a communist united front on Garvey was to have his white communist friend Rose Pastor Stokes address the convention. She expatiated on Russia's desire to free Africa and on the need for black-white working class unity. She then called on Garvey to take a stand in relation to her communist overtures. Garvey was polite but noncommittal. The final stroke in Briggs' strategy was to have ABB delegates to the convention introduce a motion for endorsement of the communist program. The motion was debated and tabled.[66] The ABB, piqued at this setback, then immediately published a *Negro Congress Bulletin* on August 24, almost entirely devoted to a scurrilous misrepresentation of the UNIA convention. This was brought to the convention's notice and an explanation was requested from the four ABB delegates. Their names were called but there was no response. An examination of the delegates' cards was about to be made when, in the words of the *Negro World,* "a man was seen to rise hastily and scurry across the hall, plunge through the doorway, beating his way in precipitate flight towards Seventh Avenue. The erstwhile indignant House rocked with laughter." It was then unanimously voted that the ABB delegates' cards should be withdrawn.[67] Such a blunt and in many ways insulting power play could only have been due to political ineptitude on Briggs' part or a disdain for Garvey's great knowledge of political infighting.

In any event, Garvey used the ABB's Bolshevism to justify his case
against them, even though he praised Lenin and Trotsky during the same
convention in a speech that urged his hearers to do for Africa what Lenin
and Trotsky had done for Russia in overthrowing Czarist despotism.[68]
This distinction between Lenin and Trotsky, whom he usually endorsed,
and American communists, whom he avoided, represented Garvey's normal position. Some time later he said, "I am against the brand of Communism that is taught in America. . . . In America it constitutes a group
of liars, plotters and artful deceivers who twist—a one third truth to a
whole big lie, and give it out to the unthinking clientele for consumption.
Communism among Negroes in 1920-1921 was represented in New York
by such Negroes as Cyril Briggs and W. A. Domingo, and my contact with,
and experience of them, and their methods are enough to keep me shy of
that kind of communism for the balance of my natural life."[69]

Briggs, for his part, consoled himself on his defeat by arguing that
Garvey had engineered his expulsion to prevent the ABB program from
being officially represented to the delegates, whom, he said, were favorably
disposed towards it.[70]

This turn of events meant that if even the communist desire for a
united front with the UNIA had failed, the communists were assured of
the next best thing, the cooperation of what were now some of Garvey's
most vitriolic enemies. The Briggs-Garvey feud descended to its most
acrimonious less than two months after the abortive ABB coup when the
Negro World carried an advertisement entitled "WHITE MAN NEGRO
FOR CONVENIENCE." It read, "A White Man in New York by the name
of CYRIL BRIGGS has started the 'AFRICAN BLOOD BROTHERHOOD'
to catch Negroes, no doubt. To make it succeed he claims to be a Negro,
and continuously attacks the Universal Negro Improvement Association
and its founder, Marcus Garvey. Negroes, take notice and govern your-
selves accordingly."[71] For this indiscretion Briggs (who was indeed light
of hue) had Garvey arrested and tried for criminal libel, and Garvey reacted by showing Briggs' letter of cooperation to the judge.[72] Briggs
remained unmollified by a favorable decision, for the next month's
Crusader was a veritable Garvey special. At least ten of the sixteen editorials dealt with Garvey, as did several other articles. Readers were informed that Garvey had left his wife, that his father had died in a poor
house (a point which was also utilized by Du Bois and the British govern-

ment in anti-Garvey campaigns), that a Briggs letter to the Bureau of
Navigation had met with a response suggesting that there was no record
of two ships claimed by the Black Star Line, and more. He also quoted a
Garvey statement acknowledging favorable comment on the UNIA from
some European socialist publications to show that Garvey might have
changed his mind since repudiating the ABB position on linking up with
white workers for the liberation of Africa. One editorial even claimed
that Garvey had raped a "little white girl in a friend's office" in England.[73]
For this last indiscretion Briggs was in his turn arrested on a criminal libel
charge brought by Garvey.[74]

   At about this time three high-ranking estranged Garveyites joined
forces with the ABB. They were Cyril Crichlow, J. D. Gordon, a former
assistant president-general, and Bishop McGuire.[75] The last two later
returned to the UNIA.[76] Their presence did not seem to help the ABB
much. At a 1922 ABB meeting in Baltimore, for example, Garveyites
resorted to one of their favorite tactics against enemy gatherings. They
packed the meeting with UNIA members. They listened awhile to the
speaker but as soon as he attacked the UNIA he was met with the advice,
"Stop there, brother; don't you say anymore." The police were called,
but since the atmosphere was peaceful they left. The Garveyites then
turned it into a UNIA meeting.[77]

   In 1923 Garvey accused the ABB of being implicated in the police
raid on the New Orleans UNIA.[78] Yet in 1924 Briggs acted as an agent
for Garvey's Black Cross Navigation and Trading Company in helping it
procure a ship. Garvey later attacked one of his own subordinates,
William L. Sherrill, for having been responsible for this.[79]

   Briggs' relationship with Garvey took another strange twist when in
1926 Briggs wrote a letter to the *Negro World.* This letter stated that
Briggs was no friend of Garvey and had attacked him often. Nevertheless,
he still had a letter from Garvey thanking him for supporting the First
International Convention. He also indicated that he and ABB members
W. A. Domingo and Richard B. Moore had attacked the "Marcus Garvey
Must Go" campaign of Chandler Owen and his associates. Briggs even
expressed sympathy for Garvey, now that he had seen, he said, the incompetent help Garvey had in the management of his most recent steamship line. The main point of the letter seemed to be contained in Briggs'
assertion that "to me it is evident that the UNIA will soon be on the

rocks *unless some drastic change of control and policy* can be effected
quickly. And I believe it would be a great disaster to the race to have
the UNIA disintegrate."[80] [Emphasis mine.] This letter was published
just two weeks after Garvey's attack on Sherrill for employing Briggs
had appeared and it was probably yet another communist attempt at
UNIA cooption. Briggs' interest in the UNIA followed Garvey to Jamaica
and included calls to Garveyites to join the communist League of Struggle
for Negro Rights.[81]

In 1931 Briggs published a lengthy analysis of the Garvey movement.
Garvey was pictured as the usual petit-bourgeois bogeyman who diverted
revolutionary black nationalist sentiment into "utopian, reactionary,
'Back to Africa' channels." The leadership of the UNIA, he wrote, "consisted of the poorest stratum of the Negro intellectuals—declassed elements, struggling business men and preachers, lawyers without a brief,
etc.—who stood more or less close to the Negro masses and felt sharply
the effects of the crisis." The undeniable mass following built up by
Garvey was contrasted with "the small advanced industrial proletariat,
who were experienced in the class struggle" (presumably the ABB) for
whom the UNIA had little appeal. Briggs also put forward here what has
become something of a standard communist argument, namely that
Garvey had been progressive and willing to struggle in the United States
in the beginning, but that after his exclusion from the United States in
1921 he had taken fright and become party to an abject capitulation to
the imperialists. In concluding he recognized "certain progressive achievements" of the UNIA, one being the fact that it "undoubtedly helped to
crystalize the national aspirations of the Negro masses."[82]

Shortly afterward the *Negro World* poked some fun at the communists'
newfound position on the national question by suggesting that, in adopting
this position, Briggs was in fact preaching Garveyism. Briggs hotly denied
this, claiming, among other things, that "unconditional equality of the
Negro people" was alien to Garveyism.[83]

Briggs repeated many of his former charges against Garvey in 1932.[84]
Garvey replied immediately from the pages of his *New Jamaican,* which
editorialized, "As usual, we have been made the object of ridicule by the
official organ 'The Negro Worker' of the International Trade Union Committee of Negro Workers. In their August issue they have published an
article, below the name of one Cyril Briggs under the caption, 'How

Garvey Betrayed the Negroes.' " The editorial continued, "Briggs has been a stubborn opponent of our rational method of the solution of the Negro problem in America. He and others have always tried to rope us in with communism."[85] Briggs' antagonism remained unbridled in the face of Garvey's death. A premature obituary under the caption "Marcus Garvey Dies in London," put out by Briggs' Crusader News Agency announced, in typically distorted fashion, that "during his stay in Jamaica, he made peace with the British imperialists and joined white employers in their attacks on Jamaican unions."[86] This obituary was based on wrong information concerning Garvey's death. Garvey in fact died the following month.

The pattern of hostility interspersed with apparently friendly gestures exhibited by the ABB in its relationship with Garvey was typical of communists generally, and particularly those in the United States. He was frequently described as a "charlatan." But perhaps the most frequent term of abuse used to describe Garvey was the term "Zionist." Claude McKay had described Garvey as Zionist in an interview published in the Russian *Izvestia* in 1922.[87] Trotskyist C. L. R. James in the 1930s considered Garvey's program "essentially Back to Africa" and therefore "pitiable rubbish."[88] A host of others said basically the same thing. The most convincing argument against this "Negro Zionism" charge came, strange to say, from the pen of another communist, Robert Minor. Minor, covering Garvey's 1924 International Convention for the communist *Daily Worker,* reported a speech in which Assistant President General William Sherrill had advocated autonomy for the black man in Africa. At this point, said Minor, a reporter for "a Hebrew Zionist newspaper" whispered across the press table, "This is Negro Zionism." Minor considered this, "despite all the superficial resemblance, the wildest folly." He considered the two different for several reasons,

1. The Great Powers and the League of Nations can cheerfully give a few thousand Jews a chance to settle in Palestine.
2. The great imperialist governments of the world can smile happily over Jewish nationalist propaganda which takes Jewish workers' minds away from proletarian revolution.
But:
1. The Great Powers, Britain, France, Belgium—and now the United States—cannot smile over any suggestions of surrendering Rhodesia

and the Rand, the Kamerun, the Congo and the Nile and Morocco and
Tunis and Algeria—to any movement for independent Negro nationalism, no matter how fantastic Garvey's red and green robes may be,
nor how unseaworthy his ships.

2. The Great Powers cannot tolerate for one instant the propaganda
for Negro independent nationalism in any quarter of Africa—not even
in the Negro states of Abyssinia and Liberia, especially not in the
"fanatical" form in which alone this movement is found.

3. No, the Negro nationalist movement is more readily to be compared to the Turkish nationalism of recent years, than to Jewish
Zionism.[89]

Communists attacked Garvey on many other points. These attacks
were typically characterized by lies and distortions and often reduced
Garvey to some kind of a tool of imperialism. A 1921 article in *The
Communist* was typical. It claimed that "the kings of finance hold Mr.
Garvey in great esteem for the work he has done in keeping the Negro's
mind off the real problems before him and busying him with such tom-
foolery as knighthoods and court receptions."[90] Communist attacks were
also often opportunistic to the point where they could accuse Garvey of
lack of racial solidarity in not supporting black communist candidates at
election time.[91]

Yet praise from communist circles, though often part of a cheap ma-
neuver to lull Garvey into complacency, was nevertheless sometimes based
on an appreciation of the anti-imperialist implications of Garvey's ideas
and career. This was possibly the reason for a statement issued in 1925
by the praesidium of the International Peasants Council (Krestintern)
in Moscow expressing solidarity with Garvey after his imprisonment in
the United States. The statement read in part, "The capitalists realized
that the movement led by Garvey, the movement for Negro independence,
even under the modest slogan of 'Back-to-Africa' contained the embryo of
the future revolutionary movement which, in alliance with the workers
and the peasants, is to threaten the reign of capital." It described Garvey's
trial as "an orgy of revengeful capitalism."[92]

One of the most interesting attempts at an objective, and on occasion
even favorable communist analysis of the Garvey movement came in
Robert Minor's coverage of Garvey's 1924 convention for the *Daily*

Worker. The convention was the occasion for a major communist attempt to smother Garvey with overtures of friendship, and Minor's articles must be seen in this light. Prior to 1924 the *Daily Worker* and its predecessors (*The Worker, The Toiler* and *The Ohio Socialist*) were largely devoid of any references to the race question. From the beginning of 1924, however, a program of extensive coverage of race affairs was launched. This coverage was orchestrated to provide a supportive role for an equally intense Workers party effort of that year to "bore from within" the major black organizations.

The year began with a series of articles on the race question by Lovett Fort-Whiteman, a communist and ABB member. In February the paper announced that the ABB and the Workers party would be attending the imminent Sanhedrin in Chicago. The Sanhedrin, organized by Kelly Miller, was a black convention in which over fifty race groups participated. The opening of the conference was greeted on February 11 by a laudatory article by Fort-Whiteman who announced that the ABB's two delegates would work closely with the Workers party's five (of whom Fort-Whiteman was one) since both organizations were "wholly class conscious." He pointedly noted that the UNIA would be a conspicuous absentee from the conference, no doubt because the Sanhedrin was "concerned primarily for winning rights for Negroes where they live" while the UNIA was purportedly concerned primarily with a return to Africa.[93] One week later, after having apparently emerged somewhat less than victorious from several clashes with the Sanhedrin's organizers, the *Daily Worker* expressed utter disenchantment with Kelly Miller and the "capitalist Negroes" who helped run the affair. So great was their disenchantment that they now grudgingly agreed with Garvey's decision to remain aloof from the convention. The paper lamented, "The hope of the oppressed Negro workers does not lie in the present set of Negro leaders. Marcus Garvey says they are too old. The workers say they are too bourgeois."[94] Nevertheless the real intention of the communists, here, and later at the UNIA convention, was revealed about four months later at the fifth Comintern congress in Moscow, where an American delegate boasted that despite the domination of this assembly by ecclesiastical and petit-bourgeois types, the communists "were successful in the last two days of the congress in provoking a split."[95] The next dress rehearsal for the UNIA convention came in July when Minor, a staff writer and cartoonist

for the paper, covered the NAACP conference in Philadelphia. Then on
July 28 the paper noted the forthcoming preconvention meeting of the
Chicago UNIA in an item unusually free of anti-UNIA rhetoric.

The preconvention overtures to Garvey continued on July 29 with a
remarkable reversal of the traditional communist distortion of Garvey's
program. A front-page article noted that, "Altho the ultimate program
of the Garvey organization calls for the establishment of a Negro Nation
in Africa, with the gradual migration of the Negroes to that country,
the convention realizes the necessity of dealing with American conditions
until their final ideals are realized." The same issue stated, in very explicit
language, the respect which Garvey's powerful position compelled, even
of his opponents. "Garvey," it declared, "altho his organization declares
for an independent Negro nation, has succeeded in banding almost half
a million Negroes together in the largest mass movement the American
Negroes have ever had. The Universal Negro Improvement Association
must therefore be reckoned with as a force in the problems which confront
the Negro as a part of American society."[96] An editorial of July 29,
though reverting to the normal phraseology of the "Utopianism that
characterizes the fantastic projects of reclaiming Africa as the home of
the Negro race," nevertheless relegated this to the status of a "surface
phenomenon" of Garveyism. "The real social content of the movement,"
it asserted, "is the awakening of millions of exploited workers to the
fact of their exploitation, of their subjection, social and economic, by
sinister forces that rule society." The editorial, while upholding the
primacy and ultimate triumph of class struggle for black workers, nevertheless went so far as to recognize as "inevitable" the "racial tendency,
rather than a class one" induced by the peculiar oppression of Afro-
Americans.

The preconvention build-up continued with cautious approval on
July 30 of a Garvey speech denouncing United States imperialism in
Brazil and Haiti. Yet another editorial in this issue considered Garvey's
African program "a curious mixture of error and sound insight," a partial
about-face from the editorial of only one day previously. On July 31, in
the last article of the massive preconvention build-up, a mass meeting of
the Chicago UNIA was reported. Two thousand persons had assembled at
a farewell meeting for the Chicago delegates to the 1924 International
Convention of Negro Peoples of the World. J. J. Peters, president of

Chicago division no. 23, was quoted as saying, "My Communist white friends who are sitting on my left disagree with the nationalism of our association." He continued, "I have argued this point with them for several years, frequently coming to theoretical swordpoints with them; but still we are the best of friends."

The first reports from Garvey's August convention were from a special correspondent, but on August 5 the *Daily Worker* announced that Minor had left for New York to cover the rest of the proceedings. His articles were clearly designed to spearhead the Workers party effort to influence Garvey's convention, for readers were asked to circulate Minor's forthcoming convention articles among black workers, as well as the issue of August 5, which contained the Workers party salutation "To the Fourth International Convention of the Universal Negro Improvement Association Meeting at Liberty Hall, New York, August, 1924." "Its value depends on wide distribution," readers were urged, "Do your Communist duty."

By this time the attention given by the *Daily Worker* (and hence the Workers party) to Garvey's convention had already far exceeded that given to Kelly Miller's Sanhedrin and the NAACP's Philadelphia conference. The front-page preamble to the official salutation read, "Realizing that the only hope of emancipation for Colored and White workers is universal solidarity of labor, the Workers Party sends its ardent greetings to the representatives of the oppressed Negro Race who are gathered together in Liberty Hall, New York, under the banner of the Universal Negro Improvement Association."

The statement was signed on behalf of the Workers Party of America by William Z. Foster, national chairman, and C. E. Ruthenberg, national executive secretary. It was a lengthy one. It began by expressing the hope that "this historic convention" might be "fruitful for the liberation of your Race." The UNIA was reminded that capitalist profit is the basis of all colonial and domestic oppression. The times were characterized as troubled ones for imperialism. The fall of the old regime in Russia was seen as symptomatic of this. Garveyites were informed that these struggles would spread to the colonies and that Africa's opportunity was approaching. Thus far the statement revealed a common characteristic of Garvey's enemies and rivals, namely a stubborn reluctance to acknowledge (or a lack of knowledge of) the reality of Garvey's accomplishments. Whereas in 1919, two years before the founding of the Workers party, Garveyites

had been in the vanguard of major anticolonial struggles in such places
as British Honduras, Trinidad and South Africa, here was the party in
1924 informing Garvey that such ferment was imminent. Similarly,
Garvey hardly needed the Workers party to tell him that Africa's opportunity was approaching at a time when he had already expended many
years and much money and energy trying to seize that opportunity.

The statement then advised Garvey to struggle against the imperialists
in Africa without sacrificing rights in the United States and agreed with
a convention proposal for independent educational material for black
people. Garvey's Negro Political Union, the agency which would coordinate
the UNIA excursion into domestic politics, was enthusiastically supported,
as was his Third-World solidarity, which also antedated the formation of
the Workers party. "Your militant solidarity with the oppressed colonial
peoples internationally is an honor to your organization," the statement
read. The Workers party also commended the class composition of the
UNIA and its advocacy to black people of not fighting in future imperialistic wars. The convention's intention to petition presidents, kings and
the like of imperialist countries was dismissed as a waste of time, as was
the intention to petition the League of Nations. Garvey was advised that
the Communist International was a much more worthwhile body to
appeal to than the league. At the Communist International the UNIA
would be "honored guests." Furthermore communists were the enemies
of Garvey's enemies, and therefore should be his friends. Communist
parties, like the UNIA, were in all countries organized against the ruling
classes and against colonialism. And there was the example of Russia,
which had freed its subject nationalities.

The statement continued its systematic evaluation of Garvey's past
performance and the convention program. It disapproved of the convention intention to discuss a solution to the southern race problem "to the
satisfaction of all concerned" on the ground that all concerned could
not be pleased. (Garvey, of course, would see separation of the races as
such a mutually acceptable solution.) On Garvey's denunciation of discrimination in American labor unions the statement was especially enthusiastic, and it issued him an invitation to joint struggle—"We should especially
like to co-ordinate our efforts with yours in a drive to open the doors of
all labor unions (or such of them as now discriminate) to the full and
equal admission of Negro workers." It acknowledged that this would re-

quire reeducating white workers. Finally, Garvey's denunciations of preachers and missionaries as capitalist agents were used to hope that the convention would move away from religion to "modern, scientific thot [sic]."[97]

At the convention itself Minor interviewed Garvey, gave vivid descriptions of the pomp and ceremony and the "music of exceptionally fine quality," blamed the Republican party for having Garvey arrested during the convention, and puzzled over what struck him as paradoxes inherent in Garvey's anticlerical stance versus his religiousness, his anti-imperialism versus his reluctance to unconditionally denounce the Ku Klux Klan.[98]

This August offensive, for all its obvious preparation and its large scale, was not without its stupid blunders of the magnitude of the ABB's 1921 offensive. The favorable tenor of Minor's articles from New York were from time to time offset by editorials from the Chicago headquarters which were hostile enough to make any intelligent reader wonder at the sincerity of the newfound friendliness toward the UNIA. On August 8, for example, in the same issue bearing an effusive story of a black woman peering over the shoulder of a *Daily Worker* reader in a streetcar and being won over to the paper's readership, there appeared an article captioned "Daily Worker Seeks to Win Marcus Garvey's Followers to the Communist Program." The item consisted of a letter from one Israel Zimmerman expressing shock at the paper's friendly attitude toward Garvey a mere two years after Comrades Briggs, Owen and Randolph had campaigned against him. To Zimmerman's demand for an explanation, the paper explained, "We have not changed our fundamental attitude towards Marcus Garvey. We are today as much opposed to his schemes for a Negro promised land in Africa as we ever were. We not only do not endorse but totally repudiate all schemes like Garvey's 'Black Star Line' as means of liberating the oppressed and exploited Negro masses." The only reason for its new spirit of cooperation with the UNIA, the paper explained, was to win over Garvey's followers to a "virile, class conscious" (i.e., Workers party) leadership. Thus were the blunders of the 1921 ABB offensive repeated. Once more the communists had sought to win Garvey's friendship, steal his followers, and insult his intelligence, all at the same time.

It is difficult to conceive of how the Workers party expected to achieve its goals after this article, but the attempt continued. Minor, obviously impressed by the spectacle and the indication of power that was a UNIA convention, was moved to great feats of lyrical expression. He wrote,

I heard Garvey speak last night. He is one of the most powerful personalities that I have ever seen on the platform. He is one of the rare types
that history finds rising in every unsettled period to express new currents among the masses of men. For weal or woe, Garvey is of the
stuff that leaders (or very powerful misleaders) are made of. Not the
kind of leaders who rise in times of quiet and fit their environment
as a fashion model fits the gowns of the day, but the kind of leaders
who rise in times of storm and stress, who do not fit their environment,
who look and feel and act out of place in the order of the day—who
are called uncouth, who are jeered as misfits, and yet who may form
the heads of the battering rams which smash down the walls of their
environment.

I cannot vouch for the integrity of Marcus Garvey. But I know that
the worst set of scoundrels that I know on earth hate Garvey.[99]

The Workers party, perhaps desiring to create a split in the UNIA convention as they had boasted of doing at the Sanhedrin, moved after two
weeks to the tactic of direct intervention in the Liberty Hall deliberations. The *Daily Worker* on August 14 carried a new official Workers
party statement to the convention. For this attack the communists
utilized the convention resolution on the Ku Klux Klan, which considered
the Klan's attitude to black people "fairly representative" of white feelings generally, and which pointed out that alleged Klan atrocities were
not very significant when compared with outrages perpetrated by white
workers in the North. The statement sought to establish the communists'
credentials, as it were, by quoting from a resolution from the fourth
Comintern congress of 1922 praising struggles of black workers. Garvey
was also assured that the communists "are engaged no less than you in
the struggle against the imperialism which is enslaving Africa." They
therefore regretted the convention's Klan resolution, which they construed
as a refusal to fight for equality in the United States.

This Workers party communication was duly debated by the convention and provided a good example of Garvey's handling of the American
communist challenge. Garvey opened the discussion by reminding the
delegates that the UNIA was a very liberal organization. At a previous
convention, he said, they had allowed Rose Pastor Stokes to try to in-
doctrinate the organization, and now they were going to give the Workers

party a hearing. To a motion asking that the Workers party statement be tabled, Garvey objected, saying that it was an important question and should be answered in the same spirit of friendliness as proffered. If the communists were so desirous of fighting the Klan, Garvey argued, let them take their proposal to the Jew and the Catholic, both of whom were in a much stronger economic position than the black man and not dependent on Klan types for employment. "I think it is all right to let the white groups fight among themselves," he said. "The more rogues fall out, the more the other people can get their dues. And therefore I would advise the Workers party to send their communication to the Jews and Catholics, and advise them to fight on, and fight on, and fight on."[100] Workers party delegates who attended the convention and participated in its deliberations were not present, for some unexplained reason, at this session.[101]

As the convention wore on Minor considered that Garvey might destroy himself on the Klan question but that the organization would continue with other leaders.[102] And toward the end of the month an editorial took the white press to task for giving much coverage to the small meeting of the National Negro Business League while ignoring Garvey's massive convention. In the same editorial the large-scale communist effort during Garvey's convention was acknowledged and explained thus: "In the sessions of the Universal Negro Improvement Association there are even more working class elements represented than there were in the Sanhedrin and an even stronger attempt was made by the communists to unify the struggles of the exploited workers regardless of their color."[103]

Garvey's attitude toward communism was complex. Though resisting the crude advances of the ABB and the Workers party, his writings and speeches are nevertheless often interspersed with nonhostile and even favorable references to communism. His publications also frequently carried news of an anti-imperialist nature from communist sources. Even sources actively hostile to Garvey, such as Cyril Briggs' Crusader News Service and the *Negro Worker*, were utilized for news items. *Negro World* columnists also occasionally wrote favorably on communism.

Garvey's ambiguities concerning communism may be partially explained, as already noted, by the fact that he normally distinguished between communism in Russia, especially under Lenin, and communism in America. He was once quoted as suggesting a pact with Lenin and

Trotsky to take Africa during a Liberty Hall speech of August 1920.[104]
In 1922 he referred to the experiment in "social democracy" in Russia
as one that would probably prove "a boon and a blessing to mankind."[105]
But Garvey's most extensive appreciation of the revolutionary experiments
in Russia came in 1924, just seven months before the Workers party offensive. The proximity of these two events highlights Garvey's different attitudes to the two Communisms. The occasion was Lenin's death in January 1924. Garvey's first response was a telegram to the All Soviet Congress which said in part, "To us Lenin was one of the world's greatest
benefactors. Long life to the Soviet Government of Russia."[106] This was
followed by a lengthy speech at Liberty Hall entitled, "The Passing of
Russia's Great Man," in which he called Lenin "probably the greatest
man in the world between 1917 and the hour of 1924 when he breathed
his last." He expressed the view also that the whole world was destined
ultimately to assume Russia's form of government. He presumed that the
UNIA's message of condolence would be treated with respect, even though
"unfortunately, we have not yet sent an ambassador to Russia." He explained that Lenin represented the class that comprised the majority of
mankind. He continued,

> Therefore Lenin stands out greater than all because he was the rep-
> resentative of a larger number of people. Not only the peasantry of
> Russia mourn for Lenin at this hour, but the peasantry of all of
> Europe, the peasantry of the whole world mourn for Lenin, because
> he was their leader. And we also, as Negroes, mourn for Lenin. Not
> one but the four hundred millions of us should mourn over the death
> of this great man, because Russia promised great hope not only to
> Negroes but to the weaker peoples of the world. Russia through her
> social democratic system promised a revolution to the world that
> would truly and indeed emancipate the souls of men everywhere.
> Negroes have not yet gotten to realise the effect of certain world
> changes. We of the Universal Negro Improvement Association who
> lead have studied carefully and keenly the activities of Lenin and
> Trotsky. We have never before committed ourselves to any public
> opinion as touching the system of government now existing in
> Russia because we did not believe it wise. The social democratic
> soviet government of Russia is not yet recognised by all the other

governments of the world. Only a few recognised governments have recognised Russia. The governments of the capitalist class, the governments of the privileged class have refused to recognise Russia as a government. They are still seeking and hoping that another revolution will be enacted in Russia that will take the power and control of government out of the hands of the peasantry and pass it back into the hands of the privileged class. At that hour all the other governments not yet recognising Russia will recognise her government. But we of the Universal Negro Improvement Association, as I said, had our own opinion and our own idea in the matter of the new government of Russia. And it is without any hesitancy, without any reserve, we could not but favor the existence of a social democratic government in Russia or in any other part of the world, because we are of the class that rules in Russia and naturally our sympathy should be with the people who feel with us, who suffer with us.[107]

It was partly for sentiments such as these that European, North American and Latin American governments often considered Garvey communist. The fact that this was a period when radicalism was often equated with Bolshevism in official minds doubtless exaggerated this tendency. And Garvey of course was not loathe to proclaim himself a radical—"They talk about Garvey being radical," he said on one occasion. "How can a Negro be conservative? What has he to conserve? What have you but pain, suffering and hardship? It is time for the Negro to be radical and let the world know what he wants."[108] Thus he could be variously described by the British authorities as backed by the Industrial Workers of the World, by a provincial governor of Costa Rica as Bolshevik, by J. Edgar Hoover as pro-Bolshevik, by the Belgian imperialists as having Bolshevik connections, and by one United States official as being president of a communist party.[109] By 1932, however, the British Home Office had finally discovered that "available information goes to show that Marcus Garvey's organization is regarded by Moscow as 'bourgeois.' "[110]

Garvey's attitude toward American communists may have been influenced by the white chauvinism that existed within their ranks. Claude McKay had charged white American communists with racism at the fourth Comintern congress.[111] Similar charges were made during the sixth congress in 1928, and were acknowledged by the highest Comintern circles, in the person of Nikolai Bukharin, who warned his comrades "to adhere in the given sphere to a correct line mercilessly combatting the slightest manifestation of 'racial chauvinism.' "[112] Garvey remained convinced, however, that in a place like America, "the reign of executive communism would be no improvement on the reign of executive democracy."[113]

Garvey's hostility to American communism was also conditioned by his stubborn refusal to have his organization coopted by anybody, whether on the right or left. Writing in 1932, Garvey recalled the repeated communist attempts to seize his organization. He said,

> Communists have been our bitter foes for the last ten years. They have done us a great deal of harm in the United States. They made attempts several times to operate an organization of four million coloured people, of which we were head, and when we stopped them and stubbornly resisted them all around, they initiated a vile and wicked propaganda against us calling us Capitalists, Bourgeoisie, Opportunists and Uncle Toms.[114]

Garvey was sure that in the United States the communists would merely "use the Negro's vote and physical numbers" to elevate the position of their own kind. The black man would then discover that the majority race was still in power, "not only as communists but as whitemen."[115] This kind of thinking led *Negro World* editor H. G. Mudgal in 1932 to scoff at the selection of black James W. Ford as a communist candidate for vice-president of the United States. He argued that Ford was chosen because the communists knew they had no chance of winning.[116] Garvey's suspicions of communist duplicity had an unusual possible corroboration in a British military intelligence report of 1920. The communication, originating in New York, dealt with radical propaganda among black people and concluded that blacks were "being used to serve the ulterior purposes of the reds" and were then to be discarded. The evidence for this assertion was provided by circulars allegedly "sent out to 'Distributors of I. W. W. literature' " and obtained from an unnamed "reliable source." The circulars were said to contain the following information:

Extra activity in reaching the negroes is desired. We do not exactly want him in the organization, but we want him to help stir up unrest and general disorder. The negro is rapidly rising to a high position in useful citizenship and social standing. We need to break this up. If we can disassociate him from his present tendency to what they call good citizenship and get capital down on him we can drop him out of the association later.[117]

Friction between Garveyites and communists continued after Garvey's imprisonment and deportation. Despite his absence he left behind a firm ideological grip on masses of black people in America. Cyril Briggs admitted this fact in 1931 when he wrote that "the Garvey movement, while in decline and on the verge of collapse, still represents a most dangerous reactionary force, exercising considerable ideological influence over large masses of Negroes."[118]

Even in this period though, communist tactics were characterized by the same combination of open hostility and simultaneous attempts to impose "united front" alliances on the UNIA. The friendly approach was articulated by James W. Ford as follows: "How do we approach the Garveyites, and the other nationalistic elements. . . . We approach them in a friendly manner, and Negro Communists say: 'We Communists are defenders of our people, defenders of the Ethiopian people. . . .' "[119]

Such tactics were often aimed at UNIA leaders. In 1926 we find a committee including Workers Party representative C. E. Ruthenberg, Manuel Gomez, secretary of the Anti-Imperialist League and others arranging to have George Weston, New York UNIA leader, sent on a trip to an anti-imperialist conference in Brussels. They were also considering the possibility of throwing in a trip to the U.S.S.R. after the conference.[120] Weston was at the time leading a UNIA faction of his own in a dispute with the rest of the organization.

A more serious attempt to create strife through befriending the leaders came in 1935, when a Provisional Committee for the Defense of Ethiopia (PCDE) was formed in Harlem. The founding conference was held at the New York UNIA headquarters, and Captain A. L. King, leader of the UNIA New York Central Division, was unanimously elected chairman. The executive secretary was to be A. W. Berry of the communist-

organized League of Struggle for Negro Rights, while the publicity director was William Fitzgerald of another communist organization, International Labor Defense.[121] Among the members of the PCDE were James
W. Ford, at this time secretary of the Harlem branch of the Communist
party of the U.S.A. Ford used this opportunity to cultivate King's cooperation. In November he invited King to join a delegation to Mayor LaGuardia
to protest police invasion of a Harlem dance sponsored by the Communist
party at which seventy-four persons were arrested. The next month he
invited King to a meeting of top Harlem leaders with an Anti-Fascist
Committee.[122]

Such cooperation between King and the communists caused dissension
in UNIA ranks. A movement developed to crush King on this account.
The dissidents reaffirmed their loyalty to Ethiopia but refused to serve
on the same committee as communists. They accused King of dictator-
ship and of trying to turn the New York UNIA communist.[123] They
apparently contacted Garvey, and King was forced to write Garvey in
explanation. He assured Garvey that the sole reason for his participating
in the PCDE was to buy publicity which the organization could not
afford. He explained that several organizations belonged to the PCDE
and that the UNIA held the balance of power. This in his opinion did not
amount to consorting with the communists.[124] If King's explanation
was honest, what this meant was that the UNIA was trying to use the
communists in exactly the same way as the communists were simultaneously trying to use the UNIA. King's contact with the communists continued a while longer, for in February 1936 he was invited by the American Friends of the Soviet Union to send a UNIA representative with an
American delegation to the U.S.S.R.[125]

Relations between the two groups were not always so cordial after
Garvey's imprisonment. The communist press, headed by the *Liberator,*
regularly published appeals to Garveyites to join such communist bodies
as the League of Struggle for Negro Rights. Such appeals were accompanied
by scurrilous and otherwise hostile articles on Garvey and the UNIA and
were backed up by active proselytizing in black communities. Here, however, the presence of Garveyites proved a constant stumbling block. A
report by a member of the Young Liberators (a Communist group) in
1931 gave indication of this. While recruiting on Chicago's South Side
the group had encountered young Garveyites, who informed the Liberators

that white sons of slavemasters and rapists would never help black people. The Liberators tried for three hours to establish a distinction between white capitalists and white workers. The Garveyites were not convinced, but the Liberators entertained hopes of eventually winning them over since they were "sincere and militant."[126] Communist recruitment on the South Side had had a long history of frustration by Garveyites, going back at least as far as 1924.[127]

These types of encounters were accompanied by more serious ones. In 1927 the *Negro World* editorially attacked the communist American Negro Labor Congress.[128] And in 1930 occurred the most serious clash of all, resulting in a street fight that claimed the life of communist Alfred Levy. This particular brawl was the culmination of a bitter feud between the two groups in the New York area in 1930. William Grant, leader of the UNIA Tiger Division, had been assaulted some time before by persons he identified as communists. He had the police arrest the black communists whom he charged were his attackers. The communist International Labor Defense arranged to defend the accused.[129] The Tiger Division subsequently proclaimed its hostility to "Communists and Crooks."[130] The scene of Levy's death was a street corner UNIA meeting on Harlem's Lenox Avenue. Communists attacked the meeting, according to the Garveyite version, and one tried to mount the speaker's platform. The police, who were on hand, attempted to restrain the communists but without success. Fighting broke out and the police "entreated" the Garveyites to provide assistance. A free-for-all ensued and Levy was killed. The next day Garveyites met again at the same corner and declared their intention to break up any meeting on Lenox Avenue which spoke against the Garvey movement. Garvey's *Blackman* announced from Jamaica, "Their action can be readily understood for Garveyism forms one of the chief targets of communist hate and vindictiveness, the sowers of red propaganda branding their peaceful brothers as 'imperialist agents,' 'traitors to their race' and 'bourgeois.' "[131] The communists meanwhile retired to 144 Street and Lenox Avenue where the body of Alfred Levy lay in state under a constant communist guard. After two days a mass rally was addressed at the scene by Otto Huiswoud, who utilized the opportunity to attack Garvey. Levy was finally buried to the strains of the "Internationale."[132]

Relations were particularly strained for the two years or so after this. The *Negro World* carried an occasional letter alleging communist practice

of jim crow, or like one from Farrell, Pennsylvania, reporting that communists were telling people that they were working together with the
UNIA and that Garveyites should therefore join the communists.[133] In
1931 a Chicago Liberty Hall refused permission to August E. Poansjoe,
a Communist party candidate for city treasurer who desired to speak
there.[134]

And the communists in 1931 brought their biggest propaganda guns,
as represented by the Scottsboro case, to bear on the UNIA. In the Scottsboro case nine innocent black youths had been framed on charges of
raping two white ladies of ill repute and had been sentenced to death in
Alabama. The ILD had captured the defense from the NAACP and had
reaped a windfall from the international indignation felt at this travesty
of justice. The Scottsboro windfall became a powerful propaganda weapon.
A *Negro World* editorial of 1931 expressed an often-voiced view that the
communists would never have supported the accused were it not for the
publicity. It doubted their sincerity in view of their hostility to UNIA
divisions and other race groups trying to help.[135] Mrs. Ada Wright, mother
of two of the accused, was utilized to attack Tiger Division leader William
Grant in a speech to Garveyites in New York.[136] The *Liberator* published
an open letter attacking Grant and inviting UNIA members to join the
Scottsboro fight.[137] The UNIA attitude was summed up as follows: "Let
Communists agitate, congregate, and propagate—if they must; but let us
remain on the 'side lines' until something is started that will provide us
the opportunity that we need for making our grand 'getaway.' "[138]

The *Liberator* kept up its intensive campaign against Garvey in this
period. A successor to the *Negro Champion,* its contributing editors contained such well-known ABB and black communist names as Otto Hall,
Otto Huiswoud and J. W. Ford. The stridency of its attacks doubtless
owed something to the fact that Cyril Briggs was editor. Its attacks were
frequently comprised of wild exaggerations and distortions. On Garvey's
being barred from Cuba the *Liberator* commented in 1930 that he was
nevertheless still an imperialist tool but was being treated in this manner
by the imperialists because they were now "served by other interests"
and no longer needed Garvey "as a peddler of his particular illusions."[139]
In 1931 the paper editorialized that the League of Struggle for Negro
Rights (successor to the American Negro Labor Congress as a black communist alternative to other race organizations) "must expose this out-

rageous attempt to hoodwink the Negro masses." It continued, "meetings
must be held, leaflets distributed, contacts made with the Garvey masses,
and a smashing attack carried out against these peddlers of illusions, and
apologists for imperialism, and to win the workers in the Garvey organizations for real struggle."[140]

The *Liberator* was ably supported on the international level by a constant anti-Garvey barrage emanating from the *Negro Worker*. This journal,
published initially in Hamburg, Germany, and later at other locations,
was the organ of the International Trade Union Committee of Negro
Workers (ITUC-NW), a creation of the Red International of Labor Unions
(Profintern). The Profintern had set the tone for *Negro Worker* attacks
on Garvey by declaring in its 1931 "Special Resolution on Work among
Negroes in the United States and the Colonies" that "Of all forms of
ideological deceit, the most dangerous is 'Garveyism,' denying the class
struggle, and the possibility of the revolutionary struggle of the Negro
masses for self-determination."[141] Even before this, an ITUC-NW statement made at its founding conference in Hamburg in 1930 had declared
war on "Negro capitalist misleaders" such as Garvey, Du Bois, and a host
of others, as well as on "the white trade union faker, Captain Cipriani,
in the West Indies."[142] In 1933 Garvey was moved to comment on the
Negro Worker campaign. He wrote, "The Communists, through their
Negro section, are publishing a Monthly Magazine from Germany, called
'THE NEGRO WORKER.' We recognize members of the editorial staff
as Negroes we have met at different places. We think these Negroes are
doing their race a great deal of harm at the present time, by trying to
influence them toward assuming the responsibility of propagating Communism."[143] Garvey argued here that communism had "a great chance in
influencing a change in the political systems of the world," but black
people should still not be "sacrificed at the early stages of the battle"
by the communists.

The *Negro Worker* and other ITUC-NW materials were read by black
people who, while admiring the militancy of these publications, did not
always appreciate the denunciations of Garvey. A letter from such a reader
in British Guiana was published in 1932 together with a reply from the
editor. An extensive exchange took place in 1936 and 1937[144] between
the editor, at this time Charles Woodson (in fact Otto Huiswoud, according to a United States intelligence source)[145] and a veteran UNIA leader

from Dominica, J. R. Ralph Casimir. Casimir at this time was the Dominica
agent for the *Negro Worker* and threatened to quit performing this service
due to the misleading attacks on Garvey. He particularly disliked the
journal's tendency to play down the role of the imperialists in thwarting
Garvey's Liberian plans. The journal devoted several pages to Casimir's
letters and the editorial responses. Several anti-Casimir letters were also
published, including one from Garvey's veteran foe W. A. Domingo.

The Trotskyist wing of the communist movement also contemplated
ways of getting around Garvey's influence in the 1930s. Toward the end
of the decade their black spokesman, C. L. R. James (hiding under the
pseudonym J. R. Johnson), suggested a black united front organization
for mass struggle which would show that it was "fighting as a Negro organization, but has nothing to do with Garveyism."[146]

Nowhere is the unusual blend of tolerance and rabid hostility that
characterized the Garveyism-communism relationship better seen than
in the series of formal debates which took place between the two groups
in this period. Such exchanges had a long history. The *Negro World* of
September 20, 1919, had contained an exchange of letters between Harlem
literary figure Claude McKay and William H. Ferris, literary editor of
Garvey's paper. McKay had argued in favor of Bolshevism, suggesting
that black toilers would automatically be freed in the wake of a white
proletarian revolution. Informal debates between Workers party members
and UNIA members in Chicago have already been referred to. At Garvey's
International Convention held in Jamaica in 1929 a formal debate took
place between Garvey himself and Otto Huiswoud in yet another communist attempt to influence a UNIA convention. The topic resolved that
"The Negro Problem Can Only Be Solved by International Labor Cooperation between White and Black Labour." Garvey obviously argued
against and obviously won. The audience was judge.[147] In February 1931
the editor of the *Negro World,* H. G. Mudgal, engaged a Mr. Welch, described as associate editor of the *Revolutionary Age,* in a formal debate.
A large crowd of communists and Garveyites turned up at the Frederick
Douglass International Forum in Brooklyn to hear them debate the topic,
"Garveyism vs. Communism: Which Will Best Solve the Negro Problem?"
Mudgal won, probably because there must have been more Garveyites in
the audience than communists. Welch argued that the Negro problem was
essentially a class problem, while Mudgal argued that "No Non-Negro

could pretend to give a philosophy to just suit the needs and moods of the black masses."[148] Mudgal won a similar debate later that year against Albert Weisbord, editor of the left-wing communist *Class Struggle*. In December of that year the Cleveland division reported a similar debate, with both sides argued by Garveyites. In 1932 the *Liberator* reported that UNIA organizer Mme. De Mena had refused a communist challenge for a debate while on tour due to lack of time.[149]

Garvey's attitude toward the communists was vindicated to some extent in the 1930s and the 1940s when several prominent black communists became disenchanted and dropped out of the movement over such issues as Stalin's downgrading of work among black people, the U.S.S.R.'s sale of oil to the Italian fascists, which was used during their invasion of Ethiopia, and the hostility of American communists to black civil-rights activity during World War II. The common problem in such cases was the question of what to do when black nationalism ran counter to party interest. Many of these persons had been attracted to communism in the first place because of the potential they perceived in it for oppressed black peoples, as stressed in communist propaganda concerning Russia's favorable treatment of minorities, self-determination in the Black Belt, and so on. A very excellent example of all this, and one which shows the appeal that Garvey continued to exert over race-conscious black people, even in the communist hierarchy, was the case of George Padmore.

As a youth in Trinidad, Padmore had probably been a reader of the *Negro World* and impressed by the uprising there in 1919 which was led by Garveyites. C. L. R. James thinks that Padmore was "profoundly influenced by Garvey" at this time.[150] Certainly by the time Padmore migrated to the United States in 1924 Trinidad was the second most UNIA-organized island in the Caribbean, after Cuba. In the United States Padmore became a communist around 1927.[151] Yet in 1928 he led a protest at Howard University against the presence of British ambassador Sir Esme Howard on campus because the latter had played an important role in Garvey's deportation from the United States and Canada. Lengthy mimeographed sheets were distributed to this effect, bearing Padmore's name as secretary of the International Anti-Imperialistic Youths' League.[152] Padmore soon afterward journeyed to Moscow where he became head of the Negro Bureau of the Profintern. During the early 1930s he edited the *Negro Worker* and churned out several pamphlets and other materials

presenting communist views on various matters relevant to black workers.
Whatever lingering affinities he may have had to Garvey in 1928 were not
visible in most of these writings (mostly published in 1931). Indeed he
denounced Garvey with monotonous regularity in standard communist
rhetoric—"The struggle against Garveyism," he wrote, by way of example,
"represents one of the major tasks of the Negro toilers in America and
the African and West Indian colonies." Or again, "Like Zionism and
Gandhism, it (Garveyism) is merely out to utilize racial and national
consciousness for the purpose of promoting the class interests of the
black bourgeoisie and landlords." Another typical piece of abuse explained that Garvey was "the greatest fraud and racketeer who has ever
imposed himself upon an oppressed people."[153]

Yet in the same year that Padmore was parroting these stock communist expressions of abuse he gave an inkling of a lingering sympathy
with Garvey in a pamphlet entitled *American Imperialism Enslaves
Liberia.* Here he fleetingly departed from his distortions to admit that
Garvey's Liberian scheme "was defeated through the intervention of the
U.S. Government." He also repeated the "rumour" that W. E. B. Du Bois
was used by President Coolidge to help defeat the scheme.[154]

Padmore discontinued his various communist affiliations in 1933 and
was then formally expelled from the movement amid much strident comment from his successors in the *Negro Worker.* He had departed because
of his conviction that the partial phasing out of the Comintern's anticolonial program in Asia and Africa was a "betrayal of the fundamental
interests of my people."[155] In expelling him his ex-colleagues accused
him of many of the things that he had accused Garvey of. The ITUC-NW
published a lengthy statement of "very serious charges" summed up in
the following extract—"At a meeting on February 23, 1934, the International Control Commission decided to expel Padmore from the Communist Party for contacts with a provocateur, for contacts with bourgeois
organizations on the question of Liberia, for an incorrect attitude to
the national question (instead of class unity striving towards race unity)."[156]
A later *Negro Worker* statement showed how the Garveyite race-first
position had affected Padmore. It charged, "In a most feeble effort to
justify his position and a profound lack of confidence in the revolutionary
white workers, he claims, 'what you white comrades have never understood and will never be able to understand, is the psychology of the

Negro.' "[157] The same statement, in criticizing his fund-raising activities on behalf of Liberia, lumped him together with Garvey "the father of such an idea, who introduced the 'back to Africa movement' in the same manner."[158] Yet a later article on "The Rise and Fall of George Padmore As a Revolutionary Fighter," again compared him with Garvey declaring, in what was intended as abuse, that he had "two souls, that of the anti-imperialist and that of the Negro nationalist."[159] Padmore would have considered this a compliment, as would most black revolutionaries, Garvey included.

Once the communist movement had become a thing of Padmore's past, his attitude to Garvey once more underwent a modification. As a contributor to Afro-American papers from 1938 on, his articles sometimes assumed a Garveyite tone.[160] In 1947 he was actually listed as "our European correspondent on Colonial questions" by the Garveyite journal *The African*.[161] The year 1952 found him paying homage to Garvey as the inspirer of Jomo Kenyatta's "Africa for the Africans."[162] Shortly afterward in his major work *Pan-Africanism or Communism?* he called Garvey "the greatest black prophet and visionary since Negro Emancipation."[163] In this same work he apparently admitted Garvey's influence on his departure from communism in what may have been a veiled reference to himself when he said, "Garvey's anti-Communist tirades had a demoralizing effect upon neophyte Negro party members, some of whom were expelled for 'black nationalist deviations.' "[164] He also repeated here Garvey's often-expressed view that communists regarded black workers and peasants as "revolutionary expendables."[165]

Although the greatest battles between Garveyism and communism were waged in the United States, the struggle between these two ideologies was, of course, worldwide. And the place that most closely approximated the United States in its objective racial situation was South Africa. Here too there was jim crow (apartheid), a small communist party led by white radicals, and massive black movements in the African National Congress (ANC) and the Industrial and Commercial Workers Union (ICU), both of which had close links with the UNIA (See Chapter 7).

South Africa, too, was affected by the 1928 Comintern decision to adopt a nationalist line on the race question. Together with the imposition of the slogan for self-determination in the Black Belt in the United States, the 1928 congress sought to impose on the South African comrades the slogan of an "independent native South African republic based on the organization of the laborers and peasants guaranteeing (at the same time) the rights of the national minorities." S. P. Bunting, the South African party's white spokesman (mistakenly thought to be black by United States officials monitoring the congress), resisted this slogan. He stuck stubbornly to a preference for class struggle over racial struggle and claimed that South Africa had no effective national movement. He claimed that of the party's 1,750 members, 1,600 were black (up from only 200 the previous year).[166] The majority of the South African Central Committee shared this view and were attacked by the Comintern's executive committee for their "stubborn opposition to the correct slogan proposed by the Comintern."[167] Bunting and his colleagues seem nevertheless to have made some attempt to implement the Comintern's desires, for in 1930 they were in turn attacked within the party for preaching "Native Republicanism," which was seen as "Marcus Garveyism" under a different name. The black editor of the Cape Town communist weekly *Umsebenzi*, replying to this attack, argued that any white socialist who could not "acknowledge the right of the exploited and sjambokked Natives to complete national autonomy" must be considered a white chauvinist, "however many lectures he may have delivered before Native audiences."[168] The editor of the *Negro World* expressed the wish that black United States communists could be similarly independent of spirit and added, "We are glad to see Garveyism triumph not only over imperialism of the capitalists but also over the imperialism of the Communists."[169]

On occasion the purely American aspect of the struggle between the two ideologies spilled over into South Africa, as in 1931 when the *Negro World* poked fun at Cyril Briggs' article published in a South African communist paper. Briggs had in that article attacked a *Negro World* editorial. The *Negro World* taunted Briggs with preaching "unadulterated Garveyism" by advocating "Negro rights" worldwide. "But the only difference," the editorial suggested, "is that Briggs is willing to take orders from Moscow and Garvey is not willing to take orders from anyone whatsoever." The editorial continued with a taunt the like of which was to cause people like George Padmore to leave the communist ranks. It said, "We hope this expose of Cyril Briggs would not cost him his place as a betrayer of the orthodox Communist philosophy which denounces Briggs' idea as jimcrow nationalism. Wish you luck, Cyril, and hope those Communist bosses of yours will not notice this item."[170]

George Padmore summarized Garvey's struggles against the communists when he wrote, "The biggest mistake that the white Communists made was to attack Garvey openly and try to disrupt his movement before they had won confidence among the Negroes . . . . By fighting the Communists with their own weapons of half-truths, villification and thuggery, Marcus Garvey was the first black leader to force them to keep their hands off Negro organizations."[171]

NOTES

1. *Daily Worker,* August 23, 1924.
2. Ibid., August 9, 1924.
3. Theodore Draper, *American Communism and Soviet Russia* (New York: The Viking Press, 1960), p. 320.
4. Ibid.; William Z. Foster, *The Negro People in American History* (New York: International Publishers, 1954), p. 455.
5. *The Communist,* 13 [1920] : 4.
6. Foster, *The Negro People,* p. 455.
7. Draper, *American Communism,* p. 320.
8. Ibid., pp. 320, 321.
9. "Theses on the National and Colonial Question Adopted By the Second Comintern Congress, July 28, 1920," in Jane Degras, ed., *The Communist International, 1919-1943* (New York: Oxford University Press, 1956), I: 142. The "etc." after "Negroes" does not appear in this version but is incorporated from a shorter quotation in Draper, *American Communism,* p. 337.
10. Claude McKay, "Soviet Russia and the Negro," *Crisis* 27 (December 1923): 64; Draper, *American Communism,* p. 321; Claude McKay, *A Long Way From Home* (New York: Harcourt, Brace & World, 1970), p. 206.
11. Draper, *American Communism,* p. 326; Degras, *Communist International,* pp. 398, 399.
12. Degras, *Communist International,* I: 398-401.
13. Foster, *The Negro People,* p. 457.
14. U. Steklov, "The Awakening Race," *Izvestia,* November 16, 1922, RG 59, 861.00—Congress, Communist International, IV/2, National Archives.
15. Degras, *Communist International,* II: 97.
16. Draper, *American Communism,* pp. 328, 329.

17. Ibid., p. 334.

18. Summary from Moscow *Pravda,* July 17, 1928, RG 59, 861.00–
Congress, Communist International VI/13.

19. *Pravda,* July 26, 1928, speech by Dunne, RG 59, 861.00–Congress, Communist International VI/19.

20. Summary based on *Pravda,* August 18, 1928, RG 59, 861.00–
Congress, Communist International VI/13.

21. Ibid., summary from *Pravda,* August 24, 1928.

22. Ibid., *Pravda,* August 25, 1928.

23. Degras, *Communist International,* II: 552-557.

24. Foster, *The Negro People,* p. 463. A slightly different wording is
suggested in Draper, *American Communism,* p. 344.

25. George Padmore, *Pan-Africanism or Communism?* (New York:
Roy Publishers, 1956 [?]), pp. 305, 306.

26. *Negro Champion* 1 (August 27, 1928): 8.

27. This and preceding quotations from Degras, *Communist International,* III: 124-135.

28. McKay, *A Long Way From Home,* p. 208.

29. George Breitman, ed., *Leon Trotsky on Black Nationalism and
Self-Determination* (New York: Merit Publishers, 1967), pp. 14, 18, 25,54.

30. Amy Jacques Garvey, ed., *The Philosophy and Opinions of
Marcus Garvey* (London: Frank Cass, 1967), II: 315.

31. *Negro World,* March 24, 1923.

32. Ibid., September 4, 1926.

33. Marcus Garvey, *The Tragedy of White Injustice* (New York:
A. J. Garvey, 1927), p. 14.

34. Charles Latham to Secretary of State, August 24, 1921, RG 59,
811.108 G 191/24.

35. Garvey to Rt. Hon. Phillip Snowdon, Chancellor of the Exchequer,
February 27, 1930, CO 318/399/76634, Colonial Office Records, Public
Record Office, London.

36. *Negro World,* November 1, 1924.

37. *Blackman,* September 12, 1929.

38. *Negro World,* December 1, 1923.

39. Garvey, *Philosophy and Opinions,* II: 69.

40. Amy Ashwood Garvey, "Prophet of Black Nationalism," p. 73.
Theodore G. Vincent, *Black Power and the Garvey Movement* (Berkeley:
Ramparts Press, 1971 [?]), p. 98.

41. Charles L. Latham to Secretary of State, September 12, 1920,
RG 59, 811.108 G 191/1; Alves introduced Garvey at a meeting in the
Ward Theatre, Kingston in 1921–*Negro World,* April 16, 1921.

42. *Daily Gleaner,* June 2, 1921, quoted in Adolph Edwards, *Marcus Garvey* (London: New Beacon Publications, 1967), p. 15.

43. *Blackman,* May 14, 27, 28, 29, 30, 1929.

44. Ibid., December 31, 1929, March 10, March 17, 1930.

45. Ibid., January 11, April 12, 1930.

46. Ibid., April 26, 1930. A Garvey message on behalf of Jamaica's workers and labourers received scant attention from the British Colonial Office—E. B. Boyd to Rt. Hon. Lord Stamfordham, September 20, 1930, CO 318/399/76634.

47. *Black Man,* 3 (July 1938): 6. In 1941 the *National Negro Voice* (July 19, 1941, p. 5) considered Garvey together with Bustamante, Ken Hill and S. Kerr Coombs (publisher of the *Jamaica Labour Weekly*) as outstanding labor figures of the period. This paper also said that Garvey had created a Jamaica Labour Union in 1935 (August 9, 1941, p. 3).

48. Governor Wilfred Collet of British Guiana to Viscount Milner, October 8, 1920, Collet to Rt. Hon. Winston Churchill, June 7, 1921, CO 318/356. Critchlow himself mentions workers turning to Garveyism during hard times in the 1920s. See Hubert Critchlow, "History of the Trade Union Movement in British Guiana," in George Padmore, ed., *Voice of Coloured Labour* (Manchester: PANAF Service Ltd. [1945]), p. 51. At a 1921 UNIA meeting held by travelling commissioner R. H. Tobitt, Critchlow and a Mr. Andrews of the B.G. Labour Union were on the platform, together with G. S. Primo, Local UNIA head, J. Johnson, Vice-President, E. M. Seaton, Secretary and others—*Negro World,* July 2, 1921, reprinted from *The Tribune* (B.G.), May 22, 1921. In 1922 Tobitt was guest of honor at the third anniversary meeting of the B.G. Labour Union—*Negro World,* March 11, 1922.

49. Governor Charles Bain of Barbados to Secretary of State, Colonial Office, January 16, 1923, FO 371/8450.

50. C. E. Rappolee, Governor, U.S. Virgin Islands, "Report on activities of one D. Hamilton Jackson," February 10, 1923, RG 59, 811 G 00/37.

51. Basil Brentnol Blackman, Secretary-Treasurer, Caribbean Congress of Labour, lecture at St. Ann's Community Workshop, Trinidad, July 7, 1969.

52. Garvey, *Philosophy and Opinions,* II: 244.

53. Draper, *American Communism,* p. 333.

54. *The Communist,* 13 [1920]: 4.

55. Rose Pastor Stokes, "The Communist International and the Negro," *The Worker,* March 10, 1923.

56. Degras, *Communist International,* II: 557.

57. Robert Bruce and J. P. Collins, "The Party and the Negro Struggle," *The Communist* 1 (November 1921): 15.

58. Draper, *American Communism*, p. 329.

59. Ibid., pp. 323-325; *Crusader*, 3 (January 1921): 31; 5 (November 1921): 22; *New York Amsterdam News*, November 16, 1921; *The Worker*, August 11, 1923.

60. Cyril Briggs, "The Decline of the Garvey Movement," *Communist*, (June 1931): 550; Draper, *American Communism*, pp. 325, 326.

61. *The Worker*, August 5, 1922.

62. Congress, Communist International IV/5, minutes of "Session of the Commission on the Negro Question," November 28, 1922, enclosed in F. W. B. Coleman, U.S. Legation, Riga, Latvia, to Secretary of State, December 22, 1922, RG 59, 861.00–Congress, Communist International IV/5.

63. *The Worker*, August 18, 1923.

64. *Crusader* 4 (February 1921): 9.

65. Ibid. 5 (November 1921): 5.

66. *Negro World*, August 27,1921: Vincent, *Black Power*, p. 81; Garvey, *Garvey and Garveyism*, p. 64; *Crusader* 5 (November 1921): 5.

67. *Negro World*, September 3, 1921.

68. Garvey, *Philosophy and Opinions*, I: 73.

69. Ibid., II: 333, 334.

70. *Crusader* 5 (November 1921): 8.

71. *Negro World*, October 8, 1921.

72. *New York Herald*, October 21, 1921; *Crusader* 5 (November 1921): 5.

73. *Crusader* 5 (November 1921): passim.

74. *New York Times*, December 3, 1921.

75. *Negro World*, December 31, 1921. McGuire handed over *Negro World* subscription lists to Briggs, who sent anti-Garvey circulars to subscribers—ibid., January 14, 1922.

76. *Philosophy and Opinions*, II: xiv; Vincent, *Black Power*, p. 221.

77. *Negro World*, February 25, 1922.

78. Garvey to Harry M. Daugherty, U.S. Attorney General, January 22, 1923; Garvey to Daugherty, January 24, 1923, RG 60, 198940.

79. *Negro World*, March 20, 1926.

80. Ibid., April 3, 1926.

81. *Blackman*, August 2, 1930; *Liberator*, April 25, 1931.

82. *Communist* (June 1931): 547-552.

83. *Negro World*, August 29, 1931. See also ibid., February 27,1932.

84. *Negro Worker* 2 (August 1932): 14.

85. *New Jamaican,* September 20, 1932.
86. Crusader News Agency, week of May 20, 1940.
87. Summary from *Izvestia,* November 18, 1922, RG 59, 861.00—Congress, Communist International IV/4.
88. C. L. R. James, *A History of Pan-African Revolt* (Washington, D.C.: Drum and Spear Press, 1969), p. 79.
89. *Daily Worker,* August 18, 1924.
90. John Bruce and J. P. Collins, "The Party and the Negro Struggle," *The Communist* 1 (October 1921): 19.
91. *Negro Champion,* 1 (October 27, 1928): 5.
92. *Negro World,* November 7, 1925, from typewritten copy in Amy Jacques Garvey papers.
93. *Daily Worker,* February 11, 1924.
94. Ibid., February 18, 1924.
95. Degras, *Communist International,* II: 97. Degras says here that there were ten communists at the convention. She does not refer to the Sanhedrin by name but describes it as having taken place in Chicago in February 1924.
96. *Daily Worker,* July 29, 1924.
97. Ibid., August 5, 1924.
98. Ibid., August 6, August 13, August 18, 1924.
99. Ibid., August 13, 1924.
100. Ibid., August 23, 1924; *Negro World,* August 30, 1924.
101. *Daily Worker,* August 23, 1924; references to a black Workers party delegate, Mrs. Olivia Whiteman, are in reports of August 15, 1924, and August 19, 1924.
102. Ibid., August 29, 1924.
103. Ibid., August 25, 1924.
104. *New York Age,* September 4, 1920; *New York Tribune,* August 20, 1920.
105. Garvey, *Philosophy and Opinions,* II: 94.
106. *Negro World,* February 2, 1924.
107. Ibid., February 2, 1924. Editor T. Thomas Fortune did not share Garvey's views. Ibid.
108. Ibid., August 23, 1924.
109. Minute of September 15, 1920, FO 371/4567; "Unrest Among the Negroes," October 7, 1919, RG 28, Box 53 unarranged, file 398; American Consul, Port Limon, Costa Rica to Secretary of State, August 24, 1919, RG 59, 818.4016/orig.; J. Edgar Hoover, "Memorandum for Mr. Ridgely," October 11, 1919, RG 60, 198940; Home Office to Secretary o' ·

State Foreign Office, July 20, 1932, FO 371/16355; Frank Burke to A. J. Frey, September 1, 1921, RG 32, 605-1-653.

110. Home Office to Secretary of State, Foreign Office, July 20, 1932, FO 371/16355, Foreign Office Records, Public Record Office, London.

111. Draper, *American Communism*, p. 327.

112. *Pravda*, July 25, 27, August 4, 1928, RG 59, 861.00, Congress, Communist International VI/9.

113. *Black Man* 2 (July-August 1936): 8.

114. *New Jamaican*, September 5, 1932.

115. Garvey, *Philosophy and Opinions*, II: 69.

116. *Negro World*, June 11, 1932.

117. M.I. l.c. New York, "Special" General Report, January 6, 1920, "Negro Agitation," FO 371/4567.

118. *Communist* (June 1931): 551.

119. Quoted in Wilson Record, *The Negro and the Communist Party* (Chapel Hill, University of North Carolina Press, 1951), p. 135.

120. Lovett Fort-Whiteman to Pickens, September 11, 1926, Pickens Papers, Box 1.

121. UNIA Central Division (New York) Files, Box 15, G.

122. James W. Ford to Capt. A. L. King, November 28, December 8, 1935, UNIA Central Division (New York) Files, Box 13, e. 149.

123. Handbill, n.d., UNIA Central Division Files, Box 9, d. 41.

124. Ibid., King to Garvey, December 19, 1935, Box 8, d. 23.

125. Ibid., Mary Dalton, Executive Secretary, New York District, American Friends of The Soviet Union to King, February 19, 1936, Box 13, e. 149.

126. *Liberator*, April 25, 1931.

127. *Daily Worker*, September 12, 1924.

128. *Negro World*, July 16, 1927.

129. *Liberator*, April 25, 1931.

130. *Negro World*, August 9, 1930.

131. *Blackman*, July 12, 1930.

132. Ibid., July 19, 1930.

133. *Negro World*, November 22, 1930, May 23, 1931.

134. *Liberator*, April 25, 1931.

135. *Negro World*, May 23, 1931.

136. *Liberator*, July 4, 1931.

137. Ibid., June 13, 1931.

138. *Negro World*, January 30, 1932.

139. *Liberator,* February 8, 1930.

140. Ibid., March 28, 1931.

141. *Negro Worker* 1 (February 1931): 19.

142. George Padmore, *Negro Workers and the Imperialist War* (Hamburg: ITUC-NW, 1931), p. 16.

143. *Black Man* 1 (December 1933): 4, 5.

144. *Negro Worker* 6 (December 1936); 7 (April 1937).

145. Purport Book, RG 59, 844 g. 00/27.

146. Breitman, *Leon Trotsky on Black Nationalism*, p. 40.

147. *Daily Gleaner,* August 15, 1929; *Negro World,* September 14, 1929; Nembhard, *Trials and Triumphs of Marcus Garvey,* p. 140. Huiswoud represented the American Negro Labor Congress.

148. *Negro World,* February 14, 21, 28, 1931.

149. Ibid., October 17, 24, December 12, 1931; *Liberator,* July 15, 1932.

150. C. L. R. James, "Document: C. L. R. On the Origins," *Radical America* 2 (July-August 1968): 24.

151. James R. Hooker, *Black Revolutionary* (London: Pall Mall, 1967), p. 6.

152. *Negro World,* December 22, 1928; Hooker, *Black Revolutionary,* p. 7.

153. George Padmore, *The Life and Struggles of Negro Toilers* (London: ITUC-NW, 1931), pp. 125, 126; *Negro Worker* 1 (December 1931): 7.

154. George Padmore, *American Imperialism Enslaves Liberia* (Moscow: Centrizdat, 1931), pp. 6n, 33, 34.

155. Hooker, *Black Revolutionary,* p. 31.

156. *Negro Worker* 4 (June 1934): 14.

157. Ibid. 4 (July 1934): 6.

158. Ibid., p. 9.

159. Ibid. 4 (August 1934): 17.

160. James R. Hooker, "Africa for Afro-Americans: Padmore and the Black Press," *Radical America* 2 (July-August 1968): 14-19.

161. *The African* 5 (June-July 1947).

162. *Daily Gleaner,* October 23, 1952, quoted in A. J. Garvey, *Black Power in America,* p. 33.

163. Padmore, *Pan-Africanism or Communism?,* p. 87. There was still much hostility to Garvey expressed in this book, however.

164. Ibid., p. 304.

165. Ibid., p. 289.

166. Summary from *Pravda,* August 24, 1928, RG 59, 861.00—Congress, Communist International VI/13.

167. Degras, *Communist International,* II: 553; speech by Kuusinen, *Pravda,* September 1, 1928, RG 59, 861.00—Congress, Communist International VI/13.

168. *Umsebenzi,* September 26, 1930, quoted in *Negro World,* November 8, 1930.

169. *Negro World,* November 8, 1930.

170. Ibid., August 1, 1931.

171. Padmore, *Pan-Africanism or Communism?* 304, 305.

11

Of the NAACP and Integrationists, and Garvey and Separatists, or, The Integrationist Onslaught

Marcus Garvey is, without doubt, the most dangerous enemy of the Negro race in America and in the world. He is either a lunatic or a traitor.

—W. E. B. Du Bois[1]

I had promised not to waste much more of the space of the Negro World *on the cross-breed Dutch-French-Negro editor of the* Crisis, *the official organ of the National Association for the Advancement of "Certain" People, because it was like washing powder on blackbirds, but this one-third Dutchman, who assumes the right to dictate to the Negro people what they should do and should not do, has become so brazen and impertinent that it leaves me no other course than to deal with him as he deserves. In certain society, when we meet individuals of this kind, we do not waste time arguing with them, but give them a good horse whipping. . . .*

DuBois is speculating as to whether Garvey is a lunatic or a traitor. Garvey has no such speculation about DuBois. He is positive that he is a traitor.

—Marcus Garvey[2]

The National Association for the Advancement of Colored People, founded in 1909, was, by the time of Garvey's arrival in the United States, perhaps the most powerful of the large number of civil-rights and race-uplift organizations in the field. This reason alone would have given it sufficient cause to feel threatened by the rapid rise of the UNIA. But the rivalry and hostility which developed between these two organizations were fed by other considerations as well. Much of this disagreement was embodied in the acrimonious feud which was waged throughout Garvey's American period and afterward between Garvey and W. E. B. Du Bois, major black spokesman for the NAACP.

The major point of disagreement between the two organizations was undoubtedly the race question. The NAACP had been formed largely through the exertions of white socialists and liberals and Du Bois had been the sole black member of its initial national executive committee. Its national hierarchy in Garvey's time continued to be dominated by whites. Not unnaturally, therefore, the NAACP believed in interracial cooperation rather than in exclusively black organization. NAACP integrationism was not very different in this respect from the "progressive assimilationist tendencies" of the communists, and Garvey was opposed to both. He was particularly opposed to the position of control exercised by whites in the NAACP. He described this state of affairs as an insult and thought that the NAACP's white leaders "wish Negroes to go only so far and no further." He considered them "spies for the rest of the white race"[3] and saw them as a brake on the black man's self-reliance and a hindrance in the quest for black nationalism. In a speech entitled "Beware of Greeks Bearing Gifts," he said:

> The greatest enemies of the Negro are among those who hypocritically profess love and fellowship for him, when, in truth, and deep down in their hearts, they despise and hate him. Pseudo-philanthropists and their organizations are killing the Negro. White men and women of the Moorfield Storey, Joel Spingarn, Julius Rosenwald, Oswald Garrison Villard, Congressman Dyer and Mary White Ovington type, in conjunction with the above mentioned agencies, are disarming, dis-visioning, dis-ambitioning and fooling the Negro to death. They teach the Negro to look to the whites in a false direction . . . at the same time distracting the Negro from the real solution and objective of securing nationalism.[4]

Two years before this bitter statement Mary White Ovington, chairman of the NAACP's board of directors, had expressed herself privately (perhaps in jest) in a way that seemed to go along with Garvey's accusations. In a letter to Arthur B. Spingarn, at the time an NAACP vice-president, she said, "Only black people ought to live in these soft coal cities anyway! My lungs are daily growing as grey as the dingy curtains at my window."[5]

NAACP principles deviated from Garvey's not only on the question of white hegemony over race-uplift organizations but also over the question of attitudes to light-skinned black people. James Weldon Johnson, during Garvey's American period one of the handful of important national black NAACP officers, considered Garvey's major blunders to have included his alleged distinctions "between people of colour and blacks" and his black God, which, in Johnson's view, helped drive a wedge between blacks and lights.[6] This is not surprising, since in 1924 Garvey had published some of Johnson's *Autobiography of an Ex-Colored Man* in his daily newspaper to show that Johnson wanted to be white.[7] The NAACP also did not appreciate Garvey's contact with white segregationists.[8]

Garvey's Pan-African thrust provided another area of divergence between the two organizations. Despite Du Bois' well-known interest in the larger black world, the NAACP more typically saw itself as a specialist in the Afro-American field. James Weldon Johnson, writing during Garvey's 1920 convention, disagreed with the idea of Afro-American involvement in African liberation. He argued that Africans should be allowed to wage their own struggles. The best way that Afro-Americans could help, he thought, would be to take care of their own business at home.[9] Ten years later he argued that "The main reason for Garvey's failure with thoughtful American Negroes was his African scheme." He found it "difficult to give the man credit for either honesty or sanity in those imperialistic designs" unless his intention had been to stage a coup in Liberia.[10] This NAACP preoccupation with Afro-America led to some imbibing of the general attitudes of nativism which characterized America at large in the postwar years. Du Bois the Pan-Africanist was, strangely, one of the greatest offenders in this respect, at least in his attacks on Garvey, but other black NAACP leaders shared his pique at Garvey's foreignness. They never forgave Garvey for being first a foreigner, second bold enough to presume to lead an Afro-American movement, and third possessed of the temerity to assail James Weldon Johnson's

"thoughtful American Negroes." Johnson expressed much of this feeling
in a 1924 press release. He said: "Mr. Garvey, who is not an American
citizen, has taken it upon himself to go before the white people of this
country advocating that the American Negro abdicate his constitutional
rights, quit this country and go to Africa. Mr. Garvey apparently does not
know that the American Negro considers himself, and is, as much an
American as anyone. . . ."[11]

Garvey's ideological differences with the NAACP were translated into
a continuous succession of battles between the two. There was little that
either side did that did not result in condemnation from the other side.
One such contentious issue was the Dyer antilynching bill. The widespread public mutilation and execution of black people by lawless white
mobs, with the connivance of law enforcement personnel, was a subject
that exercised the minds of all black leaders in America. There were,
nevertheless, different approaches to solving the problem. In June 1919
a *Negro World* editorial attacked an NAACP resolution to fight lynching
by contributing to an antilynching fund and promised that the UNIA
would respond to lynching by physical means rather than by relying on
white philanthropy. With the appearance of the Dyer bill, however, the
UNIA decided at first on a policy of cooperation despite the fact that
the NAACP was spearheading the campaign for the bill's passage, and
even though it came at a time of escalating conflict between the two
organizations. The issue was obviously considered too important to allow
for considerations of organizational rivalry.

UNIA support was maintained through 1922, when the bill made it
through the House of Representatives only to be stifled afterwards in
the Senate. Thus in January Garvey despatched a telegram to Congress
urging the bill's passage. In February he took some of the credit for the
bill's passage in the House of Representatives. In March a *Negro World*
editorial by William Ferris praised the NAACP for its work on the bill.
About the same time a mixed audience meeting in support of the bill in
Wilmington, Delaware, was surprised to see a large UNIA contingent in
attendance, complete with seventy-five uniformed Black Cross Nurses
wearing their red, black and green buttons. They were there on the invitation of the NAACP, whose William Pickens was the principal speaker.
S. A. Haynes, UNIA commissioner for Delaware, also spoke. In May the
Negro World viewed favorably the visit to Washington, D.C., of a delegation led by William Monroe Trotter who hoped to dig the bill out of

committee, where it had become bogged down. In June the UNIA joined the NAACP, YMCA, and several other organizations in a parade from Harlem downtown into white Manhattan in support of the bill. And in November William H. Lewis, a black ex-assistant attorney general, spoke at Liberty Hall on the antilynching issue. A few months later Lewis was to engineer a visit by W. E. B. Du Bois to Liberia. On this occasion, however, he was effusive in his praise for Garvey.[12]

Even in the midst of this cooperation, though, occasional misgivings could be heard in the UNIA ranks. Garvey, ever suspicious of temporary palliatives where more lasting measures should be applied, declared in April that only at such time as the black man obtained a powerful government in Africa would lynching be eradicated. In May, John Edward Bruce, considering the lynching of a fifteen-year-old black youth in Texas by a crazed white mob of two thousand, exploded in disgust: "A thousand Dyer Anti-Lynching Bills cannot change the murderous instinct of these cattle." Soon afterward, Garvey began to criticize the NAACP's handling of the campaign, especially their attacks on the Republican administration while simultaneously trying to have the Republicans support the bill and their tendency to claim too much credit for whatever successes the bill did have.[13]

It was not until 1923, however, that Garvey became totally hostile to the antilynching campaign. By this time the NAACP and allied campaign to effect Garvey's imprisonment and deportation was at its height. He had also received further evidences of white hypocrisy. He wrote: "If Dyer does not know, let me tell him that I was in his Congressional District in St. Louis two weeks ago and could not get a soda served even by a dirty Greek, who kept his so-called white soda fountain in a Negro section, the section represented by the 'famous' antilynching advocate. Oh! The hypocrisy of this world!" Garvey's pique was increased by the fact that Dyer, in speeches for the NAACP, had expressed satisfaction at Garvey's conviction.[14]

Garvey now argued that Dyer's bill duplicated laws already on the books that could be enforced if the authorities so wished. Furthermore any laws Dyer proposed would still have to be enforced by white friends of the lynchers. (Some of Garvey's arguments here received an unusual vindication from the NAACP's Mary White Ovington. Whites, she wrote in a private letter, would not pass a bill to punish whites for lynching blacks.)[15]

Garvey saw the sinister hand of the NAACP behind most of his problems—from the 1921 attempt to exclude him from the country to the thwarting of his Liberia scheme, to his trial and imprisonment. He blamed the Black Star Line's problems on sabotage by certain "organizations calling themselves Negro Advancement Associations." James Weldon Johnson asked for a retraction of this statement and issued a press release on the matter. Garvey replied, no doubt tongue in cheek, that he had not referred specifically to the NAACP. "Those who have clear consciences," he admonished, "are not disturbed when anything not relating to them is said or published."[16]

Some of Garvey's bitterest accusations concerned the NAACP connections of Judge Mack and special agent Amos at his 1923 trial. He also charged that "a powerful banana and citrus fruit trust engaged in tropical trade" (apparently a reference to the United Fruit Company) had contributed to his trial and conviction. This trust employed large numbers of Black Star Line stockholders, and he identified the NAACP president, Moorfield Storey, as an "attorney or stockholder" of the fruit company.[17] The NAACP at one stage issued a press release denying a *Negro World* charge that Storey had visited the district attorney's office the same day that Garvey's case was called in order to secure a conviction.[18]

One of the more unusual of the NAACP-UNIA squabbles developed out of the visit to the United States in 1924 and 1925 of Prince Kojo Tovalou-Houénou of Dahomey. Kojó was a longtime associate of the UNIA and was feted at Liberty Hall. This caused him, according to some reports, to run the risk of forfeiting a tour of the country arranged for him by the NAACP. He therefore said uncomplimentary things about the UNIA, which had the effect of reinstating him in the good graces of the NAACP. In 1925 the prince lost two teeth while being forcibly ejected from a white Chicago restaurant, whither he had been taken by white NAACP members, in whose company he was at the time. The *Negro World* commented drily that it hoped he would now appreciate the slogan "Africa for the Africans."[19]

In the midst of their feud with Garvey the NAACP was occasionally chagrined by instances in which unknowing persons confused the two organizations. As early as 1919 Du Bois had run into this problem in Europe. When early in 1922 the *New York Times* and several other papers were misled by a news agency into calling Garvey "President of the

Association for the Advancement of the Colored Race," some NAACP officials counseled suit against them, and much energy was expended extracting retractions from the errant papers. The association explained to these editors that it comprised "white and colored people of the finest sort" and was not connected with Garvey.[20]

To add to the NAACP's discomfiture it received a steady stream of letters for and against Garvey. Many were from people who wanted to know whether Garvey was honest. One person wanted to know whether the NAACP endorsed the UNIA. Students at Howard University wanted material for a debate on the subject, "That the Marcus Garvey Movement is the best solution to the Negro Problem." The student body was said to be split between the two organizations. The editor of the *Nation* wanted confidential information on Garvey. Some, on the other hand, wrote abusive letters such as one man who returned his NAACP membership card, declaring "I am for Marcus Garvey." Another informed the association that it was a damned shame that their bunch of white men had nothing better to do than harass Garvey, the greatest black man of the age.[21] Most of the correspondents were referred by NAACP officials to anti-Garvey articles in the *Crisis, Crusader* and *Messenger.*

Yet some other rank-and-file members of the organizations were quite happy to tolerate both. In 1924, for example, Garvey spoke at Howard University under the auspices of the University's NAACP and Caribbean Clubs, both of which, it so happened, were led by the same individual.[22] Again, in 1921 Herbert J. Seligman of the NAACP received a sharp rebuke from a black lady in Boston for an article he had written on Garvey. The lady professed membership in the Boston NAACP, the National Equal Rights League, and the UNIA since they were all working for race uplift. She presumed that Seligman was white, and she expressed agreement with Garvey's views on the insincerity of white motives. "If Garvey fails and we all lose our money, it is *our business,*" she fumed, "and we have *sense enough to know* and to realise that there is a possibility of failure in everything in life save death." Seligman could manage only a weak reply about his right to criticize black as well as white and the "facts" upon which his article was based.[23] Dual membership in the rival organizations may have become more difficult after 1924, for that year's UNIA convention unanimously passed a resolution to the effect that any person joining the UNIA found to be an NAACP member would have to withdraw from one of the two.[24]

The struggle between the NAACP and the UNIA achieved its highest embodiment in the personal feud between Du Bois and Garvey. Prior to Garvey's arrival in the United States Du Bois had for many years been engaged in a celebrated ideological altercation with Booker T. Washington, undisputedly the most powerful black man in America for the two decades or so prior to his death in 1915. Apart from the very real ideological differences between the two men, Du Bois' initiatives against Washington could be construed as an attempt to wrest the mantle of unofficial supreme race leader from him. With Washington's death it may have seemed for a season that Du Bois was now free from serious competition. Yet, within four months of Washington's burial Garvey had arrived obscurely in the United States, and by 1920 he had established beyond all reasonable doubt, the fact that the country once more had a race leader of sufficient stature to clearly overshadow his contemporaries. He had appeared from nowhere and had overtaken the incumbent leadership with lightning strides. The battle which developed between himself and Du Bois far surpassed in acrimony the earlier Washington-Du Bois debate. The latter had, at least externally, been a rather genteel affair. The Du Bois-Garvey battle soon degenerated into a no-holds-barred contest in which all pretensions to decorum were dispensed with.

What was most fascinating about the Garvey-Du Bois struggle was that it was in a most real sense a continuation of the Washington-Du Bois debate. The ideological questions raised were largely the same. Furthermore Garvey was very self-consciously a disciple of Washington. Along with his admiration for Washington, Garvey had early imbibed a dislike for Du Bois. He therefore saw himself as the heir to Washington's fight against Du Bois and never missed an opportunity to compare the two, to the detriment of Du Bois.

It is impossible to pinpoint the exact date on which Garvey first became aware of Washington's ideas. The West Indies of Garvey's childhood had long been exposed to debates on the question of industrial education, the type popularized by Washington. Such debates in the West Indies had antedated Washington by many years. Yet, in the West Indies, as in America, Washington's influence provided a source of increased interest in industrial and agricultural schools. As a boy Garvey lived in St. Ann's Parish on Jamaica's north coast where in 1909 pioneer Barbadian Pan-Africanist Dr. Albert Thorne started an industrial school.[25] By this time interest in Washington's educational experiments was widespread in the islands and West Indian students were attending Washington's Tuskegee Institute. Several West Indian delegates attended Washington's International Conference on the Negro held at Tuskegee in 1912. Among them were a group of Jamaican educators, including the island's director of education. A resolution presented to the conference by British West Indian delegates, among them teachers and students at Tuskegee, called for the erection of a Tuskegee in the West Indies and for a visit to the islands by Booker T. Washington.[26] It was not long after this conference (reported in the London-based *Africa Times and Orient Review* for which Garvey worked) that Garvey read Washington's autobiography, *Up From Slavery*. This had a profound effect on him and it is from this event that, as he put it, his "doom" of being a race leader dawned on him.[27]

A Garvey letter to Washington in 1915 referred to a previous letter of 1914 and to Washington's reply inviting Garvey to Tuskegee. Garvey expressed his intention of leaving Jamaica in May or June 1915 for a speaking tour which would be confined mostly to race audiences in the South. This was to be a fund-raising tour to provide the wherewithal for alleviating suffering in Jamaica. He wrote, "I need not reacquaint you of the horrible condition prevailing among our people in the West Indies as you are so well informed of happenings over Negrodom." He enclosed a UNIA manifesto which stated among its "local objects" (as opposed to international objectives) the establishment of industrial colleges.[28] Washington replied two weeks later promising to do whatever he could to make Garvey's stay in the United States as profitable as possible.[29] Less than seven months later, however, Washington was dead.

Garvey therefore postponed his visit and held a memorial meeting for Washington at Kingston's Collegiate Hall. He also busied himself lecturing throughout the island bringing Washington's life and work to the attention of, in his words, "the sleeping Jamaica Negro public." He informed Washington's associate Emmett J. Scott that he would soon be undertaking his tour to raise funds for his "Industrial Farm and Institute Scheme."[30] By now Garvey was immersed in Washington's ideas. By February 1916 the letterhead on his stationery bore a Washington quotation to the effect that the man on top could not hold down the man below without keeping himself down too. He reiterated, in a letter to Washington's successor, R. R. Moton, his desire to set up an Industrial

Farm and Institute in Jamaica along Tuskegee lines to teach "race pride, race development, and other useful subjects." He even referred in Washingtonian terms, to minor assistance obtained from "cultured white people."[31] When Moton paid a brief visit to Jamaica shortly after this letter Garvey managed a few fleeting words with him despite efforts to prevent any such contact on the part of persons who by now considered Garvey a nuisance.[32]

This brief encounter with Moton was in March 1916, the same month in which Garvey left Jamaica for the United States. During his first tour of the states he went to Tuskegee and met Emmett J. Scott, who provided him with introductions to influential persons.[33] Garvey returned to Tuskegee late in 1923. This time he remained a few days, addressed the students and left what the student newspaper called a "substantial contribution" of fifty dollars to the scholarship fund. He made a promise of an annual gift. "Language fails me," he wrote at the end of his visit, "to express my high appreciation for the service Dr. Washington has rendered to us as a people."[34]

Washington was, of course, and continues to be, a controversial historical figure. Many have seen him primarily as a great accommodator willing to compromise with racism to buy time for the black man in his struggle for survival. Garvey was not oblivious of this aspect of Washington's career. He believed that Washington's reluctance to indulge in open agitation for political rights and his dependence on white philanthropy may have been inevitable during Washington's lifetime. In the new reality of the postwar world, however, "The industrially educated Negro would himself evolve a new ideal, after having been trained by the Sage of Tuskegee." Rather than attack Washington on these points, he preferred to argue that Washington himself would have made these kinds of adjustments if he had lived.[35]

Garvey became increasingly intolerant of Washington's successor, R. R. Moton, when it became clear that he would not make the required adjustments to the new age. Garvey openly denounced him in the late 1920s and in 1929 he wrote, "Dr. Moton is kept by white philanthropists, therefore, such a black man has absolutely no right talking on behalf of the Negro race."[36]

Garvey, therefore, was aware of and did not necessarily approve those elements in Washington's program which have caused him to be labeled an accommodator. What he more typically saw in Washington's career were self-reliance and race pride, both qualities that he professed not to see in Du Bois. For whereas Washington was "an originator and builder who, out of nothing, constructed the greatest educational and industrial institution of the race in modern times," Du Bois was "a bombast and iconoclast" full of "vicious and malicious criticisms of other men." Washington, he said, was therefore worth more than two million Du Boises.[37] Similarly, Garvey saw in the UNIA a continuation of Washington's hostility to "social equality,"[38] as the generalized social intermingling between the races was often called. Another aspect of Washington's career which Garvey also admired was the worldwide scope of his influence.[39]

If Garvey became disenchanted with R. R. Moton, in T. Thomas Fortune, editor of the *Negro World,* he had a close associate who had been for many years a close aide to Washington. Indeed Fortune thought that he must have known Washington more intimately than anyone else during the eighteen years of their relationship. Hardly a day passed during that period, he said, without the two being in direct contact, either personally or by letter or telegram.[40] On Fortune's death in 1928 the *Negro World* sketched the links between Washington, Fortune and Garvey. The paper said:

> . . . Mr. Fortune was for many years guide, philosopher and friend to the greatest industrial educator, whom white men delighted to praise and black men idolized. Then a happy fate decreed that he should be helpmeet to the only man who either here or abroad surpassed in girth Washington's greatness—who, starting where Washington left off, carried fast and high the torch of true emancipation for the Negro race. . . .[41]

Contact between Du Bois and Garvey began innocently enough. Du Bois recalled, "I heard of him first when I was in Jamaica, in 1915 when he sent a letter 'presenting his compliments' and giving me 'a hearty welcome to Jamaica, on the part of the United Improvement and Conservation Association [*sic*].' "[42] In a pamphlet published around the same time Garvey included Du Bois in a long list of race heroes.[43] Garvey's esteem for Du Bois was to be short lived, however. Du Bois said many years later that on this trip to Jamaica he was "surprisingly well-received by colored people and white."[44] Possibly because of this, and possibly because of the apparent absence in Jamaica of the more blatant aspects of American racism, he may have been temporarily fooled, as has many an unwary North American visitor, into thinking that the Jamaican race problem had been solved. For in February 1916 Garvey, now seemingly disenchanted with Du Bois, wrote in a letter to Moton at Tuskegee, "Don't you believe like coloured Dr. Du Bois that the 'race problem is at an end here' except you want to admit the utter insignificance of the black man." Garvey continued, significantly, "I personally would like to solve the situation on the broadest humanitarian lines. I would like to solve it on the platform of Dr. Booker T. Washington."[45] Garvey later attributed Du Bois' misreading of the Jamaican race situation on this occasion to the fact that he had associated on this visit mostly with the local light-skinned caste.[46]

The NAACP's official organ, the *Crisis,* of which Du Bois was editor for the whole of Garvey's American period, acknowledged Garvey's presence shortly after his arrival in the United States. A brief statement in the May 1916 issue noted: "Mr. Marcus Garvey, founder and president of the Universal Negro Improvement Association of Jamaica, B.W.I., is now on a visit to America. He will deliver a series of lectures on Jamaica in an effort to raise funds for the establishment of an industrial and educational institution for Negroes in Jamaica."

By the time this appeared Garvey had already visited Du Bois' office (on April 25, 1916) with a request that Du Bois chair his first UNIA meeting in the United States. This meeting was scheduled for May 9, 1916, at St. Marks Hall at 57 West 138 Street in Harlem. The subject was to be "Jamaica." Garvey at this stage was presumably willing to overlook his disagreement with Du Bois in view of the prestige that the editor of the *Crisis* would lend to his gathering. In any event Du Bois, who was not in when Garvey called, declined, pleading an out of town engagement.[47] Garvey later claimed to have been "dumbfounded" by what he saw at the office. He was unable to tell, he said, "whether it was a white show or a colored vaudeville he was running at Fifth Avenue."[48]

By 1919 Garvey had already emerged as one of the more important of Harlem's militant New Negroes and even though, as Du Bois himself admitted, he tried for as long as he could to "explain away the Garvey movement and ignore it,"[49] he could not totally pretend that Garvey did not exist. For one thing, the occasional reference to Garvey, sometimes explicit, sometimes veiled, intruded into the *Crisis*. During Du Bois' absence in France in 1919, for example, a long editorial considered favorably the new demand of Africa for the Africans and even advocated limited Afro-American migration to Africa, though not at the expense of the struggle at home.[50] A brief *Crisis* report later that year carried news of Garvey's conflict with the district attorney in New York.[51] In the same year, a UNIA commissioner in France crossed Du Bois' path and actually attended the latter's hastily organized Pan-African Congress.[52] And in December the *Crisis* felt obliged to affirm the right of the *Negro World* and other radical black papers to publish, in the face of an onslaught against the black press by southerners in Congress, backed by the attorney general.[53]

By 1920 Garvey was very near, if not at the peak of his career, so that even though Du Bois continued to try, it was now becoming very difficult indeed to ignore him. For one thing, two of Du Bois' former associates were now among Garvey's closest colleagues. They were John Edward Bruce and William H. Ferris, both of whom had been among the fifty-nine who issued the call to the founding meeting of Du Bois' well-known Niagara Movement in 1905. Both were knighted by Garvey. Bruce also had been president of the Negro Society for Historical Research, founded in Yonkers, New York, in 1911. Du Bois had been a corresponding member of that society. So was Mrs. Marie DuChatellier of Bocas del Toro, Panama, by 1920 a UNIA organizer, and Duse Mohamed Ali, Garvey's former employer in England and himself connected for a time with the UNIA. Garvey's staunchest Liberian supporter, Chief Justice James J. Dossen, a former vice-president of Liberia, was an honorary member.[54] Du Bois could not have been unaware of the Garveyite connections of at least some of this impressive list of the highly educated element whom he called the "talented tenth."

From the beginning of 1920, then, Du Bois began to direct some *Crisis* editorials toward Garvey. Even at this point, however, he still wanted to ignore his new rival and confined himself to thinly veiled references to Garvey without actually naming him. In January 1920 he editorialized favorably on the new mood of separatism and race consciousness expressed in such slogans as "Asia for the Asians" and "Africa for the Africans." He suggested that the white man should get out of

black communities all over the world or provide "utter justice for all."
"Here is the choice," he wrote. "Which will you have, my masters?"[55]
In March, though, in response to criticisms of the NAACP's interracial
character from an unnamed source, a *Crisis* editorial argued that black
people could not strive for equality in white society and separation at
the same time and vigorously defended white participation in the
NAACP.[56] Shortly thereafter Garvey sneered at Du Bois' receipt of the
Spingarn Medal for founding the Pan-African Congress. He considered
William Monroe Trotter (who had broken with Du Bois) to have performed a worthier task in presenting a petition of his National Equal
Rights League to the Paris peace conference. Trotter, he pointed out,
had been too radical for the NAACP's white point of view.[57]

Two weeks before the start of his 1920 convention Garvey wrote to
Du Bois:

> Dear Dr. DuBois:
>   At the International Convention of Negroes to be held in New York
> during the month of August, the Negro people of America will elect
> a leader by the popular vote of the delegates from the forty-eight
> States of the Union. This leader as elected, will be the accredited
> spokesman of the American Negro people. You are hereby asked to
> be good enough to allow us to place your name in nomination for
> the post.

Du Bois remained outwardly calm in the face of this assault on his ego.
"I thank you for the suggestion," he replied, "but under no circumstances
can I allow my name to be presented." He then retaliated with a series
of requests from Garvey for detailed information on UNIA finances,
membership, property, "activities and accomplishments" and more, for
a "critical estimate" to be published in the *Crisis.*[58]

Soon after the start of the convention it was announced that Du Bois
had attended an early session. This brought forth a Garvey denunciation
of Du Bois which drew the day's most enthusiastic applause. In a reference
to two of the latter's well-known publications, Garvey declared that
Du Bois could not preach "close ranks" (with white America) one day
and "dark water" the next.[59] To add to his discomfiture, Du Bois had
been mistakenly blamed by the *Chicago Tribune* for the "Back to Africa"

riot in that city, in which Garvey had supposedly been implicated.[60] Halfway through the convention Garvey informed an interviewer for the National Civic Federation that Du Bois represented the "ante-bellum Negro" as opposed to the militant postwar New Negro. Four days later Du Bois told the same interviewer that Garvey was not sincere. He also said here what was to become something of an obsession with him, namely that Garvey's followers were "the lowest type of Negroes, mostly from the Indies" and that the UNIA could in no way be considered an Afro-American movement. He also denounced Garvey as an ally of Bolsheviks and Sinn Feiners.[61]

Despite this forthright denunciation of Garvey made in private Du Bois continued his policy of veiled public attack in the *Crisis,* the September issue of which carried an editorial on West Indians directed, on Du Bois' own admission, at Garvey and the UNIA.[62] By this time Du Bois' efforts at ignoring Garvey had come to the attention of Chandler Owen and A. Philip Randolph, whose *Messenger* in an editorial entitled "A Record of the Darker Races" (a takeoff on the subtitle of the *Crisis*) pointed out that the *Crisis* did not live up to its subtitle. The *Messenger* showed that although the *Crisis* had mentioned minor race events, it had allowed Garvey's spectacular happenings in New York City to go unreported.[63] Perhaps in response to this criticism the November *Crisis* finally took cognizance of Garvey's August convention in a few brief lines hidden away in the midst of several brief and relatively unimportant news items.[64] This same issue carried yet another Du Bois editorial against attacks from unnamed sources on his advocacy of social equality. This time Du Bois attempted to use Booker T. Washington against the Garveyite neo-Washington camp by suggesting that Washington himself, the great opponent of social equality, had participated in functions with white people.[65] The usual Garveyite response to this kind of argument was, of course, that Washington took the white people's money but built himself an independent black power base with it. Garvey probably did not know it, but his contempt for Du Bois' history of dependence on whites was shared by Mary White Ovington, who privately contrasted Du Bois' influence among white people with his lesser influence among black people, even within the NAACP. She then remarked, with a contempt hardly less than Garvey's, "His career has been made by the whites; first Dr. Bumstead [the Atlanta University president who hired Du Bois], next various mem-

bers of the NAACP."[66] Ovington herself maintained an unlikely relationship with the *Negro World,* which in 1921 and 1922 regularly carried
her "Book Chat" column.

His attempt to publicly pretend that Garvey was not there having
failed to secure Garvey's disappearance, Du Bois in November 1920 decided that the time had come to call off the pretense. He wrote W. A.
Domingo, by now a known enemy of Garvey: "May I ask if you have any
information concerning Mr. Marcus Garvey and his organizations which
you would be willing to give me?" He inquired also after the address of
Eliezer Cadet, the Haitian UNIA commissioner who had attended his
1919 Pan-African Congress in Paris. The letter was returned to him and
he sent it off to historian Arthur A. Schomburg in the hope that Schomburg could locate Domingo and forward it.[67] The letter seems to have
gotten no further than Schomburg but the December *Crisis* nevertheless
featured a Du Bois article entitled, "Marcus Garvey." The battle was now
irrevocably joined.

In this article, as in most but by no means all of his published comments on Garvey, Du Bois affected the pose of the impartial scholarly
observer—a posture that never prevented his analyses of Garvey from
being to varying degrees distorted and inaccurate. It did, however, mislead
many commentators on the Du Bois-Garvey conflict for the next half-
century into thinking that Du Bois was in fact always fair and detached.
Whereas in August Du Bois had privately denounced Garvey as an in-
sincere Bolshevik sympathizer leading a bunch of ignorant West Indians,
now his public pose was somewhat more mellow. He characterized Garvey
as "essentially an honest and sincere man" but possessed of a long list
of character defects. Several of his major objections to Garvey were
stated. Inveterate snob that he was, he scoffed at what he considered
Garvey's defects of training, much as he had long flayed all those, including Washington, who would not acknowledge the near-divine right of the
"talented tenth" to lead the race. Again, as always, Garvey was described
as a leader of Jamaica's black peasantry but not as a leader of Afro-
Americans. The continuing conflict between the Pan-African Congress
and the UNIA also got a preview. In attempting to establish that Garvey
could not get along with his fellow workers he overreached himself,
adducing as proof the fact that none of the fifteen names of Garvey's
officers in 1914 appeared on a similar list for 1918.[68] The truth of the

matter was, of course, that the 1914 list comprised Garvey's earliest Jamaican executive, while the 1918 list represented his American organization. John Edward Bruce attacked Du Bois on this point.[69] Du Bois published a second installment of this critique in January. Here he attacked Garvey on the black versus light-skinned question and accused him of raising this question in a land where, according to Du Bois, it was a non-question. He also objected to Garvey's antagonism of the British imperialists and released the information that in July 1920 he had sent "a courteous letter of inquiry" to Garvey asking for financial data on the UNIA and Black Star Line. He had expected Garvey to furnish him with this information and was upset because his letter remained unacknowledged and unanswered. He again overreached himself, this time describing the Black Star Line's *Yarmouth* as a wooden rather than a steel vessel.[70] Du Bois later published a retraction of this statement at the suggestion of Arthur B. Spingarn, head of the NAACP's legal committee.[71] By this time the controversy between the two men had elicited enough interest for a "debate" to be arranged at the Mother Bethel AME Church in Philadelphia. Du Bois presented his views on April 4, 1921. Garvey, scheduled to speak the following week, could not do so, being still stranded in the West Indies.[72]

After these two articles Du Bois returned to his policy of attacking Garvey without naming him. In one such attack in May 1921 he introduced the question of a concentration on purely Afro-American struggle versus a move to immediate linkages among African communities worldwide. Du Bois, after blowing away the "hoard of scoundrels and bubble-blowers, ready to conquer Africa, join the Russian revolution, and vote in the Kingdom of God tomorrow," came out in favor of "a program which says: the battle of Negro rights is to be fought right here in America." He expressed the sanguine expectation, which he himself was to repudiate in the next decade, that twenty-five more years of "intelligent fighting," such as the NAACP was engaged in, would free the race in America.[73] Such isolationist sentiments from the founder of the Pan-African Congress were not as unusual as may appear at first glance. For Du Bois at this time seems to have conceived of this organization more as an international social club for the talented tenth rather than a body engaged in real worldwide grass-roots struggle such as was the purpose of the UNIA. He himself said as much in a letter to Secre-

tary of State Charles Hughes one month after the appearance of this article.
He told Hughes, "The Pan-African Congress is for conference, acquaint-
anceship and general organization. It has nothing to do with the so called
Garvey movement and contemplates neither force nor revolution in its
program." He continued, "We have had the cordial cooperation of the
French, Belgium and Portuguese governments and we hope to get the
attention and sympathy of all colonial powers."[74] What is interesting
about this letter, apart from its evidence of Du Bois' very nonmilitant
conception of Pan-Africanism, is that it was written at the time when
Hughes and the Department of State were trying to keep Garvey out of
the United States. It may possibly have reinforced Hughes' conviction of
Garvey's undesirability. Garvey, for his part, was quite convinced that
Du Bois had a hand in his exclusion. Du Bois wrote a similar letter to
the British ambassador in Washington.[75] The purpose of these letters
was to obtain governmental support for the 1921 Pan-African Congress
in London.

The Pan-African Congress was scheduled for August and September
and may have represented an attempt to distract some attention from
Garvey's annual August convention. On the eve of the UNIA convention
Garvey, only recently back from his ordeal in the Caribbean, issued a
call for unity and invited Du Bois, R. R. Moton, Kelly Miller and Emmet
J. Scott to attend.[76] He could not have been too serious, however, for
he almost simultaneously described Du Bois as "leader of the opposition" to the UNIA and an "exponent of the reactionary class" who "kept
Negroes in serfdom and peonage."[77] Moreover, the convention all but
commenced with a resolution denouncing the Pan-African Congress. This
was passed amidst loud cheers.[78] During the convention the *Negro World*
published an account of the UNIA finances. This information, long sought
by Du Bois, was diligently transcribed from the paper at the NAACP headquarters.[79] And Garvey's convention once more rated a fleeting mention
among the *Crisis* news briefs.[80]

In Europe, meanwhile, the Pan-African Congress was widely mistaken,
despite Du Bois' efforts, for a Garveyite affair, much to the chagrin of
its founder and to the joy of Garvey, who exulted in the free publicity
accruing to the UNIA from Du Bois' hapless predicament. Every second
word said at Du Bois' congress had been "Marcus Garvey" he boasted,
and he cited a large collection of clippings from European papers to sup-

port his contention.[81] Du Bois had not considered it necessary to invite
any UNIA participation because he considered the Garvey program too
"dangerous" and "impracticable."[82] Garvey's ideas and influence nevertheless continued to haunt the proceedings. At the London session a
Nigerian student read a paper proposing "An African Program," which
was nothing but warmed-over Garveyism, complete with New World
African migration to the mother continent, a Liberian loan, and establishment of a beachhead in Liberia to lead eventually to a United States of
West Africa.[83] But the "most unkindest cut of all" came when the person
left in charge of the permanent secretariat set up in Paris after the conference became infected with Garveyite ideas. Du Bois himself thusly
explained this episode: "Just as the Garvey movement made its thesis
industrial cooperation, so the new young secretary of the Pan-African
movement, a coloured Paris public school teacher, wanted to combine
investment and profit with the idea of Pan-Africa. He wanted American
Negro capital for this end. We had other ideas."[84] Du Bois added that
this Garveyite influence almost wrecked his organization.

The problems of Du Bois' 1921 Pan-African Congress were not made
any less worrisome by a stream of hostile comments emanating from
the *Negro World* editorials of William H. Ferris. Du Bois, Ferris argued,
must surely be indulging in poetic license when he dared call his gathering a Pan-African Congress even though such people as British colonial
official and Africanist scholar Sir Harry Johnston were among the spon-
sors. It was Johnston, Ferris reminded his readers, who in his arrogance
had said that not a single Afro-American knew anything about Africa.
Du Bois' misnomer was also emphasized by presenting a long list of
African territories (the vast majority on the continent) unrepresented
at the congress. "There has been no 'Pan-African' Congress in Europe
this year," this editorial concluded, "because ALL AFRICA didn't respond to the Du Bois call." Ferris wrote off Du Bois' gathering as a joke,
a "racial adulteration," an "exclusive college function," comprising thirty
delegates and two thousand white so-called "audiences."

Furthermore, Ferris saw in this latest Du Bois endeavor merely the
most recent example of Du Bois' long-standing tendency toward plagiar-
ism. He argued that Du Bois had incorporated Ida Wells-Barnett's antilynching program without giving her credit for it. Eight years after William
Monroe Trotter's *Guardian* and race organization had appeared, Ferris

continued, Du Bois had started a magazine and organization along similar lines. The only credit he gave Trotter for his idea was to call him a fanatic. Du Bois' short history of the Negro was but a shorter version of one published nine years earlier by a black man whom Du Bois had referred to as an upstart. Ten years previously Duse Mohamed Ali had written Booker T. Washington, Dr. W. S. Scarborough and Du Bois informing them of the impending appearance of his magazine designed to draw closer together the darker races of the world. The first two had sent encouraging replies. Du Bois' reply had been described by Mohamed as pointless and disappointing. Yet Du Bois later copied Mohamed's idea. Now, after having found fault with Garvey's 1920 convention, he was busy discussing the same things at his congress and trying to set up a permanent organization.[85]

Back in America after the congress Du Bois ran into a storm of criticism from Garvey and others, including Garvey's adversary Cyril Briggs, over a widely circulated Associated Press report. This report had quoted Du Bois as having said during the congress that not only did Afro-Americans have no desire to oust the colonialists from Africa, but they could hardly migrate there since they could not stand the climate. Garvey commented, "One editor and leader went so far as to say at his so-called Pan-African Congress that American Negroes could not live in Africa, because the climate was too hot."[86] Du Bois later attempted to extricate himself from this statement. He denied it but diluted his denial somewhat by adding that because one's great-grandfather might have been African it did not follow that the African climate would hold no terrors.[87]

On his return Du Bois also had to face continuing embarrassing disclosures in the pages of the *Negro World* concerning his Pan-African Congress. One report, translated from a Portuguese paper, recalled Du Bois' invitation to the Portuguese colonialists to attend his conference. The article claimed that only hand-picked Africans, members of the Liga Africana (African League), had been allowed to attend. These delegates had then returned to Portuguese-controlled Africa, where two of them, Nicolan Santos Pinto and Jose de Magalhanes [sic] , were heckled and forced to stop speaking when they tried to extol the virtues of the Pan-African Congress. They were confronted by shouts of "Long live Marcus Garvey and the African National Party (UNIA)." The audience denounced Blaise Diagne (conservative Senegalese president of the congress) in particular and the congress in general.

Another article, translated from a French magazine, was by a Paris attorney, a Mr. Alcandre, who had attended the Paris session of the congress. The article reproduced a resolution introduced at the congress calling upon the body to invite Garvey to its next meeting instead of attacking him unjustly in his absence. Diagne, presiding over the meeting, had at first refused to read it. When he did read it, it was in a semi-understandable fashion at the very end of the session. Alcandre, the resolution's sponsor, was not sure whether it passed or not.[88]

The end of 1921 found Du Bois vainly attempting to persuade the NAACP hierarchy to move its headquarters uptown into Harlem.[89] The dispute with Garvey may well have heightened the disadvantages of a downtown location on the white side of New York City.

Thus ended the first full year of increased hostility between the two leaders. During the year their followers and supporters had increasingly joined in the fray. One Garveyite, Wheeler Sheppard, had actually published a book attacking Du Bois because he thought that Garvey had not been firm enough with him. The book bore the self-explanatory title, *Mistakes of W. E. B. Du Bois, Being an Answer to Dr. W. E. B. Du Bois' Attack upon the Honourable Marcus Garvey.* The author described himself as a "Voluntary Field Speaker of the UNIA," and emphasized that Du Bois was "dubious" and an adept at "scientific lying," an apparent reference to Du Bois' tactic of framing distortions in apparently scholarly, dispassionate language.

Du Bois accelerated his campaign against Garvey's philosophy and personality in 1922. The beginning of the year found Garvey on his annual list of "debits" "In Account With The American Negro." Garvey shared Du Bois' list of debits together with President Harding's Birmingham speech and the lynching of fifty-nine black people during the year. Among the "credits" were the Dyer Antilynching Bill and, naturally, the second Pan-African Congress.[90] Garvey's response was to call his adversary a "crazy lunatic or a soulless employee" in the pay of an alien race for suggesting that his ships were liabilities rather than assets.[91] A few pages after the list of debits and credits Du Bois slipped in another attack on Garvey in the midst of a eulogy of Afro-American Colonel Charles Young, who had died in West Africa. He wrote of Young, "But Africa needed him. He did not yell and collect money and advertise great schemes and parade in crimson—he just went quietly, ignoring appeal and protest." As if this was not enough, Du Bois included yet another camouflaged anti-Garvey editorial on the same page. This one, entitled "Africa for the Africans," suggested that "Africa should be administered for the Africans and, as soon as may be, by the Africans." He emphasized that he did "not mean by this that Africa should be administered by West Indians or American Negroes."[92] Thus whereas Garvey was clamoring for immediate African government, with West Indians and Afro-Americans providing a supply of extra skilled personnel, Du Bois in 1922 seemed content to go along with the colonialist lie that they were gradually training presently incompetent Africans for eventual self-government. Several Africans protested this and other similar statements emanating from Du Bois and Blaise Diagne.[93]

On the domestic scene, Garvey's criticisms seem to have brought about a sharpening of Du Bois' analysis of the Afro-American reality. For whereas in 1921 he had argued that Garvey had all but introduced intraracial color antagonism onto the American scene where it practically did not exist,[94] now Garvey's success made him think again. In yet another lengthy attack on Garvey without expressly naming him, he referred to his adversary as "the Demagog." "From now on in our new awakening," he declared, "our self-criticism, our impatience and passion, we must expect the Demagog among Negroes more and more. He will come to lead, inflame, lie and steal. He will gather large followings and then burst and disappear. Loss and despair will follow his fall until new false prophets arise." Yet he acknowledged that his supposedly hypothetical demagogue would in 1922 find a fertile field of growing cleavage "between our incipient social classes." White oppression, he argued, had artificially restrained class differences among black people. But these differences, though not as great as they would be in the absence of such discrimination, were there all the same. "Nevertheless," he argued, "the ties between our privileged and exploited, our educated and ignorant, our rich and poor, our light and dark, are not what they should be and what we can and must make them."[95] Du Bois' admission that antagonisms existed in Afro-American society between "light and dark" is important because prior to this, and indeed afterward too, he preferred to treat it as a taboo subject not to be discussed, except to blame Garvey for introducing it.

After this spate of sniping attacks during the first half of 1922 Du Bois decided that the time had come for another article openly directed at Garvey. He therefore set about from July gathering information for an article on the Black Star Line. On July 27 he wrote the chairman of the

United States Shipping Board for information on Garvey's attempts to
buy ships from the board. He explained to the chairman that Garvey had
collected perhaps half a million dollars in connection with his shipping
line and hinted at the possibility of fraud. The chairman declined to
divulge any information but suggested he try Joseph P. Nolan, who had
acted as attorney for the Black Star Line in some of these transactions.[96]
Undaunted, Du Bois then wrote to the Department of State. He was requested to furnish a statement explaining his interest in the matter before
a decision could be made on whether to grant his request. He complied
with this suggestion, explaining that "the Black Star Line was promoted
by a West Indian agitator named Marcus Garvey. He collected from the
colored people in America and the West Indies nearly $800,000." Many
persons, he suggested, had lost money in the process. Among these were
Crisis readers. He therefore now wanted to publish the truth and warn
readers against such schemes. Once more, however, the information was
refused. He was informed that the files were confidential.[97] While awaiting these replies Du Bois went ahead and wrote the article anyway, and
obtained legal advice before sending it to press to ensure that it was not
libelous.[98]

Much of this activity was going on during August, the month of
Garvey's convention. An earlier Garvey invitation to Du Bois to attend
and let "the real leadership" lead the race was apparently not taken up.
Nor was Garvey's invitation to the NAACP to participate in the convention parade together with a banner bearing the association's name.[99]

The Black Star Line article appeared in the September *Crisis*. It was
carefully documented to avoid the possibility of libel proceedings, with
most of the important information in the form of direct quotations from
the *Negro World* and the Orr case (where a stockholder had sued the
Black Star Line, resulting in public exposure of the line's great financial
losses). Many of Du Bois' arguments here were later repeated by the
prosecution in the 1923 trial. Here for once in his dealings with Garvey
Du Bois was able to harness his rage long enough to effectively employ
his considerable scholarly talents. And coming as it did in the midst of
the "Marcus Garvey Must Go" campaign and at a time when Garvey had
already been arrested and indicted for alleged fraud in connection with
the shipping line, the result was the most devastating of Du Bois' attacks.
Du Bois in effect presumed guilt and passed judgment on a matter which

was *sub judice.* This, together with his letters to government officials
and his friendship with the judge who was soon to preside over Garvey's
trial, must certainly have prejudiced Garvey's chances of an impartial
hearing. Garvey considered this attack to be particularly unfortunate
since, he explained, the Black Star Line represented not a venture in the
interest of individuals but an effort to lift up a struggling race. "If," he
therefore lamented, "Du Bois were a constructive leader, since he possesses
all the knowledge in the world, he would help Marcus Garvey, the Universal Negro Improvement Association, and the Black Star Line to make
good."[100] Du Bois attempted to help the line make good all right. He
wrote the secretary of state for two ships to, in effect, take the line over.[101]

The Black Star Line article marked the beginning of an escalated series
of open attacks on Garvey. One of these articles appeared in November
and concerned Dr. Leroy Bundy's defection from the NAACP to the
UNIA. Bundy had been arrested during the 1917 massacre of black
people in East St. Louis for encouraging the black community to arm in
self-defense and charged with murder and incitement to riot. He collaborated for a while with the NAACP, which organized a defense fund and
prepared to defend him. Somewhere along the line, Bundy fell out with
the NAACP and defected to the UNIA camp. During the 1922 convention he was knighted by Garvey, and the convention elected him first
assistant president general. In response to the incessant NAACP accusations of financial mismanagement, Garvey countered with an accusation
of his own. What, the *Negro World* inquired, had become of the $50,000
collected by the NAACP for Bundy's defense? Only $150 had been spent
on Bundy, the paper charged. The NAACP's legal director, Arthur
Spingarn, had suggested that Du Bois publish a "very brief resume of the
disbursements and expenditures in the Bondy [*sic*] matter."[102] Du Bois
published a six-page article on the affair, which was duly repudiated by
two Ferris editorials in the *Negro World.*[103]

The year 1923 was greeted by a Du Bois attempt to prove that the
UNIA had fewer than 18,000 members.[104] To do this he published a
UNIA financial report which he claimed had been suppressed up to that
time. The figure for subscriptions was relatively small and Du Bois presumed that all branches had sent in all their subscriptions and that paid-
up members and active members were necessarily the same. When he discovered that only around 200 delegates had voted at the 1922 convention,
he concluded that this was an indication of the small number of delegates

present, not realizing that votes were cast by delegation rather than by individual. Du Bois' conclusions concerning membership here were obviously a gross understatement. When white papers could conservatively estimate 20,000 to 25,000 persons attending the first session of Garvey's 1920 convention or 3,000 people at one meeting of the Chicago branch alone, or 100,000 people parading and jamming the sidewalks of Harlem in 1926 demanding Garvey's release, then the enormity of Du Bois' underestimate becomes clear.[105]

Garvey at this stage issued *An Answer to His Many Critics* refuting, among other things, the charge that his following represented "the ignorant and gullible." This Garvey statement appeared about the same time as an NAACP press release of January 25[106] giving advance publicity to Du Bois' most elaborate onslaught against Garvey, a ten-page article appearing in the February issue of the white *Century* magazine. The article portrayed Garvey as a semicomic figure. It began: "There was a long, low, unfinished church basement, roofed over. A little, fat black man, ugly, but with intelligent eyes and big head, was seated on a plank platform beside a 'throne,' dressed in a military uniform of the gayest mid-Victorian type. . . . Among the lucky recipients of titles was the former private secretary of Booker T. Washington!" In this article Du Bois restated most of his ideological and other differences with Garvey. There was first the question of race. He insisted contradictorily that intraracial color lines were essentially a West Indian phenomenon, "despite the near-white aristocracies of cities like Charleston and New Orleans, and despite the fact that the proportion of mulattoes who were free and who gained some wealth and education was greater than that of blacks because of the favor of their white parents." He even admitted that after emancipation in America "color caste tended to arise again" and that in his own time it was fashionable for light-skinned Afro-Americans to pose as Spanish or Portuguese. In the face of all this voluntary evidence to the contrary he stubbornly insisted that intraracial color antagonism was practically unknown in Afro-America because all-pervading white racism forced light-skinned folk to refer to themselves as Negroes. That this position was due largely to his own feeling of vulnerability as a person of very light hue was apparently unconsciously admitted when he stated, "Colored folk as white as the whitest came to describe themselves as negroes. Imagine, then, the surprise and disgust of these Americans when Garvey launched his Jamaican color scheme." For someone as sensitive about

his color as Du Bois was, the intraracial color question was best treated
by silence. He said so in this article, though he foisted his idea upon the
bulk of Afro-Americans. He said, "it came to be generally regarded as
the poorest possible taste for a negro even to refer to differences of color."
Coupled with his refusal to admit of a home-grown color question
within the race, Du Bois came very near in this article to a condescending,
amused, and even offensive treatment of Garvey's blackness. Garvey,
of course, often accused Du Bois of hating the black blood within him
and of hankering after white society. This facet of Du Bois' experience
was later given scholarly treatment by the eminent Afro-American sociologist E. Franklin Frazier. Frazier's analysis came close to that of Garvey.
He defined Du Bois as a "marginal man." He wrote:

> He was born in New England, where his mulatto characteristics per-
> mitted him a large degree of participation in the life of the white
> world. During his short sojourn in the South as an undergraduate at
> Fisk University, where he was under New England white teachers, he
> never was thoroughly assimilated into Negro life. His return to New
> England afforded him a more congenial environment where he thor-
> oughly absorbed the genteel intellectual tradition of Harvard. . . .

> But Du Bois, aristocrat in bearing and in sympathies, was in fact a
> cultural hybrid or what sociologists call a "marginal man." Once back
> in America and Atlanta, he was just a "nigger." Fine flower of western
> culture, he had here the same status as the crudest semi-barbarous
> Negro in the South. In the *Souls of Black Folk* we have a classic state-
> ment of the "marginal man" with his double consciousness: on the
> one hand sensitive to every slight concerning the Negro, and feeling on
> the other hand little kinship or real sympathy for the great mass of
> crude, uncouth black peasants with whom he was identified. For, in
> spite of the way in which Du Bois has written concerning the masses,
> he has no real sympathetic understanding of them. The *Souls of Black
> Folk* is a masterly portrayal of Du Bois' soul and not a real picture of
> the black masses. When he takes his pen to write of the black masses
> we are sure to get a dazzling romantic picture. Someone has remarked
> aptly that the Negroes in *The Quest of the Silver Fleece* are gypsies.
> The voice of Du Bois is genuine only when he speaks as the represent-
> ative of The Talented Tenth. . . .[107]

In the *Century* article Du Bois restated his contention that Garvey was essentially a leader of West Indian peasants who was uninterested in and not very knowledgeable about Afro-American struggles. Recurring here also was his typical disdain for Garvey and all others who had not been educated at Harvard and Berlin. "Garvey," he said, "had no thorough education and a very hazy idea of the technic of civilization." He again voiced his disapproval of Garvey's anti-imperialist attitude and accused Garvey of trying to take over Liberia. The seesaw struggle in his mind between separation and integration was now firmly on the side of integration. "Not in segregation," he pontificated, "but in closer, larger unity lies interracial peace." And with his insistence against segregation he recognized the affinity between Booker T. Washington and Garvey. He disposed of them jointly with the claim that

> The present generation of negroes has survived two grave temptations, the greater one, fathered by Booker T. Washington, which said, "Let politics alone, keep in your place, work hard, and do not complain," and which meant perpetual color caste for colored folk by their own cooperation and consent, and the consequent inevitable debauchery of the white world; and the lesser, fathered by Marcus Garvey, which said: "Give up! Surrender! The struggle is useless; back to Africa and fight the white world."

The *Century* attack, Du Bois' most comprehensive, did not go unanswered. Garvey's reply was swift and bitter. He addressed himself first to the racial slurs. The *Negro World* headline proclaimed, "W.E. BURGHARDT DU BOIS AS A HATER OF DARK PEOPLE." A subtitle followed: "Calls His Own Race 'Black and Ugly,' Judging From the White Man's Standard of Beauty." Garvey declared, "This 'unfortunate mulatto,' who bewails every day the drop of Negro blood in his veins, being sorry that he is not Dutch or French, has taken upon himself the responsibility of criticizing and condemning other people while holding himself up as the social 'Unapproachable' and the great 'I AM' of the Negro race." Garvey, himself no mean wielder of a vitriolic pen, continued to heap scorn and abuse on Du Bois' racial remarks. "How he arrives at his conclusion that Marcus Garvey is ugly, being a Negro, is impossible to determine," he raged, indulging his fondness for referring to himself in the third person, "in that if there is any ugliness in the Negro race it

would be reflected more through Du Bois than Marcus Garvey, in that
he himself tells us that he is a little Dutch, a little French, and a little
Negro. Why, in fact, the man is a monstrosity." Garvey could not see
why "this professor, who sees ugliness in being black, essays to be a
leader of the Negro people." He supposed that Du Bois' equation of
blackness with ugliness and whiteness with beauty explained "why he
likes to dance with white people, and dine with them, and sometimes
sleep with them." In Du Bois' racial attitude he preferred to find an
explanation "for the bleaching processes and the hair straightening escapades of some of the people who are identified with the National
Association for the Advancement of Colored People in their mad desire
of approach to the white race." It was for these reasons too, no doubt,
that "the erudite Doctor" kept a "French Beard." Garvey also took
credit for having embarrassed the NAACP after his 1916 visit to their
offices into hiring black James Weldon Johnson and William Pickens.
Pickens, he asserted, must have been ugly to Du Bois because he later
came to Garvey seeking employment.

Garvey also used his differences with Du Bois on race to answer his
rival's disparaging references to Liberty Hall as a "low, rambling basement of brick and rough stone." Du Bois had contrasted this structure
with several nearby buildings that he considered beautiful. Garvey was
able to demonstrate that every building Du Bois praised was wholly or
partly white-owned. Liberty Hall, he argued, at least represented black
self-reliance. Du Bois, on the other hand, was a "lazy dependent mulatto."
Du Bois' jeering at Garvey's knighthoods was also seen as a lack of racial
consciousness, for he certainly would have exulted in a similar honor from
a white potentate. (In fact, it will be remembered, Du Bois had in 1920
been the recipient of a Spingarn Medal, named after a white NAACP
leader, and certainly no less silly than a Garveyite honor. And he certainly exulted later in the gilded, frock-coated pageantry that surrounded
his brief stint as a United States representative in Liberia.)[108]

On Du Bois' incessant harpings on the educational disabilities of his
rival Garvey also had his say. "If Du Bois' education fits him for no better
service than being a lackey for good white people," he commented, "then
it were better that Negroes were not educated." The reason for the fuss
over Du Bois' educational accomplishments he saw as stemming from
the fact that "he was one of the first 'experiments' made by white people

on colored men along the lines of higher education." Despite the
vehemence of his reply, Garvey did not address himself to some of
Du Bois' accusations. He ignored the charge that he was a black Jamaican
peasant uninterested in the Afro-American struggle. He ignored, too, Du Bois'
assaults on his Liberian program and on his anti-imperialist attitude.[109]
Garvey repeated many of these arguments in the months that followed.
During these months his trial took place and he was imprisoned awaiting
bail. He was out of jail in time for Du Bois' third Pan-African Congress,
however. Du Bois blamed Garvey for the poor showing of this congress.
He wrote later that "The unfortunate debacle of his over-advertised
schemes naturally hurt and made difficult further effective development
of the Pan-African Congress idea."[110] Nevertheless both Kelly Miller in
America and Casely Hayford's *Gold Coast Leader* came out at this time
in favor of Garvey's African program over Du Bois' Pan-African Congress.[111]
     In London meanwhile the Pan-African Congress ran into trouble and
could not raise a quorum for its last session; Garvey's representative in
London reported an attendance of eleven. Du Bois' report of a larger representation Garvey attributed to double counting and the inclusion of a
few curious people who looked in briefly. Of all the Africans in the
world, Garvey lamented, Du Bois could not get twenty to meet with him.
Instead the principal speakers, apart from Du Bois himself who was principal speaker at most sessions, were "white persons having peculiar ideas
about the Negro, especially Sir Sydney Olivier and H. G. Wells." "Why a
Pan-African Congress in such company?" Garvey wanted to know. "The
thing is unholy and is bound to die the death of the unrighteous."[112]
Similar criticisms were voiced by A. Philip Randolph and Chandler Owen
of the *Messenger* which editorialized, "Dr. Du Bois represented the twelve
millions of American Negroes, without their consent, and Mr. H. G. Wells,
together with some other white English liberals, doubtless, constituted
the voice of the African section of Great Britain."[113] Garvey made the
same point more picturesquely: "Du Bois had no more right or authority
to have called a Pan-African Congress than a cat had to call together a
parliament of rats."[114] And the *Negro World* quoted the *Manchester
Guardian* on the unconcern shown for the congress by most of Britain's
prominent Africans.[115]
     Du Bois' London failure was followed by a session of his congress in
Lisbon, Portugal, hosted by the Liga Africana. From there he journeyed

to Liberia, where he was to be special minister plenipotentiary and envoy
extraordinary representing President Coolidge at the second inaugural of
President King of Liberia on January 1, 1924. Garvey reported that
Du Bois on his return home was honored at a banquet at which Judge
Mack, who presided over Garvey's 1923 case, was special guest.[116] And
in September Secretary of State Charles E. Hughes informed President
Coolidge, after reading a UNIA petition for assistance in going to Liberia,
that Du Bois' following was much larger and more respectable than
Garvey's.[117] The *Messenger,* by this time well into the "Marcus Garvey
Must Go" campaign, approved of Du Bois' actions, arguing that if he had
done nothing else in Liberia than thwart Garvey's plans, then his trip
would have been worthwhile.[118]

In May Du Bois published the most venomous of all his attacks on
Garvey. This notorious editorial, "A Lunatic or a Traitor," showed once
again that the differences between the two men were overshadowed by
their differences on race, particularly the question of intraracial color
antagonisms and separation as opposed to integration. The editorial condemned Garvey as a lunatic or traitor who had overstayed his welcome
in America and must now be "locked up or sent home." It alleged that
"No Negro in America ever had a fairer and more patient trial than Marcus
Garvey." Garvey, he claimed, had convicted himself by his own "swagger-
ing monkey-shines" and threats of violence, and was for the latter reasons
refused bail. He admitted that J. W. H. Eason (whom he did not actually
name) had been responsible, after he broke with Garvey, for giving the
Crisis the UNIA financial statement which Du Bois had published.

The immediate reason for this outburst was a symposium which
Garvey had mailed to influential white people. The symposium sought
to secure a favorable sentiment among white people for racial separation
and African colonization. It argued in effect that black people would
never be tolerated as equals in America, and hence the NAACP program
of integration could lead only to race war. Du Bois was not the only
integrationist driven to fury by this symposium. The communists blasted
it on the front page of the *Daily Worker* and the black socialist integrationists of the *Messenger* group also attacked it bitterly.

It is interesting to note that Du Bois was in the midst of severe internal
difficulties within the NAACP, at this time, a fact of which Garvey was
aware. He had been forced out of the 1923 annual NAACP conference

and now he was accusing James Weldon Johnson, Walter White and Mary White Ovington of trying to keep him out of the 1924 conference starting in June.[119]

This latest Du Bois attack contained several factual inaccuracies, and the *Negro World* devoted much space to counterattacks and refutations. T. Thomas Fortune editorially described the latest Du Bois effort as an "orgy of inaccurate detraction and vituperative abuse."[120] But the most imaginative response came in a special editorial by Norton Thomas, associate editor of Garvey's paper, entitled "With Apologies to Shakespeare." This was in fact an adaptation from Shakespeare's *Julius Ceasar.* It began at "Act XCIX. Scene IX. Harlem. Seventh Avenue." It continued:

Enter William Pickens, William Du Bois and Weldon Johnson.

Du Bois (Nervously)

Another general shout!
I do believe, that these applauses are
For some new honors that are heaped on Garvey.

Johnson

Why, man, he doth bestride the world of Negroes
Like a Colossus; and we petty men
Walk under his huge legs, and peep about
To find ourselves dishonourable graves,
Men at some time are masters of their fates;
The fault, dear Du Bois, is not in our stars,
But in ourselves, that we are underlings.
Du Bois and Garvey: What should be in that Garvey?
Why should that name be sounded more than yours?
Write them together, yours is as fair a name;
Sound them, it doth become the mouth as well;
Weigh them, it is as heavy; conjure with them,
Du Bois will start a spirit as soon as Garvey.
Now, in the names of all the Gods at once,
Upon what meat doth this our Garvey feed,
That he is grown so great?

Du Bois

> Enough, faithful one. (Sighs) What you have said,
> I will consider; what you have to say,
> I will with patience hear: and find a time
> Both meet to hear, and answer, such high things.
> Till then, my noble friend, chew upon this:
> Du Bois had rather be a Nordic,
> Than to repute himself a son of Ham
> Under these hard conditions as this time
> Is like to lay upon us.
>
> (Exeunt Du Bois and Johnson.)[121]

The editorial continued with a Pickens soliloquy.

With the "Lunatic or Traitor" editorial, the controversy between these two leaders descended to a new low. Garvey, to be sure, was never sparing in abusiveness, but of outright falsehoods Du Bois seems to have maintained a monopoly. This editorial represented about the worst example of Du Bois' propensity to let the truth get away from him. For this he was assailed by several black publications.[122] Communist Robert Minor also attacked him severely on this editorial, even though he enjoyed cordial relations with some NAACP members. He wrote:

> I would think long before I would dispute the judgment of the Negro scholar, Dr. W. E. B. Du Bois. But when Dr. Du Bois writes that the United States Government gave Garvey "a fair and patient trial" and that Garvey was refused bail "because of the repeated threats and cold-blooded assaults charged against his organization," and that "he himself openly threatened to get the district attorney," etc., I get a different reaction from that intended by Dr. Du Bois. I am obliged to look beyond the details at the apparent fact that a government which hates the working class, and which has never been unforgiving to grafting schemes, that such a government does not find a friend in Garvey.

And above it all towers the fact that the Universal Negro Improvement Association, the largest organization of Negroes in the world,
is made up almost entirely of the working class.

I am waiting for some Negro leader who has organized more Negroes
than Marcus Garvey has organized, to criticize Garvey—and I frankly
confess that if such a leader has been given a longer term in Leavenworth than Garvey received, I will listen to him more attentively.

The lickspittles of capitalism in Washington do not love Marcus Garvey.
This alone ought to make one of the working class think twice before
condemning the man. His enemies say the government condemns Garvey
for using questionable financial methods for the purpose of fleecing the
masses of uneducated Negro workers. But I don't think the Teapot Domers
at Washington have any objections to the fleecing of the Negro masses.

I think their solicitude is based on something else.

The fact that Garvey is organizing many thousands of Negroes of the
class that is destined to take over the earth, and makes a militant demand
for a sweeping international liberation of colonial peoples, seems to me to
be a more likely reason why Mesrs. Coolidge, Daugherty and, yes, Mr.
Hughes of the State Department have interested themselves in Garvey.[123]

Shortly after the "Lunatic or Traitor" editorial, Du Bois and Garvey
actually came face to face with each other for a brief and frightening
moment. Du Bois, in the company of one W. P. Dabney, was waiting to
enter a hotel elevator when out stepped a bevy of splendidly dressed
ladies accompanied by "a stout dark gentleman, gorgeously costumed"
in military attire. "Ye gods!" wrote Dabney afterwards, "Twas Garvey.
He saw me, a smile of recognition, then a glance at Du Bois. His eyes flew
wide open. Stepping aside, he stared; turning around, he stared, while
Du Bois, looking straight forward, head uplifted, nostrils quivering,
marched into the elevator. . . ." In response to a Dabney inquiry, Du Bois
claimed that he did not see Garvey. His nostrils were quivering, he explained, because he smelled food.[124]

One result of the events of 1923 and 1924 was that both Garvey and
Du Bois took the irreconcilability of their views to mean that total black
unity was not only an impossibility, but a goal not even worth striving for.
At the Sanhedrin in February 1924 Alain Locke of Howard University
and other prominent black persons had called for a rapprochement between the two rivals.[125] Responding to such views before the start of
the Sanhedrin, Garvey had argued that he and Du Bois could not come
together on any constructive basis in such an all-embracing convention.
For Du Bois was a "modern extremist" preaching an integration ideal
that might materialize in two thousand years time when all races had
achieved equal material and cultural strength. For the time being, Garvey
explained, "The Negro has got to develop apart, and create his own government and industrial foundation" in order to catch up with a world that
respected only political and economic strength.[126] Du Bois in July came
out equally strongly against unity, arguing that diversity, and even some
"personal bickering" were "absolutely essential in the present situation
of the Negro race." The NAACP, he argued, wanted the black man to
become "a full fledged American citizen" and disagreed with contrary
views. "Under such circumstances," he declared, "to talk unity and
agreement is nonsense. If the National Association for the Advancement
of Colored People is right, these other people are wrong. If one group is
walking North and the other group walking South then unity would mean
an abdication of its position by one group." Only such people as were
willing to accept its program were welcome to unite with the NAACP.[127]

The "Lunatic or Traitor" editorial was followed by a few relatively
low-key *Crisis* attacks later in 1924, but the UNIA moved on to officially
ostracize Du Bois from the race. This was done by a resolution, unanimously carried, at the end of the 1924 UNIA convention. News of
Liberia's final frustration of UNIA colonization had been received during
the convention and the delegates saw in this the consummation of Du Bois'
efforts. The resolution stated:

> In view of the fact that W. E. B. Du Bois has continually attempted to
> obstruct the progress of the Universal Negro Improvement Association
> to the loss and detriment of the Negro race and that he has on several
> occasions gone out of his way to try to defeat the cause of Africa's

redemption, that he be proclaimed as ostracized from the Negro race as far as the Universal Negro Improvement Association is concerned, and from henceforth be regarded as an enemy of the black people of the world.[128]

With Garvey in jail from early in 1925 the battle subsided somewhat. Garvey continued to accuse Du Bois and the NAACP of helping him to jail and Du Bois no doubt felt that he had accomplished his purpose, since he had lent his voice to those calling for Garvey's incarceration and deportation. He planned a fourth Pan-African Congress to be held in the West Indies in 1925, which may or may not have been a move to increase his influence in the only area in which he acknowledged the existence of a powerful Garvey following. However his plans were frustrated. Strange to say, he thought the colonialists were behind this failure.[129] In previous years he had blamed Garvey for his congress setbacks.

In 1927, however, Du Bois did succeed in holding a congress in that greatest of all Garveyite strongholds, Harlem. The initiative had come largely from black women's organizations. Garvey was, of course, still in jail and had decreed that there should be no UNIA convention that year. So, in the UNIA convention month of August, Du Bois rushed in to fill the breach. His congress went so far as to borrow Garvey's famous slogan and pass a resolution advocating "Africa for the Africans."[130]

It would have been strange indeed if Du Bois could have held a congress, even a four-day one, in Harlem without some Garveyite interest. From the pages of the *Negro World*, Kelly Miller pointedly called Garvey a political prisoner, a greater race leader than all his predecessors and the greatest ever advocate of African redemption. He called on the Pan-African Congress to demand clemency for Garvey. T. Thomas Fortune dropped in on the closing session to see for himself what was going on and returned to his office to write an editorial about it. He disagreed with much of what he heard, including "The opinion of Professor Logan that it was not possible nor would it be good to hope that the Europeans could or would be driven out of Africa," and that the Africans should cooperate with the white man. "The old theory of the lion and the lamb lying down together without a row," Fortune mused, "because the lamb was inside the lion. It is the Red Indian in contact with the European whites on the Western Continent all over again."

One of the last items of business for the congress was the adoption
of resolutions. Du Bois had kept tight control over this phase of the
business. He drew up the resolutions himself and they were approved
by a committee. While he was reading them to the audience a Reverend
Walker, pastor of an AME Church in Cleveland, Ohio, interrupted to
suggest that the congress should issue a call for clemency for Garvey.
The idea was roundly applauded and put in the form of a formal
motion, accompanied by an effusive and well-received eulogy of Garvey.
Du Bois suggested that the resolution go back to committee, where he
could kill it, rather than be voted on by the whole gathering. After a
warm debate which, Fortune reported, indicated that most of the audience supported the resolution, it was maneuverd into committee from
which it did not return. But this did not stop "the brazen-faced doctor"
as one report put it, from proclaiming "Africa for the Africans."[131]

Garvey was nevertheless released from jail and deported three months
after the congress. Du Bois celebrated with a review of his controversy
with Garvey "not to revive forgotten rancor but for the sake of historical
accuracy." The article was in fact yet another distortion and anything
but historically accurate. In claiming that the *Crisis* had published a
mere five articles on Garvey he conveniently forgot those that were
obviously devoted to Garvey but did not name him, as well as several
minor *Crisis* articles. Du Bois even forgot the date of one of his own
articles, claiming that extracts from a 1924 article had appeared in
1922. His claim that "the impression that the NAACP has been the
persistent enemy of Marcus Garvey" was "without the slightest basis
of fact" was at the very least a gross exaggeràtion. He contrasted this
sweet innocence on the NAACP's part with "Garvey's attacks on the
NAACP [which] have been continuous, preposterous and false."[132]
About this time it seems that Du Bois took his campaign against Garvey
into fiction, for Alain Locke, reviewing his *Dark Princess*, spotted "perhaps a thinly varnished Garvey" among the characters.[133]

Du Bois lived for ninety-five years. His life was in many ways the sad
and tortuous story of a man drawn by training and upbringing to white
aristocracy, yet too sensitive to ignore the racism that buffeted him and
his race. During his life he moved impatiently from one tactic to the
next, from one philosophy to the next, in a frustratingly vain quest for
the elusive formula that would overcome the formidable monster of

white racism, and more especially American white racism. And so it was
that Du Bois came to Garveyism.

When Garvey was deported from the United States in 1927, Du Bois
was already an old man, less than three months short of his sixtieth
birthday. He had already tried intellectualizing the race problem away.
He had long given that up in favor of agitating it away. He had tried
socialism, and integration, and more. Yet some time around 1930, Du Bois
began going the way that George Padmore was soon to follow. The major
difference between the two was that Padmore was more honest about
the influence of Garvey on causing black communists to reconsider their
positions than Du Bois was in the case of his own switch from integration to separation.

No sooner was Garvey out of the way than Du Bois was overcome
by a deep disillusionment with the integration that he had defended so
stubbornly. He increasingly came to realize that for all his effort, for all
the effort of the NAACP, integration was making little headway. De
facto school segregation had increased in the North and lynchings, though
less frequent, were no less brazen. He therefore now began to argue that
since integration was an apparent impossibility for the time being at
least, then black people might as well make the most of separation. He
talked of a nonprofit cooperative "racial economy" that would operate
within American capitalism but not be of it. This racial economy would
in time incorporate the West Indies. He even began, with the terrible
tragedy of the depression, to voice Garvey's pessimism about the survival
of the African race in America. Du Bois had in the past threatened separation if America denied the black man equality but these were but fleeting glimpses of his uncertainty. Now, however, it was different.

One of the first to notice the change in Du Bois was Garvey himself.
After reading a Du Bois commencement speech at Howard University
Garvey, from Jamaica, loudly accused Du Bois of now preaching Garveyism. This was in 1930, and Du Bois had referred in that speech to the
need for a black economic base.[134] In 1931 the *Negro World* made the
same point. Page 1 headlines declared, "Dr. Du Bois agrees with UNIA
Leader—Takes Program Over Finally—But Does Not Openly Confess It.
Emphasizes Negro-Owned INDUSTRIES, BUSINESS."[135]   This new line
of thinking led inevitably to a break between Du Bois and his integrationist employers at the NAACP. Du Bois, in his own words, was now "ad-

vocating new, deliberate, and purposeful segregation for economic defense."[136] In 1934 he and the NAACP parted company, leaving the *Crisis* in the capable integrationist hands of Roy Wilkins and George W. Streator. Garvey, alluding to Du Bois' late arrival at the philosophy of racial economic self-reliance commented, "It is no wonder Du Bois has resigned from the National Association for the Advancement of Coloured People. He can go no farther. Can he continue abusing the white man when the American Negro is at the white man's Soup Kitchen?"[137] Du Bois meanwhile, while steadfastly refraining from giving Garvey credit for his new position, sought to make his peace with the ghost of Booker T. Washington, claiming now that he had not opposed Washington on segregation grounds.[138]

Other observers, however, noted the Garveyite sound of Du Bois' new pronouncements. George Streator wrote soon after, "It is significant that the Garvey idea, however much it was ridiculed by Negro intellectuals during the heyday of the movement, has not downed. On the contrary it reappears in the most unexpected quarter, for example, in the currently expounded Du Bois doctrine of a black economy. . . ."[139] And sociologist E. Franklin Frazier, himself no great lover of Garvey, observed, "When Garvey proposed a grandiose scheme for building a black commercial empire Du Bois ridiculed his naivete. But what could be more fantastic than his own program for a separate non-profit economy within American capitalism?" Frazier, having written Du Bois off as the marginal man who could not discover his identity, prophesied, correctly as it turned out, that Du Bois would not remain a separatist for too long. He wrote in scathing tones:

> Du Bois' racial program needs not to be taken seriously. . . . He has only an occasional romantic interest in the Negro as a distinct race. Nothing would be more unendurable for him than to live within a Black Ghetto or within a black nation—unless perhaps he were king, and then probably he would attempt to unite the whites and blacks through marriage of the royal families. When Garvey attempted his genuine racial movement no one was more critical and contemptuous than Du Bois of the fantastic glorification of the black race and all things black. Garvey's movement was too close to the black ignorant masses for Du Bois. On the other hand, he was more at home with the colored intellectuals who gathered at the Pan-African Congresses.[140]

In England, meanwhile, Garvey summed up his conflict with Du Bois. He summarized Du Bois' great shortcomings in a sentence: "He has no racial self-respect, he has no independent ideas, he has nothing of self-reliance about him and that is his great trouble." In Du Bois, moreover, Garvey saw no evidence of any independent long-range thinking on strategies to emancipate the race, such as had characterized Booker T. Washington's program. Garvey saw Du Bois' outstanding contribution rather as a negative hostility to the most important programs for liberation in his time. Garvey wrote in 1935:

> When Du Bois dies he will go down in his grave to be remembered as the man who sabotaged the Liberian colonization scheme of the Negro, the man who opposed the American Negro launching steamships on the seas, the man who did everything to handicap the industrial and commercial propositions of the American Negro, the man who tried to wreck the industrial, educational system of Tuskegee, the man who never had a good word to say for any other Negro leader, but who tried to down every one of them.[141]

The short-range, more spontaneous nature of the Du Bois-NAACP conception of a program of liberation was well expressed by Du Bois himself in 1921 when he explained that "the NAACP is organized to agitate, to investigate, to expose, to defend, to reason, to appeal. This is our program and this is the whole of our program."[142] This is exactly what Garvey meant when he said that Du Bois had no program. Concerning the charge of constant hostility to the programs of Garvey and others Du Bois wrote later, "In his case, as in the case of others, I have repeatedly been accused of enmity and jealousy, which have been so far from my thought that the accusations have been a rather bitter experience."[143]

The Du Bois-Garvey conflict dominated the conflict between the NAACP and Garvey. But Garvey had his occasional exchanges with other NAACP leaders. In the case of one of them, William Pickens, an extended controversy developed which was second in intensity only to Garvey's struggle with Du Bois. The case of Pickens is important because not only was the personal animosity generated as great, but the ideological disagreements which surfaced were the same as those of the Du Bois-Garvey conflict. The coincidence of the positions of Du Bois and Pickens in their separate conflicts with Garvey underlines the real ideological character of the differences between the NAACP and the UNIA. Pickens joined the NAACP in 1920 as associate field secretary. He was a graduate of Yale, class of 1904, and like some of Garvey's associates, had been a member of Du Bois' Niagara Movement. When he joined the NAACP he was a vice-president of Morgan State College.[144]

Even before he joined the NAACP, if Pickens' very unreliable later testimony can be believed, he had received an offer or offers from the UNIA.[145] After about a year with the NAACP Pickens began expressing dissatisfaction with the organization. He was counseled by Du Bois in March 1921 to be loyal nevertheless.[146] He decided, however, to explore the possibility of alternative employment with the UNIA. Amy Jacques Garvey recalls that he phoned Garvey and subsequently visited his apartment twice. He told Garvey that his pay was insufficient even though he did more work than his colleagues, and he was being discriminated against because of his color. Garvey offered him a job until the August convention, at which time he could run for office.[147] Pickens, however, had no real intention of joining Garvey at this juncture but was merely skillfully, and with extreme callousness, using Garvey in an attempt to exact more money and a position of greater authority from the NAACP. He was therefore able to temporize with Garvey until safely after the August convention, although he addressed a Liberty Hall audience on August 30.[148] On September 12, however, when his conflict with the NAACP was reaching a head, he wrote Garvey an effusively flattering letter, which, in the light of later events, was a calculated deceit of the greatest magnitude. The letter claimed that Pickens was doing well and really did not need a change of job except for "the great feeling of the great opportunity to aid the supreme enterprise which you are undertaking, and which you have been urging me for some time to consider." Undaunted by his intended treachery he assured Garvey, "I know you have dealt with many traitors and have still traitors to meet. They infest the world. But trust me. If I never worked in the same organization with you, I should still be your brother."[149]

A mere five days later, on September 17, Pickens submitted his resignation to the NAACP board of directors effective not later than November 1, but preferably on October 1. He claimed that he would continue to uphold the aims of the association, strange talk for a prospective

Garveyite.[150] It transpired that the October 1 preference was due to his promise to speak to the "colored people of New York" on October 2.[151] On September 25, doubtless in response to NAACP attempts to settle his problems, he informed the associations's treasurer that whereas he would have received substantially more had he succumbed to earlier offers, his biggest current offer was only about the same as his current salary plus his earnings from occasional lectures.[152] On September 29 he refused an invitation to attend a meeting of the NAACP's executives to discuss his resignation. "The next move," he scribbled on the bottom of the invitation, "belonged to them and I let them take it."[153] The executives nevertheless refused to accept the resignation and appointed a committee to investigate. The committee recommended an increase in pay and a reorganization of field work to give Pickens "a larger directional part," thus overcoming his two major grievances.[154] Pickens' ploy had thus succeeded. That he had merely used the UNIA he himself confirmed. Concerning Garvey's offer of temporary employment until the 1921 convention he explained, "This I decided to try out for all it was worth, IF I should have to leave the NAACP, which I never wanted to do, if it could be reasonably avoided."[155]

Sometime during the course of these intrigues Pickens wrote an article for the *Nation* at that magazine's request. It was written before the resolution of his conflict with the NAACP. The result was so effusively pro-Garvey that the magazine's editors suspected a hoax. On October 11, one day after the NAACP board of directors accepted the recommendation to increase Pickens' pay and authority, he had to assure the *Nation*'s editors that he had not in fact taken them for a ride. He claimed that the article had been written before he began to entertain the possibility of joining Garvey and that he would write exactly the same article now that his conflict with the NAACP was settled.[156] The *Nation* published an expurgated version in December. The *Negro World* published the full article a week and a half earlier. It also appeared in the black *California Voice* on December 31, 1921, together with a Pickens Christmas greeting to the UNIA. The California paper introduced the article with the headline, "Field Secretary N.A.A.C.P. Analyzes and Endorses Garvey Movement."[157]

The article itself praised Garvey's emphasis on race, defended his regalia while not agreeing that it was necessary, supported his business methods, his steamship line and his honesty, and saw no necessary contradiction between the international operations of the UNIA and the domestic emphasis of the NAACP. Pickens even argued that there was no reason why the same person could not belong to the Urban League, the UNIA, and the NAACP "and yet talk consistently in an 'interracial congress' in Atlanta, Georgia." The unexpurgated version even suggested that a West Indian leader and a black movement in the United States were the perfect combination for racial emancipation at that particular time. Where there was criticism, as on the light-skinned question, it was mild. In February 1922 Garvey proclaimed his "high regard" for Pickens, whom he considered "above meanness of any kind." In March a *Negro World* editorial came to Pickens' defense when the Cleveland *Call* inquired, "What Side of the Fence is Pickens On?"[158]

Pickens seems not to have informed Garvey of his intention to remain with the NAACP, even after receiving his increased salary and settling his dispute, for in May 1922 Garvey again extended an offer to him.[159] In June, Pickens privately made a fairly favorable appraisal of Garvey. He praised Garvey's international organization but this time opted for the NAACP's domestic struggle as a quicker remedy for emancipation of the race in America. He opposed emigration to Africa but conceded that Garvey's program was the greatest menace of the time to the white world. His remarks are important because they came just before the "Marcus Garvey Must Go" campaign, of which Pickens was shortly to become one of the leaders. Perhaps as a harbinger of things to come, he seemed to anticipate the persistence of the "Garvey idea" after the departure of Garvey himself. He wrote:

> As to the Garvey Movement, it is not perfect. No movement is— but Garvey has the right idea that ALL NEGROES of all countries and especially of the Western World, should be in touch and organization with each other. I know Garvey personally, and I do not regard him as a crook. He is somewhat of a visionary; all such men are. He will not FAIL, altho he himself will not see the great success of his plans. The idea he has injected into the Negro masses will stay, even if Garvey should be jailed or hung. The whole world today, the large white world, outside of places like Shreveport and Mississippi, are more concerned over the "Garvey idea" than over any other move

the Negro has ever made for power in the modern world. They know that to effect an international organization is to reach out for REAL power, especially thru MASSES of men.

But I am with the N.A.A.C.P., altho I have been offered as much as TEN THOUSAND DOLLARS a year to join other forces, and the offer still stands. I believe in the EARLIER FRUITION of the sowings of the N.A.A.C.P., for the good of Negroes in the U.S.A.

Colored Americans will make regrettable mistakes, if they help white Americans to fight the "Garvey idea." The idea is all right, if only Garvey can get rid of some of the crooks that have infested his organization, and speak plain about ORGANIZATION of the racial group, and not try to fool anybody about the "back to Africa" myth.[160]

On July 10 Garvey invited Pickens to accept an honor at the forthcoming August UNIA convention for his exemplary endeavors in the service of the race. By this time, however, the "Marcus Must Go" campaign was firing its first broadsides at Garvey and Pickens had aligned himself with it. On July 24 he replied angrily. His reply showed quite clearly that, like Du Bois, he could be driven to great rage by Garvey's more extreme separatist manifestations, in this case the summit conference with the Ku Klux Klan.[161] Pickens considered absurd any deal with the Klan by which, as he said, America was accepted as a white man's country in exchange for assistance in making Africa truly a black man's continent. He believed, he said, in Africa for the Africans, black and white, and in America for all colors.

Up to this time Pickens had done nothing worse than mislead Garvey to obtain a salary increase. From now on he was to be a central figure in the most vituperative campaign ever waged by Afro-American leaders of importance against a major rival.

MARCUS GARVEY MUST GO!!!

The "Marcus Garvey Must Go" campaign represented essentially a temporary alliance of convenience between black socialists, represented principally by A. Philip Randolph and Chandler Owen, some black Urban

League officials, the NAACP, and miscellaneous other black integrationists. It represented a formidable coalition of the most influential black
integrationist leaders in the land. Many of them had previously crossed
swords with one another in their competition for leadership of the Afro-
American masses, and many were to cross swords after the removal of
Garvey, but for the moment they were willing to cooperate in the face
of the Garvey steamroller which threatened to crush them all.

Among the more important personalities leading this campaign were
first of all Randolph and Owen. They represented the radical wing of the
noncommunist integrationists, being more prone to intemperate speech
and voluble pratings concerning the class struggle and the "scientific"
nature of their program. In many respects, however, they differed little
from the mainstream integrationists in the NAACP. The NAACP's major
representatives in this campaign were Pickens and Robert W. Bagnall, its
director of branches, with Du Bois, of course, playing a key supporting
role. The executive board of the National Urban League in New York
provided two of the campaign's leaders in John E. Nail and Harry H.
Pace.[162] The Urban League, too, was mainstream integrationist.[163]

Many of the campaign's leaders had previously been engaged in acrimonious disputes with Garvey. Bagnall, a preacher, had almost attempted
to throw Garvey out of his church in Detroit when Garvey tried to "inte-
grate" it by sitting up front among the light-skinned folk during his early
years in the United States.[164] Robert S. Abbott, editor of the *Chicago
Defender* and another leader of the campaign, had been sued for libel
by Garvey in 1919 for attacks on what he called the "Jim Crow" Black
Star Line. Abbott, as the editor of one of the leading Afro-American
newspapers, presumably did not appreciate the competition from the
fast-growing *Negro World* and Garvey's attacks on his race-demeaning
advertisements. In 1920 Abbott engineered Garvey's arrest on a technicality while he was on tour in Chicago.[165] Garvey's previous contacts
with Randolph and Owen went back much further.

Randolph claims the distinction of having given Garvey his first opportunity to address a Harlem audience. The year was 1916, and Randolph
was addressing a large gathering from his soapbox at the corner of 135
Street and Lenox Avenue. Someone pulled on his coat and said that a
young man from Jamaica wished to speak. Garvey did speak, and, according to Randolph, "you could hear him from 135th to 125th Street."

After his speech Garvey sat down near the platform with paper, stamps and envelopes, busily engaged in sending out his propaganda.[166] Garvey's 1917 speech denouncing the East St. Louis riot was presided over by Chandler Owen. This cordial relationship continued into 1919. From July 1919 W. A. Domingo, himself a socialist, was listed as a contributing editor of the *Messenger* while simultaneously editing the *Negro World*. Many of his articles appeared in the *Messenger* up to and beyond his resignation from the paper. In 1919 Randolph was actually chosen by Garvey as one of his representatives to the Paris peace conference. The trip never materialized. Randolph later claimed, at the height of the campaign against Garvey, that the first big mass meeting ever held by the UNIA was under the pretext of sending him to this conference.[167]

Garvey's collaboration with these socialists was doomed from the start because of the incompatibility of their advocacy of integrationist interracial class struggle with his own ideas of race first. His dismissal of Domingo therefore coincided with a break with Owen and Randolph over these principles. The *Messenger* itself in December 1920 acknowledged the ideological nature of the split. It editorialized: "At one time, the editors of the MESSENGER spoke from the same platform with the moving spirit of the organization in question. Then, the Black Star Line idea was no part of its effects. Nor were the slogans 'Negro first,' and 'African Empire,' 'Back to Africa,' and extreme race baiting prominent in its program." Siding with Garvey in this schism was Hubert H. Harrison who left the Socialist party, as he explained in 1917, because as a firm believer in "the American doctrine of 'Race First,' he wished to put himself in a position to work among his people along lines of his own choosing."[168] (Harrison was referring to himself here in the third person.)

Increasing the ranks of these dedicated integrationists of long standing was the inevitable occasional opportunist who seized the time to grind some personal axe against Garvey. The outstanding representative of this category was J. W. H. Eason. Elected UNIA leader of the American Negroes in 1920, Eason had maintained this position until his expulsion during the 1922 convention. Eason it was who in 1920 had been slated to occupy the UNIA Black House in Washington, D.C., a most unintegrationist gesture. A few months before his departure from the UNIA he had expressed a fervent desire to go to Africa. "But if I never go," he implored his UNIA audience, "I want you American Negroes, when you make your future exodus from this country, to take my bones with you and bury them in the motherland." Four months later he was saying that he left the UNIA because there were enough problems in America without having to get involved in Africa, or anywhere else. In June he claimed to be impressed by white Mississippi segregationist Senator McCallum, whom he had interviewed. McCallum had suggested that black people should see about their own affairs. In August, on the eve of his expulsion, he was accusing Garvey of joining the KKK.[169]

The truth of the matter was that Eason had been formally impeached and expelled from the UNIA for ninety-nine years in lengthy legal proceedings at the 1922 convention. His impeachment had arisen out of charges of a large number of financial and other irregularities, some of which he admitted. These matters had come to the attention of Garvey and had been substantiated by his auditor J. Charles Zampty during an extensive tour throughout the United States prior to the convention.[170] Once expelled, he reinforced the integrationist campaign by holding anti-Garvey meetings all over the country under the nominal auspices of his hastily organized Universal Negro Alliance. He traveled through many of the same areas that he had only recently toured on behalf of the UNIA, this time repudiating his former Garveyite opinions. Sometime during this period it was announced that he would be the star witness against Garvey in the latter's forthcoming trial.

The swiftness and comprehensiveness of his about-face did not go down well with Garvey's supporters. At a Chicago meeting thirty-one of the thirty-five who turned up to hear him were loyal Garveyites keeping a wary eye on him. After this meeting shots rang out leading many to believe, in the words of the *Negro World,* that Eason had "paid the price of the traitor." The shots in fact were the result of some unconnected altercation. The following night he had an audience of six. In New Orleans in October he spoke to thirty-two persons where a few months previously, as Garvey's representative, he had on four occasions addressed full houses. Worse was yet to come. In January 1923 he was shot dead after addressing an Emancipation Day meeting, again in New Orleans. The *Negro World* called his murder a "dastardly act" and suggested an illicit amorous entanglement as the probable cause. Two Garveyites were arrested and charged with the murder. The UNIA initiated a defense fund for them and they were eventually acquitted. A third suspect was almost cornered at a UNIA meeting in Detroit, but detectives inquiring after him were detained at the door by members of the Universal African Legions long enough to enable the suspect to escape through a rear exit. The UNIA meanwhile disclaimed any complicity in the assassination.[171]

As in the case of Du Bois, the integrationist coalition made Garvey's separatism and allied doctrines its main objects of attack. There was also the very nonideological question of what one study has called the "crisis of confidence" in the Urban League (and certainly in other organizations) when, despite white philanthropic help, they could not raise anywhere near the sums that Garvey could from his black followers.[172] (Indeed both John E. Nail and Harry H. Pace, the two major Urban League figures in the anti-Garvey campaign, were at the time members of the Urban League's finance committee.)[173]

The effect of Garvey's doctrine of racial separation in forcing these integrationists to come together is highlighted by the squabbling that went on among them prior to, and for a short while after his rise to prominence. In 1917, for example, the *Messenger* had attacked Du Bois, Pickens and others. In 1918 it called Du Bois, Pickens, James Weldon Johnson and others "a discredit to Negroes and the laughing stock among whites." Similar attacks came in 1919 when Randolph referred to these three as typical Negro reactionaries. In December 1919 Pickens, responding to attacks from Owen and Randolph, said that he respected socialism, but not the cheap brand practiced by these two. He advised the white socialists to find more suitable material for work among black people or face continued failures. And as late as December 1920 the first overt Du Bois comment on Garvey charged that early in 1919 Chandler Owen had presided over a large mass meeting in Harlem's Palace Casino. At that meeting, Du Bois charged, Garvey and Randolph addressed the audience and $204 was collected on a claim that Du Bois had obstructed Garvey's high commissioner in France by repudiating Garvey's statements on American lynching and injustice. (The *Messenger* had attacked Du Bois in September.)[174] By the time of Du Bois' article, however, Pickens had begun to make his peace with Owen and Randolph.[175] He had also, if he is to be believed, already been approached by Garvey.

One of the earliest muffled shots in the coalition's campaign came in May 1920 when the founding meeting of the Friends of Negro Freedom took place in Washington, D.C. This group was to play an important role, at least nominally, in the campaign. The meeting was convened at the initiative of Owen and Randolph, who were to become its joint executive secretaries. The list of those invited showed that already there had been some closing of integrationist ranks, for several NAACP local officials were among them. These included Archibald Grimké, president of the Washington, D.C., chapter, who had formerly been written off as reactionary by Owen and Randolph. Among the other invitees were Robert W. Bagnall, Carl Murphy, editor of the Baltimore *Afro-American,* and historian Carter G. Woodson who, unlike most of the others, usually managed to discreetly avoid becoming involved in attacks on Garvey. Later on this Owen-Randolph inspired integrationist coalition reached out to embrace the communist assimilationists, for the name of Cyril Briggs appeared on the Friends of Negro Freedom letterhead.[176] The precampaign hostility of Owen and Randolph to the communists (which was reciprocated in equal measure) was as great as that toward other elements of this coalition.

The first meeting of the Friends of Negro Freedom was scheduled to be held less than two weeks after the 1920 national convention of the Socialist party. Here Owen and Randolph, together with W. A. Domingo and Thomas E. A. Potter, were seen as playing the same kind of role as the African Blood Brotherhood was to play for the communists. They were to spearhead the socialist drive among the black masses.[177] The Friends of Negro Freedom were doubtless, among other things, a manifestation of this role. The new organization was also thoroughly integrationist, it being specified that it should be interracial though black-led.

In the months that followed, Owen and Randolph continued their attacks on Garvey's separatist program. Owen declared in August 1920, "we educated scientific-minded and higher minded Negroes do not want a Negro nation. It would forever kill our dream of world equality." The *Messenger* also opposed the slogan "Africa for the Africans" because, it argued, oppression knows no color.[178] By October 1920 the magazine had come to the conclusion that the UNIA was "not a promise but a definite menace to Negroes." Among Garvey's menacing attributes were his advocacy of a black political party in the United States.[179] Garvey's African program especially came under repeated attack. Randolph argued that Africa was almost totally colonized and so could not be taken. Garvey, he thought, was a tool of white racists in that he diverted black aspirations into unattainable goals. On this point Randolph compared Garvey unfavorably with the Zionists, whom, he claimed, did not advocate conquest. "The keen mentality of the Jew," he pontificated, "recognizes the suicidal folly of such a policy." He did recognize, however, that Garvey had made a useful contribution in his "necessary and effective criticism on Negro leadership," in his popularization of black history, in his instilling of an attitude of resistance towards whites, and in motivating black people to follow black leadership.[180]

These attacks, serious as they were, were but a prelude to the real campaign, which may be said to have gotten underway with the appearance of the July 1922 *Messenger.* The very first editorial screamed starkly, "Marcus Garvey!" Once again, and not for the last time, Garvey's separatist utterances had driven the integrationists into a frenzy. This time the casus belli was a Garvey speech in New Orleans. He was quoted as saying, in terms reminiscent of Booker T. Washington, that America was a white man's country and the black man could not insist on riding the white man's jim crow streetcar, since he had not built any streetcar of his own. This was too much for the *Messenger.* Before the month was through, Randolph had commenced his anti-Garvey speeches in Harlem.[181]

Once the decision for all-out war had been made, Owen and Randolph dropped all pretensions to propriety in their attacks. Like Du Bois, they exploited to the full the most vulnerable chink in Garvey's armor, namely his foreignness, and this despite having previously disassociated themselves from attacks on Garvey's nativity.[182] Garvey's incarceration and deportation were henceforth to be the main objectives of the campaign. "This fool talk, too," the opening salvo declared, "emanates from a blustering West Indian demagogue who preys upon the ignorant unsuspecting poor West Indian working men and women who believe Garvey is some sort of Moses." All "ministers, editors and lecturers who have the interests of the race at heart" were urged "to gird up their courage, put on new force, and proceed with might and main to drive the menace of Garveyism out of this country." And just in case the message still had not been made clear, the following declaration of uncompromising hostility appeared: *"Here's notice that the* MESSENGER *is firing the opening gun in a campaign to drive Garvey and Garveyism in all its sinister viciousness from the American soil."*[183]

At this point Pickens entered the campaign. The black Philadelphia *Public Journal*, for which he was a contributing editor, and the August *Messenger* both carried reprints of the July 1922 exchange of letters between himself and Garvey. In response to Garvey's offer of an award at the August UNIA convention he had replied that he wanted no award from the KKK organization.[184] By suppressing his former correspondence with Garvey, he created the impression that Garvey's advances were a one-sided affair, although he later admitted to having "discussed" a job possibility.[185] He supported his entry into the campaign with a steady flow of news releases and editorials, many of them scurrilous, against Garvey.[186] Garvey, for his part, lamented Pickens' about-face. "We believed that he was really a race patriot," he wrote, "and could have been harnessed for service to his race, but we find him, black as he is, smarting under the lash of a prejudiced crowd that has more venom than sense, more malice than race loyalty." Garvey also regretted his dishonesty in not publishing a further addition to the correspondence in which Garvey had rejected accusations of a link with the KKK and had challenged Pickens to a public debate.[187]

August, the month of Pickens' anti-Garvey debut in the *Messenger*, was also the month of Garvey's convention. The back page of the *Messenger* proclaimed, as thousands of handbills were soon to do, "Marcus Garvey Must Go!!!" There followed notice of anti-Garvey meetings in Harlem for each of the four Sundays in August. The speakers would be Pickens, Bagnall, Randolph and Owen. Handbills described this quartet as "four of the most distinguished scholars, nationally noted orators, famous debaters, deep thinkers, faithful, unselfish, fearless, devoted and incorruptible public servants in the cause of Negro freedom." The NAACP's involvement was underscored by the addition of Du Bois and James Weldon Johnson to the names of the four speakers as persons who had taken the correct line while in the South, which Garvey allegedly had not. It was made clear that the attacks would largely revolve around the Black Star Line (and hence the African program) and the Ku Klux Klan question.[188] The meetings were held under the auspices of the Friends of Negro Freedom.

The UNIA convention not unnaturally opened amid much tension. A large police contingent was on hand for the opening parade, during which a few minor skirmishes took place between marchers and bystanders who were brave enough to echo the charges of the rival camp.[189]

During the course of the month, Garvey challenged the campaigners to a public debate; Randolph was reported as having said that the Afro-American would be just as out of place in Africa as the white man; three Africans wrote to the *New York Times* protesting Pickens' denigration of the Motherland during an anti-Garvey meeting; and Walter White, assistant secretary of the NAACP, sent an unnamed gentleman from the West Indies to Randolph with interesting anti-Garvey information that Randolph was glad to receive.[190]

Around this time Randolph received through the mail a packet containing a human hand. The hand had red hair on it and was therefore presumably that of a white person.[191] An accompanying letter scolded Randolph for not being able to unite with his own and gave him a week to join his "nigger improvement association." It was signed "KKK." Whether the hand came from the Klan or Garvey or was posted by Randolph to himself has never been established. In any event Randolph concluded that "the Klan has come to the rescue of its Negro leader, Marcus Garvey." He conveniently omitted from the article which drew these conclusions the fact that the hand was white.[192] This event was balanced by rumors that the campaigners were considering having Garvey assassinated.[193]

In between the abuse, the very real ideological objections to Garveyism continued to surface, among them being his African program. "Africa for the African," said Randolph, was "devoutly to be wished," which did "not imply that we recognize the ability of the Africans to assume the responsibilities and duties of a sovereign nation, at the present."[194]

In November the *Crisis* came to the assistance of the campaign by attacking a UNIA handbill distributed through Harlem countering the charges of Randolph and company and the *Messenger* published a list of the "Twelve Smallest Persons in America." Garvey naturally headed the list, followed by such persons as a Ku Klux Klan leader, Jack Johnson, and one John S. Williams of Georgia, who had buried thirteen black people alive.[195]

Throughout the campaign the brunt of the attack was borne by Owen and Randolph and to a lesser extent by Pickens and Bagnall. A useful indication of how little they had been able to carry prominent non-Garveyite and even anti-Garveyite Afro-American opinion with them was provided by Owen and Randolph themselves. They sent a questionnaire to twenty-five of the most prominent Afro-Americans, including

some nominal members of the Friends of Negro Freedom and some of
the most active campaign members. The recipients of the questionnaire
included Du Bois, Carter G. Woodson, Bagnall, Kelly Miller, Emmett J.
Scott, Robert S. Abbott, Carl Murphy, Archibald Grimké and others.
The questionnaire was accompanied by a letter of so-called "facts"
alleging Garvey's involvement with the Klan and responsibility for the
human-hand affair. Fourteen persons replied. Of this number, Du Bois
referred them to the *Crisis* and declined to answer further, and Woodson
discreetly pleaded lack of sufficient knowledge of the Garvey movement
to answer meaningfully. Of the remaining twelve, no less than five were
soon to be signatories of the notorious anti-Garvey letter to the attorney
general and thus were among the most strongly committed of the anti-
Garvey campaigners. Yet out of a total of twenty-five questionnaires and
fourteen responses resulting in twelve effective replies, heavily biased by
the inclusion of anti-Garvey campaign members, only four agreed with
Owen and Randolph that Garvey should be deported. Among those
against deportation were Emmett J. Scott, Carl Murphy, Kelly Miller,
Archibald Grimké and campaign member John E. Nail, who would soon
be coaxed into changing his mind and signing the prodeportation letter
to the attorney general. Abbott of the *Chicago Defender,* another signer,
declined to answer that question. Those who favored deportation were
Harry H. Pace of the Urban League, Bagnall of the NAACP (both signers
of the letter to the attorney-general), Thomas W. Talley of Fisk University
and J. B. Bass, editor of the *California Eagle.*[196]

The beginning of 1923 found both Pickens and Bagnall listed as contributing editors to the *Messenger.* The year opened disastrously for the
anti-Garvey campaign. J. W. H. Eason was shot dead in January. At this
stage the campaign was in a very precarious position indeed. For about
six months the campaigners had poured forth a torrent of anti-Garvey
rhetoric backed up by meetings all over the United States and in Canada.
Garvey's great influence over the mass of people was evident everywhere.
In New Orleans, Chicago, Toronto, Harlem, and elsewhere, they were
subjected to threats, harassments and intimidations by Garveyites. Their
meetings regularly had to be held under police protection. The campaigners' list of complaints was impressive. An Eason meeting in Philadelphia stopped by the police to prevent bloodshed after persons attempting to attend were knocked down and insulted by Garveyites congregat-

ing outside; a "veritable riot" in Cleveland, Ohio, led by Garvey's deputy
Dr. Leroy Bundy against anti-Garvey elements; Chandler Owen narrowly
saved by the police from Garveyites rushing the streetcar on which he
was riding in Pittsburgh; Pickens intimidated by Garveyites in Toronto;
a Chicago policeman shot by a Garveyite during a fracas after an anti-
Garvey meeting; campaign meetings in New York invaded by "scores"
of Garveyites; a campaign speaker slashed after an anti-Garvey meeting
in Cincinnati; and now Eason dead.[197]

It was at this stage that the anti-Garvey crusaders decided to enact
one of the strangest episodes in Afro-American history. They decided
to write and publicize widely a letter to the attorney general. In effect,
they were moving to openly enlist the support of the United States
government in overcoming their major rival. Concerning this episode
Garvey commented, "It is said that there is honor even among thieves,
but it is apparent that there is no honor and self-respect among certain
Negroes."[198]

The notorious letter to Attorney General Harry M. Daugherty, signed
by eight leaders of the "Marcus Garvey Must Go" campaign, was dated
January 15, 1923. This seems to be the date on which the draft was composed. It was in fact posted or delivered later, although the original date
was not changed. Though signed by eight, the principal drafters were
four—the same four who had provided the initiative and most of the
energy for the campaign so far. They were Randolph, Owen, Pickens
and Bagnall. The preeminent role of these four was stated by Bagnall
in a letter to Arthur B. Spingarn, a national vice-president and chairman
of the legal committee of the NAACP. This letter to Spingarn proves, as
if any proof were needed in light of the role of Pickens and Bagnall, that
the NAACP was deeply implicated in the whole affair. In fact, Bagnall
enclosed the draft to the attorney general and requested legal advice. This
was before the other eventual signers had endorsed it. Bagnall's letter read:

> The enclosed is an open letter to Attorney General Daugherty which
> we plan to have signed by influential colored people in various parts
> of the country. It was drawn up by a group of us, among whom Owen,
> Randolph, Pickens and I were the principals. We wish to guard against
> any illegal statement, and we shall appreciate your advice on that
> point and as to the whole matter.[199]

Spingarn (or somebody else at the NAACP office) did examine the draft
very carefully. Several overexuberant portions were deleted. It seems
quite safe to say that the version which eventually went to the attorney
general was finalized in the NAACP office, in all probability by Arthur B.
Spingarn. It was apparently seen by other NAACP officials too, most
probably Johnson and White, secretary and assistant secretary, respectively, though they claimed that the NAACP "as an organization" had
nothing to do with it.[200]
    The letter attacked Garvey's anti-integration position. It said, "there
are in our midst certain Negro criminals and potential murderers, both
foreign and American born, who are moved and actuated by intense
hatred against the white race. These undesirables continually proclaim
that all white people are enemies of the Negro." The UNIA was described
as "just as objectionable and even more dangerous" than the KKK, "inas-
much as it naturally attracts an even lower type of cranks, crooks and
racial bigots, among whom suggestibility to violent crime is much greater."
    Garvey's foreignness was once more exploited. His followers were de-
scribed as mostly foreigners and voteless, the inference being that the
government would not have to worry about losing their votes. To make
the proposition even more attractive, Du Bois and Domingo were quoted
as authorities on the worldwide membership of the UNIA, which was
put at "much less than 20,000." The letter also revealed the same type
of integrationist elitism and snobbery which characterized Du Bois. The
phenomenon of masses of black workers and peasants militantly organized
and not afraid of violence if necessary was a specter as terrifying to black
integrationists as it was to white people. The letter declared, "The UNIA
is composed chiefly of the most primitive and ignorant element of West
Indian and American Negroes," and more than half of the letter was
devoted to a catalog of their violent acts. The UNIA constitution was
quoted to show that Garvey frowned on criminals except where their
crimes were committed in the interests of the organization. This pro-
vision would doubtless have covered cases such as the conviction of UNIA
members for resisting police attacks on their meeting places. It was presented here, however, as a positive incitement to crime.
    In two cases where matters were pending before the courts, the letter
attempted to impress upon the country's chief law officer the probability
of Garveyite guilt. These were the Eason case, where the UNIA officers

arrested had professed their innocence though rejoicing in his death, and
Garvey's own pending mail fraud case. They begged the attorney general
to "vigorously and speedily push the government's case against Marcus
Garvey for using the mails to defraud" since "hosts of citizen voters" of
both colors "earnestly" desired it. The letter asked finally for Depart-
ment of Justice surveillance of the UNIA and requested "that the Attorney-
General use his full influence completely to disband and extirpate this
vicious movement." The eight signatories were Harry H. Pace of the
Urban League and president of a phonograph corporation; Robert S.
Abbott, publisher and editor of the *Chicago Defender*; John E. Nail of
the Urban League and president of a real estate company; Dr. Julia P.
Coleman, president of a cosmetic manufacturing company; William
Pickens, field secretary of the NAACP; Chandler Owen, co-editor of the
Messenger and co-executive secretary of the Friends of Negro Freedom;
Robert W. Bagnall, the NAACP's director of branches; and George W.
Harris, editor of the *New York News* and a member of the board of
aldermen of New York City.[201] Conspicuously absent from the list of
signatories was the name of A. Philip Randolph despite his major role
in the affair.

The attorney general was requested to address his reply to Owen, the
secretary of the committee of signatories. For Owen especially, this was
a most sorry turn of events. His *Messenger* in its early days had unashamed-
ly proclaimed itself the only radical black journal. And in 1919 the then
Attorney General A. Mitchell Palmer had branded it the most radical
Afro-American publication. Now the socialist radical was begging the
attorney general to get rid of his rival Garvey.

On January 26 Owen wrote another letter to the attorney general.
He suggested that the letter of the eight be not given to the press since
it was to be released throughout the country on February 1.[202] On January 30 Carl Murphy, editor of the Baltimore *Afro-American,* inquired
of the attorney general what steps had been taken to disband the UNIA
in accordance with the wishes of the eight.[203] On February 4 Garvey,
now aware of the letter, informed the chief law officer that there was
"absolutely no truth" in the allegations contained therein. The UNIA,
he wrote, stood for the uplift of a downtrodden race. There was nothing
disloyal about that. The Bolsheviks and socialists among his detractors
he considered the real disloyal elements.[204] Then on February 20 a re-

markable thing happened. The attorney general's office drafted a detailed
reply to Owen endorsing his hostile analysis of the Garvey movement
and promising possible further legal action against Garvey. The letter
was apparently drafted by Assistant Attorney General John W. H. Crim.
Crim, it is interesting to note, was later accused by Garvey of remarks
prejudicial to his mail fraud case while it was still *sub judice*. Somebody,
perhaps Attorney General Daugherty, had second thoughts about the
reply and it was not sent. The unsent draft read:

> The Department is in receipt of your communication of the 15th
> ultimo addressed to the Attorney General by yourself and several
> others with particular reference to Marcus Garvey and the organiza-
> tion known as the Universal Negro Improvement Association.
>
> The Department appreciates thoroughly the facts recited in your
> letter with regard to the activities of this alien. The Department of
> Justice is very well acquainted with the details of his operations and
> is thoroughly satisfied that his schemes were formulated and have
> been executed to the great detriment of thousands of colored American
> citizens who have fallen as dupes and turned over to him innocently
> their meager savings in the hope that he would accomplish the im-
> possible. Garvey has known this impossibility from the start, but, like
> so many other organizations that have sprung up throughout the
> country the propaganda has been a means of livelihood more satisfy-
> ing than an honest occupation. It is unfortunate that so many of
> Garvey's dupes have been American citizens, a number of them the
> poorer negroes who could least afford to lose their meager life
> savings.
>
> It was with this knowledge that the government succeeded in having
> Garvey indicted in New York for the misuse of the mails in a scheme
> to defraud. As you are aware, this case is set for trial at a very early
> date and the Department has sufficient confidence to believe that
> the ends of justice will most certainly be satisfied before the entire
> matter is concluded.
>
> The Government is thoroughly aware of the fact that Garvey does
> not and never has represented the American negro. For many months

prior to the preparation of this joint letter, the Government has not been idle or unmindful of this colossal fraud and at all times it is anxious to receive from the substantial elements of your race any information which will assist it in enforcing the laws of the nation and the suppression of movements such as the Garvey scheme.

The details of your letter are being given very careful attention and if sufficient evidence can be obtained on the several instances recited, you may rest assured that still additional action will be taken.[205]

This draft was replaced by a brief, more formal note of two sentences. Even this note, however, ended, "Please keep us advised in the event additional facts come to your attention."[206]

It is hardly surprising that the original draft was not sent. It would undoubtedly have found its way into the *Messenger* and the rest of the anti-Garvey press. And even in the context of Garvey's case, already hopelessly prejudiced by the efforts of Du Bois, the Friends of Negro Freedom and others, this would have been a little too much. On February 26 Owen, the would-be socialist radical, thanked Crim for his reply and reminded him that the eight represented "the most distinguished and responsible businessmen, educators and publicists among the colored people of the United States."[207]

The letter of the eight to the attorney general was paralleled by one from Du Bois to the secretary of state branding Garvey as "a thoroughly impractical visionary, if not a criminal, with grandiose schemes of conquest."[208]

Garvey responded at length to the charge of the eight. "My enemies," he said, "and those opposed to the liberation of the Negro to nationhood are so incompetent and incapable of meeting argument with argument and tolerance with tolerance that they have cowardly sought the power of Government to combat and destroy me." He concluded that this was proof of "their weakness and inability to stand up under the onward march of African redemption and real Negro freedom." Like the "good old darkies" that they were, "they believe they have some news to tell and they are telling it for all it is worth."

He denounced them as a bunch of assimilationists who wanted to hurdle the barrier into the white race. The UNIA was not in his opinion

a hater of white people because it believed in the rights of all races. And
he could not see how his maligners could simultaneously accuse him of
stirring up ill feeling between the races and seeking an alliance with the
Ku Klux Klan. Their main problem, he thought, was their inability to
tolerate any organization that did not have white members. Concerning
the alleged "primitive" and "ignorant" following of the UNIA he was
no less indignant. "Were it not for the ignorant element of Negroes," he
retorted, "these very fellows would have starved long ago, because all of
them earn their living either by selling out the race under the guise of
leadership or by exploiting the race in business." He reaffirmed the ability
of the UNIA to marshal more votes than all other black organizations
in the United States put together and affirmed that "every second Negro
you meet, if not an actual member, is one in spirit." And he prophetically
warned them that by their actions "a precedent will be set for the destruction of all Negro organizations that seek in any way to improve the condition of the Negro race."

    Garvey's reply included a pen portrait of the eight. One was a "busi-
ness exploiter" who appealed to race patriotism while overcharging for
his products. Another was "a race defamer of Chicago" whose paper
loved to highlight the crime and vice of the race. "He was the man who
published in his newspaper for over one year a full page advertisement
showing the pictures of two women, a black woman and a very light
woman, with the advice under the photograph of the black woman to
'lighten your black skin.' " The next was a "real estate shark" who
charged higher rents than white landlords. Then came "a hair straightener
and face bleacher, whose loyalty to the race is to get the race to be dissatisfied with itself." On the "turn coat and lackey" who had used him
to get a raise in a rival organization, he was particularly severe. Then
came the "grafter Socialist" who had started sundry enterprises among
black people without accounting for the funds. The seventh signer was
Garvey's old adversary, the ex-pastor of a "Blue Vein Society Church in
Detroit, Mich.," who was relieved of his charge for alleged immorality.
Finally there was the "unscrupulous politician" who had lost the respect
of the masses. The response ended with an appeal to UNIA members to
close ranks against this onslaught. By way of postscript Garvey noted
that all the signers were octoroons or married to octoroons. The sole

exception, "a mulatto and Socialist" (Owen), had tried to marry a white woman but had been dissuaded by UNIA criticism.[209] John Edward Bruce, ever faithful to Garvey, composed a poem for the occasion entitled "Seven Little Colored Men." A typical two lines went "Three little colored men a sitting in a row,/Remarked one to the other dis Garvey man must go."[210]

The campaign continued unabated after the letter. Bagnall, showing that integrationist dislike for Garvey's physical features shared by Du Bois, described him as "A Jamaican Negro of unmixed stock, squat, stocky, fat and sleek with protruding jaws, and heavy jowls, small bright pig-like eyes and rather bulldog-like face. Boastful, egotistic, tyrannical, intolerant, cunning, shifty, smooth and suave, avaricious. . . ."[211]

Yet, due no doubt to the stress of the campaign, splits began to appear among Garvey's foes. For one thing, the campaign's strident anti-West Indian onslaught now began to embarrass its chief West Indian member, W. A. Domingo. While maintaining his anti-Garvey position Domingo now openly attacked the *Messenger* on this score. Owen defended the *Messenger*'s position amid more rancorous integrationist nativism.[212] Another fissure resulted in the dismissal of Floyd J. Calvin from his post as associate editor of the *Messenger*. Calvin's mistake had been to suggest that Randolph and Owen should not seek to bring about the destruction of the whole of Garvey's organization merely because Garvey may have erred. Mild as this criticism was, it cost him his job.[213] As if to underscore their disagreement with Calvin, the *Messenger* editors declared in April 1923, "Our work is bearing fruit. The Black Star Line is completely gone. Every one of his stores is closed. His *Negro Times* is suspended, and well-nigh all of his former employees are suing him for pay."[214] The campaign had by now degenerated to the point where a *Messenger* cartoon could depict Garvey as a donkey and describe him as "A Well Known Jackass."[215] The campaign did not let up during Garvey's trial, and during the posttrial imprisonment without bail the *Messenger* urged the total destruction of the UNIA now that Garvey was in jail, since it represented a continuance of Garvey's spirit.[216]

Garvey was out of jail in time to congratulate his supporters for having contributed to George Harris' defeat in Harlem primaries. Harris, one of the eight, had some time previously been the lone objector to a UNIA sponsored celebration, even though his white colleagues on the board of aldermen had given their approval.[217] And Pickens, after publishing an article in which he reversed the good he had to say about Garvey in 1921, wrote the prosecutor expressing his impatience at the delay in disposing of Garvey's case now that he was out on bail.[218]

Du Bois' "Lunatic or Traitor" attack in 1924 was warmly applauded by the *Messenger*, which came to his defense in the face of the widespread disagreement it generated. The editors were so pleased that they said they felt like rescinding all their previous criticisms of Du Bois. Du Bois, they said, was an intellectual giant. Garvey was but a "Low Grade Moron."[219]

Garvey lost his appeal in February 1925 and Pickens rejoiced.[220] An interesting aside on the tragedy and comedy of Pickens' role in this campaign is the fact that late in 1924 he again extracted a salary increase from the NAACP by using the same tack as in 1921. He claimed that he had passed up a chance to get a substantial increase from a similar organization.[221] In his first application for pardon in June 1925, Garvey pointed out that Pickens had acted in a provoking and unbecoming manner in the courtroom during the trial and that Abbott, another of the eight, had brought the first Mrs. Garvey back into the country and featured her pronouncements in his *Chicago Defender* in order to prejudice his trial.[222] By 1926 George Harris was not above boosting the circulation of his *New York News* by organizing a "petition" supposedly on behalf of Garvey and publishing Garvey's "memoirs," the latter in fact written by a prosecution witness at Garvey's trial.[223]

As in the case of the communists, who adopted a form of black nationalism once Garvey had departed America, and as in the case of Du Bois, who began preaching separatism in the 1930s, so it was with some of the eight. Amy Jacques Garvey noted in 1927 that George Harris had warned the white world that it would have to reckon with Garvey's radical ideas and stop exploiting black people. And the *Negro World* noted an Abbott editorial on African redemption, complete with Garvey phraseology.[224] Of the eight, however, it was Pickens, always the most erratic and unpredictable, who came out openly for Garvey's release in 1927. He said, however, that he would have preferred deportation to prison for Garvey from the beginning.[225]

The "Marcus Garvey Must Go" campaign, as has been noted, was essentially an alliance of convenience between integrationists, many of whom had been at loggerheads with one another before Garvey's successes drove them to temporary unity. Once Garvey had gone, the basis for their unity went with him. Thus less than a year after Garvey's imprisonment the *Messenger* was editorially attacking Abbott. Even before that they had turned on former Attorney General Daugherty who was now, in their opinion, "notorious for his crooked, shady political dealings." And in 1928 Owen and Randolph launched an attack on yet another of the eight, George Harris.[226]

The relationship between the UNIA and the integrationists was one of overwhelming but not unrelieved hostility. Occasionally, as in the case of the Dyer bill, they were willing to cooperate where the interests of black people might otherwise suffer severely. Thus in 1922 at the height of Du Bois' attacks, John Edward Bruce was willing to join him on a "Fair Play League," which would visit police stations in Harlem to try to ensure the proper treatment of black prisoners.[227] As in the case of relations with the communists, however, this type of cooperation was more likely to take place after Garvey's deportation from the United States when the UNIA gradually receded as a threat to the integrationist establishment. In 1931 the *Negro World* sided with the NAACP against communist exploitation of the Scottsboro case and in the middle of the decade a meeting sponsored by the UNIA and the Provisional Committee for the Defense of Ethiopia featured Walter White and Du Bois (now in his separatist phase) as speakers.[228] In 1944, the same year in which he rejoined the NAACP, Du Bois actually solicited the help of Amy Jacques Garvey in attracting delegates to the fifth Pan-African Congress.[229] When the congress convened in Manchester, England, in 1945, the Jamaica UNIA was among the delegations represented.[230]

These instances of cooperation were, however, relatively minor and mostly very late in the day. They in no way detract from the fact that a major portion of the responsibility for Garvey's imprisonment and deportation must be attributed to the integrationist onslaught, especially as manifested in the campaigns of Du Bois and the NAACP, and the black Socialists Owen and Randolph.

NOTES

1. *Crisis* 28 (May 1924): 8.
2. *Negro World,* May 10, 1924.
3. Ibid., October 6, 1928.
4. Amy Jacques Garvey, ed., *The Philosophy and Opinions of Marcus Garvey* (London: Frank Cass, 1967), II: 70.
5. Ovington to Spingarn, February 8, 1921, Arthur Barnett Spingarn Papers, Box 2, Library of Congress.
6. James Weldon Johnson, *Black Manhattan* (New York: Atheneum, 1968), first pub. 1930, p. 257.
7. *Messenger* (June 1924): 184. Garvey said he welcomed anyone with one-sixteenth or more black blood, provided they worked for the unity of the race—*New York World,* August 24, 1920.
8. In August 1924 Walter White, NAACP Assistant Secretary, wrote a letter of introduction for Communist Mrs. Robert Minor to one Louis R. Glavis in New York. Glavis supposedly had "authoritative data" on Garvey's dealings with the Ku Klux Klan—Assistant Secretary to Louis R. Glavis, August 28, 1924, NAACP Administrative Files, Library of Congress, Box C-304.
9. *New York Age,* August 21, 1920.
10. Johnson, *Black Manhattan,* p. 258.
11. NAACP press release, March 21, 1924, NAACP Files, Box C-304, Manuscript Division, Library of Congress.
12. *Negro World,* June 7, 1919, January 7, 14, February 4, March 4, May 27, June 10, November 4, 1922.
13. Ibid., April 8, May 27, July 15, December 16, 1922.
14. Ibid., October 27, 1923.
15. Ovington to Spingarn, February 8, 1921, Spingarn Papers, Box 2.
16. Johnson to Garvey, January 20, 1922, Garvey to Johnson, January 21, 1922, NAACP Files, Box C-304.
17. Garvey, *Philosophy and Opinions,* II: 261.
18. Press release June 22, 1923, NAACP files, Box C-304.
19. *Negro World,* January 3, June 6, 1925.
20. Assistant Secretary to Mr. Allen Dawson, ed., *New York Tribune,* February 17, 1922, and related correspondence, NAACP Files, Box C-304; Walter White to Spingarn, February 18, 1922, Spingarn Papers, Box 2.
21. A. A. Maney to James W. Johnson, December 2, 1921; Norman Thomas, associate editor of the *Nation* to Johnson, August 31, 1921;

Edgar Collier to Johnson, March 12, 1921; J. K. Marshall to NAACP, August 24, 1924, and many others, NAACP Files, Box C-304.

22. *Negro World*, February 2, 1924.

23. Alice Woodby McKane, M.D., to Seligman, December 21, 1921, Seligman to McKane, December 27, 1921, NAACP Files, Box C-304.

24. *Negro World*, September 6, 1924.

25. Graham Knox, "Political Change in Jamaica (1866-1906) and the Local Reaction to the Policies of the Crown Colony Government," p. 161; Lewis, "A Political Study of Garveyism," p. 14.

26. *Africa Times and Orient Review* 1 (July 1912): 10-12.

27. *Negro World*, December 8, 1923.

28. Garvey to Booker T. Washington, April 12, 1915, Booker T. Washington Papers, Container 939, Library of Congress.

29. Washington to Garvey, April 27, 1915, Washington Papers, Container 939.

30. Garvey to Emmett J. Scott, in Daniel T. Williams, *Eight Negro Bibliographies* (New York: Kraus Reprint Co., 1970).

31. Garvey to R. R. Moton, February 29, 1916, in Williams, *Eight Negro Bibliographies*.

32. R. N. Murray, ed., *J. J. Mills, His Own Account of His Life and Times* (Kingston: Collins and Sangster, 1969), p. 110.

33. Amy Ashwood Garvey, "Prophet of Black Nationalism," p. 80.

34. Garvey to Moton, October 23, 1923, Garvey to Secretary, Tuskegee Institute, November 2, 1923, Principal, Tuskegee Institute to Garvey, November 6, 1923, in Williams, *Eight Negro Bibliographies; Negro World*, November 17, 1923; *The Tuskegee Student* 33 (December 1923): 2.

35. Garvey, *Philosophy and Opinions*, I: 41; *New York World*, August 3, 1921.

36. *Blackman*, April 22, 1929; *Southern Workman* 57 (October 1928): 425.

37. *Negro World*, November 10, 1923.

38. Garvey, *Philosophy and Opinions*, II: 38.

39. *Negro World*, November 17, 1923.

40. Ibid., April 19, 1924.

41. *Negro World*, June 9, 1928.

42. W. E. B. Du Bois, *The Autobiography of W. E. B. Du Bois* (New York: International Publishers, 1968), p. 273.

43. Garvey, *A Talk With Afro-West Indians*, p. 3.

44. W. E. B. Du Bois, *Dusk of Dawn* (New York: Schocken, 1968), p. 277.

45. Garvey to Moton, February 29, 1916, in Williams, *Eight Negro Bibliographies.*

46. Garvey, *Philosophy and Opinions,* II: 60.

47. Herbert Aptheker, ed., *The Correspondence of W. E. B. Du Bois* (Amherst: University of Massachusetts Press, 1973), I: 214, 215.

48. Garvey, *Philosophy and Opinions,* II: 57, 311.

49. Du Bois, *Dusk of Dawn,* p. 278.

50. *Crisis* 17 (February 1919): 165, 166.

51. *Crisis* 18 (August 1919): 207.

52. C. G. Contee, "The Worley Report on the Pan-African Congress of 1919," *Journal of Negro History* 55 (April 1970): 141.

53. *Crisis* 19 (December 1919): 46.

54. The list of members is reprinted in Martin Kilson and Adelaide Hill, *Apropos of Africa* (Garden City, N.Y.: Doubleday, 1971), pp. 203-205.

55. *Crisis* 19 (January 1920): 107.

56. *Crisis* 20 (March 1920): 6-8.

57. *Negro World,* June 12, 1920, quoted in Elliott M. Rudwick, "Du Bois versus Garvey: Race Propagandists at War," *Journal of Negro Education* 28 (1959): 424.

58. Aptheker, *Correspondence,* pp. 245, 246.

59. *New York World,* August 4, 1920; *Negro World,* August 14, 1920. Garvey says that Ferris informed him of Du Bois' presence.

60. *Crisis* 20 (August 1920): 189.

61. National Civic Federation Papers, Box 152, New York Public Library.

62. *Crisis* 20 (September 1920): 214-215; National Civic Federation Papers, Box 152.

63. *Messenger* (September 1920): 84, 85.

64. *Crisis* 21 (November 1920): 35.

65. Ibid., p. 16.

66. Ovington to Spingarn, July 24, 1921, Spingarn Papers, Box 2.

67. Du Bois to Schomburg, November 9, 1920, enclosing Du Bois to Domingo, November 6, 1920, Schomburg Papers, Box 2.

68. *Crisis* 21 (December 1920): 58-60.

69. Bruce Papers, Group D-9E, 14-9.

70. *Crisis* 21 (January 1921): 112-115.

71. *Crisis* 21 (March 1921): 213; Spingarn to Du Bois, February 9, 1921, Spingarn Papers.

72. *Negro World,* April 9, 1921.

73. *Crisis* 22 (May 1921): 8.

74. Du Bois to Hughes, June 23, 1921, RG 59, 540 C2/original, National Archives. Du Bois published Hughes' cordial reply in the *Crisis* 22 (August 1921): 150.

75. Garvey to Sir A. Geddes, British Ambassador, Washington, June 16, 1921, quoted in Robert G. Weisbord, "Marcus Garvey, Pan-Negroist: The View from Whitehall," *Race* 11 (1970): 426.

76. *New York Call,* August 1, 1921.

77. *Negro World,* July 30, 1921.

78. *New York World,* August 2, 1921.

79. Typewritten copy, NAACP Files, Box C-304.

80. *Crisis* 22 (September 1921): 225.

81. W. E. B. Du Bois, *The World and Africa* (New York: International Publishers, 1965), p. 237; Du Bois, *Dusk of Dawn,* p. 278; *Negro World,* October 8, 1921.

82. *Negro World,* July 2, 1921.

83. *Crisis* 24 (May 1922): 33.

84. W. E. B. Du Bois, "The Pan-African Movement," in George Padmore, ed., *History of the Pan-African Congress* (London: Hammersmith Bookshop, [1945]), pp. 21, 22.

85. *Negro World,* July 2, October 1, 1921.

86. Garvey, *Philosophy and Opinions,* I: 50; *New York Tribune,* September 15, 1921, reprinted in *Crusader,* 5 (November 1921): 24, 25.

87. *Crisis* 23 (February 1922): 154.

88. *Negro World,* October 29, December 17, 1921.

89. Minutes of a December 21, 1921, meeting, Spingarn Papers, Box 37.

90. *Crisis* 23 (February 1922): 151.

91. *Negro World,* February 1922.

92. *Crisis* 23 (February 1922): 155.

93. *Negro World,* October 1, 1921, February 11, 1922.

94. *Crisis* 21 (January 1921): 114.

95. *Crisis* 23 (April 1922): 252.

96. Du Bois to Chairman, U.S. Shipping Board, July 27, 1922, A. D. Lasker, Chairman, to Du Bois, July 31, 1922, RG 32, 605-1-653.

97. Du Bois to Department of State, August 3, 1922, Wilbur J. Carr, Director of Consular Services, to Du Bois, August 18, 1922, Du Bois to Carr, September 6, 1922, Carr to Du Bois, October 5, 1922, RG 59, 195.7 Kanawha.

98. Du Bois to Charles Studin, August 8, 1922, Spingarn Papers, Box 52.

99. *Negro World,* February 4, 1922, quoted in Rudwick, "Du Bois versus Garvey," p. 427; Garvey to Secretary, NAACP, July 14, 1922, NAACP Files, Box C-304.

100. *Negro World,* November 4, 1922.

101. Du Bois to Hon. Charles Hughes, January 5, 1923, in Aptheker, *Correspondence,* p. 261.

102. Walter White to Spingarn, August 16, 1922, Spingarn to White, August 17, 1922, White to Spingarn, August 18, 1922, Spingarn Papers, Box 2; *Negro World,* August 19, 1922.

103. *Crisis* 25 (November 1922): 16-21; *Negro World,* October 28, November 4, 1922.

104. *Crisis* 25 (January 1923): 120-122.

105. The author has interviewed old men in Harlem who considered themselves Garveyites but were never paid-up members of the UNIA. One such informant says that he regularly took time off from work to attend UNIA parades and functions; Ferris refuted this Du Bois allegation in the *Negro World,* January 6, 1923.

106. NAACP Files, Box C-304.

107. *Race* 1 (Winter 1935-1936): 11, 12.

108. Du Bois, *Dusk of Dawn,* p. 124.

109. Garvey, *Philosophy and Opinions* II: 310-320, reprinted from *Negro World,* February 13, 1920.

110. Du Bois, *Dusk of Dawn,* p. 278.

111. *Negro World,* December 15, October 6, 1923, reprinted from the *Gold Coast Leader,* n.d.; *Negro World,* January 26, 1924, reprinting editorial from *Gold Coast Leader* of December 1, 1923.

112. *Negro World,* November 24, December 1, 1923.

113. *Messenger* (January 1924): 5.

114. *Negro World,* December 29, 1923.

115. Ibid., December 15, 1923.

116. Ibid., August 27, 1927; Garvey, *Philosophy and Opinions,* II: 243.

117. Memorandum, September 6, 1924, in Hughes to the President, September 6, 1924, RG 59, 882.5511/10.

118. *Messenger* (October 1924): 313.

119. Du Bois to Johnson, April 15, 1924, Spingarn Papers, Box 3. For attempts to settle this dispute see Harry E. Davis to Spingarn, June 16, 1924; Du Bois to Spingarn, June 23, 1924, enclosing Johnson to Du Bois, June 23, 1924 and Du Bois to Johnson, June 23, 1924; Garvey

referred to Du Bois' NAACP problems in the *Negro World,* September 9, 1922 and November 4, 1922—see Rudwick, "Du Bois versus Garvey," p. 427.

120. *Negro World,* May 10, 1924.

121. Ibid.

122. *Pittsburgh Courier,* n.d., quoted in *Negro World,* May 17, 1924; *Hotel Tattler,* n.d., reprinted in *Negro World,* May 24, 1924; Gary *Sun,* n.d., reprinted in *Negro World,* May 24, 1924.

123. *Daily Worker,* August 13, 1924.

124. Cleveland *Gazette,* n.d., reprinted in *Negro World,* June 7, 1924.

125. *Daily Worker,* February 14, 1924.

126. *Boston Chronicle,* n.d., reprinted in *Negro World,* February 2,1924.

127. *Crisis* 28 (July 1924): 103, 104.

128. *Negro World,* September 6, 1924; *New York Times,* August 29, 1924.

129. Du Bois, *World and Africa,* p. 242.

130. Ibid., p. 243.

131. *Negro World,* September 3, 1927, January 14, 1928.

132. *Crisis* 35 (February 1928): 51.

133. *New York Herald Tribune Books,* May 20, 1928.

134. *Negro World,* July 19, 1930.

135. Ibid., November 7, 1931.

136. Du Bois, *Autobiography,* p. 298.

137. *Blackman* 1 (November 1934): 9.

138. Newspaper clipping, n.d., Du Bois Scrapbook, Schomburg Collection, New York Public Library.

139. *Race* 1 (Winter 1935-1936): 14.

140. Ibid., pp. 12-14.

141. *Black Man* 1 (late July 1935): 6-8.

142. *Crisis* 22 (August 1921): 151.

143. Du Bois, *Autobiography,* p. 273.

144. *New York Age,* February 1920.

145. Pickens to J. E. Spingarn, September 25, 1921, Pickens Papers, Schomburg Collection, Box 1.

146. Du Bois to Pickens, March 28, 1921, Pickens Papers, Box 1.

147. Amy J. Garvey to E. David Cronon, March 28, 1955, Amy Jacques Garvey Papers. A. J. Garvey, *Garvey and Garveyism,* p. 249; Garvey, *Philosophy and Opinions,* II: 307; *Negro World,* August 27, 1927. Here Mrs. Garvey suggests that Pickens may have visited Garvey several times.

148. *Negro World,* September 10, 1921.

149. Pickens to Garvey, September 12, 1921, quoted in Sheldon Avery, "Up from Washington: William Pickens and the Negro Struggle for Equality, 1900-1954" (Ph.D. diss., University of Oregon, 1970),p. 82.

150. Pickens to Board of Directors, NAACP, September 17, 1921, Pickens Papers, Box 1.

151. Ibid., "Memorandum to Mr. Bagnall," n.d.

152. Ibid., Pickens to J. E. Spingarn, September 25, 1921.

153. Ibid., Robert W. Bagnall, Secretary pro tem, to Pickens, September 29, 1921.

154. Minutes of meeting of the Board of Directors, October 10, 1921, Spingarn Papers, Box 37.

155. Pickens to Mr. Gruening and Mr. Thomas, editors of the *Nation,* October 11, 1921, Pickens Papers, Box 1.

156. Ibid.

157. *Nation* 113 (December 28, 1921): 750-751; *Negro World,* December 17, 1921; *California Voice,* December 31, 1921.

158. *Negro World,* February 25, March 11, 1922.

159. Garvey to Pickens, May 5, 1922, Pickens Papers, Box 7.

160. Pickens to Dr. H. Claude Hudson, June 4, 1922, Pickens Papers, Box 1.

161. Garvey to Pickens, July 10, 1922, Pickens to Garvey, July 24, 1922, Pickens Papers, Box 7.

162. Bulletin, New York Urban League, Inc., *Annual Report 1921,* p. 1.

163. *National Urban League, Report 1920,* 3 (January 1921): 14. The "League's Ideal" stated here reads: "Let us work not as colored people nor as white people for the narrow benefit of any group alone, but TOGETHER as American citizens. . . . "

164. Garvey, *Philosophy and Opinions,* II: 58.

165. Marcus Garvey v. Robert S. Abbott Publishing Company, Federal Court Records, New York, FRC 536137; Garvey, *Philosophy and Opinions,* II: 78, 321.

166. Jervis Anderson, *A. Philip Randolph* (New York: Harcourt Brace Jovanovich, 1973), p. 122; William H. Ferris, "Garvey and the Black Star Line," *Favorite Magazine,* 4 (July 1920): 397.

167. *Messenger* (August 1922): 467-471.

168. Hubert Harrison, *The Negro and the Nation* (New York: Cosmo Advocate Publishing Company, 1917), p. 3.

169. *Negro World,* May 6, June 10, September 20, 1922; *New York Times,* September 11, 1922.

170. Interview with J. Charles Zampty, Highland Park, Michigan, April 17, 1973; *Negro World,* September 2, 1922.

171. Interview with J. Charles Zampty, Highland Park, Michigan, April 17, 1973; *Negro World,* October 14, 1922, January 13, 20, 1923.

172. Guichard Parris and Lester Brooks, *Blacks in the City—A History of the National Urban League* (Boston: Little, Brown and Co., 1971), p. 200; Owen and Randolph expressed the same fear—NCF Papers, Box 152.

173. *Negro World,* January 28, 1922.

174. *Messenger* (November 1917): 31, (January 1918): 23, (May-June 1919): 9, 10, 26, 27, (December 1919): 21, (September 1920); *New York Age,* December 13, 1919; *Crisis* 21 (December 1920): 60.

175. *Messenger* (December 1920): 178.

176. *Messenger* (April-May 1920): 3, 4, Chandler Owen to Hon. Harry M. Daugherty, January 26, 1923, RG 60, 198940.

177. *Revolutionary Radicalism* (Albany, New York: J. B. Lyon, 1920), p. 2007.

178. NCF papers, Box 152; *Messenger,* September 1920, pp. 83, 84.

179. *Messenger,* October 1920, December 1920.

180. Ibid., September 1921, January 1922.

181. *Negro World,* July 29, 1922.

182. Ibid., May 13, 1922, quoting from the *Messenger,* n.d.

183. *Messenger* (July 1922): 437.

184. Ibid (August 1922) 472; *The Public Journal,* July 29, 1922; Garvey to Pickens, July 10, 1922, Pickens to Garvey, July 24, 1922, Pickens Papers, Box 7; Pickens to Garvey, n.d., July 1922, NAACP files, Box C-304.

185. *The Public Journal,* clipping, n.d.

186. Undated clippings from *The Public Journal,* Pickens Papers, Box 7.

187. *Negro World,* August 12, 26, 1922.

188. "Marcus Garvey Must Go!!!" handbill; *Messenger,* August 1922. The *Messenger* advertisement had one exclamation mark.

189. *New York World,* August 2, 1922.

190. Ibid., August 6, 1922; *New York Times,* August 7, 1922; A. J. Garvey, *Garvey and Garveyism,* pp. 96, 97; Assistant Secretary to Randolph, August 7, 1922, Randolph to White, August 25, 1922, NAACP Files, Box C-304.

191. *New York Times,* September 6, 1922.

192. *Messenger,* October 1922.

193. *Negro World,* August 19, 1922.

194. *Messenger* (November 1922): 523.

195. *Messenger,* November 1922.

196. Ibid. (December 1922): 550-552.

197. Garvey, *Philosophy and Opinions,* II: 296-298.

198. Ibid., p. 294.

199. Bagnall to Spingarn, January 16, 1923, Spingarn Papers.

200. The draft is now lodged in a file with material largely written by Johnson and White. NAACP Files, Box C-304. See also ibid., White to Johnson, May 17, 1923, NAACP press release, May 18, 1923, Johnson to Hon. Julian W. Mack, May 19, 1923.

201. Chandler Owen et al. to Hon. Harry M. Daugherty, January 15, 1923, RG 60, 198940; Garvey, *Philosophy and Opinions,* II: 293-300.

202. Owen to Daugherty, January 26, 1923, RG 60, 198940.

203. Ibid., Murphy to Daugherty, January 30, 1923.

204. Ibid., Garvey to Daugherty, February 4, 1923; John W. H. Crim, Assistant Attorney General to Garvey, February 7, 1923.

205. Ibid., Assistant Attorney General to Owen, February 20, 1923.

206. Ibid., Crim to Owen, February 23, 1923.

207. Ibid., Owen to Crim, February 26, 1923.

208. Du Bois to Hon. Charles Hughes, January 5, 1923, in Aptheker, *Correspondence,* p. 261.

209. Garvey, *Philosophy and Opinions,* II: 300-309.

210. Bruce Papers, Group D, P 3-10, Schomburg Collection, New York Public Library.

211. *Messenger* (March 1923): 638.

212. Ibid., pp. 639-645.

213. *New York Amsterdam News,* March 7, 1923; *Messenger,* March 1923.

214. *Messenger* (April 1923): 748.

215. Ibid. (March 1923): 647.

216. Ibid. (August 1923): 782.

217. *Negro World,* October 6, 1923. It was to be a "Rose Day" ("Race Day" according to at least one report).

218. Ibid., October 20, 27, 1923; Pickens (simply "W.P." on this unsigned carbon copy) to Mattuck, December 19, 1923, NAACP Files, Box C-304.

219. *Messenger* (July 1924): 210, 212.

220. *New York Amsterdam News,* February 11, 1925.

221. Pickens to Spingarn, September 16, 1924, Spingarn Papers.

222. Garvey, *Philosophy and Opinions,* II: 243, 253.

223. *Negro World,* February 6, 1926.

224. Ibid., August 27, 1927.

225. *New Republic,* 52 (August 31, 1927): 46, 47.

226. *Messenger* (January 1926): 16; *Negro World,* August 27, 1927. *Messenger* (February 1928): 41, 45.

227. R. E. Enright, Commissioner of Police to Bruce, June 2, 1922, Bruce Papers; *Negro World,* June 10, 1922.

228. *Negro World,* May 23, 1931; handbill, n.d., UNIA Central Division (New York) Files, Box 14, F. 4.

229. Vincent, *Black Power and the Garvey Movement,* p. 246. Vincent quotes here the following letters from the A. J. Garvey Papers—Du Bois to A. J. Garvey, April 8, 1944, and A. J. Garvey to Du Bois, April 24, 1944.

230. Padmore, *History of the Pan-African Congress,* p. 62.

12

The Ku Klux Klan, White Supremacy, and Garvey — A Symbiotic Relationship

Between the Ku Klux Klan and the Moorfield Storey National Association for the Advancement of "Colored" People group, give me the Klan for their honesty of purpose towards the Negro. They are better friends to my race, for telling us what they are, and what they mean, thereby giving us a chance to stir for ourselves, than all the hypocrites put together with their false gods and religions, notwithstanding. Religions that they preach and will not practise; a God they talk about, whom they abuse every day—away with the farce, hypocrisy and lie. It smells, it stinks to high heaven.

—Marcus Garvey[1]

A black man who advocates racial integrity cannot be opposed by a white man who advocates racial integrity. They are drawn to each other, for they fight in a common cause.

—Earnest Sevier Cox, of the White America Society[2]

The most widely publicized of Garvey's dealings with white segregationists and supremacists involved his summit conference with the Ku

Klux Klan in 1922. As head of a black organization with branches all over the United States, Garvey continually came face to face with the racist reality of the KKK and similar groups. In 1920 the formation of a UNIA division in Key West, Florida, caused whites in the area to organize a KKK branch as a countermeasure. The local UNIA leader, Reverend T. C. Glashen, was given twenty-four hours to leave town by the president of the chamber of commerce. When he refused he was arrested and jailed. After intervention by the UNIA parent body in Harlem, a judge visited him in jail and begged him to leave to avoid a racial clash between the UNIA and white mobs. Glashen finally left for New York via Havana, Cuba, since he was warned by the judge that he would be pulled from the train if he attempted to travel overland.[3]

Again, in 1922, R. B. Mosely, UNIA high commissioner for Texas, was jailed and fined for "vagrancy" while on an organizing tour. On his release from jail he was whipped by a gang of eight white men.[4] At the UNIA convention that year several delegates related first-hand experiences of white racist fury, including some near escapes from lynch mobs. A Mr. Davis of Homestead, Alabama, told of attempts by white mobs to intimidate and break up the UNIA in his town, these efforts culminating in the lynching of a young man selling stock in UNIA enterprises.[5]

It was because of incidents like these that Garvey initially not only supported the Dyer antilynching bill but also adopted a position of open hostility toward the KKK. He was quoted in 1920 as threatening to whip the Klan if it came North,[6] and several *Negro World* editorials in 1920 and 1921 were directed against this organization.[7] A banner at the 1921 convention parade proclaimed, "The New Negro is Ready for the Ku Klux."[8]

In June 1922, however, while on an extensive tour of the United States, Garvey stopped in Atlanta for a conference with Edward Young Clarke, acting imperial wizard of the Klan. The initiative had come from Clarke who relayed a request to the local UNIA to meet with the UNIA leader. Garvey accepted this invitation because he considered it in the best interests of his organization, given the history of conflict between the UNIA and white segregationists.

The meeting lasted two hours. During this time, each side outlined its philosophy. Clarke emphasized that America was a white man's country, that his organization stood for racial purity, and denied that the

Klan was responsible for all the incidents of racial intolerance attributed
to it. Garvey outlined the UNIA's philosophy. He said afterwards, "I was
speaking to a man who was brutally a white man, and I was speaking to
him as a man who was brutally a Negro."[9] As a result of the discussions
Clarke expressed sympathy for the aims of the UNIA, while Garvey was
reinforced in his suspicion that the Klan represented the invisible government of the United States. He became convinced that this organization
represented the white American majority viewpoint and was impressed
by Clarke's assertion that the Klan was stronger in the North than in the
South. Both principals agreed to publish a memorandum of the meeting
in their respective organs and Garvey invited Clarke to Liberty Hall to
further clarify the Klan's position. In the meantime Garvey seems to
have gotten an assurance from Clarke that the Klan would refrain from
harassing the UNIA, especially since the UNIA did not represent a threat
to their phobia concerning intermarriage. Clarke even said, according to
Garvey, that he was against white men raping black women. And Garvey
approvingly cited the case in Baton Rouge, Louisiana, where UNIA members had flogged some white men they found sleeping with black ladies.
For this action the UNIA members had been complimented by a KKK
judge. The end result of all this was that Garvey concluded that it would
henceforth be more worthwhile to push forward with the UNIA program
to build a strong government in Africa which would redound to the benefit of black people everywhere, rather than waste time attacking the Klan,
an idea which he had been contemplating since 1921.[10]

The immediate result of this UNIA-KKK summit conference was an
avalanche of protest from black integrationist leaders, and white ones
too. A. Philip Randolph went so far as to call Garvey the Klan's "Negro
leader," a sentiment echoed by communist Robert Minor, who declared
Garvey "chief defender of the Klan."[11]

The federal government got into the act too when, during their prosecution of the mail fraud case against Garvey, they forced Clarke to appear
under subpoena before a federal grand jury in New York. Garvey protested that this was an attempt to further prejudice his case, since his
dealings with the Klan were irrelevant to the charges against him.[12]

In the face of this hue and cry, Garvey tried, largely in vain, to counter
the simplistic views put forward concerning his meeting with the Klan.
Less than a month after the meeting he defended it this way:

I repeat, knowing the power and influence and intention of the Klan, I interviewed them for the purpose of getting them, if possible, to adopt a different attitude toward the race and thus prevent a repetition in many ways of what happened during the days of reconstruction. Because of this, my effort to stave off an impending danger by a better understanding of the attitudes of this organization, this unthinking bombast [George Harris] steps out in the full authority of his ignorance to accuse me of surrendering to the Wizard and forming an alliance with the Klan. This has been the attitude of a large number of Negro editors all over the country, and especially those editors who live in the North, who do not come in daily contact with the Ku Klux Klan, as the millions of our people do in the Southern States. These wiseacres and so-called race-patriots remain 1,500 and 2,000 miles away and write all kinds of stuff against the South, against the Ku Klux Klan, and against people with whom they do not come in contact, leaving the people who really come in contact with them to suffer from the result of their senseless and hypocritical propaganda. Some Negro men who talk and write up North will make a big noise as far as Washington, but whenever the conductor requests of them to change cars they become as mum as an oyster.[13]

Several individual segregationists got Garvey's support when their views seemed to coincide with his. A few months before his meeting with the Klan in 1922, for example, Garvey urged support for a resolution introduced into the Mississippi State Senate by Senator McCallum. This resolution called upon the Mississippi legislature to memorialize the president and congress to secure by treaty, purchase, or other negotiation a piece of Africa where the Afro-American could move toward independence under the tutelage of the United States government. He suggested that a European nation might be induced to part with such an area in exchange for some of the Allied war debt owed to the United States.[14] Garvey agreed with a similar idea put forward at about the same time by Senator Joseph I. France of Maryland. This plan envisaged the giving over to the United States of ex-German East Africa, again in exchange for the war debt.[15]

Garvey cooperated also with John Powell of the Anglo-Saxon Clubs of America. Powell visited Garvey in jail shortly after his incarceration

in Atlanta in 1925 and thereafter let it be known that Garvey had assured
him of "the fullest support of his organization." *Negro World* editor T.
Thomas Fortune considered this a little too much and sought to confine
Garvey's support to the doctrines of race purity and Africa for the Africans.
Garvey thereupon telegraphed a rebuke from Atlanta. "I know nothing
of the spirit of the editorial," he fumed, "which I regard as mischievous."
Fortune insisted that his editorial was written in good faith and that
there was "nothing in it to modify or retract." Garvey's response was to
arrange, from jail, for Powell to speak at Liberty Hall. There Powell explained, among other things, that he had introduced a resolution into
the Richmond, Virginia branch of the Anglo-Saxon Clubs expressing
indignation at Garvey's imprisonment.[16]

One of Garvey's most extensive contacts with white segregationists
was his relationship with Theodore G. Bilbo. By the time their paths
crossed in the late 1930s, Bilbo had already had a long and notorious
public career in Mississippi. He had been state senator, lieutenant governor and governor. By the time of his contacts with Garveyism he was
serving as Democratic senator to the United States Senate from
Mississippi.[17]

Bilbo had long been one of the country's most outspoken racists. He
once admitted having been initiated into the Ku Klux Klan. In 1926 he
declared, "Let us treat the negro fairly; give him justice; teach him that
the white man is his real friend; let him know and understand once and
for all that he belongs to an inferior race and that social and political
equality will never be tolerated in the south." Two decades later he wrote,
"Historically and scientifically, the inferiority of the Negro race when
compared to the white race, is both a proved and obvious fact," though
he claimed here to have "always dealt fairly and sympathetically with
the Negro." As a United States senator he was active in moves to prevent
black people from participating in Mississippi primaries. In 1947 the
Eightieth Congress, acting in response to a loud clamor from civil-rights
and church groups, trade unions and other organizations, moved to prevent him from being sworn in for his third term. The motion was tabled
because he was already stricken with a fatal illness.[18]

Like Garvey, one of Bilbo's pet hates was miscegenation, or mongrelization, as he preferred to call it. To demonstrate the iniquity of race mix-
ing he was willing to falsify history, arguing that ancient Egypt had original-

ly been Caucasian but had subsequently declined owing to race mixture. "The desire to mix, commingle, interbreed or marry into the white race" he blamed mostly on "mulattoes or mongrels" who were "now to an alarming degree found within the Negro race in this country." Not surprisingly, he deplored the marriage of a white girl "to the corpulent, fraudulent, pot-bellied, coal-black, seventy year old Negro who calls himself Father Divine." At one point he introduced a bill to prohibit intermarriage in Washington, D.C.[19]

Bilbo's links with Garvey and Garveyites revolved around the proposed Greater Liberia Act which he introduced in the United States Senate in 1939. The act called for the voluntary repatriation of Afro-Americans to West Africa with assistance from the United States government. Bilbo had not always considered repatriation to be feasible. In 1923 he had scoffed at "Senator T. G. McCallum's scheme to move negroes of the United States to darkest Africa" as "wonderful to contemplate, a fact to be devoutly wished for, but . . . an idle dream."[20]

Several factors had caused him to modify his opinion. For one thing he had become impressed by Garvey, whom he considered "the most conspicious [sic] of all the organizers of his race" and "a noted and world-renowned Negro leader."[21] Garvey, he said, had "definitely succeeded in establishing the fact that there is an overmastering impulse, a divine afflatus among the masses of Negroes in the United States for a country of their own and a government administered by themselves."[22]

He had become impressed, too, by the activities of the Peace Movement of Ethiopia. This organization, which spearheaded the drive for Afro-American repatriation during the 1930s, was led by Mrs. Mittie Maude Lena Gordon of Chicago, a former UNIA member and an undying admirer of Marcus Garvey. Mrs. Gordon saw emigration as the only way out from the suffering which descended on black people during the depression. In a touching letter to Bilbo she pledged her support for his bill because, she said, she was tired watching children die.[23] In 1933 the Peace Movement of Ethiopia had petitioned President Roosevelt for assistance in getting to Africa. The petition pointed out that the cost of helping black people lay the foundation for a modest living in Africa would be less than the charity they were forced to subsist upon in America through no fault of their own.[24] Bilbo claimed that commissioners of the movement had journeyed to Liberia and had been assured by the country's president that "millions of acres" were awaiting Afro-Americans.[25] Mrs. Gordon later incurred the disfavor of Bilbo and his patriotic fellow segregationists when she was arrested for allegedly collaborating with the Japanese during World War II.[26]

Bilbo changed to advocacy of repatriation too because Africa was, or so he affected to believe, the richest continent in the world. He related in wondrous terms the story of an emigrant from Mississippi who reaped twelve crops of sweet potatoes a year in the balmy Liberian climate.[27] He added to these reasons his fear of "a mongrel race" developing in America and the fact that the Afro-American had picked up skills during his enforced sojourn in the white man's land which would increase his ability to make good in Africa. Finally, during World War II he foresaw "so much trouble with the negro race in every part of the country" at the war's end that there would surely be "a crying demand for passage of my legislation."[28]

Bilbo envisaged the removal of five to eight million black people over a period of fifteen to twenty-five years. By concentrating on persons of productive age and young persons it was expected that those who remained would die out in the normal course of things.[29] To avoid a possible loophole, he specifically made provisions for black aliens within the United States to participate in his repatriation scheme.[30] And when the emigrants were settled in West Africa, he declared, he would make Eleanor Roosevelt, wife of the United States President, "Queen of Greater Liberia," this presumably an indication of his dislike for the first lady's liberal tendencies.[31]

Garvey's support for Bilbo's bill was extensive. In August 1938 the Eighth International Convention of the UNIA meeting in Toronto, Canada, passed a unanimous resolution of support. Garvey sent copies to President Roosevelt and to Bilbo.[32] The Virginia UNIA shortly afterward wired the President in support.[33] The leaders of the UNIA in New York, Philadelphia and elsewhere entered into correspondence with Bilbo, sent delegations to Washington, distributed copies of the bill, and organized mass meetings in support of it. By April 1939 the UNIA had contributed 50,000 signatures to the two million Bilbo said he collected. Bilbo at one stage tried to obtain funds to send some of his Harlem supporters on a speaking tour.[34] The UNIA even staged a public debate on the bill in Brooklyn.[35] And Garvey from England appointed a special

committee to lobby in Washington during the bill's introduction.[36]
UNIA leaders from New York, Philadelphia and Cleveland later formed
themselves into a "Lobby Committee on Greater Liberia Act."[37]

Garvey, as usual in his dealings with segregationists, took the position
that since what the senator was proposing was what he wanted, then
Bilbo's motives were irrelevant. "The Senator's desire for carrying out
the purpose of his Bill may not be as idealistic as Negroes may want,"
Garvey argued, "but that is not the point to be considered. What is wanted
now is the opportunity of the Negro to establish himself and there is no
doubt that this Bill offers such an opportunity."[38]

Bilbo's bill, after two readings in the Senate, was referred to the Committee on Foreign Relations since it involved negotiations with a foreign
power. This, for all practical purposes, was the end of it. In 1946 he expressed an intention of resuscitating it in the coming congress, but death
intervened.[39]

Closely related to Garvey's support of the Bilbo bill was his long-
standing association with Earnest Sevier Cox, a tireless worker in the
cause of the White America Society and a close friend and associate of
Bilbo. Cox, a resident of Virginia, claimed to have first become interested in racial matters when he came into contact with black people
while a graduate student at the University of Chicago. This interest, he
said in 1931, caused him to spend $60,000 of his own money. He claimed
also to have traveled widely in Africa.[40] Perhaps for this reason, he supported Garvey's African program, even considering white colonization
in that continent "impractical and . . . unfair to the Negro."[41] He had
the closest contacts with the UNIA rank and file of any segregationist.
Not only did he address the occasional UNIA meeting but he claimed
to be in correspondence with Garveyites in twenty-six states, as well as
Jamaica, Panama, Honduras, Cuba, Haiti, Santo Domingo and elsewhere.[42]
Garveyites in Detroit sold 17,000 copies of his book *White America,*
mostly to white people.[43] His association with the UNIA, begun in the
early 1920s, was still very much alive in 1961.[44]

Cox dedicated his book *Let My People Go* to Garvey and discussed
him approvingly in another, *The South's Part in Mongrelizing the Nation.*
Like Garvey, however, he resented the simplistic view which saw in the
relationship between black advocates of race purity and white advocates
of race purity some sort of all-embracing alliance. Thus when the *Norfolk*

Journal and Guide suggested that there was an alliance between the two men and that Cox was Garvey's disciple, his refutation was as emphatic as Garvey's annoyance at being called a member of the Klan. He pointed out that there was an understanding between the two men on the question of racial integrity, and that was all.[45]

Most of Cox's collaboration with the UNIA revolved around his espousal of Afro-American emigration to Africa. He saw himself as a successor to racist white American statesmen like Thomas Jefferson and Ben Tillman, as well as the "great emancipator" Abraham Lincoln, all of whom had favored repatriation of the Afro-American.[46] As a resident of Virginia he was especially aware of the state's historical antecedents to his work. Virginia had been the home of Thomas Jefferson. The Virginia assembly had also supported the American Colonization Society, which was responsible for settling Afro-Americans in Liberia from the early nineteenth century.

In 1932 Cox engineered the introduction into the Virginia state legislature of a resolution suggesting that the federal government be memorialized to assist in emigration to Liberia. The resolution was couched in language almost identical to Abraham Lincoln's second message to Congress. It engendered much opposition and died in committee.[47] In 1936 his efforts were more successful. The state of Virginia on this occasion did memorialize congress for federal assistance to the Greater Liberia idea. Cox later thanked the governor of Virginia on behalf of the UNIA, the Peace Movement of Ethiopia, the National Union for People of African Descent and a group of black Virginians.[48]

Cox worked closely with Bilbo for the popularization of Bilbo's bill and both men tried strenuously to get Garvey back into the United States. In the case of Cox these efforts went back at least as far as 1931.[49] By 1938 the effort was intense due to Bilbo's conviction that Garvey's presence, even on a temporary permit, would greatly enhance his bill's chances of success.[50] Cox had another reason for wanting Garvey back, namely to offset the influence of the NAACP.[51]

The most bizarre episode in the story of the attraction which Garveyism exerted upon white segregationists came from novelist Thomas Dixon whose literary efforts glorifying the Ku Klux Klan and white supremacy had long earned him a notoriety that rivaled, if it did not exceed, that accruing to Bilbo. It was Dixon whose libelous novel *The Clansman* had called forth massive opposition from the NAACP and other civil-rights groups when it appeared in 1915 as the motion picture *Birth of a Nation*. The movie, like the book, sought to present the emancipation and granting of civil rights to Afro-Americans during reconstruction as a great mistake.

In 1939, the year of the Bilbo bill, Dixon published a novel entitled *The Flaming Sword*. The novel was wild, fast moving, exciting after a fashion and very long. Dixon, considering the novel to be "the most vivid and accurate form in which history can be written," presumed "to give an authoritative record of the Conflict of Color in America from 1900 to 1938."[52] The novel was essentially an epic diatribe against what the dust jacket called "the one unsolved problem of America which threatens our existence as a civilized people." This problem, of course, was race mixture. Dixon warned in his preface that he had "been compelled to use living men and women as important characters." He warned further, with remarkable aplomb, "If I have been unfair in treatment they have their remedy under the law of libel. I hold myself responsible." Having thus cleared the air he proceeded to fill his book with all manner of vile insults against "the junta fighting for intermarriage," to wit, Du Bois, James Weldon Johnson, A. Philip Randolph, communists James W. Ford and Earl Browder, the African Blood Brotherhood, Claude McKay, Carl VanVechten, J. E. Spingarn, Moorfield Storey, and others. The book's frontispiece bore a Du Bois quotation from which Dixon had extracted its title: "Across this path stands the south with flaming sword."

Dixon did not fail to highlight the normal racist stereotypes of happy, contented slaves and lascivious black "beasts" lusting after white women. One such killed a white man and his two dogs, gagged his child, raped a white woman to death in the dead man's house, and was eventually lynched. After finishing off the woman the rapist was made to say, "A nigger in Harlem sent me a little book dat say I got de right ter marry a white gal ef I kin get her. Can't marry her down here, but by God, I got her." It turned out that his inspiration had been a poem by James Weldon Johnson entitled "The White Witch" and containing the following lines:

And I have kissed her red, red lips
And cruel face so white and fair;
Around me she has twined her arms,
And bound me with her yellow hair.[53]

The story, such as it was, was merely an excuse into which Dixon could inject his ideas on race relations. His basic contention was that the good work started by Booker T. Washington and continued by Garvey was in danger of being destroyed by Du Bois and the integrationists. He contrasted the almost-white Du Bois to Washington, who

> in spite of the tinge of yellow in his darker skin, was unmistakably African in every line of his face and body. And not of the handsomer type. His hair, inclined to kink in spite of modern lotions, was coarse and plainly Negroid. His large ears were inclined to flop. His nose was large and flattened. His jaw was heavy. Every feature stamped him a Negro of Negroes. Only from his grave forceful eyes flashed the light of leadership. He was heavily built and sprawled Negro fashion when seated.[54]

He considered Garvey the "logical successor" to Abraham Lincoln and Thomas Jefferson because of his emigrationist efforts and also "the greatest Negro of the modern world." His heroine, on a trip to Harlem, happened to hear a Garvey speech and was won over to the idea of repatriation. She was reinforced in this opinion when she read Earnest Sevier Cox on white superiority and the necessity for black repatriation. Near the end of the book the hero died and bequeathed a $10 million trust fund for establishment of a Marcus Garvey Colonization Society for the "peaceful, voluntary colonization of the Negro race." The book closed with America caught off-guard in the throes of a communist revolution. Thus ended undoubtedly the strangest tribute ever paid to Marcus Garvey. Earnest Sevier Cox considered it "the first colonizationist novel since Uncle Tom's Cabin."[55]

There were other instances of Garvey's affinity with segregationists. The German Emergency League Against the Black Horror supposedly sought his aid in 1921 for the removal of French African troops from the Rhineland.[56] Garvey had previously objected to the presence of these troops, but for different reasons—he thought that the French were afraid to send them home since their military training might augur ill for French colonialism.[57]

In 1921 also Garvey controversially endorsed President Harding's Birmingham, Alabama, speech which eschewed "racial amalgamation," suggested that blacks should no longer vote solidly Republican and appealed to southern whites not to vote solidly Democrat. Garvey was doubtless impressed by Harding's suggestion that the black man should be "the best possible black man and not the best possible imitation of a white man."[58]

The story of Garvey and white supremacy is a most unusual one and susceptible of easy misinterpretation. What the story proves is that Garvey must surely be the most singleminded black separatist of all time. His fierce love for his own race placed him in the unlikely position of sharing, with America's most notorious white racists, a hostility to integrationists and an advocacy of emigration. People like Bilbo and Cox continued to preach white superiority for the benefit of their kinsmen, but in their direct dealings with Garvey and his representatives there was no hint of racial arrogance. Each side was aware of the other's position and preferred to dwell as far as possible on areas of common concern. As Garvey said of his interview with the Klan's representative, "I was speaking to a man who was brutally a white man, and I was speaking to him as a man who was brutally a Negro."

NOTES

    1. Amy Jacques Garvey, ed., *The Philosophy and Opinions of Marcus Garvey* (London: Frank Cass, 1967), II: 71.

    2. *Negro World,* September 26, 1931.

    3. Ibid., July 16, 1921.

    4. Ibid., June 3, 1922.

    5. Ibid., September 16, 1922.

    6. *Afro-American,* November 19, 1920, quoted in Theodore Vincent, *Black Power and the Garvey Movement* (Berkeley: Ramparts [1971]), p. 19.

    7. *Negro World,* September 24, 1921.

    8. *New York World,* August 2, 1921.

    9. *Negro World,* July 15, 1922.

    10. Interview with J. Charles Zampty; interview with Mrs Amy Jacques Garvey; *Negro World,* July 1, 15, 1922; Garvey's application for executive clemency, June 5, 1925, RG 204, 42-793, National Archives; *Negro World,* October 8, 1921.

    11. *Messenger* (October 1922) 500; *Daily Worker,* August 23, 1924.

12. *New York Times,* February 8, 1923; application for executive clemency, June 5, 1925, RG 204, 42-793, National Archives.

13. *Negro World,* July 22, 1922.

14. Ibid., February 11, 18, March 18, 1922.

15. Ibid., May 13, 1922.

16. Ibid., August 15, 22, October 24, 1925; Garvey, *Philosophy and Opinions,* II: 340-342.

17. Thurston E. Doler, "Theodore G. Bilbo's Rhetoric of Racial Relations" (Ph.D. diss., University of Oregon, 1968), pp. 31ff.

18. Ibid., pp. 1, 2, 69, 135; Theodore G. Bilbo, *Take Your Choice: Separation or Mongrelization* (Poplarville, Miss: Dream House Publishing Co., 1947), p. 86; *Living Age* 358 (June 1940): 333.

19. *Living Age* (June 1940): 334; Bilbo, *Take Your Choice,* preface (n.p.); Bilbo to Earnest Sevier Cox, May 19, 1944, Theodore G. Bilbo Papers, University of Southern Mississippi.

20. Doler, "Bilbo's Rhetoric," p. 107.

21. Bilbo, *Take Your Choice,* pp. 271, 254.

22. Ibid., p. 271.

23. Gordon to Bilbo, October 15, 1939, quoted in Doler, "Bilbo's Rhetoric," p. 247.

24. *Living Age* (June 1940): 328; Gunnar Myrdal, *An American Dilemma* (New York: Harper and Row, 1944), p. 813.

25. *Living Age* (June 1940): 330.

26. Earnest Sevier Cox to Gordon, September 28, 1942, Bilbo Papers.

27. *Living Age* (June 1940): 330.

28. Ibid., p. 334; Bilbo to Elzy Johnson, January 24, 1940, Bilbo to Cox, October 2, 1942, Bilbo Papers, University of Southern Mississippi.

29. *Living Age* (June 1940): 330; Bilbo, *Take Your Choice,* p. 275; Bilbo Papers, Cox to Bilbo, February 20, 1938.

30. Bilbo, *Take Your Choice,* p. 304.

31. Doler, "Bilbo's Rhetoric," p. 115.

32. Garvey and Ethel Collins, Secretary-General to President, U.S.A., August 13, 1938, RG 59, 880.5211/21.

33. Minutes of meeting October 4, 1938, UNIA Central Division (New York) Files, Box 6, c. 26.

34. Ibid., Capt. A. L. King to Garvey, April 28, 1939, Box 8, d. 23; King to C. Jacobs, May 9, 1939, Box 8, d. 5; handbill, n.d., Box 14, f. 19; Bilbo to Cox, November 21, 1939, Bilbo Papers.

35. Andronicus Jacob to King, July 19, 1939, UNIA Central Division (New York) Files, Box 8, d. 8; handbill, n.d., Box 14, f. 19.

36. Ibid., Box 8, d. 23, *op. cit.*

37. Ibid., Cox to King, January 11, 1940, Box 12, e. 95.

38. *Black Man* 3 (November 1938): 19.

39. Doler, "Bilbo's Rhetoric," p. 108; UNIA Central Division (New York) Files, Box 8, d. 5; Bilbo to Cox, August 2, 1946, Bilbo Papers.

40. *Negro World,* November 28, 1931.

41. Ibid., September 26, 1931.

42. Earnest Sevier Cox, *Lincoln's Negro Policy* (Richmond, Va.: The William Byrd Press, 1938), p. 30; *Negro World,* November 28, 1931.

43. Garvey, *Philosophy and Opinions,* II: 342.

44. *Minutes of the Fourteenth Annual Convention of the UNIA, August 13-20, 1961, Brooklyn, N.Y.,* p. 6.

45. *Negro World,* August 15, 1925.

46. Cox to Bilbo, May 14, 1944, Bilbo Papers.

47. *Negro World,* September 26, 1931, March 5, June 18, 1932.

48. *Richmond Times-Despatch,* January 27, 1940; Cox to Governor James H. Price, December 29, 1939, UNIA Central Division (New York) Files, Box 8, d. 10.

49. *Negro World,* September 26, 1931.

50. Bilbo to King, February 23, 1938, UNIA Central Division (New York) Files, Box 16, h. 10.

51. Cox to Bilbo, February 20, 1938, Bilbo Papers.

52. Thomas Dixon, *The Flaming Sword* (Atlanta: Monarch Publishing Co., 1939), preface, n.p.

53. Ibid., pp. 175, 178.

54. Ibid., p. 248.

55. Cox to Bilbo, December 12, 1939, Bilbo Papers.

56. *Nation* (December, 28, 1921): 769.

57. Garvey, *Philosophy and Opinions,* II: p. 113.

58. *New York Times,* October 27, 1921.

Afterword

My work is just begun, and as I lay down my life for the cause of my people, so do I feel that succeeding generations shall be inspired by the sacrifice that I made for the rehabilitation of our race. Christ died to make men free, I shall die to give courage and inspiration to my race.

—Marcus Garvey [1]

If Garvey dies, Garvey lives. . . .

—Marcus Garvey [2]

Marcus Garvey has as good a claim as anyone to the distinction of being the greatest black figure of the twentieth century. Insofar as his program was foiled short of its ultimate realization in his own lifetime, his career represents a monumental tragedy, an epic of heroism and courage overcome by catastrophe. Yet the larger tragedy in no way detracts from the multitude of successes that were Garvey's accomplishments.

That Garvey was a powerful charismatic figure there can be no doubt. Unlike many charismatic leaders, however, he had the additional gift of organizational ability. He has no rival in Afro-American history for the international scale on which he was able to establish units of his organization.

Garvey bestrode the black world like no one else and all those in power there, or aspiring to influence therein, were forced to deal with him. In a way his legacy continues to bestride the black world. An impressive array of tendencies within the black revolution of the 1960s and 1970s have identified him as a formative influence. Whether it is the Muslims, with Elijah Muhammad's Garveyite origins, or Afro-Americans in mainstream electoral politics, or Malcolm X, whose father was a UNIA organizer, or Kwame Nkrumah and Jomo Kenyatta in Africa, or the Rastafarians in Jamaica—it seems that there is a Garveyite lurking in the past of many a contemporary black political activist or organization.[3]

Yet, incredibly, for two decades or so after his death Garvey was all but relegated to the position of an unperson. Afro-American, West Indian and African history books, with few exceptions, failed to mention him or glossed over his career in embarrassed and contemptuous haste. Here and there pockets of nationalists stubbornly kept his name alive but their efforts were unnoticed except by a few. It took the Black Power revolution of the 1960s with its revival of Garvey's red, black and green, his race pride, his self-reliance, his separatism, his anti-imperialism and his revolutionary nationalism, to belatedly return to Garvey the recognition he deserves as a major, if not the major black figure of the century.

NOTES

1. Amy Jacques Garvey, ed., *The Philosophy and Opinions of Marcus Garvey* (London: Frank Cass, 1967), II: 218.
2. *Negro World,* May 26, 1923.
3. See the epilogue to the Collier Books edition of Amy J. Garvey's *Garvey and Garveyism.* At least two members of the Congressional Black Caucus, Shirley Chisholm and Charles C. Diggs, are the children of Garveyites—Shirley Chisholm, *Unbought and Unbossed* (New York: Avon Books, 1971), pp. 26, 27; interview with J. Charles Zampty, Highland Park, Mich., April 1973.

Appendix

This appendix has been compiled from membership cards in the UNIA Central Division (New York) files, Schomburg Collection, New York Public Library. In most cases the spelling appearing in the cards has been followed.

UNIA BRANCHES IN THE UNITED STATES, CIRCA 1926

ALABAMA

Divisions: Birmingham, Fair Hope, Gadsden, Inverness, Mobile, Neenah, Prichard, Selma, Whistler.

Chapters: Mobile, Northside (Mobile).

ARIZONA

Divisions: Mesa, Phoenix, Prescott, Somerton.

ARKANSAS

Divisions: Amoriel, Blackton, Blythe, Blytheville, Burdett (Blytheville), Burton Spurr, Brickeys, Calexico, Clear Lake, Cotton Plant, Council,

Crawfordville, Cypert, Duncan, Earl, Fort Smith, Good Hope, Gosnell, Green Brier, Hickman, Holly Grove, Howell, Hughes, Indian Bay, Jefferson, Lake Hall, Lexa, Madison, Moten, Oneida, Pine Bluff, Pine City, Round Pond, New Home (Round Pond), Simmsboro, Twist.

Chapters: Holly Grove, Pine Bluff.

CALIFORNIA

Divisions: Allensworth, Bakersfield, Calipatria, Duarte, Fresno, Los Angeles, Oakland, Pixley, San Diego, San Francisco, San Jose, Sawtelle, Victorville, Wasco, Watts.

Chapters: Los Angeles.

COLORADO

Divisions: Colorado Springs, Denver, East Denver.

CONNECTICUT

Divisions: Bridgeport, East Graanby, Hartford, New Britain, New Haven, Norwalk, Norwich, Portland, Rockville.

Chapters: New Haven.

DELAWARE

Divisions: Belvidere, Wilmington.

Chapters: Western Section (Wilmington).

DISTRICT OF COLUMBIA

Divisions: Washington, D.C.

Chapters: Washington, D.C.

FLORIDA

Divisions: Bocaratone, Boynton, Cocoanut Grove, Dania, Del Ray, Deerfield, Denver, East Jacksonville, Fort Pierce, Hallandale, Jacksonville, Jensen, Key West, Lakeland, Leisburg, Merritt, Miami, Odessa, Otter Creek, Pompiano, St. Petersburg, South Jacksonville, Stuart, Tampa, Wabasse, West Palm Beach, West Tampa.

Chapters: Campbell Hill, Jacksonville, Jacksonville (Hearns), North Jacksonville, West End.

GEORGIA

Divisions: Alma, Atlanta, Baker County, Baxley, Brunswick, Camilla, Charity Grove, Clyatville, Coverdale, Fitzgerald, Gardi, Haylow, Jessup, Kinsborough, Limerick, Moultrie, Oakfield, Patterson, Pooler, Powellton, Savannah, Shingler, Sylvester, Ty Ty, Waycross.

Chapters: Waycross.

ILLINOIS

Divisions: Alton, Cairo, Chicago, Chicago Heights, Champaign, Colp, Danville, Decatur, East St. Louis, Freeman Spurr, Georgetown, Hill Crest, McClure, Madison, Morgan Park, Olmstead, Robins, Springfield, Tamms, Hodges Park (Unity), West Chicago.

Chapters: Chicago Heights, East St. Louis.

INDIANA

Divisions: East Chicago, Evansville, Fort Wayne, Gary, Indiana Harbor, Indianapolis, Richmond, Terre Haute, West Indianapolis.

Chapters: East Chicago, East Indianapolis, Highland (North Terre Haute), Irvington.

IOWA

Divisions: Buxton, Waterloo.

KANSAS

Divisions: Coffeyville, Frankford, Independence, Kansas City, Parsons, Rosedale.

Chapters: Sunny Side.

KENTUCKY

Divisions: Benham, Coxton, Daniel Boone, Florence, Louisville, Madisonville, Sergent.

Chapters: Oakland Addition (Louisville).

LOUISIANA

Divisions: Algiers, Amite, Amite City, Armistead, Bajou Goula (the sepa-
rate entry for Bayou Goula has a different division number), Baker,
Baskin, Batchelor, Baton Rouge, Eaden Park (Baton Rouge), Bayou
Goula, Belle Chase, Bermuda, Brusly, Clarence, Clouterville,
College Grove, Convent, Cypress Hall, Derry, Donaldsonville, Donner,
Dutch Bajou (Reserve), Frenier, Funisberg (Lower Algiers), Geismer, Gilbert,
Good Hope, Gretna, Gross Tete, Jesuit Bend, Jordan Stream, Kenner,
La Place, Livania, Lemonville, Lockport, Luling, Luna, Lutcher,
Marero, Maringouin, Melrose, Modeste, Montz, Morganza, Natchez,
Natchitoches, New Orleans, Oaknolia, Phoenix, Plaquemine, Robeline,
St. Bernard, St. Mary, St. Rose, Scotlandville, Taft, Trinity, Union,
Westwego, White Castle, Winnsboro, Zachary.

Chapters: Baton Rouge, Carrolton, Comite River, Lee Station (Gentilly),
New Orleans (Chapter 27), New Orleans (Chapter 54), Phoenix,
Plaquemine, Rosebud, South Baton Rouge.

MARYLAND

Divisions: Annapolis, Baltimore, Chase, Marley Neck, Middle River, Mt.
Winnanis, Queen Anne County, Waverly.

Chapters: East Baltimore, South Baltimore.

MASSACHUSETTS

Divisions: Boston, Brocton, Cambridge, Malden, New Bedford, Springfield, Winthrop.

MICHIGAN

Divisions: Albion, Ann Arbor, Branch, Detroit, Flint, Hamtramck, Idle-
wild, Jackson, Macomb, Pontiac, Quinn Road, River Rouge, Ypsilanti.

Chapters: Detroit.

MISSISSIPPI

Divisions: Aberdeen, Askew, Baltzer, Biloxi, Canton, Clarksdale, Cleveland, East Cleveland, East Drew, East Mound Bayou, Evansville,

Forest, Greenville, Gulfport, Lambert, Macel, Marks, Maltson, Meridan, Merigold, Mound Bayou, Mt. Calvary, Myrtle, Natchez, Pace, Poplarville, Renova, Shelby, Stillmore, Sumner, Symond, Turkey Creek, Tutwiler, Vance, Vicksburg, Water Valley, Webb, West Boyle, Wiggins.

Chapters: East Merigold, Elizabeth, Merigold, West Cleveland, West Merigold.

MISSOURI

Divisions: Bertrand, Charleston, Clayton, Commerce, Crowden, Dexter, Essex, Hermandale, Kansas City, Lilbourn, New Madrid, Parmo, Point Pleasant, Poplar Bluff, St. Louis, Saymos, South Kinlock, Tyler, Wyatt.

Chapters: Kensington, Webster Grove.

NEBRASKA

Divisions: Omaha.

NEW JERSEY

Divisions: Asbury Park, Atlantic City, Bayonne, Burlington, Camden, Cliffwood, East Orange, Egg Harbor City, Elizabeth, Glasboro, Hackensack, Jersey City, Kenilworth, Milmay, Montclair, Newark, Newark (two Newark divisions are listed, Division 888 and Division 66), Perth Amboy, Pleasantville, Rahway, Roselle, Scotch Plaines, Trenton, Vauxhall, Westwood, Whitesboro, Wildwood, Woodbine, Woodbridge.

Chapters: Newark (Chapter 13A), Newark (Chapter 18A).

NEW YORK

Divisions: Albany, Beacon, Brooklyn, Buffalo, Flushing, Freeport, Lackawanna, Middleton, New York Local, Newburg, Niagara Falls, Rochester, Syracuse, Yonkers.

Chapters: East Brooklyn, New York.

NORTH CAROLINA

Divisions: Ashville, Aulander, Bailey, Belhaven, Bethel, Broadway, Charlotte, Columbia, Council, Duke, Fayetteville, Gardners Town, Gaylord,

Goodwin, Goldsboro, Greensboro, Jamesville, Kinston (Division 757), Kinston (Division 277), Lidling, Mackeys, Magnolia, Matthews, Merry Hill, Morgantown, New Bern, Norwood, Pantego, Parmele, Raleigh, Randleman, Ransomeville, Red Springs, Roanoke (Littleton), St. Matthew, Salisbury, Sandford, Spencer, Spring Hope, Warrentown, Warsaw, Whittaker, Wilmington, Wilson, Winston-Salem, Zebulon.

Chapters: Winston-Salem.

OHIO

Divisions: Akron, Alliance, Barberton, Barton, Canton, Cincinnati, Cleveland, Columbus, Dayton, Duncanwood, Franklin, Hamilton (Division 68), Hamilton (Division 863), Lorain (Division 622), Lorain (Division 810), Massillon, Medina, Middletown, New Plymouth, Pomeroy, Sandusky, Santoy, Springfield, Steubenville, Struthers, Swartsville, Toledo, Warren, Waynesburg, Xenia, Youngstown.

Chapters: Highland Heights (Bedford), Walnut Hill (Cincinnati), Cleveland, College Hill, American Addition (Columbus), South Side (Columbus), Hamilton, St. Clair.

OKLAHOMA

Divisions: Apex, Boggs, Weleetka (Bookertee), Binger, Bristow, Broken Arrow[?], Brownsville, Crescent, Dapew, Guthrie, Haskell, Wellston (Lincoln City), Mt. Canaan, Muskogee, New Hope, Oklahoma City, Okmulgee, Porter, Red Bird, Sapulpa, Tabor, Tallahassee, Tulsa, Sunshine (Wagoner), Wewoka.

Chapters: Arizona Chapel, Hopewell (Lincoln City), Hattie's Chapel (Porter).

OREGON

Divisions: Portland.

PENNSYLVANIA

Divisions: Ambler, Avonmore, Blairsville, Braddock, Burgettstown, Chester, Clairton, Coatsville, Connelsville, Conora, Dinsmore, Duquesne, Edric, Elmwood, Fairbanks, Germantown, Glassmere, Greensburg, Harris-

burg, Herron Hill, Irwin, Johnstown, Leechburg, Longhorn, Mason-
town, Midland, Homestead (Munhall), McKeesport, New Castle, New
Kensington, Northside, Pittsburgh, East Liberty (Pittsburgh), Point
Perry, Sharon Hill, Uniontown, Wheatland, Wilkes Barre, Crestmont
(Willow Grove), Woodlawn.

Chapters: Elmwood, Friendship, North Philadelphia, Philadelphia,
Sharon Hill.

RHODE ISLAND

Divisions: Newport, Providence.

SOUTH CAROLINA

Divisions: Anderson, Beaufort, Charleston, Chehan, Church Parish,
Coosaw Island, Georgetown, Green Pond, Labaco, Lake View, Mid-
land Park, Mount Holly, Pineopiolis, Rock Hill, St. Andrew, Strawberry,
Union Heights, Yemassee.

Chapters: Ashley Junction, Charleston, Dale, Marysville, Murry Hill,
Ten Mile Hill.

TENNESSEE

Divisions: Alcoa, Chattanooga, Henry County, Knoxville, Memphis,
Nashville.

Chapters: Hyde Park, Knoxville, South Nashville.

TEXAS

Divisions: Acliff Heights, Cameron, Dallas, Egypt, Elmo, Glen Fawn,
Mill City, Waco, Whitney.

UTAH

Divisions: Ogden.

VIRGINIA

Divisions: Arringdale, Bacon's Castle, Bells Mill, Munden (Berkley),
Berkley Station, Campostella, Capron, Danville, Dewitt, Ettricks, Fairfax,

Franklin, Grafton, Grove, Hopewell, Kenbridge, Lebanon, Meherrin, Munden, Newport News, East End (Newport News), Norfolk, Oakwood (Norfolk), Tidewater (Norfolk), Oakwood Park, Oyster Point, Petersburg (Division 854), Petersburg (Division 174), Pocahontas, Portsmouth, Prospect, Rappahannock, Richmond, Roxbury, Smithfield, Somerset, Suffolk, Titus Town, Warfield, Waverly, Tabbs (York County), Zimi.

Chapters: Berkley, Kecoughtan City, Jefferson Point (Newport News), West End (Norfolk), Royal, Virginia.

WASHINGTON

Divisions: Seattle, Tacoma.

Chapters: Seattle.

WEST VIRGINIA

Divisions: Anawalt, Baxton, Beckley, Broomfield, Capels, Carbon, Carolina, Cedar Grove, Charleston, Clarksburg, Coalwood, Collier, Elkins, Enterprise, Everetteville, Farmington, Fairmont, Four State, Grant Town, Gypsy (Division 743), Gypsy (Division 627), Hutchinson, Ida May, Killam, Litwar, Laura Lee, Manayka, Meadowbrook, Monongah, Montana Mines, Mt. Clare, New Chiefton, Paden City, Parkersburg, Purseglove, Rosemont, Shinnston, Sprague, Wellsburg, Wheeling, Whipple.

Chapters: Despard (Clarksburg), Farmington, Nuterford.

WISCONSIN

Divisions: Milwaukee.

MISCELLANEOUS

The cards for these branches appeared at the end of the United States cards and were not filed with any particular state, though some indicate their geographical location. Two are probably not in the United States at all. One (Mullins River) is also listed under British Honduras.

Divisions: West St. Louis, Marianna, Zanesville [?] [Ohio], Union Mills, Garvey Club (Charleston, South Carolina), Garvey Club (Columbus, Ohio).

Chapters: Mullins River (Stann Creek), Far West Side.

UNIA BRANCHES OUTSIDE THE UNITED STATES, CIRCA 1926

ANTIGUA
Divisions: St. John's.

AUSTRALIA
Divisions: Sidney.

BARBADOS
Divisions: Bridgetown, Crab Hill (St. Lucy), Indian Ground (St. Peters).
Chapters: Bridgetown

BERMUDA
Divisions: Bermuda Division.

BRAZIL
Divisions: Porto Vello.

BRITISH GUIANA
Divisions: Charlestown, Georgetown, Lacytown, Parika, Pomeroon, Vergenogen.
Chapters: Georgetown.

BRITISH HONDURAS
Divisions: Belize, Corozal, Stann Creek.
Chapters: Mullins River (Stann Creek).

CANADA
Divisions: Calgary (Alta) [?], Donatville (Alberta), Edmonton (Alberta), Jenkins, Keystone (Alberta), Montreal, New Aberdeen, Sydney (Nova Scotia), Upper Big Tracadie (Nova Scotia), St. Catherine (Ontario), Toronto, Windsor (Ontario), Vancouver (British Columbia), Winnipeg (Manitoba).
Chapters: New Waterford (C.B.S.).

COLOMBIA

Divisions: Barranquilla, Bienaventura, Bottom House, Gaugh, North End, Santa Marta.

COSTA RICA

Divisions: Cahuita, Cairo, Cedar Creek, Estrada, Estrella Valley, La Africa, La Germania (Division 85), La Germania (Division 88), Liverpool Spur, Madre de Dios, Manzanillo, Matina, New Castle, Old Harbor, Pacuarito, Pocora, Port Limón, Puerto Viego, Púntarenas, San José, Siquirres, Talamanca, Waldeck 28 Miles.

CUBA

Divisions: Almirante, Antilla Nipe Bay, Banes, Bartle (Oriente), Caigo Mambi, Camaguey, Central Elia, Central Francisco (Camaguey), Central Isabell (Oriente), Central Macareno, Central Manate (Oriente), Central Mariano, Central Mirande (Oriente), Central Palma, Central Socores, Central Velasco, Central Vertuentes, Cespedes, Chaparra, Ciego de Avilla, Cueto (Oriente), Delicias, Florida (Camaguey), Guanaboca (Havana), Guantanamo (Oriente), Hatuey [?] , Havana, Ingenio Rio Canto, Jababo (Oriente), Jatibonico, Las Minas, Marcane, Mariano, Moran Camaguey, Nueva Gerona, Nuevitas, Palmarito de Canto, Placetas, Puerto Padre, Remedios, Sagua la Grande, San Cristobal, San German, San Geronimo, San Manuel (Oriente), San Pedro, Santa Cruz del Sur, Santiago, Sola (Camaguey), Victoria de las Tunas.

Chapters: Guantanamo (Oriente), Santiago.

DOMINICA
Divisions: Dominica.

DOMINICAN REPUBLIC
Divisions: Barona, La Romana, San Pedro de Macoris, Sanchez, Santo Domingo.
Chapters: Consuela Estate.

DUTCH GUIANA
Divisions: Suriname.

ECUADOR

Divisions: Guayaquil.

ENGLAND

Divisions: London, Manchester.

GOLD COAST

Divisions: Accra, Amanpupong.

GRENADA

Divisions: Grenada.

GUATEMALA

Divisions: Guatemala City, Los Amates, Morales, Puerto Barrios.

Chapters: Livingston.

HAITI

Divisions: Port au Prince.

JAMAICA

Divisions: Bog Walk, Kensington, Kingston, Montego Bay, Morant Bay, Port Antonio, Resource, St. Thomas (Golden Grove), Spanish Town, Swift River.

Chapters: St. Andrews.

LIBERIA

Divisions: Monrovia (no division number), Monrovia (Division 216).

MEXICO

Divisions: Tampa, Tampico Alto.

Chapters: Consuela, Olivia (Bocas).

NASSAU (BAHAMAS)

Divisions: Gambier, Nassau.

NEVIS

Divisions: Charleston.

NICARAGUA

Divisions: Bluefields, Great River, Greytown, Pearl Lagoon.

Chapters: Bluefields.

NIGERIA

Divisions: Lagos.

PANAMA

Divisions: Almirante, Baranco, Bocas del Toro, Colon, David, Dos Camos, Gamboa, Gatum, Guabito, New Providence, Panama City, Paraiso, Pedro Miguel, Farm 1 (San Blas) (Division 822), Farm 2 (San Blas), Farm 3 (San Blas), Farms 4 and 9, Farm 5 (San Blas), Farm 1 (San Blas) (Division 875), Victoria.

Chapters: Alvira, Baranero, Belleview, Farm 4 (Bocas del Toro), Farm 6 (Bocas del Toro), Caterina, Chumcubali, Clarita, Costa Rica, Elena, Guachapali, Helen, La Celia, Las Delicias, La Palma, La Zaiala, Laire, Margarita, Farm 2 (Bocas del Toro), Farm 5, San San, Sepoyn, Shepard Island, Sibuli, Suretka, Tavala [?] , Virginia.

CANAL ZONE (PANAMA)

Divisions: Las Cascadas, New Hope.

PUERTO RICO

Divisions: San Juan.

ST. KITTS

Divisions: Basseterre.

ST. LUCIA

Divisions: Castries.

ST. THOMAS

Divisions: St. Thomas.

ST. VINCENT

Divisions: Stubbs (St. Vincent).

SIERRA LEONE

Divisions: New Hope, Freetown.

Chapters: West Ward.

SOUTH AFRICA

Divisions: Basutoland (filed with South Africa in the cards), Cape Town, Claremont (Cape), Woodstock (Cape Town), Evaton (or New Clare, Johannesburg), Goodwood, Pretoria, West London.

SOUTH WEST AFRICA

Divisions: Luderitz, Windhoek.

SPANISH HONDURAS

Divisions: El Porvenir, La Ceiba, Puerto Cortes, Tela, Traversia, Truxillo.

Chapters: La Ceiba, San Juan Tela.

TRINIDAD

Divisions: Balandra Bay, Carapichaima, Caroni, Cedros, Chaguanas, Couva, D'Abadie, Enterprise, Gasparillo, Guaico, La Brea, Los Bajos, Mucurapo, Matura, Morne Diablo, Penal, Port-of-Spain, Princes Town, Rio Claro, St. Mary (Moruga), Ste. Madeleine, San Fernando, Siparia, Tableland, Victoria Village.

Chapters: Iere Village, Lily of the Nile (Port-of-Spain), Marabella, Palmira, Williamsville.

VENEZUELA

Divisions: El Callao.

WALES

Divisions: Barry Dock (Glamorgan, South Wales), Cardiff.

MISCELLANEOUS

Divisions: El Centro, Baguanos, Brewerville (W.C. Africa).

Bibliography

A vast amount of material is available to the Garvey scholar. It is unfortunately scattered all over the world in private and public collections of all sorts. Garvey's activities reached into every area inhabited by black people and his organization was watched by all manner of governments and law-enforcement bodies. There must be few newspapers or periodicals published in North, Central or parts of South America, Africa, or the West Indies between 1918 and 1940 that do not contain some references to Garvey or the UNIA. The newspapers and periodicals of Europe also had their fair share of news concerning Garvey. Garvey's activities were known in such places as Japan, India and Australia. Several prominent Garveyites from Garvey's time and thousands of the rank and file who followed him are still alive, their memories often remarkably undimmed by age. And for the researcher desirous of catching an echo of the Liberty Hall meetings of Garvey's time, it is still possible to attend UNIA meetings in surviving Liberty Halls, listen to the orators, sing the Universal Ethiopian Anthem, occasionally see a uniformed member of the Universal African Legions and, in Harlem, watch the annual Garvey Day parade. Survivors from Garvey's heyday, now mostly in their seventies and eighties, still demonstrate all the fierce loyalty and devotion to their leader and his ideas for which Garvey's following was legendary.

By far the single most important source of information on Garvey and the UNIA is the *Negro World*. Once thought to be irretrievably lost, it is now possible, by piecing together the holdings in several locations, to see practically the whole run of this UNIA organ from 1921 to 1933. The author has also seen several issues for 1920 and a few for 1919. 1918 is the only year for which this author has so far been unable to locate a single copy. The work of the *Negro World* was admirably supplemented and continued by the *Blackman,* the *New Jamaican* and the *Black Man* magazine. Together these publications provide as full a record as any researcher could hope for of Garvey's activities, speeches and even correspondence at times. They also provide an outstanding record of the UNIA.

Of extreme importance also are the National Archives of the United States and the Public Record Office in London. Both these places contain large amounts of testimony to the impact which Garvey had on the most powerful governments in the world. In the former there are still occasional secret files whose contents must await a later generation of researchers. The FBI files, in particular, will probably yield valuable new information. At the Public Record Office almost as many files relating to Garvey have already been officially destroyed as those surviving.

The other primary sources used in this study have also been very useful. Among the published primary sources the *Philosophy and Opinions,* compiled largely from *Negro World* material, still occupies a place of preeminence.

A recent request to gain access to Garvey's personal correspondence retained at the Atlanta penitentiary was passed on by the Bureau of Prisons to the late Mrs. Amy Jacques Garvey, who objected strenuously to its release. She explained that the correspondence was private and coded, and that it consisted mostly of letters written by Garvey to her.* Mrs. Garvey's own papers will doubtless be an important addition to existing material if they are ever made fully available. The author was only allowed to see items deemed relevant to his study by Mrs. Garvey.

Secondary sources proliferate. They must, however, be approached with extreme caution for they are very often to a greater or lesser degree inaccurate. Much of the material written in Garvey's own time was authored by black rivals who had a vested interest in his downfall or

*Amy Jacques Garvey Papers, Amy J. Garvey to Dr. Vincent Harding, September 7, 1970.

white journalists whose understanding of the aspirations of oppressed black people was as remote as could be. Later secondary sources too often fed on these inaccurate sources and compounded the mischief. This was especially true since the second round of secondary-source authors all thought that the *Negro World* was gone forever and were unable, or unwilling, for various reasons, to utilize the wealth of primary material that is now available.

PUBLICATIONS OF THE GARVEYS

Articles, Pamphlets and Books

Garvey, Amy Jacques. "Africans at Home and Abroad." *The African* 3 (October 1945): 14.

———. "An Appeal for African Names and their Meanings." *The African* 5 (October-November 1947): 13.

———. "Be Prepared." *The African* 4 (May 1946): 12, 13, 22.

———. *Black Power in America*. Kingston: A. J. Garvey, 1968.

———. "Bread Plus Butter—A World Battle." *The African* 4 (August 1946): 11.

———. *Garvey and Garveyism*. Kingston: A. J. Garvey, 1963. Reprint. New York. Collier Books, 1970.

———. "Garvey and Panafricanism." *Black World* 21 (December 1971): 15-18.

———. "Is Yours a Home?" *The African* 3 (April 1945): 10.

———. "Man's Disposition Causing Self-Destruction." *The African* 5 (June-July 1947): 11, 14.

———. *Memorandum Correlative of Africa, West Indies and the Americas, Sent to the Representatives of the United Nations*. Jamaica, 1944.

———. *Message to the Seminar on the Realities of Black Power*. London: West Indian Students' Union, 1968.

———. "Mrs. Amy Jacques Speaks at Liberty Hall on Garvey's Day." *National Negro Voice* (September 6, 1941): 6.

———. "Political Activities of Marcus Garvey in Jamaica," *Jamaica Journal* 6 (June 1972): 2-4.

———. "A Resurrected Art." *The African* 5 (September 1947): 13.

———. "Salute to Youth." *The African* 3 (July-August 1945): 7.

———. *United States of America vs. Marcus Garvey—WAS JUSTICE DEFEATED?* New York: A. J. Garvey, 1925.

———. "What Are You Living For?" *The African* 4 (September 1946): 11, 18.

————. "What's Wrong with Our World?" *The African* 5 (January 1947): 18, 19.

————. "Where Are My Children?" *The African* 4 (June 1946): 11, 20.

————. ed. *Philosophy and Opinions of Marcus Garvey or Africa for the Africans.* 1923, 1925. Reprint. London: Frank Cass, 1967.

*Garvey, Marcus. *Aims and Objects of Movement for Solution of Negro Problem Outlined.* New York: Press of the UNIA, 1924.

————. *An Answer to His Many Critics,* UNIA Press Release, January 1923.

————. *An Appeal to the Soul of White America.* New York: Press of the UNIA, 1924.

————. "The British West Indies in the Mirror of Civilization." *Africa Times and Orient Review* (October 1913): 158-160.

————. *Conspiracy of the East St. Louis Riots.* New York: UNIA, 1917.

————. *Eight Uncle Tom Negroes and W. E. Burghardt Du Bois As A Hater of Dark People.* New York: Press of the UNIA, 1923.

————. *Grand Speech of Hon. Marcus Garvey at Kingsway Hall, London, Denouncing the Moving Picture Propaganda to Discredit the Negro.* London: Black Man Pub. Co. [1939?].

————. *Minutes of Proceedings of the Speech by the Hon. Marcus Garvey at the Century Theatre.* London: Vail and Co., 1928.

————. "The Negro's Greatest Enemy." In *Three Articles on the Negro Problem.* New York: Press of the UNIA, 1924.

————. *Renewal of Petition of the Universal Negro Improvement Association and African Communities' League to the League of Nations.* London: Vail and Co., 1928.

————. *Selections from the Poetic Meditations of Marcus Garvey.* New York: A. J. Garvey, 1927.

————. *Speech Delivered by Marcus Garvey at Royal Albert Hall on Wednesday Evening, June 6th, 1928, In Setting Forth "The Case of the Negro for International Racial Adjustment, Before the English People."* 1928. Reprint. London: Poets and Painters Press [1968?].

————. *Speech of Hon. Marcus Garvey Delivered at 71st Regiment Armory.* New York, 1922.

————. *A Talk With Afro-West Indians—The Negro Race and its Problems.* [Kingston?]: African Communities League [1915?].

*In publications up to 1917, and on at least one occasion thereafter, Garvey's articles bear the name Marcus Garvey, Jr. (or Jnr. or Junr.). The Jr. is omitted here.

———. *The Tragedy of White Injustice*. New York: A. J. Garvey, 1927.
———. *Universal Negro Improvement Association Convention Hymns*. [Kingston], 1934.
———. "The West Indies in the Mirror of Truth." *Champion Magazine* 1 (January 1917): 267, 268.

Phonograph Records

Garvey, Amy Ashwood. "Up You Mighty Race." N.p., n.d.
Garvey, Marcus. "Speech by Hon. Marcus Garvey On His Return to United States" (208-A) and "Explanation of the Objects of the Universal Negro Improvement Association" (208-B). The L. H. Bourne Recording Co., See See Be Record, "Made Exclusively for the UNIA." [New York, 1921].
———. "Hon. Marcus Garvey on His Return to the U.S.A." (LHR 701-A) and "Explanation of the Objects of the Universal Negro Improvement Association" (LHR 701-B), London House Records, Newark, "Made Exclusively for Vanguard Local UNIA-ACL."[ca. 1960s].

Extant Newspapers and Magazines Published by Marcus Garvey

Black Man (magazine).
Blackman (newspaper).
Daily Negro Times.
Negro World.
New Jamaican.

MANUSCRIPT AND ARCHIVAL COLLECTIONS

American Colonization Society Records. Manuscript Division, Library of Congress.
Theodore G. Bilbo Papers. University of Southern Mississippi, Hattiesburg.
John E. Bruce Papers. Schomburg Collection, New York Public Library.
Court Records. Federal Building, New York, New York.
Amy Ashwood Garvey Papers. London, England.
Amy Jacques Garvey Papers. Kingston, Jamaica.
National Archives of the United States, Washington, D.C. and Suitland, Maryland.
NAACP Administrative Files. Manuscript Division, Library of Congress.
National Civic Federation Papers. New York Public Library.

National Urban League, Southern Regional Office Records. Manuscript
    Division, Library of Congress.
William Pickens Papers. Schomburg Collection, New York Public Library.
Public Record Office, Colonial Office and Foreign Office Records. London,
    England.
Arthur A. Schomburg Papers. Schomburg Collection, New York Public
    Library.
Arthur B. Spingarn Papers. Manuscript Division, Library of Congress.
UNIA Central Division (New York) Files. Schomburg Collection, New
    York Public Library.
Booker T. Washington Papers. Manuscript Division, Library of Congress.
Carter G. Woodson Papers. Manuscript Division, Library of Congress.

FORMAL INTERVIEWS AND MEETINGS ATTENDED

Interviews Conducted by the Author

Casimir, J. R. Ralph. Roseau, Dominica, August 1974.
Garvey, Amy Jacques. Kingston, Jamaica, March 1972.
Moore, Queen Mother Audley. Flint, Michigan, November 1971.
Whiteman, Herbert. Bronx, New York, December 1971.
Zampty, J. Charles. Highland Park, Michigan, April 1973.

Interviews Conducted by Other Persons

Garvey, Amy Jacques. Transcript of conversation with John Henrik
    Clarke, Kingston, Jamaica, August 1970.
"Marcus Garvey the Man." Tape of conversation with Garveyites in
    Detroit, Michigan, by V. A. Chavous [ca. 1969].

Meetings Attended

Vanguard Local, UNIA; Harlem, New York, 1971.
International Convention, UNIA; Youngstown, Ohio, 1971.
UNIA Detroit, Michigan, division, 1973.

COLLECTIONS OF NEWSPAPER CLIPPINGS AND MISCELLANY

African Nationalist Pioneer Movement. Schomburg Collection, New York
    Public Library.
Du Bois, W. E. B. Scrapbooks. Schomburg Collection, New York Public
    Library.

Garvey, Amy Jacques. Schomburg Collection, New York Public Library.
Garvey, Marcus. Moorland Collection, Howard University, Washington, D.C.
———. Schomburg Collection, New York Public Library.
Garvey, Marcus (Movement). Schomburg Collection, New York Public Library.
Gibson, Joseph D. Schomburg Collection, New York Public Library.

BOOKS, ARTICLES, PAMPHLETS, THESES AND PROCEEDINGS

"Africa for the Africans." *Messenger* (September 1920): 83, 84.
African Nationalist Pioneer Movement. *Marcus Garvey Day!!!* [1964].
African Nationalist Pioneer Movement (Detroit). *Garveyism A Political Creed*. A.N.P.M., Detroit, n.d.
African Studies Association of the West Indies. *International Seminar on Marcus Garvey, 2-6 January 1973*. Mona, Jamaica, 1973.
———. "A Summary of the International Seminar on Marcus Garvey." *Black Scholar* 4 (February 1973): 58-60.
Akpan, M. B. "Liberia and the Universal Negro Improvement Association: The Background to the Abortion of Garvey's Scheme for African Colonization." *Journal of African History* 14 (1973): 105-127.
"Alleged Garvey Intrigues in Liberia: Mr. Elie Garcia's Confidential Notes for the 'President General's' Guidance." Supplement to *The African World*, March 31, 1922.
Anderson, Jervis. *A. Philip Randolph*. New York: Harcourt Brace Jovanovich, 1972.
Aptheker, Herbert, ed. *The Correspondence of W. E. B. Du Bois: Vol. I*. Amherst: University of Massachusetts Press, 1973.
Association for the Advancement of Caribbean Education, Inc. *Synopsis of Life of the Honorable Marcus Garvey*. N.p., n.d.
Avery, Sheldon. "Up From Washington: William Pickens and the Negro Struggle for Equality, 1900-1954." Ph.D. dissertation, University of Oregon, 1970.
Bagnall, Robert W. "The Madness of Marcus Garvey." *Messenger* (March 1923): 638, 648.
Barrett, Leonard E. *The Rastafarians*. Rio Piedras: Institute of Caribbean Studies, University of Puerto Rico, 1968.
Bayen, Malaku E. "Is Marcus Garvey Faithful to Himself?" *The Voice of Ethiopia* 1 (January 1937): 1-3.
"A Betrayer of the Negro Liberation Struggle." *Negro Worker* 4 (July 1934): 6-10.

Bilbo, Theodore G. "An African Home for Our Negroes." *Living Age* 358 (June 1940): 327-335.

————. *Take Your Choice: Separation or Mongrelization.* Poplarville, Mississippi: Dream House Pub. Co., 1947.

"Mr. Bilbo's Afflatus." *Time* (May 8, 1939): 14, 15.

"Black Magic Fails Again." *The Independent* 120 (June 23, 1928): 586, 587.

"A Black Moses and His Dream of a Promised Land." *Current Opinion* 70 (March 1921): 328-331.

"Blaming It on Garvey." *Crusader* 4 (February 1921): 9.

Boris, Joseph J., ed. *Who's Who in Colored America.* New York: Who's Who in Colored America Corp., 1927.

Breitman, George, ed. *Leon Trotsky on Black Nationalism and Self-Determination.* New York: Merit, 1967.

Briggs, Cyril V. "Briggs Pokes Fun at Garvey." *Crusader* 5 (November 1921): 16, 17.

————. "Briggs' Reply to Garvey Editor Who Claims Garveyism and Communism Are Kindred." *Liberator* (August 8, 1931): 7.

————. "The Decline of the Garvey Movement." *Communist* (June 1931): 547-552.

————. "Garvey Turns Informer." *Crusader* 5 (November 1921): 5.

————. "How Garvey Betrayed the Negroes." *Negro Worker* 2 (August 1932): 14-17.

————. "Lessons in Tactics." *Crusader* 5 (November 1921): 15, 16.

Brisbane, Robert H. *The Black Vanguard.* Valley Forge, Pennsylvania: Judson Press, 1970.

————. "His Excellency: The Provincial [*sic*] President of Africa." *Phylon* 10 (1949): 257-264.

————. "Some New Light on the Garvey Movement." *Journal of Negro History* 36 (January 1951): 53-62.

Bruce, John, and Collins, J. P. "The Party and the Negro Struggle." *Communist* 1 (October 1921): 18-20.

Bruce, Robert [*sic*], and Collins, J. P. "The Party and the Negro Struggle." *Communist* 1 (November 1921): 15-17.

Buell, Raymond Leslie. *The Native Problem in Africa.* New York: Macmillan, 1928.

Bunche, Ralph J. "The Programs, Ideologies, Tactics and Achievements of Negro Betterment and Interracial Organizations," Manuscript prepared for the Carnegie-Myrdal study, *The Negro in America,* June 7, 1940, Schomburg Collection, New York Public Library.

Casimir, J. R. Ralph. *Farewell (And Other Poems)*. Dominica: J. R. Ralph Casimir, 1971.

————. "Greetings From Dominica." *Crusader* 5 (November 1921): 29-31.

Chaka, Oba. "Marcus Garvey—The Father of Revolutionary Black Nationalism." *Journal of Black Poetry* 1 (1970-1971): 82-96.

Chalk, Frank. "Du Bois and Garvey Confront Liberia." *Canadian Journal of African Studies* 1 (November 1967): 135-142.

Christy, Dr. Cuthbert. "Liberia in 1930." *The Geographical Journal* 77 (June 1931): 515-540.

Clarke, John Henrik. *Marcus Garvey and the Vision of Africa*. New York: Random House, 1974.

————. "The Neglected Dimensions of the Harlem Renaissance." *Black World* 20 (November 1970): 118-121.

Contee, Clarence G. "Du Bois, the N.A.A.C.P., and the Pan-African Congress of 1919." *Journal of Negro History* 57 (January 1972): 13-28.

————. "The Worley Report on the Pan-African Congress of 1919." *Journal of Negro History* 55 (April 1970): 140-143.

Convention Program, New York Local, UNIA, Sunday, August 15 to 21, 1926.

CORE, 3 (Fall-Winter 1973). Special Garvey Issue.

Coulthard, G. R. *Race and Colour in Caribbean Literature.* London: Oxford University Press, 1962.

Cox, Earnest Sevier, *Let My People Go*. Richmond, Virginia: The White America Society, 1925.

————. *Lincoln's Negro Policy*. Richmond, Virginia: The William Byrd Press, Inc., 1938.

————. *The South's Part in Mongrelizing the Nation*, 1926.

Critchlow, Hubert. "History of the Trade Union Movement in British Guiana." In Padmore, George, ed., *The Voice of Coloured Labour*. Manchester: PANAF Services Ltd. [1945?].

Cronon, Edmund D. *Black Moses*. Madison: University of Wisconsin Press, 1955.

Crusader News Agency, New York. News releases. 1935-1940.

Cruse, Harold. *The Crisis of the Negro Intellectual*. New York: Morrow, 1967.

————. *Rebellion or Revolution*. New York: Morrow, 1969.

Cunard, Nancy, ed. *Negro Anthology*. London: Wishart and Co., 1934.

Davis, Helen. "The Rise and Fall of George Padmore as a Revolutionary Fighter." *Negro Worker* 4 (August 1934): 15-17, 31.

Dego. "Amy Jacques Garvey." *Tom-Tom* [1973].

Degras, Jane, ed. *The Communist International, 1919-1943, Documents.* New York: Oxford University Press, 1956, 1960, 1965. 3 vols.

De Warnaffe, Ch. du Bus. "Le Mouvement Pan-Nègre Aux Etats-Unis et Ailleurs." *Congo* (May 1922): 1-15.

Dixon, Thomas. *The Flaming Sword.* Atlanta: Monarch Pub. Co., 1939.

Doler, Thurston E. "Theodore G. Bilbo's Rhetoric of Racial Relations." Ph.D. dissertation, University of Oregon, 1968.

Domingo, W. A., and Owen, Chandler. "The Policy of the *Messenger* on West Indian and American Negroes—W. A. Domingo vs. Chandler Owen." *Messenger* (March 1923): 639-645.

Dowd, Jerome. *The Negro in American Life.* New York: Century Co., 1926.

Drake, St. Clair, and Cayton, Horace R. *Black Metropolis.* New York: Harper and Row, 1962.

Draper, Theodore, *American Communism and Soviet Russia.* New York: Viking Press, 1960.

Du Bois, W. E. B. *Autobiography of W. E. B. Du Bois.* New York: International Publishers, 1968.

———. "Back to Africa." *Century Magazine* 105 (February 1923): 539-548.

———. "The Black Star Line." *Crisis* 24 (September 1922): 210-214.

———. "A Correction." *Crisis* 21 (March 1921): 213.

———. *Dark Princess.* New York: Harcourt, Brace, 1928.

———. *Dusk of Dawn.* New York: Schocken Books, 1968, first pub. 1940.

———. "Leroy Bundy." *Crisis* 25 (November 1922): 16-21.

———. "A Lunatic or a Traitor." *Crisis* 28 (May 1924): 8, 9.

———. "Marcus Garvey." *Crisis* 21 (December 1920): 58-60.

———. "Marcus Garvey." *Crisis* 21 (January 1921): 112-115.

———. "The Pan-African Movement." In George Padmore, ed. *History of the Pan-African Congress.* London: Hammersmith Bookshop, n.d.

———. "The Social Equality of Whites and Blacks." *Crisis* 21 (November 1920): 16-18.

———. "The U.N.I.A." *Crisis* 25 (January 1923): 120-122.

———. *The World and Africa.* 1946. Reprint. New York: International Publishers, 1965.

Dworkin, Martin S. "Liberia Again." *The Span* 6 (1948): 27-31.

Edmondson, Locksley. "The Internationalization of Black Power: Historical and Contemporary Perspectives." *Mawazo* 1 (December 1968): 16-30.

Edwards, Adolph. *Marcus Garvey.* London: New Beacon, 1967.

Elkins, W. F. "Suppression of the Negro World in the British West Indies." *Science and Society* 35 (Fall 1971): 344-347.

―――. " 'Unrest Among the Negroes:' A British Document of 1919." *Science and Society* 32 (Winter 1968): 66-79.

Elmes, A. F. "Garvey and Garveyism—An Estimate." *Opportunity* 3 (May 1925): 139-141.

Essien-Udom, E. U. *Black Nationalism.* New York: Dell, 1964.

"Expulsion of George Padmore from the Revolutionary Movement." *Negro Worker* 4 (June 1934): 14, 15.

Fax, Elton C. *Garvey.* New York: Dodd, Mead and Co., 1972.

Federal Writers Project. *New York Panorama.* New York: Random House, 1938.

Ferris, William H. "After Marcus Garvey What?" *The Spokesman* (August 1927): 12, 13.

―――. "A Colored American's Estimate of the *Africa Times and Orient Review.*" *Africa Times and Orient Review* 1 (April 14, 1914): 77, 78.

―――. "Garvey and the Black Star Line." *Favorite Magazine* 4 (July 1920): 396-398.

Fierce, Milfred C. "Economic Aspects of the Marcus Garvey Movement." *Black Scholar* 3 (March-April 1972): 50-61.

Ford, Arnold J., ed. *Universal Ethiopian Hymnal.* New York: Beth B'nai Abraham Pub. Co., 1920, 1921, 1922.

Foster, William Z. "The Garvey Movement." *Political Affairs* 33 (February 1954): 15-23.

―――. *The Negro People in American History.* New York: International Publishers, 1954.

Frazier, E. Franklin, *Black Bourgeoisie.* London: Collier, 1962.

―――. "The Du Bois Program in the Present Crisis." *Race* 1 (Winter 1935-1936): 11-13.

―――. "Garvey: A Mass Leader." *Nation* 123 (August 18, 1926): 147-148.

Fremmer, Ray. *Jamaica's Heroes and Patriots.* Kingston: United Printers Ltd., 1963.

Garvey, Amy Ashwood. "Marcus Garvey—Prophet of Black Nationalism." Unpublished manuscript. N.p., n.d.

"Garvey." *Crisis* 29 (December 1924): 86.

"Garvey About Gone." *Messenger* (April 1923): 748.

"Garvey Again." *Time* (August 11, 1924): 3, 4.

"Garvey and Anarchism." *Messenger* (October 1922): 500-502.

"Garvey and the Garvey Movement." *Opportunity* 6 (January 1928): 4, 5.

"Garvey and Liberia." *Crisis* 28 (August 1924): 154, 155.

"Garvey Believes Conviction Just." *Messenger* (August 1923): 781.

"The Garvey Movement: A Promise or a Menace." *Messenger* (December 1920): 170-172.

"A Garvey Myth." *Messenger* (November 1923): 861, 862.

"Garvey Retracted Once Before." *Crusader* 5 (November 1921): 24.

"Garvey Unfairly Attacked." *Messenger* (April 1922): 387.

"Garvey's Gone!" *Messenger* (April 1923): 759.

"Garvey's Social Equality Cables." *Messenger* (October 1921): 259.

"A German Appeal to Garvey." *The Nation* 113 (December 28, 1921): 769.

Gold, Michael. "When Africa Awakes." *New York World* Magazine and Story Section, (August 22, 1920): 3, 13.

Goldman, Morris. "The Garvey Movement, 1916-1927." Masters thesis, New School for Social Research, 1951.

Graham, Stephen. *Children of the Slaves.* London: Macmillan, 1920.

Grant, George S. "Garveyism and the Ku Klux Klan." *Messenger* (October 1923): 835, 836, 842.

Green, Rev. Zebedee. *Why I Am Dissatisfied.* Pittsburgh: Quick Printing Co., 1922.

———. *Why I Am Dissatisfied–Part Two.* Pittsburgh, 1924.

"Gunning for the 'Negro Moses.' " *Literary Digest* 74 (August 19, 1922): 40-45.

Harris, Robert. "Accomplishments Under Marcus Garvey's Leadership," in *The African Nationalist Pioneer Movement presents GARVEY DAY CELEBRATION, August 17, 1967.*

Harris, Robert, and Miller, Vernon T. *Black Glory in the Life and Times of Marcus Garvey.* New York: African Nationalist Pioneer Movement, 1961.

Harrison, Hubert H. *The Negro and the Nation.* New York: Cosmo Advocate Pub. Co., 1917.

———. *When Africa Awakes.* New York: Porro Press, 1920.

Hartt, Rollin Lynde. "The Negro Moses." *Independent* 105 (February 26, 1921): 205-206, 218-219.

Haywood, Harry. *Negro Liberation.* New York: International Publishers, 1948.

Henry, Edward Barnes. *The Predictions of a Great Race Leader in Fulfillment.* New York: Edward B. Henry, 1953.

Hodges, Norman. "The Odyssey of Marcus Garvey: 1887-1940." *The Pan-Africanist* 1 (June 1971): 16-21.

Hooker, James R. "Africa for Afro-Americans: Padmore and the Black Press." *Radical America* 2 (July-August 1968): 14-19.

————. *Black Revolutionary: George Padmore's Path From Communism to Pan-Africanism.* London: Pall Mall, 1967.

"Hot Fight in Los Angeles U.N.I.A." *Crusader* 5 (November 1921):19.

Huiswoud, Otto. "Negro Leadership: A Tragedy!" *Negro Champion* 1 (October 27, 1928): 4, 5.

"In His Own Country." *Crisis* 26 (September 1923): 230.

International Convention, U.N.I.A. 1929 Garvey Club Inc. Souvenir Journal. August 4, 1946.

"Is Garveyism the Answer to the Present Problem of the American Negro?" *The American Negro* 1 (August 1955): 19-23.

"Is Marcus Garvey Learning?" *Crusader* 5 (November 1921): 12.

Isaacs, Harold R. *The New World of Negro Americans.* New York: Viking Press, 1963.

Isles, William. *Our Leader–March Song.* New York: William Isles, UNIA Building, 1921.

James, C. L. R. *The Black Jacobins.* 2d ed. New York: Vintage, 1963.

————. "Document: C. L. R. James on the Origins." *Radical America* 2 (July-August 1968): 20-29.

————. *A History of Pan-African Revolt.* Washington, D.C.: Drum and Spear Press, 1969.

Johnson, Fenton. "Harlem by Day and Night." *Favorite Magazine* 4 (July 1920): 363, 364.

Johnson, James Weldon. *Black Manhattan.* 1930. Reprint. New York: Atheneum, 1968.

Julian, Col. Hubert. *Black Eagle.* London: Jarrolds, 1964.

Kadalie, Clements. *My Life and the I.C.U.* New York: Humanities Press, 1970.

Kendal, Henry H. "A Garveyite Offended." *Negro Worker* 2 (August 1932): 21-24.

King, Kenneth J. "African Students in Negro American Colleges: Notes on the Good African." *Phylon* 31 (Spring 1970): 16-30.

————. "The American Background of the Phelps-Stokes Commissions and Their Influences in Education in East Africa, especially in Kenya." Ph.D. dissertation, Edinburgh University, 1968.

————. "Early Pan-African Politicians in East Africa." *Mawazo* 2 (June 1969): 2-10.

Knox, Graham. "Political Change in Jamaica (1866-1906) and the Local
    Reaction to the Policies of the Crown Colony Government." In F. M.
    Andic and T. G. Matthews, eds. *The Caribbean in Transition.* Rio
    Piedras: Institute of Caribbean Studies, University of Puerto Rico,
    1965.
Langley, Jabez Ayodele. "Garveyism and African Nationalism." *Race*
    11 (October 1969): 157-172.
————. "Pan-Africanism in Paris, 1924-1936." *Journal of Modern
    African Studies* 7 (April 1969): 69-94.
————. "West African Aspects of the Pan-African Movements: 1900-
    1945." Ph.D. dissertation, Edinburgh University, 1968.
Lee, Davis. *Future of the Negro.* N.p., n.d.
Leopold, James. "Is Garvey Mis-understood?" *The African* 4 (Novem-
    ber 1946): 15-16.
————. "Is Garvey Mis-understood?" *The African* 5 (September 1947):
    17-19.
Lewis, Rupert. "A Political Study of Garveyism in Jamaica and London:
    1914-1940." Masters thesis, University of the West Indies, 1971.
"Liberia." *Crisis* 29 (August 1925): 260-262.
"The Liberian Government and the Marcus Garvey Movement—Plain
    Commonsense Talk on the Situation." *Liberian News* (August 1924):
    3, 4.
Lincoln, C. Eric. *The Black Muslims in America.* Boston: Beacon Press,
    1961.
Locke, Alain. *The New Negro.* 1925. Reprint. New York: Atheneum,
    1969.
Lovett, Robert M. "An Emperor Jones of Finance." *New Republic* 35
    (July 11, 1923): 178-179.
Lugard, F. D. "The Colour Problem." *The Edinburgh Review* 233 (April
    1921): 267-283.
MacKawain, Herman W. "The Negro Thinks of War." *Negro Worker* 4
    (August 1934): 5-9.
McGuire, George Alexander. "Liberia's Appeal to the Western Negro."
    The Negro Churchman 5 (February 1927): 6, 7.
————. *Universal Black Men Catechism.* N.d., first pub. 1921.
McKay, Claude. *Harlem: Negro Metropolis.* New York: Dutton, 1940.
————. *A Long Way From Home.* 1937. Reprint. New York: Harcourt,
    Brace & World, 1970.
————. "Soviet Russia and the Negro." *Crisis* 27 (December 1923):
    61-65.

————. "What Is and What Isn't." *Crisis* 27 (April 1924): 259-262.

McKenzie, F. A. "Is There a Black Peril? The Story of Marcus Garvey, The Leader of the Negro People." *Overseas* (April 1921): 43-45.

Manoedi, M. Mokete. *Garvey and Africa.* New York: New York Age Press, n.d.

"Marcus Garvey." *Journal of Negro History* 25 (October 1940): 590-592.

"Marcus Garvey." *Messenger* (June 1922): 417, 418.

"Marcus Garvey!" *Messenger* (July 1922): 497.

"Marcus Garvey and Liberia." *Liberian News* (August 1924): 9-11.

"Marcus Garvey and the N.A.A.C.P." *Crisis* 35 (February 1928): 51.

"Marcus Garvey—The Garvey Movement: A Promise or a Menace to Negroes." *Messenger* (October 1920): 114, 115.

"Marcus Garvey Must Go!" *Messenger* (October 1922): 508.

"Marcus Garvey to William Pickens and William Pickens to Marcus Garvey." *Messenger* (August 1922): 471, 472.

"Marcus Garvey Vindicated—Adam Clayton Powell Jr. Adopts U.N.I.A. Platform." *The Centralist Bulletin* 2 (May 1944): 1, 2.

"Marcus Garvey Visits the Institute." *Tuskegee Student* 33 (December 1923): 2.

Martin, Tony. "C. L. R. James and the Race/Class Question." *Race* 14 (October 1972): 183-193.

————. "Marcus Garvey and Trinidad, 1912-1947." Paper read at the International Seminar on Marcus Garvey, Jamaica, 1973.

————. "Revolutionary Upheaval in Trinidad, 1919: Views From British and American Sources." *Journal of Negro History* 58 (July 1973): 313-326.

————. "Some Reflections on Evangelical Pan-Africanism, or, Black Missionaries, White Missionaries, and the Struggle for African Souls—1890-1930." *Ufahamu* 1 (Winter 1971): 77-92.

Miller, Kelly. "After Marcus Garvey—What of the Negro?" *Contemporary Review* 131 (April 1927): 492-500.

Minutes of the Fourteenth International Convention of the Universal Negro Improvement Association. August 13-20, 1961, Brooklyn, New York.

Minutes of the International Convention of the Universal Negro Improvement Association and Negro Peoples of the World, Held at Garvey Memorial Hall, 1609-1611 W. Columbia Avenue, Philadelphia, Penna., August 21st through 28th, 1955.

Mudgal, Hucheshwar G. *Marcus Garvey—Is He the True Redeemer of the Negro?* New York: H. G. Mudgal, 1932.

Muhammad, Elijah. *Message to the Blackman in America*. Chicago: Muhammad Mosque of Islam No. 2, 1965.

Mulzac, Hugh. *A Star to Steer By*. New York: International Publishers, 1972.

Murray, R. N., ed. *J. J. Mills—His Own Account of His Life and Times*. Kingston: Collins and Sangster, 1969.

Myrdal, Gunnar. *An American Dilemma*. 1942. Reprint. New York: Harper Torchbooks, 1964.

"A Negro Almost as Low as Garvey." *Messenger* (November 1922): 519, 520.

"Negro Deputy of France Condemns Garvey." *Messenger* (December 1922): 538-539.

"Negro Leadership in America." *The World's Work* 41 (March 1921): 435, 436.

"A Negro Moses and his Plans for an African Exodus." *Literary Digest* (March 19, 1921): 48-55.

Nembhard, Lenford Sylvester. *Trials and Triumphs of Marcus Garvey*. Kingston: The Gleaner Co., Ltd., 1940.

"Nigerian Progress Union." *The Spokesman* 1 (February 1925): 16.

Nkrumah, Kwame. *Ghana: The Autobiography of Kwame Nkrumah*. London: Nelson, 1959.

Obadende, Ibidunni Morondipe. "An African Program." *Crisis* 24 (May 1922): 33.

The Official Proceedings of the National Negro Congress, February 14, 15, 16, 1936, Chicago. Washington, D.C.: National Negro Congress [1936].

O'Neal, James. "The Next Emancipation." *Messenger* (September 1922): 481, 482.

Osofsky, Gilbert. *Harlem: The Making of a Ghetto*. New York: Harper Torchbooks, 1963.

Ovington, Mary White. *Portraits in Color*. New York: Viking Press, 1927.

Owen, Chandler. "Should Marcus Garvey Be Deported?" *Messenger* (September 1922): 479, 480.

Padmore, George. *American Imperialism Enslaves Liberia*. Moscow: Centrizdat, 1931.

———. "Bankruptcy of Negro Leadership." *Negro Worker* 1 (December 1931): 4-7.

———. *The Life and Struggles of Negro Toilers*. London: pub. by the R.I.L.U. Magazine for the International Trade Union Committee of Negro Workers, Hamburg, 1931.

————. *Negro Workers and the Imperialist War—Intervention in the Soviet Union.* Hamburg: ITUC-NW, 1931.

————. *Pan-Africanism or Communism?* New York: Roy Publishers, [1956?].

————. *What is the International Trade Union Committee of Negro Workers?* Hamburg, ITUC-NW, n.d.

————. ed. *History of the Pan-African Congress.* London: Hammersmith Bookshop [1945?].

Palmer, A. Mitchell. *Investigation Activities of the Department of Justice, Vol. XII of Senate Documents, No. 153, 66th Congress, 1st Session, 1919.* Washington, D.C.: Government Printing Office, 1919.

Parker, Nathaniel. *Negro History—Ancient Life; "Africa—At Home and Abroad."* Philadelphia: St. Clair Spencer Printing Co., 1926.

"The Passing of Garvey." *Opportunity* 3 (March 1925): 66.

Patterson, William L. "Negro Harlem Awakes." *Negro Worker* 5 (July-August 1935): 24-27.

Peet, H. W. "The American Negro and Africa—An Interview With Sir Gordon Guggisberg." *Southern Workman* 57 (April 1928): 180-183.

————. "An Interview With Marcus Garvey." *Southern Workman* 57 (October 1928): 423-426.

Pickens, William. "Africa for the Africans—The Garvey Movement." *Nation* 113 (December 28, 1921): 750, 751.

————. "The Emperor of Africa." *Forum* 70 (August 1923): 1790-1799.

Potekhin, I. I. *African Problems,* Moscow: Nauka, 1968.

Powell, Adam Clayton. *Marching Blacks.* New York: Dial, 1945.

"The Press and 'Back to Africa.' " *Crisis* 24 (October 1922): 273, 274.

Program of the Communist International. New York: Workers Library Pubs., 1936.

"Program of the United Communist Party." *Communist,* 13 [1920?] : 2-7.

Programme of First Two Days International Convention of Universal Negro Improvement Association and African Communities League, Sunday August 1st and Monday August 2nd, 1920, New York City.

"The Purple Robed Champion of 'Africa for the Africans.' " *Literary Digest* (September 4, 1920): 63.

Randolph, A. Philip. "Black Zionism." *Messenger* (January 1922): 330-331, 334-335.

————. "Garveyism." *Messenger* (September 1921): 248-252.

————. "Heavyweight Championship Bout for Afro-American-West Indian Belt, Between Battling Du Bois and Kid Garvey." *Messenger* (June 1924): 179, 184, 193.

_____."The Human Hand Threat." *Messenger* (October 1922): 499, 500.

_____. "The Only Way to Redeem Africa." *Messenger* (November 1922): 522-524, (December 1922): 540-542, (January 1923): 568-570, (February 1923): 612, 613.

_____. "Reply to Marcus Garvey." *Messenger* (August 1922): 467-471.

Record, Wilson. *The Negro and the Communist Party.* Chapel Hill: University of North Carolina Press, 1951.

_____. "The Negro Intellectual and Negro Nationalism." *Social Forces* 33 (October 1954): 10-18.

Redding, Saunders. *The Lonesome Road.* Garden City, New York: Doubleday, 1958.

Reid, C. H. "Marcus Garvey as a Social Phenomenon." Masters thesis, Northwestern University, 1928.

Reid, Ira de A. *The Negro Immigrant.* 1939. Reprint. New York: Arno Press and New York Times, 1969.

"Remember Marcus Garvey." *The West Indian-American* 1 (October 15, 1927): 12.

Revolutionary Radicalism. Report of the Joint Legislative Committee Investigating Seditious Activities Filed April 24, 1920, In the Senate of the State of New York. Albany, New York: J. B. Lyon, 1920.

Rogers, J. A. *World's Great Men of Color.* New York: J. A. Rogers, 1947.

Roome, William J. W. *Aggrey–The African Teacher.* London: Marshall, Morgan and Scott Ltd., n.d.

Rudwick, Elliott M. "Du Bois Versus Garvey: Race Propagandists at War." *Journal of Negro Education* 28 (Fall 1959): 421-429.

Rushing, Byron. "A Note on the Origin of the African Orthodox Church." *Journal of Negro History* 57 (January 1972): 37-39.

Schoell, Frank L. "La Question des Noirs aux Etats-Unis." *Crisis* 28 (June 1924): 83-86.

Schuyler, George S. "A Tribute to Caesar." *Messenger* (July 1924): 225, 226, 231.

Scott, William R. "A Study of Afro-American and Ethiopian Relations: 1896-1941." Ph.D. dissertation, Princeton University, 1971.

"See What Garvey Has Done." *Crisis* 25 (November 1922): 34-36.

Sheppard, Wheeler. *Mistakes of Dr. W. E. B. Du Bois Being an Answer to Dr. W. E. B. Du Bois' Attack Upon the Honorable Marcus Garvey.* N.p., 1921.

Shepperson, George. "Notes on Negro American Influences on the Emergence of African Nationalism." *Journal of African History* 1 (1960): 299-312.

————. "Pan Africanism and 'Pan-Africanism': Some Historical Notes."
    Phylon 23 (1962): 346-358.
Sherrill, William L. *Highlights—Sidelights and Observations at the United
    Nations Conference San Francisco.* Detroit: Negro Outlook and Asso-
    ciates, 1945.
————. *Re-Statement of Garvey's Program.* Detroit: Negro Outlook
    and Associates [1945?].
Simmons, Charles Willis. "The Negro Intellectual's Criticism of Garvey-
    ism." *Negro History Bulletin* 25 (November 1961): 33-35.
*Sixth Anniversary Drive Cincinnati Division No. 146, U.N.I.A., at Liberty
    Hall, From May 8th to 18th 1927.*
Smith, Terry. "Amy Jacques Garvey—Portrait of a Courageous Woman."
    The Jamaican Housewife 3 (Winter 1964): 22-25.
Solanke, Ladipo. "Open Letter to the Negroes of the World." *The Spokes-
    man* 1 (June 1925): 12-15.
————. "The Why of the Nigerian Progress Union." *The Spokesman* 1
    (April-May 1925): 25, 26, 30, 31.
"Special Resolution on Work Among Negroes in the United States and
    the Colonies." *Negro Worker* 1 (February 1931): 18-19, 1 (March
    1931): 14-16.
Starling, Lathan, Sr., and Franklin, Donald. "The Life and Works of
    Marcus Garvey." *Negro History Bulletin* 26 (October 1962): 36-38.
Streator, George. "In Search of Leadership." *Race* 1 (Winter 1935-1936):
    14-20.
————. "Three Men." *Commonweal* 32 (August 9, 1940): 323-326.
Strickland, Shirley Willson. "A Functional Analysis of the Garvey Move-
    ment." Ph.D. dissertation, University of North Carolina, 1956.
Sundiata, Tiki. "A Portrait of Marcus Garvey." *Black Scholar* 2 (Septem-
    ber 1970): 7-19.
"A Supreme Negro Jamaican Jackass." *Messenger* (January 1923): n.p.
"A Symposium on Garvey." *Messenger* (December 1922): 550-552.
Talley, Truman Hughes. "Garvey's 'Empire of Ethiopia.' " *World's Work*
    41 (January 1921): 264-270.
————. "Marcus Garvey—The Negro Moses?" *World's Work* 41 (Decem-
    ber 1920): 153-166.
Taylor, W. "Conditions of Negroes in the U.S.A." *Negro Worker* 3 (March
    1933): 6-8.
Things You Ought to Know. N.p., n.d.
Thrupp, Sylvia L. *Millennial Dreams in Action.* The Hague: Mouton and
    Co., 1962.

Thwaites, R. G., Jr. "Marcus Garvey, Africa and the New World Negro."
    Jamaica Journal 2 (September 1968): 2-5.
"Twelve Smallest Persons in America." *Messenger* (November 1922):
    517.
UNIA. *Constitución y Libros de Leyes de la Asociación Universal de
    Negros y la Liga de Comunidad Africana.* Guantánamo [Cuba]:
    Imprenta La Universal, n.d.
————. *Constitution and Book of Laws. Made for the government of
    the Universal Negro Improvement Association, Inc. and African Com-
    munities League, Inc., of the World, in effect July 1918. Revised and
    amended August 1920, 1921 and 1922.* New York.
————. *Excerpts of the Late Marcus Garvey.* Robbins, Illinois: Elinor
    White, Commissioner of Illinois, n.d.
————. *Petition of the Universal Negro Improvement Association and
    African Communities League to League of Nations, Geneva, Switzer-
    land.* New York [1922].
————. *Universal Negro Improvement Association Borrowing $2,000,000
    from its Members To Start Building a Nation for the Negro Peoples of
    the World.* New York [1925?].
"The U.N.I.A." *Messenger* (August 1923): 782.
"The U.N.I.A. and Progress." *The Spokesman* 1 (June 1925): 5, 6.
"The Universal Negro Improvement Association in the Liberian Legisla-
    ture." *The Liberian Patriot* 1 (May 21, 1921): 4.
Valentine, C. "Garvey Turns Informer." *Crusader* 5 (November 1921): 8.
Vincent, Theodore G. *Black Power and the Garvey Movement.* Berkeley:
    Ramparts [1971].
————. *Voices of a Black Nation.* Berkeley: Ramparts, 1973.
Walrond, Eric D. "Imperator Africanus." *Independent* 114 (January 3,
    1925): 8-11.
Walshe, A. P. "Black American Thought and African Political Attitudes
    in South Africa." *Review of Politics* 32 (January 1970): 51-77.
Warner, Robert Austin. *New Haven Negroes.* New Haven: Yale University
    Press, 1940.
Webb, James Morris. *The Black Man—The Father of Civilization—Proven
    by Biblical History.* Chicago: Fraternal Press, 1924.
Weinstein, James. "Black Nationalism: The Early Debate." *Studies on the
    Left* 4 (Summer 1964): 50-58.
Weisbord, Robert G. "British West Indian Reaction to the Italian-Ethiopian
    War: An Episode in Pan-Africanism." *Caribbean Studies* 10 (April
    1970): 34-41.

————. "Marcus Garvey, Pan-Negroist: The View From Whitehall."
    Race 11 (1970): 419-429.
Welch, Joseph O. *The Man of Destiny.* N.p. [1922?].
Wells, Ida B. *Crusade for Justice—The Autobiography of Ida B. Wells.*
    Edited by Alfreda M. Duster. Chicago: University of Chicago Press,
    1970.
"The West Indies." *Crisis* 36 (December 1929): 419, 420.
Whyte, Daisy. "Private Secretary Reveals Details of the Illness and Death
    of Marcus Garvey." *Voice of Freedom* 1 (August 1945): 1, 2.
Wickham, Clennel W. "Garveyism A World Force—What It Means and Is."
    Barbados Weekly Herald, September 29, 1923.
"Will Not Co-operate, Says Garvey." *Crusader* 5 (November 1921):
    22, 23.
Williams, C. Kingsley, ed. *Aggrey Said.* London: Sheldon, 1945.
Williams, Daniel T. *Eight Negro Bibliographies.* New York: Kraus Reprint
    Co., 1970.
Wilson, Rev. C. A. *Men of Vision.* Kingston: Gleaner Co. Ltd., 1929.
Wilson, Elaine Joan. "A Comparative Study of the Marcus Garvey and
    Black Muslim Movements." Masters thesis, Howard University, 1967.
Work, Monroe N. *Negro Year Book, 1921-1922.* Tuskegee: The Negro
    Year Book Pub. Co., 1922.
Wynter, Sylvia. *Jamaica's National Heroes.* Kingston: Jamaica National
    Trust Commission, 1971.
Young, Sidney A., ed. *Isthmian Echoes.* Panama, R.P.: Benedetti Hnos
    [1928?].

NEWSPAPERS AND JOURNALS
NOT MENTIONED ELSEWHERE
IN THIS STUDY

Africa and Orient Review.
African Opinion.
Ethiopian World.
Garvey's Voice.
New Negro Voice.
New Negro World.
People's Voice.
The Voice of the U.N.I.A.

Index

Abantu Batho, 120, 139
Abbott, Robert S., 316, 324; and
letter of eight to attorney general, 327; brings Amy Ashwood
Garvey back to United States,
332; on African redemption,
332; attacked by *Messenger,*
333
Abyssinia. *See* Ethiopia
Adam, Jean Joseph, 45, 46
Africa, 12, 24, 25, 41, 42, 44,
48, 49, 54-55, 56, 59, 60-62,
69, 72, 73, 77, 82, 92, 110-50,
152, 165, 177, 182, 220, 238,
243, 244, 247, 250, 277, 291,
292, 317, 346, 351, 354; ex-
German, 11, 45, 46, 122, 347.
See also individual countries
African, The, 263
African Abroad, The (Ferris), 82

African Blood Brotherhood
(ABB), 13, 139, 236-43, 245,
249, 251, 258, 320, 353;
membership, 238; enters Com-
munist Party, 238; founding of,
239; estranged Garveyites join, 241
African Communities League, 10
African Communities League
Peoples Cooperative Bank, 35
"African Fundamentalism"
(Garvey), 88 n.8
African Methodist Episcopal
Church, 47, 97, 117, 289, 308.
See also Christian Recorder
African Methodist Episcopal
Church of Zion, 43
African National Congress (ANC),
45, 118, 120, 263
African Orthodox Church, 71-73,
120

INDEX

Books from the Majority Press

THE NEW MARCUS GARVEY LIBRARY

Literary Garveyism: Garvey, Black Arts and the Harlem Renaissance. Tony Martin. $19.95 (cloth), $8.95 (paper).

The Poetical Works of Marcus Garvey. Tony Martin, Ed. $17.95 (cloth), $7.95 (paper).

Marcus Garvey, Hero: A First Biography. Tony Martin. $19.95 (cloth), $7.95 (paper).

The Pan-African Connection. Tony Martin. $22.95 (cloth), $7.95 (paper).

Message to the People: the Course of African Philosophy. Marcus Garvey. Ed. by Tony Martin. $22.95 (cloth), $8.95 (paper).

Race First: the Ideological and Organizational Struggles of Marcus Garvey and the Universal Negro Improvement Association. Tony Martin. $29.95 (cloth), $10.95 (paper).

The Philosophy and Opinions of Marcus Garvey. Amy Jacques Garvey, Ed. $10.95 (paper).

Amy Ashwood Garvey: Pan-Africanist, Feminist and Wife No. 1. Tony Martin. Forthcoming 1989.

African Fundamentalism: A Literary and Cultural Anthology of Garvey's Harlem Renaissance. Tony Martin, Ed. $12.95 (paper). Spring 1989.

THE BLACK WORLD

Brazil: Mixture or Massacre? Essays in the Genocide of a Black People. Abdias do Nascimento. $9.95 (paper).

Studies in the African Diaspora: A Memorial to James R. Hooker (1929-1976). John P. Henderson and Harry A. Reed, Eds. $39.95 (cloth).

In Nobody's Backyard: the Grenada Revolution in its Own Words. Vol. I, the Revolution at Home. Tony Martin, Ed. $22.95 (cloth), $7.95 (paper).

In Nobody's Backyard: the Grenada Revolution in its Own Words. Vol. II, Facing the World. Tony Martin, Ed., $22.95 (cloth), $7.95 (paper).

Order from The Majority Press, P.O. Box 538, Dover, MA 02030, U.S.A. Mass. residents add 5% sales tax.